Chinese–Japanese Competition and the East Asian Security Complex

This volume examines contemporary diplomatic, economic, and security competition between China and Japan in the Asia-Pacific region.

The book outlines the role that Sino-Japanese competition plays in East Asian security, an area of study largely overlooked in contemporary writing on Asian security, which tends to focus on US–China relations and/or US hegemony in Asia. The volume focuses on Chinese and Japanese foreign policy under President Xi Jinping and Prime Minister Shinzō Abe, and regional security dynamics within and between Asian states/institutions since 2012. It employs regional security complex theory as a theoretical framework to view Chinese and Japanese competition in the Asian region. In doing so, the volume draws on a "levels of analysis" approach to demonstrate the value in looking at security in the Asia-Pacific from a regional rather than global perspective. The vast majority of existing research on the region's security tends to focus on great power relations and treats Asia as a sub-region within the larger global security architecture. In contrast, this volume shows how competition between the two largest Asian economies shapes East Asia's security environment and drives security priorities across Asia's sub-regions. As such, this collection provides an important contribution to discussion on security in Asia; one with potential to influence both political and military policy makers, security practitioners, and scholars.

This book will be of much interest to students of Asian politics, regional security, diplomacy, and international relations.

Jeffrey Reeves is Associate Professor in the College of Security Studies at the Daniel K. Inouye Asia-Pacific Center for Security Studies in Hawaii, US.

Jeffrey Hornung is a Political Scientist in the Defense and Political Sciences Department at the RAND Corporation, US.

Kerry Lynn Nankivell is Associate Professor in the College of Security Studies at the Daniel K. Inouye Asia-Pacific Center for Security Studies in Hawaii, US.

Asian Security Studies

Series editors: Sumit Ganguly, *Indiana University, Bloomington*, Andrew Scobell, *Research and Development (RAND) Corporation, Santa Monica*, and Joseph Chinyong Liow, *Nanyang Technological University, Singapore*.

Few regions of the world are fraught with as many security questions as Asia. Within this region it is possible to study great power rivalries, irredentist conflicts, nuclear and ballistic missile proliferation, secessionist movements, ethnoreligious conflicts, and inter-state wars. This book series publishes the best possible scholarship on the security issues affecting the region, and includes detailed empirical studies, theoretically oriented case studies, and policy-relevant analyses as well as more general works.

Globalization and Security Relations across the Taiwan Strait
In the shadow of China
Edited by Ming-chin Monique Chu and Scott L. Kastner

Multilateral Asian Security Architecture
Non-ASEAN stakeholders
See Seng Tan

Chinese Foreign Relations with Weak Peripheral States
Asymmetrical economic power and insecurity
Jeffrey Reeves

Democratic Transition and Security in Pakistan
Edited by Shaun Gregory

China's Use of Military Force in Foreign Affairs
The dragon strikes
Markus B. Liegl

Regional Institutions, Geopolitics and Economics in the Asia Pacific
Evolving interests and strategies
Edited by Steven B. Rothman, Utpal Vyas and Yoichiro Sato

Chinese-Japanese Competition and the East Asian Security Complex
Vying for influence
Edited by Jeffrey Reeves, Jeffrey Hornung, and Kerry Lynn Nankivell

Chinese–Japanese Competition and the East Asian Security Complex
Vying for Influence

Edited by Jeffrey Reeves,
Jeffrey Hornung, and
Kerry Lynn Nankivell

LONDON AND NEW YORK

First published 2017
by Routledge
2 Park Square, Milton Park, Abingdon, Oxon OX14 4RN

and by Routledge
711 Third Avenue, New York, NY 10017

Routledge is an imprint of the Taylor & Francis Group, an informa business

© 2017 Selection and editorial material, Jeffrey Reeves, Jeffrey Hornung, and Kerry Lynn Nankivell; individual chapters, the contributors

The right of the editors to be identified as the authors of the editorial material, and of the authors for their individual chapters, has been asserted in accordance with sections 77 and 78 of the Copyright, Designs and Patents Act 1988.

All rights reserved. No part of this book may be reprinted or reproduced, or utilized in any form or by any electronic, mechanical, or other means, now known or hereafter invented, including photocopying and recording, or in any information storage or retrieval system, without permission in writing from the publishers.

Trademark notice: Product or corporate names may be trademarks or registered trademarks, and are used only for identification and explanation without intent to infringe.

British Library Cataloguing-in-Publication Data
A catalogue record for this book is available from the British Library

Library of Congress Cataloging-in-Publication Data
A catalog record has been requested for this book

ISBN: 978-1-138-21906-9 (hbk)
ISBN: 978-1-315-43633-3 (ebk)

Typeset in Times New Roman
by Keystroke, Neville Lodge, Tettenhall, Wolverhampton

Contents

Acknowledgements	vii
Foreword	ix
MICHAEL JONATHAN GREEN	
Notes on contributors	xiii

1 Sino-Japanese competition in East Asia's emerging security complex   1
JEFFREY REEVES

2 Framing Sino-Japan competition: drivers and responses across the military, economic, and diplomatic sectors   25
JEFFREY REEVES AND JEFFREY HORNUNG

PART I
Security institutions   51

3 Sino-Japanese competition over regional institutions in Asia   53
MIE OBA

4 China, Japan, and economic security competition (and cooperation) in the Asia-Pacific   71
RAMON PACHECO PARDO

5 Sino-Japanese competition and energy security   86
VLADO VIVODA

vi *Contents*

PART II
Security issues 101

6 **Sino-Japan relations in Asia's maritime worlds: rivalry in the East and South China Seas** 103
KERRY LYNN NANKIVELL

7 **From backdoor to bridge: Japan as a Western power in cyberspace** 128
LORA SAALMAN

PART III
Security relations 141

8 **Australia navigates Sino-Japanese competition: engaging, binding, and hedging** 143
NICK BISLEY

9 **Vietnam between China and Japan in the Asian security complex** 159
ALEXANDER L. VUVING AND THUY T. DO

10 **Navigating between the Dragon and the Sun: the Philippines' gambit of pitting Japan against China in the South China Sea dispute** 178
RENATO CRUZ DE CASTRO

11 **Vying for influence: Sino-Japanese competition in perspective** 198
JEFFREY HORNUNG, KERRY LYNN NANKIVELL, AND JEFFREY REEVES

Selected bibliography 212
Index 224

Acknowledgements

The editors would like to acknowledge their family members, all of whom were instrumental in providing the time, space, and motivation need to put this book together. The editors would also like to thank the Daniel K. Inouye Asia Pacific Center for Security Studies and the Sasakawa Peace Foundation USA for their institutional support during the writing process. The editors reserve special thanks to the volume's numerous contributors, without whom the editors could not have realized their vision.

Foreword

The post-war neoliberal order is under greater duress than at any point since the Cold War ended. International relations theorists have groped for explanations why. Is it the relative decline of American power and the rise of a new bipolarity with China? Is it the diffusion of power away from states and the emergence of a non-polar world? Is it the rise of post-modern global challenges such as climate change or terrorism that will unify former rivals around a common cause?

Thus far none of these hypotheses has been validated by the realities of international security developments on the ground. What has become unmistakably clear is that the post-war neoliberal order is under direct assault in Europe, Asia, and the Middle East by aspiring revisionist powers that seek to dilute American alliances, institutions, and norms in an effort to restore their own historic privileges. In aggregate these developments represent a profound challenge to the established international order, but it can only be truly understood region by region. This is something that theorists in search of universal truths or policy planners in search of global themes find difficult to do.

Historically, the US has often made major errors when it imposed extraregional constructs on regional problems. The Eisenhower administration's opposition to the Bandung non-alignment conference in 1955 flowed from a hardline stand against communism globally, but failed to recognize that the real driver was nationalism within post-colonial Asia – a nationalism that might have been harnessed if understood. American paralysis in Vietnam in the late 1960s was exacerbated by a preoccupation with global prestige (particularly in Europe) and the inability of the Johnson administration to look for regional solutions in Asia. Nixon and Kissinger fumbled the India–Pakistan–Bangladesh conflict in the early 1970s because they interpreted all moves through the global prism of the Sino–US–Soviet triangle instead of appreciating the drivers for the conflict within South Asia. George W. Bush rightly went after terrorist cells in Southeast Asia, but let that global imperative define relations with the region to an unhelpful degree. And Barack Obama's belief that fighting climate change would unite China under a "new model of great power relations" unsettled regional allies and ultimately contributed to US–China collisions over the South China Sea when China's great power aspirations emerged. The Trump administration has now come into office, promising a new condominium with Russia that ignores the regional dynamics in

x *Foreword*

Europe, and a new confrontation with China that avoids the regional dynamics in Asia. US policy towards major powers within regions will inevitably fail if not sufficiently aligned with the power dynamics within that region.

Yet just as it is tempting for grand strategists or theorists at the global level to boil regional dynamics down to one big player (how often have conferences *not* organized by regional experts featured panels on China rather than Asia as a whole?), it is also difficult for regional experts, usually trained in one language or country, to broaden their analysis to the context of multipolar regional dynamics, let alone the implications for the broader international system.

This book goes a long way towards remedying that problem. The editors have taken a decades' old concept – regional security complexes – but turned to a rising generation of scholars from across the Asia-Pacific region to explain how their countries of study have managed not only a rising China, but also the Sino-Japanese strategic rivalry playing out across the region. All too often scholars fall into the trap of what the editors of this volume call the "dual hierarchy" of US–China relations. Authors like Sheila Smith (*Intimate Rivals*, 2016) have broken this dual hierarchy in bilateral studies. This volume is one of the few in recent years to attempt to do so on a region-wide basis.

What emerges is a tapestry of manoeuvring around the regional-level Sino-Japanese rivalry and an effort to preserve a stable balance of power by second- and third-tier powers. From this perspective, it becomes clear that Japan has strengths in soft power, defence engagement, and strategic partnering with other major actors on China's periphery, such as Australia and India. Some of this sub-regional alignment represents hedging against declining relative US power or confidence in Washington, yet much of the behaviour coincides exactly with what strategists in Washington want, including greater networking and capacity-building among US allies and partners and greater strategic weight for Japan, Australia, and India.

The book also spotlights the intense battle between Tokyo and Beijing over Asia's emerging regional norms, institutions, strategies, energy policies, and infrastructure investment. On the one hand, Japan is now fighting a proxy battle for universal norms at the regional level. This is a remarkable departure from Japanese attitudes a generation ago, when the so-called "Washington consensus" on economic transparency and democracy seemed a greater threat to Japan's interests than did China. Internal Japanese political change and Beijing's more assertive behaviour have changed that narrative. The rest of the region lines up somewhere in between, defining rule-of-law, open societies, democracy, and human rights as important priorities, but wary of interference in internal affairs of other countries or entrapment in a Sino-Japanese battle over values.

None of this is to say that the US is becoming irrelevant. The contest between Japan and China in Asia is also a contest for and against American presence and influence in the region. Japan wants more of it, China less. For the rest of Asia, the US remains the power stabilizer of choice. Most governments seek much stronger ties with democratic and benevolent Japan in order to reduce dependence on China's economy and vulnerability to China's strategic pressure – despite painful historical memories regarding Japan. Yet governments are generally pursuing closer ties in order to supplement US power, not in any expectation that Japan will become a replacement absent the US. Still, uncertainty about the US longer-term staying power could make this once secondary competition far more pronounced down the road if the US fails to lead.

Incoming administration officials will try mightily to understand China – as they should. They will ultimately find many more actionable ideas in this book. Beijing is much more of an immutable object for the US, and to the extent Washington makes progress with Beijing, it will be based on a solid footing in the region as a whole. This book paints the landscape policy makers will face.

Michael Jonathan Green
Senior Vice-President for Asia and Japan Chair
Center for Strategic and International Studies (CSIS)

Contributors

The editors

Jeffrey Reeves is an Associate Professor in the College of Security Studies at the Daniel K. Inouye Asia-Pacific Center for Security Studies in Hawaii, US. He is the author of *Chinese Foreign Relations with Weak Peripheral States: Asymmetrical Economic Power and Insecurity* (Routledge, 2015) and co-editor (with Ramon Pacheco Pardo) of *Non-Traditional Security in East Asia: A Regime Approach* (Imperial College Press, 2015), among other works on China, Asian security, and Mongolia.

Jeffrey Hornung is a Political Scientist in the Defense and Political Sciences Department at the RAND Corporation, US. He has written about Japanese security and foreign policy issues for numerous outlets, including *Asian Security*, *The Washington Quarterly*, *Foreign Affairs*, *The Wall Street Journal*, CNN, and *The Diplomat.*

Kerry Lynn Nankivell is an Associate Professor in the College of Security Studies at the Daniel K. Inouye Asia-Pacific Center for Security Studies in Hawaii, US. Prior to working at the College of Security Studies, Ms Nankivell worked with Canada's Commander, Maritime Forces Pacific and Joint Task Force Pacific in Victoria, British Columbia. Her primary research focus is maritime security in the Asia-Pacific, and she is currently a PhD student at King's College, London, UK.

The contributors

Nick Bisley is the Executive Director of La Trobe Asia and Professor of International Relations. His research and teaching expertise are in Asia's international relations, globalization, and the diplomacy of great powers. Nick is currently Editor-in-Chief of the *Australian Journal of International Affairs*, Director of the Australian Institute of International Affairs, and a member of the Council for Security and Cooperation in the Asia-Pacific.

Renato Cruz De Castro is a Professor (on sabbatical leave) in the International Studies Department, De La Salle University, Manila, Philippines, and holds the

xiv *Contributors*

Charles Lui Chi Keung Professorial Chair in China Studies. He is currently the US–ASEAN Fulbright Initiative Researcher from the Philippines based in the East-West Center in Washington, DC, US.

Thuy T. Do is Senior Lecturer in the Department of International Politics and Diplomacy, Diplomatic Academy of Vietnam. She has been awarded visiting research fellowships at the S. Rajaratnam School of International Studies (China Programme – 2008), East-West Center (Asia-Pacific Programme – 2010), and the Japan Institute of International Affairs (ASEAN Programme – 2014).

Mie Oba is Associate Professor at Tokyo University of Science, Japan. She obtained her MA and PhD at the Advanced Social and International Studies, Graduate School of Arts and Sciences, the University of Tokyo. Her major is international relations and politics in the Asia-Pacific. She is a specialist of the development of regionalism in this region as well as theories of regional integration and regionalism.

Ramon Pacheco Pardo is a Senior Lecturer in the fields of International Relations and International Political Economy at King's College, London, UK. Dr Pacheco Pardo is also Co-director of the London Asia Pacific Centre for Social Science, a Committee Member at CSCAP EU, and an alumni of the Korea Foundation Korea-Europe Next Generation Policy Expert programme.

Lora Saalman is Director of the Stockholm International Peace Research Institute (SIPRI) China and Global Security Programme. Her research focuses on China's cyber, nuclear, and advanced conventional weapon developments in relation to India, Russia, and the US. She completed her PhD at Tsinghua University in Beijing, China, where she was the first American to earn a doctorate from its Department of International Relations.

Vlado Vivoda is Research Fellow at the Centre for Social Responsibility in Mining, Sustainable Minerals Institute, at the University of Queensland, Australia. He has an extensive publication record on a wide range of topics related to extractive industries, China, which includes two single-authored books, five book chapters, and 19 journal articles.

Alexander L. Vuving is Professor at the Daniel K. Inouye Asia-Pacific Center for Security Studies in Honolulu, US. His major areas of research range from theoretical topics such as the sources of state behaviour, the making of grand strategic change, and the workings of soft power, to regional issues such as Asian security architecture and strategies, the rise of China, the South China Sea disputes, and Vietnamese politics and foreign relations.

1 Sino-Japanese competition in East Asia's emerging security complex

Jeffrey Reeves

Looking at East Asia in early 2017, one gets the sense that the peace and stability that has defined the region for the past two decades is no longer a certainty.[1] Tensions between some East Asian states are growing in tandem with their military capabilities and their capacity to harm one another both directly and indirectly. Nationalism and identity politics have become more pronounced in East Asian states' foreign affairs, increasing the overall difficulty for state-sponsored compromise and diplomatic solutions. At the same time, the US – a pivotal lead agent in the region for the past five decades – is no longer as capable, reliable, or predictable a security actor as it once was. President Trump's approach to the region (as understood from his piecemeal policy pronouncements at the time of writing) raises worrying questions among the US's Asian allies and partners about its willingness to remain engaged. Uncertainty over the US commitment to Asia, in turn, has led regional states to consider the possibility of US abandonment at the very moment when a rising China is reshaping regional order.

In light of these developing trends, there is a pressing need for new thinking on Asian security of a kind that takes these changing dynamics into consideration. There is, unfortunately, a proclivity among security scholars and analysts, particularly those from the US, to take a parochial view of the Asian region as a whole and to relegate regional actors to secondary roles with a US-dominated landscape. More specifically, a substantial majority of analysts tend to treat Asia as a subregion of the global system where security remains contingent on US involvement and/or US–China relations, and where states are nothing more than "middle powers" forced to react to US and/or Chinese initiatives. For these writers, Asian security exists as a consequence of global-level great power spillover, not as a regional commodity in and of itself. One can see this tendency in the high-profile titles such as "Between the Eagle and the Dragon", *The Pivot: The Future of American Statecraft in Asia*, and *The Improbable War: China, the United States and Logic of Great Power Conflict* that dominate reading lists on Asian security in university courses and within policy communities. While valuable in highlighting certain characteristics of Asian security, such as global-level/great power influence in the region, this type of writing almost always either assumes continued US hegemony or a US–Chinese "dual hierarchy" in Asia, both of which preclude agency among the Asian states themselves.[2] In turn, the proliferation of such texts has led to an

2 Jeffrey Reeves

unnecessarily myopic focus on the US and/or US–China relations to the detriment of more nuanced study, resulting in a lopsided representation of Asia's regional security dynamics as a whole.

There are, in fact, a myriad of regional and sub-regional factors that contribute to East Asia's security environment exclusive of global-level security and US hegemony. Foremost among these is security competition between China and Japan. While routinely referenced as subversive to US–Chinese relations (if, indeed, referenced at all), Sino-Japanese rivalry in East Asia plays a central role in shaping and influencing regional security institutions, regional security affairs, and regional-level securitization of threats, exclusive of US involvement. Over the past five years in particular, the two states' conflicting security agendas and competing foreign policies have influenced and shaped security partnerships, security norms and values, and security poles in ways that have fundamentally altered East Asian security dynamics. Even more, Sino-Japanese security competition has consolidated, and is consolidating, East Asian security at the regional level, fundamentally reshaping security relations and patterns in the process. More specifically, the Sino-Japanese rivalry is forcing a "thickening" of security ties between East Asian states and forging a regional security complex independent of global-level security.

To demonstrate the centrality of the Sino-Japanese rivalry in East Asian security, this volume examines the two states' competition across three sectors: security institutions, security issues, and security relations. To provide a working theoretical framework for analysis, the volume employs regional security complex theory (RSCT), which prioritizes a regional approach to the study of security interconnectedness, security nodes, relations of amity and enmity, and regional-level balance-of-power dynamics aimed at combating "the tendency to overstress the role of the great powers, and to ensure that the local factors are given their proper weight in security analysis."[3] In so doing, the volume makes three essential arguments.

First, while US engagement in Asia remains of paramount important to the study of Asian security, the Sino-Japanese rivalry has widespread influence on Asian security exclusive of US activity and/or involvement. Examination of the patterns, approaches, and relationships inherent in the Sino-Japanese rivalry, therefore, provide important insight into the nature of East Asian security that one cannot get from a US-centric frame of reference. Second, the region is the most appropriate level of analysis for East Asian security as it allows for greater analytical attention to geographic adjacency, shared historic, commercial, cultural, and ethnic ties, and security linkages between states with shared security priorities. Such essential components of security analysis are often overlooked in writing that privileges the international level and global great power dynamics. Third, regional order in East Asia is far more complicated than the majority of contemporary analysis would suggest and failure to understanding its complexities is failure to understand the region's true nature. The idea of a "dual hierarchy", for instance, fails to capture Japan's influence on security and economic relations (which are closely intertwined in the region, as Ramon Pacheco Pardo's chapter on economic security demonstrates) and accords both China and the US with more influence than is perhaps warranted.

Global focus and great power relations: deficiencies in contemporary Asian security studies

Central to this volume's approach is the contention that a gap exists in writing on Asian security with regard to regional-level security dynamics. One can see this deficiency in both Western and Asian writings as well as historical and contemporary works. During the twentieth century, for instance, Western scholars viewed Asia as a peripheral area with importance only in proportion to their respective state's global interests.[4] During the Cold War, scholars of strategic studies took a narrow view of Asia, treating it as one of many geographic areas in which competition between the US and the Soviet Union defined local-level security.[5] Valuable in part as it addressed a defining security characteristic of the time, this common theoretical approach also became an obstacle for more nuanced treatment of Asia's regional-level security drivers and state relations.

Contemporary scholarship identifies a number of variables that contributed to Western scholarships' myopic approach to Asian security studies and international relations (IR). Western cultural chauvinism, for instance, led analysts to misread Asian states and Asian peoples as somehow inferior and incapable of cooperating without Western powers' involvement.[6] Lack of exposure to Asian states resulted in antiquated, even fictitious, views among some scholars as to the contemporary realities of these states' positions.[7] Post-colonial thinking influenced Western perceptions of Asian states' abilities, often in a largely paternalistic and negative way, well into the 1990s and, in some respects, beyond.[8] Lack of appropriate language skills among those working on security in Asia further contributed to bias and underdeveloped thinking on Asian-specific dynamics. The dichotomous viewpoint that dominated Western scholarship during the Cold War pervaded analyst communities to the point where they naturally gravitated towards the more simplistic "us versus them" framework inherent in great power discourse.[9]

Incidentally, scholarship in Asia over the same period closely mirrored Western scholarship's focus on Asia as a sub-region within the larger global system, albeit for largely different reasons. Until the 1990s, Asian scholars (and policy makers) viewed security in Asia largely as a byproduct of global-level competition, first between the US and the Soviet Union, and later between the Soviet Union and China.[10] Conflict between and within Asian states, such as Vietnam and Cambodia, were treated as secondary effects of global-level great power competition. Where Asian scholars did attempt to treat Asia as a distinct region, they adopted structurally determinant paradigms such as the "periphery" or "third world" to describe Asia's place within the global system.[11] Ostensibly an effort to differentiate Asia from the West and/or colonial states, self-reference of the region as a periphery or third world inadvertently reinforced the perception of Asia as a subset of global great power relations, insignificant in itself to constitute a regional analytic approach.

Predictably, such mis- and preconceptions resulted in impoverished writing on Asian security within mainstream Western scholarship. Paul Cohen argues, for instance, that Western writing on China and Asia in the decades after the Second World War uniformly applied Western biases to their studies, some of which were

4 *Jeffrey Reeves*

based in imperialistic conceptions.[12] These approaches resulted in factually incorrect conclusions about historical cause and effect and inherently paternalistic accounts of Asian historical development. Martin W. Lewis and Kären Wigen similarly argue that early Western scholarship employed overly simplistic geographic accounts of "west" and "east" to the study of Asia, resulting in diminutive assumption of Asian states' distinctness and historical origins.[13] Lewis and Wigen note that re-conceptualizing these meta-regions into more precise world regions was the starting point for more informed scholarship. Most damning, perhaps, is Edward Said's critique of Western scholarship on non-Western countries and civilizations, which argues that cultural chauvinism and bigotry among Western scholars resulted in Asian states being relegated to the periphery. States like China, Japan, the Koreas, Indonesia, and Vietnam were seen as too exotic or different from Western states to justify anything more than a secondary status in a Western-dominated international system.[14]

As with Western scholarship, Asian scholars' focus on the global level and great power dynamics was an obstacle to the development of a more nuanced study of regional-level security dynamics. Reliance on strategic-level great power politics to understand conflict in the region, for instance, overshadowed local-level sources of insecurity between states like China, the Democratic People's Republic of Korea, South Korea, Japan, Taiwan, Vietnam, Cambodia, Malaysia, and Indonesia.[15] Neither did such analysis pay appropriate attention to the development of regional norms and institutions in Asia that affected security relations and security dynamics.[16] Singular focus on the global-level great power competition also obfuscated the developing multipolarity within Asia, particularly the dynamics between China and Japan – the two states with the capacity to affect regional-level security developments irrespective of great power involvement.

Western and Asian scholarship on IR and security studies in Asia has improved markedly over the past several decades. Western scholarship now demonstrates greater understanding of Asian politics, economics, cultures, and languages that allow for more substantive writings. Asian scholars, conversely, have undertaken Asia-specific theory building in line with the region's historical and contemporary dynamics. Yet Western scholars' tendency to view Asian security as a sub-section of global security relations and as a byproduct of great power competition persists. Such writing commonly treats Asia as a sub-region within the Western-dominated international system, not as a self-contained region with specific economic, political, and, most importantly, security characteristics. While not confined to a single theoretical IR approach, contemporary scholarship on Asian security is most closely aligned with a Realist approach, which holds the anarchic systemic level as the appropriate reference point and great power politics as the fundamental force determining "global" security.[17] Prominent examples of Western and Asian writers of this type include Henry Kissinger, Thomas Christensen, Aaron Friedberg, Robert Kaplan, Michael Pillsbury, Michael Swaine, and John Mearsheimer, among others. All accomplished and talented academics and policy thinkers in their own right, these scholars share the tendency to view Asian security through the lens of US interests, China's rise, global-level security dilemmas and geopolitics, great

Sino-Japanese competition 5

power transitions, and system-level hegemonic power. Consequently, none of them offer a balanced understanding of Asian regional dynamics.

Kissinger, for example, writes that US–China competition in Asia closely resembles that between England and Germany preceding the First World War.[18] Inherent in this interpretation of Asian security dynamics is that the region's future hinges solely on US–China relations. Christensen presents a similar view of Asian security as held hostage by US–China relations and argues that the US must manage China through engagement and exchange to avoid conflict in Asia.[19] Conversely, Friedberg, Kaplan, Pillsbury, Mearsheimer, and Swaine employ power transition theory in the study of Asian IR and security, and argue, to different effect, that global-level great power competition between the declining US and rising China is the defining feature of Asian order and security.[20]

Authors including John Ikenberry and Martin Jacques identify US and/or Chinese "dominance" of Asia as the region's defining security characteristic. Ikenberry, for instance, argues that the US has developed international institutions within Asia that support its position as a security provider to such a degree that China will have little ability to shift the existing security status quo.[21] Jacques argues the adverse point, stating that China will achieve global hegemony through its economic rise and, as such, will fundamentally transform Asia's security environment.[22] Despite their conflicting interpretation of which state has or will achieve hegemonic status, both scholars follow the typical Western pattern of prioritizing the global level and great power competition in theorizing about Asian security outcomes.

Notably, one can observe a similar tendency to privilege US–China relations and US hegemony over regional-level dynamics in Chinese scholars writing on Asian security. One can see these tendencies clearly in writings by Yan Xuetong, Jia Qingguo, and Shi Yinhong, three of China's most well-known and widely cited IR scholars. Yan Xuetong's work on IR and Asian security, for example, largely follows a Realist conception of global power politics, particularly in relation to US–Chinese competition. Yan writes, for instances, that Asian security is defined by China's rise and the US's simultaneous decline, and that global-level conflict between the two states is inevitable.[23] Jia Qingguo similarly writes that US–Chinese relations are the primary source of global order, largely downplaying regional-level dynamics for the sake of great power competition.[24] As with many Chinese academics over the past five years, Shi Yinhong has written extensively on the Xi administration's proposal to establish a "new type great power relationship" with the US as an important tool to manage relations between the states. Inherently a policy prescription, Yin's writing (as well as the majority of other Chinese scholars who support Xi's initiative) is entirely informed with preconceptions about great power competition and repeatedly references the global as opposed to the regional level for analysis.[25]

Highlighting the above high-profile writers' tendency to privilege the global level and great power competition in their analysis of Asian security is not to suggest there is no value in writing on US hegemony and/or US–Chinese competition as it relates to Asian security. The US military presence in Asia,

6 Jeffrey Reeves

US military alliances, and US–China competition all have considerable impact on global- and regional-level security. As such, these topics deserve scholarly attention in proportion to their importance. Scholarship focused on the global level and on great power competition within Asia is not, therefore, misplaced or misguided. A singular focus on US hegemony and/or US–China relations does, however, devalue regional dynamics that have just as much, if not more, influence over Asia's security environment. It is inaccurate, for example, to view US involvement in Asia and/or US–China competition as the single point of failure for Asian security. The result of such preoccupation is a less developed picture of Asia's security drivers and security environment as a whole that can't be prudently applied to prognostication about future outcomes.

The applicability of a regional approach to Asian security

A starting point for more inclusive analysis of Asian security is a refocus of the level of analysis away from the global towards the regional level. Far from an arbitrary readjustment, contemporary scholarship on state relations in Asia, both historic and modern, has demonstrated the applicability and the necessity of looking at the relations between Asian states for greater understanding of Asian security dynamics. Recently scholarship on state relations in Asia, for example, suggests a historical basis for Asian regionalism long overlooked in Western accounts of Asia's regional order. Zhang Feng's work on regionalism in historical Asia, for instance, shows that for centuries states in East, Southeast, South, and Central Asia had far greater political and economic interdependence than many historians previously thought.[26] Zhang identifies robust regional-level institutions in historical Asia that contributed to regional-level norms and rules, all of which highlight historical regional cohesion. David Kang has made similar observations in his work, particularly with regard to Asian states' relations and customs.[27] Kang argues, for instance, that tributary relations and shared Confucius-derived values between China and its Asian neighbours contributed to a relatively stable and peaceful Asian regional community for several centuries. John Hobson argues further that far from being the product of Western invention, Asia existed as a separate and distinct region for centuries, going back as far as 500 BCE. Hobson even argues that Asian regionalism influenced the development of Western civilization through commercial, philosophical, and cultural expansionism.[28] Differing in their precise interpretation of historical "Asia", all three men argue that interstate relations within Asia existed before Western involvement and that Asian norms developed exclusive of Western influence. For these scholars, there is a clear historical basis for treating Asia as a distinct region outside a larger (particularly Western-dominated) global system.

More relevant to this volume's conceptual approach, however, are the contemporary conditions within Asia that have contributed to Asian regionalism over the past several decades. Economically, Asian states have become increasingly interdependent in trade, investment, aid, finance, and capital flows since 2008.[29] According to the Asia Regional Integration Center, Asian intraregional trade stood at 58 per cent of total regional trade in 2015, down slightly from previous years but nevertheless high by global standards.[30] Trade linkages between Asian states at the regional and sub-regional levels, however, suggest trade integration in Asia will grow rapidly in the near-term. The region is also becoming more consolidated around bilateral and multilateral free trade agreements (FTAs) between states, which increased from 17 in 2000 to 200 in 2015.[31] The growth of regional FTAs includes ASEAN+1 FTAs with regional states, as well as ongoing discussions between China, Japan, and South Korea to form a Northeast Asian FTA. Further, the potential exists for "mega-FTAs" such as the Regional Comprehensive Economic Partnership (RCEP), which would bring the ASEAN+6 economies together in a regional-level mechanism. Such regional-level initiatives had received greater impetus from the Trump administration's wholesale rejection of the Trans-Pacific Partnership (TPP), which would include the US but exclude China.

Fifty-two per cent of Asia-originating foreign direct investment (FDI) stayed in Asia in 2015, equalling US$277 billion.[32] Asia has increased its financial integration, with intraregional portfolio investments accounting for 18.5 per cent in 2013. Intraregional credit flows also grew in 2014 to above US$66 billion. Asian regional developments are now more important than global developments in determining Asia's capital markets.[33] Intraregional development aid has also expanded with the establishment of region-specific financial institutions, including the Asian Development Bank, the Asian Infrastructure Investment Bank, the Silk Road Fund, and a number of regional sovereign wealth funds.

Politically and diplomatically, Asia has become increasingly integrated through regional organizations including the Asia Pacific Economic Cooperation (APEC), ASEAN Regional Forum, East Asian Summit, ASEAN+3, the Shanghai Cooperation Organization, the Greater Mekong Initiative, and the South Asian Association for Regional Cooperation (SAARC), to name only the most prominent. These venues serve the critical purpose of providing regional-level platforms for dialogue and engagement and, as such, are important vehicles for the establishment and dissemination of regional political and diplomatic norms and values.[34] With regard to security cooperation, the ASEAN Defense Ministers Meeting-Plus (ADMM+) has become an increasingly important venue for cooperation between Asian states on matters ranging from transnational crime to terrorism (on which more is written below). As with its diplomatic counterparts, the ADMM+ has become instrumental in shaping regional security norms with regard to cooperation and engagement.[35]

Less than economic, political, and security drivers, Asian cultural and identity linkages also contribute to regionalism. From Lee Kuan Yew's advocacy for Asian values to Kishore Mahbubani's writing on Asian perceptions, political and intellectual thought entrepreneurs argue for the relevance and further development of a specific Asian identity, often in distinct contrast to Western concepts of individualism.[36] Controversial in scope as critics argue authoritarian states press the idea of "Asian values" to justify their paternalistic governing style, there is little arguing that Asian identity has started to coalesce around such shared experiences as South Korean television and movies, Japanese pop music, intraregional travel, and shared political affiliation within ASEAN.[37]

8 *Jeffrey Reeves*

Regional security complex theory

These historic, economic, political, and cultural indicators clearly demonstrate the value in, indeed necessity of, studying Asia at the regional level. Still unquestionably tied to the larger global level and influenced by great power politics, Asia is increasingly shaped by relationships, developments, and events that take place within the geographic confines of the region. RSCT provides the conceptual basis and operational guidance for shifting focus away from systemic-level discourse on Asian security towards a more nuanced discussion of regional-level security dynamics derived from and/or influenced by China–Japan competition.

Indeed, RSCT makes three important theoretical contributions to the study of Sino-Japanese rivalry as it relates to and affects Asian security. First, the theory outlines the value in approaching security studies from the regional rather than the global level. More specifically, RSCT advances the concept of regional security complexes, which are geographically confined security communities determined by states' shared security nodes, security interconnectedness, and security concerns. Second, RSCT draws on the concept of securitization to establish patterns of amity and enmity between states that are further necessary to justify treatment of a region as a distinct security complex. Amity and enmity, in turn, provide an operational basis for the examination of a community's nodes and interconnectedness to determine trends in security relations. Third, RSCT argues the need to examine relations between regional-level powers, or regional-level power poles, to better understand conditions within the security complex. Through these three key theoretical insights, one can establish the basis to treat a specific region as a security complex, understand the overall security environment within the complex, and identify and analyse power relations at the regional level. Each point is dealt with in more detail below.

East Asia as a region and security complex

RSCT argues that the regional as opposed to national and/or global level is the most appropriate level for security analysis as states view their security interests in line with regional dynamics. Buzan and Wæver – RSCT's principal architects – argue that the regional level is "where states or other units link together sufficiently closely that their securities cannot be considered separate from each other". These security linkages, in turn, act with centripetal force to fuse neighbouring states' institutions of national security together in a durable but flexible bond. Geographic proximity, for example, contributes to the development of security interdependence between states with histories of interaction, and is most influential over security sectors including military, political, economic, societal, and environmental security, or what Buzan, Wæver, and de Wilde call "widened" accounts of security.[38] RSCT does not argue that all regions manifest into security complexes.[39] Rather, to become a regional security complex, a group of states must first have sufficient security interdependence, usually derived from material, cultural, or historical contact, "to establish them as a linked set and to differentiate them from surrounding security regions."[40] Neither do regional security complexes neatly fit

Sino-Japanese competition 9

with existing analytically determined regions, such as the European Union or the Middle East. Regional security complexes only exist where states have sufficient security ties to justify unified analytical treatment.

These observations apply to East Asia, as defined by this volume, where security nodes and regimes exist exclusive of global-level dynamics and great power relations. East Asia is home to a number of inter-state security threats, some of which have endured to the point of becoming regional security fixtures and some of which have emerged in recent years in line with the region's rapid economic growth. Most examined in terms of military challenges are ongoing tensions on the Korean peninsula between the Democratic People's Republic of Korea (DPRK) and Republic of Korea (ROK), and the DPRK's continuous nuclear programme. A defining security characteristic of Asian security for decades, uncertainty over the DPRK's nuclear intentions and the involvement of China and Japan (Asia's two regional primary powers) continues to ensure the issue's centrality in Asian's security.[41] Territorial disputes in the East and South China Seas have also gained (or regained) prominence within Asia's regional security architecture. In particular, low-level skirmishes over ownership of land features in the maritime domain and disagreements over maritime rights as defined by the UN Convention on the Law of the Sea have become a defining feature of Asian state relations, both in terms of cooperation and conflict (on which more is written below).[42] Both contributing to and separate from these security issues is Asia's regional trend of military modernization and increased military spending. States throughout the region, from the DPRK to Australia, have undertaken internal reform in recent years to professionalize their respective militaries and to enact legislation that redefines their use of force.[43] From 2013 to 2014, military spending in Asia increased more than 6 per cent in total, placing the region at the forefront of world military spending trends.[44]

Security challenges such as organized crime, terrorism, and cybersecurity have also developed in line with regional patterns of trade, migration, and tourism to the degree that complex webs of shared security challenges tie Asian states closely together. Drug trafficking in opiates and amphetamines, for instance, has exploded within Asia, with traffickers exploiting the physical linkages states have established for trade to move their illicit goods.[45] Terrorist acts including bombings and knife attacks and terrorism-related issues such as radicalization and returned fighters has also become more prevalent through the region. Together with political violence and insurgency, the threat of terrorism is a defining feature of East Asia's security architecture.[46] Cybersecurity has also grown as a regional security characteristic, with interconnectivity increasing states' vulnerabilities to this little-understood security challenge.

Non-traditional security concerns including biosecurity, environmental security, economic security, and energy security have also led to security interdependence between states. States and societies within East Asia, for example, have securitized the actual and potential spread of pandemic disease in the region from a public health issue to a transnational security concern.[47] States have similarly raised the importance of environmental occurrences such as climate change, yellow sand,

10 *Jeffrey Reeves*

deforestation, desertification, water, air, and soil pollution, and animal and fish die-offs to the level of national and regional security – an elevation of environmental issues that has led to cooperation and conflict in the region.[48] Economic security – or security related to stability and growth in states' domestic economies and within their bilateral relations – has become a defining feature of the East Asian security landscape, the result of greater economic regional interdependence, the 1997 Asian financial crisis, and the 2008 global financial crisis.[49] Energy security, or states' access to energy sources either in Asia or further abroad, has become both a national priority for states (both energy consumers and providers) and a regional-level security regime with implications across other security sectors, including environmental and economic security.[50]

As demonstrated above, East Asia is home to multiple regional-level security nodes and extensive security interconnectedness between states. These patterns of security exist outside the larger global level and are not dependent on the great power involvement of the US, in particular. Rather, East Asia's security characteristics are largely internal to the geographic region and, as such, form the basis of an East Asian regional security complex.

Sino-Japan competition and the East Asian regional security complex

In addition to its focus on regional security nodes and linkages, securitization, and amity and enmity, RSCT argues that security complexes are home to "patterns of rivalry, balance-of-power, and alliance patterns among the main powers *within* the region" that one must examine to understand regional-level security dynamics.[51] Specifically, standard regional security complexes are home to regional powers that act as poles, creating either a bilateral or multilateral overlay to the region's security regimes. Nowhere is this pattern of state competition in East Asia clearer than between China and Japan. Both states exert a huge degree of influence over regional developments through their economic centrality and their proactive foreign policies, particularly under the Xi Jinping and Shinzō Abe administrations. As of 2014, for instance, China and Japan were the world's second and third largest economies by nominal GDP, respectively, and the first and second largest in East Asia. Global in their economic outreach, both states primarily focus on the East Asian region for economic activity ranging from trade to FDI and from provision of aid to energy relations. As such, the two serve as economic poles within East Asia that have contributed (and continue to contribute) to regional economic growth and development.[52]

China and Japan are also both within the top six countries globally in terms of military spending (the first and second largest in East Asia) and regional leaders in terms of military modernization and professionalism.[53] Such parallel development contributes to a security dilemma between both states where they view one another's military advancement as offensive in nature and seek to balance it through greater military investment and posturing.[54] Military competition between Beijing and Tokyo is heightened by ongoing conflicts between the two over the

Japanese-administered Senkaku Islands (Diaoyu Islands), where their respective navies, coast guards, and air forces regularly encounter the other in pursuit of their competing territorial claims. Military competition between the two states is a defining feature of regional security dynamics, as this volume demonstrates in detail. Both states use their military capacities for coercive and conducive means within the region, whether to encourage military partnership and cooperation with regional states or to strengthen a claim through posturing over a disputed territory.[55]

Politically, Beijing and Tokyo both have developed robust, proactive diplomatic and foreign policy approaches to the East Asian region, largely designed to balance each other's regional influence through the creation of special relations and partnerships in the economic and security spheres. Competition across the diplomatic sphere has exponentially increased since 2012, when both states underwent leadership changes. For many states in the region, managing Chinese and Japanese competition for engagement is an increasingly dominant feature of their domestic and foreign policies.

Notably, balance-of-power relations between China and Japan are not the only balance-of-power dynamics in the region worth examining. Vietnam's role as a sub-regional power in continental Southeast Asia is a subject worthy of further study, as is Indonesia's growing ability to affect regional outcomes within the ASEAN framework and maritime Southeast Asia. The China–Japan rivalry, however, dominates the region and, indeed, directly influences the overall regional environment in which sub-regional balance-of-power dynamics occur. As such, specific focus on the role the competition between China and Japan has in East Asian regional security dynamics is both entirely salient and largely overdue.

Neither is it possible to address balance-of-power relations in East Asia entirely exclusive of the US's involvement in the region, which remains central to the region's security architecture. RSCT, however, accounts for such great power involvement within regional security complexes through the concept of penetration. Those states with the capacity to operate in extraregional security dynamics – particularly the US – can, and do, influence regional security through processes including alliances, military power projection, and war. RSCT can and does account for the influence that great powers have in regional security dynamics. The theory views great power involvement within the regional security complex, however, as an external variable, albeit one with significant influence over regional dynamics.[56] As such, RSCT does not argue for the artificial construction of regional-level units of analysis, but rather advocates a regional focus for better understanding of salient threats between states exclusive of great power involvement.

RSCT as an operational approach

In addition to providing a conceptual framework for viewing security at the regional level and a theoretical justification for a focus on competition between regional powers, RSCT focus on security nodes, relations of amity/enmity, and regional power relations provide the basis for an operational approach that

12 *Jeffrey Reeves*

serve as this volume's overarching guide to the study of Sino-Japanese competition within Asia. Specifically, RSCT argues that through examination of patterns of major security nodes and interlinkages, of existing state-to-state ties of amity and enmity, and of regional balance-of-power behaviour between the region's two most dominant powers, one can map regional boundaries, understand the region's anarchic structure and polarity, and identify social construction of a regional security architecture or identity.[57] Through identification of these essential structures within a regional security complex, one can then determine whether the complex is a standard, centred, great power, and super complex. Standard complexes, for instance, are complexes in which regional poles determine power relations while centred complexes are complexes organized around the dominance of a single, all-powerful actor, whether state or institution (e.g. the European Union). Great power complexes are organized around the presence of either global or regional great powers while super complexes result from spillovers of global and regional great power competition.[58] Through understanding of the regional security complex's "type", one gains a greater understanding of regional-level dynamics that contribute to the region's overall security architecture and the regional forces that shape regional security dynamics.

One also gains insight into the evolution of regional security complexes, or what RSCT calls predictive scenarios. Through determination of security nodes, regional balance-of-power relations, and linkages of amity and enmity, for instance, one can surmise whether the region is evolving towards maintenance of its status quo, towards an internal transformation, or towards an external transformation. Status quo, of course, suggests continuity with regional dynamics at the time of analysis. Internal transition suggests developments within the existing complex, such as shifts in regional balance of power or changes in dominant patterns of amity and enmity. External transition, conversely, is transition in which the complex either expands or contracts, shifting its geographic borders through a potential inclusion or exclusion of a security actor.[59] Consideration of a regional security complex's development is essential for determining movement between actors and the potential impact states' security relations may have on their ability to form a cohesive region.

Volume structure

The remaining volume, as such, examines Sino-Japanese relations in line with regional security nodes, relations, and balance of power in East Asia to determine the region's complex type and to provide a regional-level understanding of East Asia's evolving security architecture. The volume accomplishes this through a three-part approach. First, the following chapter provides a primer on China and Japan's foreign policy development and outcomes under President Xi and Prime Minister Abe to set a basis for the volume's subsequent sections and chapters. The chapter demonstrates how Beijing and Tokyo have developed foreign policy approaches that are largely competitive in nature and how this competition is largely based around movement for influence and advantage between the two states. The chapter also shows how the states' centrality within East Asia – in material and ideational terms – positions them both within East Asian security dynamics, both in instances of cooperation and conflict. As such, Chapter 2 provides the underlying rationale for further analysis in Parts I, II, and III.

Part I examines the effects of Sino-Japanese rivalry on regional security institutions, which include not only the formal institutions discussed by Mie Oba in Chapter 3, but also economics and trade, considered in Chapter 4 by Ramon Pacheco Pardo, and energy security, dealt with in Chapter 5 by Vlado Vivoda. Part I examines in particular detail the observable patterns of Sino-Japanese amity and enmity in each, taken from the broad view of East Asia as a whole.

Examining regional institutions, Mie Oba specifically points to Sino-Japanese rivalry for influence in Asia as a catalyst for regionalism and, as a result, an outcome of such regionalism. Oba identifies the countervailing trend lines of China's economic rise and Japan's relative decline as the impetus for a shift towards an endemic regionalism driven in large part by competition between the two states for influence over East Asian institutions. Oba notes that both Beijing and Japan see themselves as the natural "leaders" of East Asian regionalism and, as such, see any loss of their prestige in largely zero-sum terms.

Oba specifically identifies Sino-Japanese competition for influence within ASEAN as a defining characteristic of post-2000s regionalism. Importantly, Oba notes that this competition has changed in line with the shifting economic dynamics between Beijing and Tokyo; a change that has privileged China over Japan since 2001. Concurrently, Oba points to the strategic dimensions of the two states' rivalry, with specific reference to China's activities in the South China Sea and how its ambiguous maritime claims have complicated its policy of outreach to ASEAN member states. Within this paradigm, Oba rightly highlights both countries' ongoing preference to engage ASEAN and its members by means that leverage their respective strengths to counter and/or exemplify the other's respective weakness.

Oba also notes how institutional competition between the two states has shaped, and is shaping, regional norms with regard to order and identity. China and Japan's competing versions of what shape the East Asia Summit should take, for instance, represented fundamentally opposing views of East Asia: one based on democracy and rule of law and one based on non-interference and respect for sovereignty. Additionally, China and Japan have fundamentally differed on the desirability of US involvement in regional affairs, although not to the extent where either state defined its own interests in line with the US or sought to advance US interests in Asia over its own.

Oba's chapter provides an important starting point for the study of the role that Sino-Japanese competition has in shaping East Asia's security environment and in consolidating East Asian state relations at the regional level. The two states' rivalry over regional order demonstrates a conscious evolution in their strategic thinking away from global engagement and towards regional influence; a strategic shift that both Beijing and Tokyo have pursued through institution-building and norm entrepreneurship. Their competition has, in turn, founded new security linkages within East Asia and between various East Asian states. Taken together, their

14   *Jeffrey Reeves*

efforts have forged a shared consensus of East Asia as the appropriate reference point for security and state relations defined, in part, by regional power competition.

Ramon Pacheco Pardo's chapter on economic security competition and co-operation between China and Japan furthers Oba's focus on regionalism through the identification of patterns of enmity and amity in regional trade and investment. Pacheco Pardo's identification of Sino-Japanese enmity across trade, development aid, and infrastructure development, for instance, illuminates regional- and domestic-level forces within East Asia that shape its overarching economic landscape and provide the structural environment in which medium and small Asian states navigate their economic strategies and shape their domestic priorities. Pacheco Pardo points to the regional proliferation of trade networks organized around both China and Japan, for example, as distinct security nodes within East Asia around which Asian states orient their trade portfolios. Insightfully, he identifies these same regional trade networks and Sino- and Japanese-centric FTAs as dominant sources of regional-level norms and rules for government trade. His conclusions about the established drivers of East Asian economic strategies around Japan and China's two dialogic poles are especially relevant in the wake of the Trump administration's vocal opposition to the TPP agreement.

Pacheco Pardo also traces the emergence of regional norms and values as shaped by competition over development aid between China and Japan, particularly as Asian states struggle to choose between China's non-conditional approach to aid allocation and Japan's use of aid conditionality. Pacheco Pardo highlights the political component of development aid as a primary outcome of the two states' competition, suggesting an aid-based rivalry for influence within Asia between the world's second and third largest economies. Sino-Japanese competition over infrastructure development is similarly oriented towards influence-building as well as a pure capital investment in overseas fixed assets. As with aid, Chinese and Japanese approaches to infrastructure development are also leading regional-level norm and value development, with the primary difference being a quantity versus quality paradigm for recipient states.

Pacheco Pardo also notes, however, that cooperation between Beijing and Tokyo in the areas of finance and development banking is leading a growing regionalization across these two essential economic sectors. China and Japan's support of financial sector management and crisis relief, for instance, has been instrumental in the establishment of regional-level mechanisms such as the Chiang Mai Initiative, which serve as distinct Asian alternatives to global financial institutions. Pacheco Pardo concludes, however, by identifying areas of potential competition within the Asian financial sector between China and Japan, such as Beijing's attempt to internationalize the RMB, that are likely to become a source of regional-level friction in the mid to long term. Regardless of the type of exchange between China and Japan, their parallel engagement within finance is driving a greater interconnectivity between states that further integrates economic security at the regional level. This conclusion provides an apt counterpoint to the notion that Sino-Japanese rivalry is primarily a liability to the development of East Asia, suggesting ways in which it may also contribute to a more robust region.

Sino-Japanese competition 15

As with Oba's chapter, Pacheco Pardo demonstrates that Sino-Japanese rivalry within East Asia's economic security realm has primary and secondary effects for regional security engagement and linkages. In pursuing their own economic and political agendas with regard to trade, aid, and infrastructure, Beijing and Tokyo have both succeeded in forging security ties, establishing security nodes, and expanding a security network throughout the region. By cooperating on finance and development banks, the two states have similarly shaped regional economic security institutions, albeit those based on shared rather than competing interests. Importantly, these economic institutions – whether based on competition or cooperation – contribute to a regional security environment in East Asia organized firmly around regional poles.

Vlado Vivado's chapter on energy security takes a more pointed view on Sino-Japanese economic rivalry. He clarifies how China and Japan's economically motivated self-help behaviour has led to a security dilemma in East Asia in which Beijing and Tokyo view access to oil and gas supplies in particular as zero-sum. Vivado expands on this understanding of energy security to suggest China and Japan are engaged in competition for access to regional energy supplies, focusing not just on overall access but on relative gains vis-à-vis one another. As such, both China and Japan have raised energy security to the top of their respective national security agendas and have contributed growing amounts of diplomatic and military resources to ensure their continued, uninterrupted access.

More specifically, Vivado identifies a desire for energy security as an essential driving force behind China and Japan's larger engagement in security relations throughout East Asia. China's intent to secure access to oil and gas, for instance, is a key rationale behind its expanded infrastructure linkages throughout East Asia. Similarly, Japan's desire to secure access to natural resources within its near-abroad is also a driving force behind Tokyo's investment strategy in East Asia. Energy security, taken in this light, provides an enduring and expanding rationale for Chinese and Japanese security relationships throughout the region. The need for secure access to energy resources also plays into both states' engagement strategies, as seen in the Australia case, and their strategic understanding of maritime security in the South China Sea, considered in the chapter by Nankivell.

Relatedly, Vivado also identifies how Beijing's and Tokyo's use of government intervention in energy markets has shaped regional-level understanding of energy security. Asian states throughout East Asia have adopted, for instance, the two states' interventionist approach in contrast to the more "Western" market-driven approach. Both China and Japan are central to this region-specific understanding of energy security and, as such, are instrumental in state securitization of the energy supply in East Asia.

Vivado's identification of Sino-Japanese rivalry as a pivotal force in Asian energy security provides further evidence that competitive relations between the two states contribute to an East Asian security complex that includes Russia, South Korea, Australia, and others. Beijing and Tokyo's competitive national security strategies towards the development of energy sources in Asia, their parallel efforts to secure access to energy supply in the near- and distant-abroad, and their

16 *Jeffrey Reeves*

respective diplomatic efforts towards energy relations have led to a web of state ties across the region. The two states' bilateral agreements with East Asian states also suggest growing energy security polarity within the region organized around the two states as alternative regional power centres. Of equal significance, the two states are driving regional values and norms regarding energy security that are largely antithetical to extraregional concepts, such as the Western-propagated market-reliant approach.

Part II looks at Sino-Japanese competition across two key security issues in Asia: maritime security and cybersecurity. Arguably the two defining security issues of contemporary Asia, each area functions as a node in which Japanese and Chinese interests, policies, and behaviours intersect. Understanding the extent to which Sino-Japanese rivalry is already a feature of these security nodes, and the specific ways in which it informs the development of these issues as a result, goes a long way to helping us appreciate Asia itself. Part II extends the institutional analysis of Part I to look at cross-cutting security issues that are key to the region's possible futures.

With regard to maritime security, Kerry Lynn Nankivell identifies Sino-Japanese rivalry in the South China Sea as a catalyst towards the regionalization of the East Asian littoral as a coherent strategic space. Nankivell argues that converging commercial and security concerns between China and Japan are forging a regional security multiplex encompassing both the East China and South China Seas – areas which both states, until recently, viewed as isolated from one another. Nankivell highlights the Japanese government's recent securitization of Chinese maritime activities in its 2015 Defense White Paper and its evolving diplomatic agenda from *safety* to *freedom* of navigation as particularly salient drivers of the regionalization process. Within this analysis, Nankivell highlights the importance for Japan for regional power relations, both within multilateral institutions under the auspices of ASEAN, and through bilateral engagement with littoral states including the Philippines and Vietnam, in both defining China's maritime security challenge and in fostering a specifically East Asian response. Japanese active engagement, in this respect, has created new and expanding security linkages between states concerned about China's ambiguous maritime claims and intentions, many of which have been institutionalized in security forums, including the North Pacific Coast Guard Forum (NPCGF), the Expanded ASEAN Maritime Forum (EAMF), and the Regional Cooperation Agreement on Combating Piracy and Armed Robbery against Ships in Asia (ReCAAP). These institutions, in turn, support the development of a security cluster between states that share concerns over Chinese maritime activity and support efforts to ensure freedom of navigation in areas claimed by China.

While China has stopped short of directly opposing Japan's expanding role in the South China Sea, Nankivell does point to Beijing's growing concern over Japanese activity in the region, measured via Chinese diplomatic protests against Tokyo's engagement. Moreover, even as Japan has deepened its engagement with the South China Sea and its littoral residents, China has increased its challenge to Japan-administered holdings in the East China Sea. While falling short of open confrontation, Japan's activities in the South China Sea and China's responses farther north are clearly trending towards overt competition. It is entirely likely that the maritime security environment in East Asia is undergoing an external transition in which the geographic edges of the salient security sub-complex are expanding. Sino-Japanese rivalry seems poised to force an evolution of regional maritime security from isolated sub-regional theatres to a single, coherent regional seascape, in which Sino-Japanese competition once confined to the East China Sea plays out across the full length of the East Asian littoral, drawing small and middle powers into its logic.

Lora Saalman's chapter on cybersecurity points to the central role Sino-Japanese competition has in shaping regional institutions, norms, and rivalries in East Asia. Saalman outlines how securitization of the other has driven domestic developments in Japan and China, both in terms of strategic thinking and force development. Beijing's conceptualization of Japan as a Western "back door" into Asia's cyber domain, for example, has informed its rush to develop indigenous information technologies. These new technologies, in turn, have laid a regional-level network for security interconnectivity between China and other Asian states in Central and Southeast Asia. Concern over Japan's ability to engage in cyber warfare, broadly defined, has also driven China's development of a cyber force and pushed the country to revise its defence strategy to elevate cybersecurity as a national security priority.

Worry over China's growing ability to engage in cyber espionage has also been central to Japan's approach to cybersecurity, in particular its engagement with Western multilateral groups and the US. While Japan's Western orientation has led to a degree of isolationism in Asia, according to Saalman, Tokyo's embrace of "Western" values in its approach to cybersecurity does provide one-half of the regional-level discourse in East Asia on cyber norms. Japan's focus on individual rights in cyberspace, for example, contrasts with China's focus on state stability and internet control. These different approaches have led to regional-level power poles, each based around different concepts of cyber sovereignty and governance.

Moving from patterns of enmity between the two states, Saalman also examines how relations of amity between Tokyo and Beijing are shaping regional power relations, with a particular focus on trilateralism with South Korea. The states' desire to establish a region-centric mechanism to deal with confidence-building in cybersecurity, to help shape cyber strategies and policies, and to inform regional-level cyber norms has also emerged as an important platform for engagement. As China and Japan remain the overwhelming powers in Asia with regard to cybersecurity, their dominant influence within the trilateral mechanism with South Korea is an important factor driving such developments.

As such, one can view Sino-Japanese rivalry as the centre of gravity in the emerging regional cybersecurity realm. The two states' competition over concepts, partnerships, and capacities, in particular, point to a regional-level great power rivalry that is shaping the very environment in which other East Asian states must respond to cybersecurity threats and challenges. As this process is ongoing and wholly new, it is also an ideal focus area for understanding the means by which

18   *Jeffrey Reeves*

competitive dynamics between Beijing and Tokyo are shaping the East Asian regional security complex.

Part III consists of three state case studies – Australia, the Philippines, and Vietnam – that highlight the role that competition for influence and access within the China–Japan dyad plays in third states' domestic and foreign policies, as well as their securitization of regional issues. Unlike in the previous two parts, the agencies of third states both complicates and offers new opportunities for both China and Japan to pursue their interests vis-à-vis one another. Each of the country studies presented here describe this triangular dynamic in some detail, and from within very different strategic and geographic positions spanning from US allies Australia and the Philippines, to Vietnam, the latter of which enjoys a comprehensive strategic partnership with China. Consequentially, these case studies provide the most tangible evidence that Sino-Japanese competition co-mingles with the national strategies of third states to contributes to a regionalization of security issues that, in turn, provides the basis for an Asian regional security complex.

Nick Bisley's chapter on Australia highlights the challenges and opportunities regional middle powers face from Sino-Japanese competition and outlines one state's policies for dealing with that competition. Bisley notes, for instance, that Canberra has been thus far successful in pursuing a hedging policy with respect to the two states, engaging with China across its economic sector and with Japan across its security and/or military sectors. Japan's concerns over challenges to the regional status quo coming from China's expanding commercial and military presence in Asia, in particular, have benefited Canberra as Tokyo has become a highly capable and eager partner for military engagement and cooperation. To date, the benefits for Australia have far outweighed any costs associated with this approach, although Bisley postulates that the cost-free balancing act Canberra has pursued to date will be increasingly difficult to maintain in the near future.

More specifically, Bisley notes that increased competition between China and Japan is decreasing Australia's room for manoeuvre within the East Asian region. Bisley argues, for instance, that China has become more vocal in criticizing Australia–Japan military engagement as it assumes – quite rightly – that the two states' security partnership is largely aimed at mitigating China's expanding presence in the region. For Australia, in this respect, Sino-Japanese competition has become a defining feature of East Asian security, influencing Canberra's regional environment, its threat perceptions, and, consequently, its security relations. Bisley specifically argues that Sino-Japanese competition now contributes to a contested regional order, or what RSCT calls an internal transition, from Australia's perspective.

Bisley's chapter also demonstrates how Sino-Japanese competition is leading to regional-level security relations between US allies, exclusive of US involvement (a point Cruz De Castro also touches on in his Philippine case study, as outlined below). Bisley's identification of this trend in security relations and power dynamics reinforces this volume's regional-level approach to understanding security linkages and nodes outside the larger US–China strategic discourse, over-dependent as it is on great power rivalries. Bisley shows, conversely, how Sino-Japanese relations inform security relationships between the region's great and middle powers, particularly those concerned with China's growing security presence in the region and Beijing's ability to reshape the existing regional order. That Australia is working with Japan directly to strengthen its strategic posture – and that Tokyo is both willing to and interested in pursuing relations to counter China's ambiguous activities in the region – is clear evidence of the importance of the regional level to security analysis in East Asia.

Renato Cruz De Castro gives a similar account via his case study on the Philippines. Cruz De Castro specifically identifies Sino-Japanese competition within East Asia as a driving force behind Manila's security relations, perceptions, and responses, and as a key rationale for the Duterte administration's shift away from engagement with the US. Indeed, Cruz De Castro goes so far as to suggest Manila's deft manipulation of Sino-Japanese tensions to increase its strategic position in the South China Sea, even as it distances itself from its treaty ally, the US. More specifically, his analysis explains how the Philippine government, over several administrations, has built upon its security concerns towards China's activities in the South China Sea to reach out to Tokyo, which has responded in kind with diplomatic and material support. Cruz De Castro notes that Manila's ability to engage in balancing behaviour comes from Japan's own desire to offset China's growing influence in the East and South China Seas, and that the resulting partnership is mutually beneficial as it increases both states' capacity to respond to a shared sense of concern towards China.

As with Bisley's writing on Australia, Cruz De Castro references the US as an important catalyst for engagement between Japan and the Philippines and correctly identifies the two states' alliance status as central in their initial willingness to deepen security engagement. Yet Cruz De Castro also notes the growing importance of Japan–Philippines relations outside the alliance system's confines, particularly with reference to Duterte's marked shift away from the US starting in 2016. Indeed, Cruz De Castro explores the growing importance of Japanese–Philippine relations with a number of regional institutions that do not include the US, such as ASEAN and its multiple sub-forums – and suggests that Washington has become more dependent on Tokyo to influence Manila than was previously the case. This shift is a significant departure in the historical pattern of East Asian security relations. Japan and the Philippines' continuous ties, in this respect, point to an important development in East Asia that is likely to further accelerate the regionalization of security relationships, following the pattern observed in so many other chapters in this volume. Such a trend would be further reinforced by a Trump administration in Washington that revamps US foreign and military policy to demand more from its traditional allies in undergirding regional stability and order.

Importantly, the Philippine case study also further hints at an emerging Asian security order in which shared security concerns and security partnerships solidify to replace the more traditional order based on the US as an external balancer. This is particularly the case with regard to the Philippines as it has been central to regional consolidation with regard to maritime rule of law (its case against China with the Arbitral Tribunal), ASEAN institutions, and regional

20 Jeffrey Reeves

partnerships. Central to this position has been the country's longstanding concern over Chinese designs on the South China Sea, and its attempt to strengthen existing security institutions and develop additional institutions to counter this effect. While Japan has been instrumental in supporting the Philippines' regional approach, so has China. In presenting Manila with a clear security challenge, Beijing has helped mobilize both the Philippine people and government to look regionally for a security solution.

Alexander Vuving's and Thuy T. Do's case study on Vietnam offers a contrasting account of Sino-Japanese rivalry's effects on the national security strategies employed by third states. Where Bisley and Cruz De Castro discuss policy evolution within US treaty allies, Vuving and Do provide a guide to understanding rivalry as manifest in a traditional Chinese partner. The authors begin by laying out Vietnam's structural and ideological dependencies on China, the result of both economic geography and a twentieth-century history that put the two communist party states on the same side of the ideological divide. Moreover, the authors note that China's sheer size combine with these two factors to ensure that Vietnam has every incentive to maintain strong and positive relations with China.

Against this backdrop of the structural inevitability of Vietnamese alignment with China, Vuving and Do discuss Japan's longstanding soft power influence. Tracing a decades-long history of Japanese investment in Vietnam and bilateral commercial exchange, the authors attribute a significant role to Japan in Vietnam's economic development trajectory. Echoing other analyses in the volume, they note Hanoi's trade-off in quality versus quantity in the evaluation of Japanese versus Chinese investment but unlike some others, their analysis demonstrates Vietnam's priority focus on the former wherever possible. For Hanoi, with a contiguous territory and ongoing sovereignty disputes with Beijing in the South China Sea, economic relations with Beijing have long been securitized. Decisions taken from within that context are naturally aimed at reducing Hanoi's dependence on Beijing without sacrificing either economic benefit or political stability in their bilateral relations, making Japan an attractive partner to hedge against Chinese dominance. The superior quality of Japanese investment and production are only additional incentives to Hanoi to seek economic partnerships with Tokyo wherever possible.

Vietnam's unique policy dilemma of a small power positioned in many ways in China's orbit contributes significantly to the volume's central proposition that regionally endogenous power structures play a powerful role in patterning the security relationships that criss-cross East Asia. In the Vietnamese case, Japan presents a useful, but somewhat weak, hedging tool. Drawn together by shared concerns about China's heavy-handed designs on East Asian seas, Vietnam has found an increasingly willing security partner in Japan. Initiatives aimed at sharing capacity – exchanging Japanese patrol boats in exchange for assured access to Vietnamese facilities at Cam Ranh Bay, for example – might yet impose costs on Vietnam's China relationship. Moreover, unlike in Australia or the Philippines, Vuving and Do confirm that Vietnam's hedging strategy will remain subordinate to its ideological affiliation with China's Communist Party through strong party-to-party and military-to-military ties, themselves underpinned by a shared

Sino-Japanese competition 21

preoccupation on regime stability. While Sino-Japanese rivalry presents a valuable opportunity to strengthen Vietnam's structural weakness vis-à-vis China, there will be firm limits to what this hedging can achieve. Nonetheless, Sino-Japanese rivalry presents a uniquely effective policy lever for a Hanoi seeking productive enmeshment with, but not engulfment by, Beijing.

The volume concludes by considering the analyses as greater than the sum of their parts, drawing some conclusions about what the comprehensive review of Sino-Japanese rivalry can reveal about the nature of that rivalry itself. Where is this rivalry most prominent and where is it more latent? How does China and Japan's mutual suspicion contribute to the development of East Asian norms, rules, and practices over particular periods? Most crucially, in what ways should we expect rivalry to be a determinant of Asian security, perhaps to the detriment of US or other external power interests? The patterns revealed by a regional examination of Sino-Japanese interaction through the lens of RSCT illustrates the salience of a regional-level approach to security studies in East Asia. It also offers texture and nuance to predictive analyses about the regional complex's future of the kind that cannot be gleaned by cleaving to great power bias. The strong regional narrative that the contributors to this volume provide is a caution to those of us that either overlook or prefer to assume away the endogenous forces that shape the contemporary Asia in which we all operate.

Notes

1 This volume employs the term "East Asia" in reference to the geographic area that includes Northeast Asia and Southeast Asia, including Australia.
2 G. John Ikenberry, "Between the Eagle and the Dragon: America, China, and Middle State Strategies in East Asia", *Political Science Quarterly*, 131 (2015); Kurt Campbell, *The Pivot: The Future of American Statecraft in Asia* (New York: Hatchette, 2015); Christopher Coker, *The Improbable War: China, the United States and Logic of Great Power Conflict* (Oxford: Oxford University Press, 2015). Other examples of this type of writing include: Thomas J. Christensen, *The China Challenge: Shaping the Choices of a Rising Power* (New York: W.W. Norton & Company, 2015); Michael Pillsbury, *The Hundred-Year Marathon: China's Secret Strategy to Replace America as the Global Superpower* (New York: Henry Holt and Co., 2015); Aaron L. Friedberg, *A Contest for Supremacy: China, America, and the Struggle for Mastery in Asia* (New York: W.W. Norton & Company, 2012).
3 Barry Buzan and Ole Wæver, *Regions and Powers: The Structure of International Security* (Cambridge: Cambridge University Press, 2003), 46.
4 Alice Miller and Richard Wich, *Becoming Asia: Change and Continuity in Asian International Relations since World War II* (Stanford: Stanford University Press, 2011), 5.
5 For examples of such writing, see: Geoffrey Jukes, *The Soviet Union in Asia* (Berkeley: University of California Press, 1973) and Ralph N. Clough, *East Asia and US Security* (Washington, DC: Brookings Institution, 1974).
6 David Schimmelpenninck van der Oye, *Russian Orientalism: Asia in the Russian Mind from Peter the Great to the Emigration* (New Haven: Yale University Press, 2010), 121; Leong Yew, *Alterities in Asia: Reflections on Identity and Regionalism* (London: Routledge, 2010), 88; Carol A. Breckenridge and Peter van der Veer, *Orientalism and the Postcolonial Predicament: Perspectives on South Asia* (Pennsylvania: University of Pennsylvania Press, 1993), 76.

22   *Jeffrey Reeves*

7   Sheridan Prasso, *The Asian Mystique: Dragon Ladies, Geisha Girls, & Our Fantasies of the Exotic Orient* (New York: Public Affairs, 2006), 3.

8   Prem Poddar and David Johnson, *A Historical Companion to Postcolonial Thought in English* (New York: Columbia University Press, 2005), 208.

9   David A. Baldwin, "Security Studies and the End of the Cold War", *World Politics* 48:1 (1995), 117–141; Kenneth N. Waltz, "Structural Realism after the Cold War", *International Security* 25:1 (2006), 5–41.

10 N. Gansen, *Bilateral Legacies in East and Southeast Asia* (Singapore: Institute of Southeast Asian Studies, 2015), 14.

11 Tuong Vu and Wasana Wongsurawat, *Dynamics of the Cold War in Asia: Ideology, Identity, and Culture* (London: Palgrave Macmillan, 2009), 91.

12 Paul A. Cohen, *Discovering History in China: American Historical Writing on the Recent Chinese Past* (New York: Columbia University Press), 147.

13 Martin W. Lewis and Kären Wigen, *The Myth of Continents: A Critique of Metageography* (Berkeley: University of California Press, 1997), 95.

14 Edward Said, *Orientalism* (New York: Knopf Doubleday Publishing Group, 2014), 285.

15 Desmond Ball, *The Transformation of Security in the Asia-Pacific Region* (London: Routledge, 2015), 176.

16 Amitav Acharya, "Thinking Theoretically about Asian IR", in David Shambaugh and Michael Yahuda, eds, *International Relations of Asia* (New York: Rowman & Littlefield, 2014), 67.

17 Donald E. Weatherbee, *International Relations in Southeast Asia: The Struggle for Autonomy* (London: Routledge, 2008), 19; Michael Mastanduno, "Realism and Asia", in Saadia M. Pekkanen, John Ravenhill, and Rosemary Foot, eds, *The Oxford Handbook of the International Relations of Asia* (Oxford: Oxford University Press, 2014), 27.

18 Henry Kissinger, *On China* (New York: Penguin, 2012), 514.

19 Thomas J. Christensen, *The China Challenge: Shaping the Choices of a Rising Power* (New York: W.W. Norton & Company, 2015)

20 Michael D. Swaine, *America's Challenge: Engaging a Rising China in the Twenty-first Century* (New York: Carnegie Endowment, 2011), 388; Aaron L. Friedberg, *A Contest for Supremacy: China, America, and the Struggle for Mastery in Asia* (New York: W.W. Norton & Company, 2012); Robert D. Kaplan, *Asia's Cauldron: The South China Sea and the End of a Stable Pacific* (New York: Random House Publishing Group, 2014); John J. Mearsheimer, "The Gathering Storm: China's Challenge to US Power in Asia", *The Chinese Journal of International Politics* 3:4 (2010), 381–396.

21 G. John Ikenberry, *Liberal Leviathan: The Origins, Crisis, and Transformation of the American World Order* (Princeton: Princeton University Press, 2012).

22 David C. Kang, *East Asia Before the West: Five Centuries of Trade and Tribute* (New York: Columbia University Press, 2012); Martin Jacques, *When China Rules the World: The End of the Western World and the Birth of a New Global Order* (New York: Penguin Books, 2012).

23 Yan Xuetong and Sun Xuefeng, *Zhongguo jueqi jiqi zhanlue* (*China's Rise and Strategy*) (Beijing: Beijing Daxue Chubanshe, 2005).

24 Jia Qingguo, "Zhong-mei guangxi de jingzheng yu weilai" (Competition and the Future of China–US Relations), *Caixin*, 22 September 2014.

25 Shui Yinhong, "Zhong-mei guanxi pingjing zaiyu quanshi fenxiang er fei huxin" (Power Sharing and Mutual Distrust are the Bottle Neck in Chinese–US Relations), *Phoenix TV*, 2 February 2015.

26 Zhang Feng, *Chinese Hegemony: Grand Strategy and International Institutions in East Asian History* (Stanford: Stanford University Press, 2015); Zhang Feng, "Rethinking the 'Tribute System': Broadening the Conceptual Horizon of Historical East Asian Politics", *Chinese Journal of International Politics*, 2:4 (2009), 597–626; Zhang Feng, "How Hierarchic was the Historical East Asian System?", *International Politics*, 51:1 (2014), 1–22.

Sino-Japanese competition 23

27 David C. Kang, *East Asia Before the West: Five Centuries of Trade and Tribute* (New York: Columbia University Press, 2012), 8.
28 John H. Hobson, *The Eastern Origins of Western Civilization* (Cambridge: Cambridge University Press, 2004).
29 Giovanni Capannelli and Masahiro Kawai, *The Political Economy of Asian Regionalism* (New York: Springer Science & Business Media, 2014), 2.
30 Asia Regional Integration Center, "Integration Indicators", https://aric.adb.org/integrationindicators/result?sort=country&filter=all&r_indicators%5B0%5D=TCINTSHR_DOT&r_indicators%5B1%5D=TRTRADER_DOT&r_reporters%5B0%5D=679&r_partners%5B0%5D=679&r_years%5B0%5D=2015, accessed December 8, 2016.
31 Asian Development Bank, "Progress in Regional Cooperation and Integration" (2015), 20, https://aric.adb.org/pdf/aeim/AEIM_2014November_Part2.pdf, accessed November 16, 2015.
32 Asian Development Bank, *Asian Economic Integration Report 2016: What Drives Foreign Direct Investment in Asia and the Pacific* (Manila: Asian Development Bank, 2016), 124.
33 Asian Development Bank, "Progress in Regional Cooperation and Integration", 24.
34 Fu-kuo Liu and Philippe Regnier, *Regionalism in East Asia* (London: Routledge, 2013), 71.
35 See Seng Tan, *Multilateral Asian Security Architecture: Non-ASEAN Stakeholders* (London: Routledge, 2015), 153.
36 Cheng Guan Ang, *Lee Kuan Yew's Strategic Thought* (London: Routledge, 2013), 82; Kishore Mahbubani, *Can Asians Think?* (Singapore: Marshall Cavendish, 2009).
37 Beng Huat Chua and Koichi Iwabuchi, *East Asian Pop Culture: Analysing the Korean Wave* (Hong Kong: Hong Kong University Press, 2008).
38 Barry Buzan, Ole Wæver, and Jaap de Wilde, *Security: A New Framework for Analysis* (Boulder: Lynne Rienner Publishers, 1998).
39 David A. Lake and Patrick M. Morgan, *Regional Orders: Building Security in a New World* (University Park: Pennsylvania State Press, 1997), 22.
40 Barry Buzan and Ole Wæver, *Regions and Powers*, 48.
41 Scott Snyder, "The Korean Peninsula and Northeast Asian Stability", in David Shambaugh and Michael Yahuda, eds, *International Relations of Asia* (New York: Rowman & Littlefield, 2014), 298.
42 M. Taylor Fravel, "Territorial and Maritime Boundary Disputes in Asia", in Saadia M. Pekkanen, John Ravenhill, and Rosemary Foot, eds, *Oxford Handbook of the International Relations in Asia* (Oxford: Oxford University Press, 2014).
43 Jo Inge Bekkevold, Ian Bowers, and Michael Raska, *Security, Strategy and Military Change in the 21st Century: Cross-Regional Perspectives* (London: Routledge, 2015).
44 Stockholm International Peace Research Institute, *SIPRI Yearbook 2015: Armaments, Disarmaments and International Security* (Oxford: Oxford University Press, 2015), 15
45 Mark Harris *et al.*, *Transnational Organized Crime in East Asia and the Pacific: A Threat Assessment* (Bangkok: United Nations Office of Drugs and Crime, 2013).
46 Rohan Gunaratna and Muh Taufiqurrohman, "Insurgency and Terrorism in East Asia: Threat and Response", in Ramon Pacheco Pardo and Jeffrey Reeves, eds, *Non-Traditional Security in East Asia: A Regime Approach* (London: Imperial College Press, 2015), 23.
47 Christian Enemark, *Disease and Security: Natural Plagues and Biological Weapons in East Asia* (London: Routledge, 2007), 12.
48 Iain Watson and Chandra Lal Pandey, *Environmental Security in the Asia-Pacific* (London: Palgrave Macmillan, 2015), 3.
49 Helen E. Nesadurai, *Globalisation and Economic Security in East Asia: Governance and Institutions* (London: Routledge, 2012), 22.
50 Michael Wesley, *Energy Security in Asia* (London: Routledge, 2007), 8.

24 *Jeffrey Reeves*

51 Barry Buzan and Ole Wæver, *Regions and Powers: The Structure of International Security* (Cambridge: Cambridge University Press, 2003), 47.
52 Edith Terry, *How Asia Got Rich: Japan, China and the Asian Miracle* (London: Routledge, 2015), 343.
53 Stockholm International Peace Research Institute, *SIPRI Military Expenditure Database,* www.sipri.org/research/armaments/milex/milex_database/milex_database, accessed November 17, 2015.
54 Richard C. Bush, *The Perils of Proximity: China–Japan Security Relations* (Washington, DC: Brookings Institution Press, 2013), 15.
55 Geopolitical Diary, "China Sees Its Competition with Japan Grow", *Stratfor*, 22 July 2015, www.stratfor.com/geopolitical-diary/china-sees-its-competition-japan-grow?0=ip_login_no_cache%3Dcd6455864dee5d3064afe92864a27322.
56 Evelyn Goh, "Great Powers and Hierarchical Order in Southeast Asia: Analyzing Regional Security Strategies", *International Security* 32:3 (2008), 113–157.
57 Barry Buzan and Ole Wæver, *Regions and Powers*, 53.
58 Ibid., 62.
59 Ibid., 53.

2 Framing Sino-Japan competition

Drivers and responses across the military, economic, and diplomatic sectors

Jeffrey Reeves and Jeffrey Hornung

Security competition between China and Japan has deepened under the Xi Jinping and Abe Shinzō administrations, both in ideational and material terms. The result of competing security claims across a range of sectors, as outlined in this volume's introductory chapter and elaborated in more detail below, the states' respective political and military leadership increasingly view one another in adversarial terms, or as the aggressive "other" against which they must mobilize their comprehensive national strength. Examination of Chinese and Japanese competition across military, economic, and diplomatic sectors in particular reveals a persistent tendency by both Beijing and Tokyo to securitize their conflicting intentions and actions through policy, through the acquisition of military platforms and diplomatic partnerships, and through economic competition. Often overlooked in security writing on Asia for the analytical sake of Sino-American relations, this security dyad sits at the centre of regional-level security affairs.

Competition between the two states also deeply impacts small and medium Asian powers as Beijing and Japan directly and indirectly compete for access and influence within the states' domestic spheres. Through their respective military strategies and deployment of military assets, for instance, China and Japan have created a regional-level environment in which states such as Vietnam, the Philippines, and Australia, among others, are either constrained or enabled through engagement with Beijing and/or Tokyo. Competition between the two states for Strategic Partnerships also creates obstacles and opportunities for smaller players, whether through bilateral or multilateral engagement. Economic competition between Chinese and Japanese firms (and the Chinese and Japanese states) also serves as a force shaping the domestic and/or regional environment in which states must act.

This chapter establishes an empirical basis of Sino-Japanese competition, which the volume's subsequent case studies examine in more detail. Specifically, it outlines the respective roles China and Japan play for one other with regard to military, economic, and diplomatic strategy. The chapter's intent is to demonstrate how threat perceptions between the two states contribute to and influence East Asia's regional security complex.[1] Specifically, the chapter highlights ways that Chinese and Japanese responses to one another construct a regional environment

26 Jeffrey Reeves and Jeffrey Hornung

in which security develops and states act. From this starting point, the volume's case studies progress.

China's "Japan" calculus: military, economics, politics, and social relations

Under President Xi Jinping's administration, China's foreign policy has moved decidedly towards Asia in what some Chinese analysts have termed China's "rebalance" to the region.[2] China's top leaders have shifted their rhetoric away from talk about "new type great power relations" towards discussion of China's win–win ties with its neighbouring states.[3] In October 2013, for instance, the Communist Party of China (CPC) held a work forum on peripheral diplomacy, the first of its kind since the People's Republic of China's founding. In his keynote speech, Chinese President Xi Jinping announced a new phase of relations between China and its peripheral states, based on common economic goals and win–win relations.[4] Following the October 2013 forum, the CPC held its fourth Central Conference on Work Relating to Foreign Affairs in November 2014. As in 2013, President Xi prioritized China's periphery diplomacy and China's "good neighbour" policy over the country's great power relations.[5] Xi also called for the formation of a "community of common destiny" in Asia, largely precluding US involvement in the region. CPC Premier Li Keqiang has similarly raised the importance of China's peripheral relations within its overall diplomatic priorities. At the 2014 Boao Forum for Asia, for instance, Li linked China's peripheral foreign policy to regional security and stability, signalling that China intended to use its central position in Asia to ensure a stable Asian environment.[6]

In practice, since 2013, China has undertaken (and is undertaking) extensive development initiatives aimed at the larger Asian region, including Central and South Asia. Within China's One Belt, One Road (OBOR) grand strategy formulation, for instance, China has worked to link its policy, facilities, trade, capital, and social sectors together with its neighbouring states in a concerted effort to cement its position as Asia's preeminent political and economic actor.[7] In support of these initiatives, China has established financial institutions, such as the Asian Infrastructure Investment Bank (AIIB) and the Silk Road Fund, and announced massive investment and aid funding through its China Development Bank. China has also established and/or re-instigated regional multilateral dialogues on Asian security and economic development, such as the Conference on Interaction and Confidence Building Measures in Asia, which outlines ways forward in Asian development that exclude the US. These efforts – among those further outlined below – are specifically targeted towards strengthening China's "pivot" to its periphery, particularly towards the region's developing states which are in need of investment, technical expertise, and further integration into the Asian regional market.[8]

Central to China's peripheral approach is Beijing's direct and indirect competition with Japan for resources, political and social influence, commercial opportunities, and control of contested territory in Asia. In 2013, for instance, the

Director General of China's Department of Asia Affairs, Ministry of Foreign Affairs, Luo Zhaohui, specifically identified Japan as a regional "trouble maker" (*mafan zhizaozhe*) in Asia and as the primary driving force behind China's peripheral diplomacy.[9] While widespread competition between the two states has been a defining characteristic of Asian security in the post-Second World War years, Chinese–Japanese competition has reached a more critical stage in recent years as the two states' material capacities, measured in economic wealth and military power and ideational appeal, viewed in line with "soft power", have reached relative parity.[10] Not the only consideration Chinese leadership employs when determining their regional foreign policy goals and actions, China's view of Japan as its only regional peer competitor does inform the Xi administration's approach to Asia.[11] This view is clearest in China's military development and strategy, its understanding of economic competition with Japan, and its view of Tokyo's role in Chinese diplomatic outreach in Asia. The remaining section addresses each sector in turn.

Military

There is a well-established tendency within Chinese writing on its security relations with Japan to conflate Japanese intentions with those of the US. Rather than view Japan as a unitary actor with agency outside Washington's control, many Chinese analysts treat Japan as a secondary variable within Sino-US military relations; one that the US controls and directs for its own security ends.[12] The US–Japan military alliance provides a rationale for such perceptions, particularly when viewed in line with global security concerns and great power relations. Closer examination of China's military development at the regional level in terms of weapons platforms, military doctrine, and military reform, however, suggest Japan's security intentions and military capabilities also influence China's regional approach to security, exclusive of US involvement. This is particularly true with regard to Sino-Japanese territorial disputes in the East China Sea, with China's desire to expand beyond its first and second island chains (or "near seas") into the Pacific, and with historical memories in China of Japanese aggression.

In his excellent study of Sino-Japanese security relations, *Perils of Proximity*, Richard Bush details how the People's Liberation Army (PLA), the PLA Navy (PLA(N)), and the PLA Air Force revised their military strategy and acquired weapons platforms in the 1990s to extend their operation coverage towards Japan.[13] This included professionalization of PLA forces and acquisition of advanced submarines (*Kilo* and *Song* class), frigates (*Jiangwei* and *Jiangkai* class), aircraft, including the J-8, J-11, J-811, Su-27SK, Su-30MKK, and MiG-19 series.[14] Developed at speed under the Jiang Zemin and Hu Jintao administrations, China's regional-level response to perceived Japanese "aggression" continues under Xi Jinping. Specifically, the Xi administration's reforms to the PLA's structure since 2014, including plans in 2016 to revamp the Central Military Commission, disband the PLA's four general departments, and consolidate its seven military regions to five theatre commands, have been at least in part to increase the PLA's operational effectiveness within Asia and towards Japan.[15] The Xi administration has also developed and deployed air and sea assets specifically with Japan in mind, as outlined in more detail below. A qualitative difference in China's contemporary approach as compared to its past approach, however, is that China has broadened its military competition with Japan from the East China Sea to the larger East Asian domain.

First, in terms of rhetoric, Chinese leadership now regularly identify Japan and Japan's military activities in East Asia as a central threat to China's regional security. From 2013 to 2015, for example, Chinese President Xi Jinping identified Japanese "militarization" (exclusive of its cooperation with the US) on five separate occasions as a direct threat to China. Specifically, Xi pointed to Japan's activities in the East China Sea around the Senkaku/Diaoyu Islands, its reinterpretation of Article 9 of its constitution, and Tokyo's inability to come to terms with its militant past as key obstacles to Asian regional peace.[16] In 2015, in conjunction with China's celebration of the 70th anniversary of its "war of resistance" against Japan, Chinese Premier Li Keqiang identified Japan's tendency to revise Asian history as a source of instability within the region.[17]

More than Chinese leadership statements, many of China's recent defence publications specifically identify Japan as China's only peer-level regional state threat. China's 2013 Defence White Paper, for instance, referenced Japan's sovereign claims over the Senkaku/Diaoyu Islands in the East China Sea as a primary security concern for China in line with terrorism and separatist activities in the Tibet Autonomous Region and Xinjiang Uyghur Autonomous Region.[18] China's 2015 Defence White Paper, "China's Military Strategy", identified Japan as an immediate regional-level threat that "is sparing no effort to dodge the post-war mechanism, overhauling its military and security policies" in East Asia.[19] Both documents commit China to the defence of its sovereign and territorial interests vis-à-vis Japanese regional "aggression", among other threats, and have elicited fierce rebuttals from the Japanese government.[20] Qualitatively, the 2013 and 2015 statements differ in China's expanding reference to Japan's regional activities in the East China Sea to a wider focus on Japanese involvement in East Asia.

Chinese media's treatment of Japan as a regional threat are closely related to Chinese defence statements and thereby an indicator of strategic intent. The Xi administration maintains strict censure over Chinese media content, which justifies analysis of media statements as related to the Chinese state's perception and treatment of Japan as a regional security rival. Of particular note is the Chinese media's increasingly virulent treatment of Japanese military activities and security intentions in Asia under the Xi administration. Since 2013, for instance, Chinese media has regularly identified Japanese military engagement with Asian states including the Philippines, Vietnam, and Australia as evidence of Japan's growing regional militarization.[21] Chinese media regularly identifies Japan as a "threat" to regional security through its constitutional "revision" and its challenge to Chinese territorial "sovereignty" in the East China Sea. Chinese media also point to Japanese statements around Chinese military modernization as the primary source of regional "China threat" rhetoric that undermines China's gains with its

Framing Sino-Japan competition 29

peripheral partners.[22] While indirect, Chinese media remains an important source of messaging for Beijing and, as such, an important reference point for examining semi-official defensive/offensive Chinese rhetoric and thinking about Japan.

More than speech acts, one can also determine Japan as a source of inspiration for China's security actions and military reform under Xi Jinping. First and foremost, China's establishment of an Air Defence Identification Zone (ADIZ) in 2013 in the East China Sea was largely directed against Japanese action around the disputed Senkaku/Diaoyu islands. Immediately after the establishment of the ADIZ, China established Tu-154 and Y-8 intelligence-gathering patrols within the zone, announced the development of its KJ-2000 Airborne Early Warning and Control system, and declared that its Su-30 and J-11 aircraft would conduct patrol flights in the East China Sea.[23] China has developed and deployed these platforms with a clear focus on Japan. Since 2013, China has also regularly dispatched its H-6 bomber to fly close to Japan's main island of Okinawa and Miyako Island and deployed its indigenous unmanned aerial vehicle, the BZK-005, to conduct reconnaissance patrols near Japan.[24]

China has also significantly expanded its Coast Guard's capabilities and presence in the East China Sea under the Xi administration. Since mid-2013, the Chinese Coast Guard, consolidating its control over China's then-disparate maritime law enforcement forces (four of the "five dragons"), increased the number and quality of its patrols in the East China Sea, and acquired sophisticated weapons platforms such as the *Zhongguo Haijing* 31239 frigate, which it has deployed in direct challenge to Japan's Maritime Self-Defence Force (MSDF).[25] Concurrently, China has developed substantial submarine capabilities aimed at deterring and challenging Japan's own submarine forces in the East China Sea, as well as creating strategic uncertainty around the Japanese home islands. Specifically, as early as 2004, open reports confirm that China has deployed nuclear-powered submarines into Japanese territorial waters.[26] Regular deep-sea patrols by Chinese submarines to the east of Japan are a feature of the North Pacific, and may already stretch to Arctic waters. As China finalizes its at-sea nuclear strike capability, this range and lethality will put considerable strategic pressure on Japan. Closer to home, China has developed its Type 039A/B *Yuan* class submarines for littoral defence in shallow, difficult-to-access waters, with direct implications for China's maritime competition with Japan.[27] Compared with Japan's *Soryu*-class submarine, China sees the Type 039A/B *Yuan* class as a versatile platform for anti-ship cruise missiles capable of supporting contingencies throughout the shallow littorals within the first island chain. Since 2013, Chinese submarines – including the *Yuan* and *Kilo* classes – have appeared sporadically in waters off Japan's coast and have spurred the Japanese government to further develop its anti-submarine warfare capacity, on which more is written below.[28]

Economic engagement

Japan is China's clearest regional-level peer economic competitor, whether in terms of market access, investment opportunity, unilateral financial engagement,

30 *Jeffrey Reeves and Jeffrey Hornung*

or promotion of the Chinese-led AIIB. Chinese leaders view Japan's economic activity in Asia as complicating China's own economic engagement strategy, with corresponding strategic implications for China's military and diplomatic activities in the region. Competition between the two countries is increasingly seen both in Beijing and Tokyo as zero-sum in nature and exceedingly intense.[29] At the core of this regional competition is China's comparative advantage in "quantity", as in overall investment, trade, and financial linkages, and Japanese comparative advantage in "quality", whether in terms of technology exports, engineering competence, or ethical engagement.[30]

To understand China's perception of Japan as an economic "spoiler", one must first understand the domestic situation behind China's contemporary economic engagement strategy. In 2014/2015, China entered a period of slower economic growth (which Chinese leaders refer to as China's "new normal" economic model) due to decreased demand for Chinese exports in developed markets (the US and EU, for instance) and diminished returns on Chinese capital within its domestic market. In response, Chinese leaders announced a reform plan to the country's economy, most clearly outlined in the Third Plenum Session of the 18th CPC Central Committee's communiqué.[31] As part of its reform efforts, China announced a regional-level plan designed to support its existing export-led economic model and to advance its move towards market-driven capital allocation. This external engagement strategy – what Chinese leaders have termed the "One Belt, One Road" – aims to develop external markets for Chinese goods in developing states, to expand Chinese exports to its regional neighbours, and to identify opportunities on its periphery for Chinese investment with greater return to capital than Chinese financial institutions and firms can receive in the country's domestic economy.

As of 2015/2016, competition with Japan for market access and investment opportunities in Asia was one of China's primary obstacles to the achievement of its OBOR economic regional-level goals. This competition is clearest with regard to the "21st Century Maritime Silk Road" component of China's OBOR strategy. China's Maritime Silk Road is a comprehensive policy that seeks to expand China's economic links with Northeast and Southeast Asian states through investment in infrastructure, deepening of market compatibility, financial cooperation in the form of commercial and non-commercial loans, and, increasingly, aid.[32] Through the Maritime Silk Road, China seeks to expand its economic position and influence in states including Australia, Cambodia, Indonesia, Laos, Malaysia, New Zealand, the Philippines, Thailand, Taiwan, and South Korea. While China has been successful in expanding trade with these states through OBOR engagement, Japan's involvement in regional economic affairs limits China's ability to fully capitalize on its strategic intentions.

Japan is a key trade partner with many East Asian states, a position which complicates China's intention of expanding its overall trade relations within Asia. Association of Southeast Asian Nations (ASEAN) trade statistics, for instance, show Japan as the bloc's second largest trade partner (9.7 per cent of total trade) behind China (13.9 per cent) and ahead of the US (9.3 per cent).[33] To focus on Indonesia as an example, Japan received 14 per cent of the country's exports while

Framing Sino-Japan competition 31

China received 13 per cent. Japanese imports to Indonesia accounted for 10 per cent of the country's total, while China's imports to the country over the same period equalled 17 per cent.[34] By way of a second example, Japan received 9.5 per cent of Vietnam's exports to China's 9.9 per cent and provided 8 per cent of the country's imports to China's 28 per cent in 2014.[35] Japan primarily exports high-value products to the region, including car components, semiconductors, and information technology goods; China's exports consist primarily of textiles, light machinery, and chemical products. While China's intermediary trade in goods with East Asia has helped it become the region's largest supplier of high-tech goods as of 2014, Japan's existing, and in some cases expanding, position in the region's high-tech export markets continues to restrict China's ability to expand its own high-value, high-tech exports.[36] More on this competition will be explored below.

Competition between the two states in Asia extends to foreign direct investment (FDI).[37] Since 2014 in particular, Beijing and Tokyo have aggressively tried to outbid one another for access to infrastructure projects in states including Indonesia, Vietnam, Thailand, Laos, and Myanmar.[38] Competition for project tenders extends to dam building, airport construction, and port development, but is most visible and zero-sum with regard to competition over high-speed and medium-speed rail development contracts. Japan's successful acquisition of projects throughout the region has complicated China's strategic intention of establishing a regional infrastructure "web" connecting China's southwestern provinces to Southeast Asia and beyond.[39] Specifically, Japan's securing of a contract for rail construction in Thailand complicates China's plan to construct a rail network from Yunnan province to Malaysia and Singapore.[40]

Central to analysis of China–Japan FDI competition is the issue of FDI quantity versus quality, as earlier mentioned. China has a relative advantage in regional infrastructure development as its state-owned firms have access to cheap capital and to inexpensive labour. Japan, however, remains a regional "gold standard" for the quality of its firms' work, as well as their ethical focus on environmental protection and human rights.[41] In 2013, the International Monetary Fund (IMF) quantified the qualitative difference between the two states' investment and economic engagement in Asian states with a shift-share analysis that showed Japanese investment contributed far more to labour productivity in the service and manufacturing sector than Chinese investment.[42] The IMF study also demonstrated that Japan's economic activity within Asian states' domestic economies contributes to greater growth for the states than does China's economic activity. For many countries in the region, the choice of whether to award Chinese or Japanese firms their contracts comes down to the question of cost versus quality, with corresponding implications for Chinese and/or Japanese comparative advantage.[43]

Last, Chinese/Japanese economic competition in Asia extends to regional development aid and/or financing, which Beijing increasingly views as an essential part of its regional economic engagement strategy. This competition is clearest in China's establishment of the AIIB in 2014/2015, which as of 2016 had an initial capital stock of US$100 billion. While Chinese leaders and the AIIB's initial 57 member states insist the AIIB is a complementary, not a competitive, partner for the Japanese-controlled Asian Development Bank (ADB), the AIIB's challenge to the ADB's regional preeminence is clear. The AIIB will offer better loan terms to Asian states, for instance, than the ADB and has announced a faster processing time for financial assistance requests.[44] The Chinese government has also stressed that the AIIB will have a more streamlined appropriate process than the ADB; a claim that has some Western analysts worried about China's ability to undercut development aid conditions and quality in Asia.[45] To be certain, as of early 2016 the AIIB remained a work in progress (with considerable setbacks). The institution's ability to challenge the Japanese-led liberal development model in Asia, however, is already well established.[46]

Diplomatic engagement

Many Chinese view Tokyo's continued military and diplomatic alliance with the US as a stumbling block for closer Sino-US relations and as a contributing factor to regional instability. Japan's partnership with the US is regularly cited in Chinese media reports and scholarship, for example, as one of the primary obstacles to China's and the US's establishment of a "new type of great power relationship", which the Xi administration has actively sought to establish with the US since 2013.[47] These writings argue that Japan constrains the US's room for manoeuvre with China and shapes Washington's view of regional security issues in Tokyo's favour. Similarly, Chinese official statements regularly identify US support for Japan as a key enabler of Japanese "aggression" and/or "militarization" within Asia. In 2014, for instance, China's Ministry of Foreign Affairs called the US– Japan alliance a "Cold War construct" that contributes to regional insecurity in the name of alliance maintenance.[48] Scholars in Chinese government-sponsored think tanks have identified a "Cold War mentality" in Japanese–US relations that underpins insecurity throughout Asia in areas as diverse as strategic trust (or lack of) and maritime security.[49]

China also views Japan's foreign policy under the Abe administration (on which more is written below) as a key challenge to its development and maintenance of foreign relations with its partner states. At the centre of China's regional-level foreign policy are Beijing's efforts to establish bilateral and multilateral comprehensive strategic/cooperative partnerships with as many Asian states and institutions as possible.[50] More specifically, China has called on its Asian partner states to establish greater government-to-government ties, to coordinate on macro-level policy decisions, to develop deeper political trust, and to develop mechanisms for cooperative consensus through OBOR engagement since 2013/2014.[51] As of early 2016, China had comprehensive strategic/cooperative partnerships with Australia, Cambodia, Indonesia, Laos, Malaysia, Mongolia, Myanmar, South Korea, Singapore, Thailand, Vietnam, and ASEAN in Asia. While each bilateral and multilateral relationship is distinct in its precise composition, Beijing's approach to comprehensive partnerships is constant. For China, comprehensive strategic/ cooperative partnerships serve the purpose of aligning the country's domestic

Framing Sino-Japan competition 33

political, economic, security, and social priorities with its partner state.[52] Formal comprehensive Strategic Partnerships are China's means of ensuring regional influence vis-à-vis other great powers in Asia, with Japan in particular.[53] They are, as such, essential components of China's foreign and security strategy outreach in Asia.

Beijing views Japan's diplomatic motivations as very similar to its own. The Chinese leadership believe that the Abe administration is intent on establishing state-to-state partnerships that enable Japan to expand its economic and security relations in the region to affect a "rejuvenation" of Japan as a great power.[54] As such, Chinese analysts view Japan's diplomatic engagement with states as contradictory to China's own strategic ends as they tend to treat intangibles such as influence and partnership as finite rather than public goods.[55] Chinese writers also view Japan's diplomatic engagement with states in Asia – including the Philippines, Australia, and Vietnam – as inherently "anti-Chinese" in nature, particularly in relation to Japan's security diplomacy.[56] Chinese scholars regularly identify this aspect of Japanese diplomacy as a source of instability within Asia, particularly as it contributes to regional sentiments that China's activities in the East and South China Seas are aggressive in nature.

China also views Japan as its principal competitor for regional soft power; a component of national strength the Xi administration is determined to further develop. Indeed, the desire to increase Chinese social influence and cultural attractiveness, or soft power, as a means of propagating the "China Dream" throughout Asia is central to all Chinese engagement within the OBOR construct.[57] To accomplish this, the Xi administration has implemented a strategy of expanding cultural exchange, education contacts, skilled-person exchanges, media cooperation, and youth exchanges within China's larger comprehensive strategic partnership approach and as part of the country's OBOR outreach.[58] China has, for instance, increased bilateral political exchange with states like Vietnam and Laos (party-to-party exchanges), Thailand (military-to-military exchange), and Malaysia and Indonesia (parliament-to-parliament exchange) through direct meetings of high-level officials. Chinese scholars argue that Japan holds a decisive "lead" over China in terms of cultural attractiveness, political and economic desirability, and education/research quality. Chinese writers on soft power argue that Asian states view Japan in largely positive terms with regard to technological savvy, manufacturing quality, and general honesty: all traits these same writers argue are lacking in China's overall image.[59]

Relatedly, Chinese academics and analysts argue that Japan is the primary source of "China threat" rhetoric in Asia, which Beijing views as the main obstacle to China's development of a more positive regional image and greater regional soft power.[60] Japanese scholars, politicians, and media, according to Chinese scholarship, perpetuate the idea that Chinese foreign policy is inherently aggressive, even when China sees its actions as defensive in nature. Japanese defence documents, such as its 2015 Defence White Paper, attribute Chinese actions in areas like the East China and South China Seas as expansionist, when China believes (rightly or wrongly) that it is acting within its sovereign rights.[61] Japanese framing

34 *Jeffrey Reeves and Jeffrey Hornung*

of Chinese intentions and actions, as such, have a profoundly negative effect on Beijing's regional-level image. For China, a diminished image has direct strategic implications for its state relations, strategic goals, and security priorities.[62] As such, competition between the two states extends to regional-level influence and attractiveness – an area where the majority of Chinese writers believe China trails Japan.

Lastly, China views Japan's energy diplomacy – used here to describe diplomatic efforts to ensure access to energy resources abroad – within Asia as inherently zero-sum in nature. Where Japan succeeds in gaining access to natural resource stocks within Asia, China typically views a loss of its own potential resource acquisition. Similarly, Chinese analysts have identified Japan's regional energy diplomacy as a potential vulnerability in Japan's regional standing, especially in areas where Japanese policy leads to negative outcomes for its partner states such as environmental degradation and/or pollution. As such, Chinese analysts have identified Japanese energy security as a potential "weak point" in Japan's regional standing which China might exploit in the event of conflict between the states.[63]

Japan's "China" calculus: military, economics, and politics

Since resuming power in 2012, Japanese Prime Minister Abe Shinzō has been active in the foreign policy realm under the banner of "Proactive Contributions to Peace". Seeing an increasingly severe security environment and confronted by grave national security challenges, the Abe administration decided that Japan needed to be more proactive, expanding its security focus beyond Japan to the larger region. This is based on the belief that "Japan cannot secure its own peace and security by itself, and the international community expects Japan to play a more proactive role for peace and stability in the world."[64] As such, Japan has become increasingly involved in regional security matters, particularly those relating to the South China Sea. This is because it believes that the "South China Sea is directly related to the peace and stability of the region and is a common concern of the international community as a whole since the issue influences the international maritime order."[65] Tokyo takes serious consideration of the fact that the Japanese archipelago and the South China Sea both fall within China's First Island Chain strategy. From Tokyo's perspective, the security of one is directly tied to the security of the other, a linkage that will be discussed in more detail in a subsequent chapter.

While there are many components to this new pro-activism, a central portion consists of a comprehensive "China strategy" meant to expand Japan's strategic operational space. This strategy consists of multiple components. Militarily, the Abe administration has worked to strengthen Japan's defensive capabilities and enhance its alliance with the US.[66] Diplomatically, the administration has deepened Japan's Strategic Partnerships with key regional countries and has engaged in the South China Sea disputes through advocacy for regional adherence to international rule of law. Economically, Abe has positioned Japan to compete with China for regional influence, particularly in the development field. Through this comprehensive approach, the Abe administration strives to provide Japan with greater room for manoeuvre in regional affairs, to limit China's freedom of action, and to prevent China's rise from overshadowing Japan's own regional position and influence.

Japan's focus on China as a regional peer competitor across its military, diplomatic and economic sectors requires contextualization. Japan's first *National Security Strategy* (NSS) in December 2013 sets the context of how the Abe administration views the country's security environment.[67] The NSS notes that "the balance of power in the international community has been changing on an unprecedented scale", driven primarily by emerging countries, particularly China. The NSS further specifies that

> risks that can impede the utilization of and free access to global commons, such as the sea, outer space, and cyberspace, have been spreading and become more serious. . .[with] an increasing number of cases of unilateral actions in an attempt to change the status quo by coercion without paying respect to existing international law.[68]

While a number of other challenges are listed, the NSS focuses primarily on threats related to China's activities. These include territorial disputes between China and other states in the South China Sea, Chinese activity in "grey zone" situations, or situations short of military encounters, Chinese military spending, and Chinese actions to coercively challenge the existing order in Asia's maritime and aerial domains.[69] The NSS clearly identifies China as Japan's principal security challenge in Asia. The Abe administration's responses to this perceived challenge across the military, diplomatic, and economic domains are outlined below.

Military

As justification for revising a set of security laws in 2015, the Abe administration pointed to the worsening security environment surrounding Japan. Explicit in its critique of China, the administration pointed to the rapid expansion and intensification of Chinese military power, increasing and expanding Chinese activity in the East and South China Seas, the normalization of Chinese military vessels advancing into the Pacific Ocean through Japanese waters, and the increase in grey zone encounters instigated by China.[70] Additionally, the 2015 Ministry of Defence's (MOD) *White Paper* critiqued China's lack of transparency about its continuous increases in its defence budget and rapid military build-up. The document highlights Beijing's "assertive actions" in the maritime domain, "as exemplified by its attempts to change the status quo by coercion", characterizing it as "poised to fulfill its unilateral demands high-handedly without compromise".[71] It states "serious concerns about China's unilateral actions to change the status quo" and references "large-scale land reclamation or construction in the South China Sea" in particular.[72]

To meet these challenges, the Abe administration has focused on building a comprehensive defence architecture and strengthening its posture for preventing

36 *Jeffrey Reeves and Jeffrey Hornung*

and responding to various contingencies.[73] Towards this end, it has continued to re-focus Japan's defence towards the country's southwestern islands most vulnerable to China, and acquire capabilities suitable for defending this maritime and aerial domain under the notion of a "dynamic joint defence force".[74] Although it would be impossible to match China's annual increases in defence spending, the Abe administration has signalled its resolve to keep pace with Beijing. Prime Minister Abe increased defence spending every year since returning to office. In 2013, he made the first defence spending increase in 11 years (0.8 per cent). He followed this with a 2.2 per cent increase in 2014 and continued increases of 0.8 per cent and 2.2 per cent for 2015 and 2016, respectively.[75] With the 2016 budget at US$42.38 billion, it marks the largest defence budget in 14 years.

Like its predecessor, the Abe administration has dedicated investments to acquire military assets to help better position the Self-Defence Forces (SDF) to respond to the various challenges that China's growing military presents to Japan, including in grey zone situations. To this end, it has sought to pursue a number of capabilities meant to offset, or at least temper, China's quantitative superiority.[76] First among these are intelligence, surveillance, and reconnaissance (ISR) capabilities. The MOD has pushed forward with installing and upgrading defence radar on Japan's outlying islands. This includes a base to house a mobile warning and control radar in Amami-Oshima, an FPS-7 fixed warning and control radar on Unishima, and a coast observation unit on Yonaguni, Japan's westernmost inhabited island. Tokyo has also acquired new E-2D airborne early-warning aircraft and three Global Hawk unmanned aerial vehicles. All of this allows the SDF to keep a better watch on Chinese activities on its southwestern flank.

Similarly, there has been a focus on anti-submarine warfare capabilities. Because submarines continue to play the dominant role in the assault force for the PLA(N), Japan has worked to blunt their effectiveness. The MSDF has acquired two 19,500-tonne helicopter destroyers (DDH), Japan's largest ships. The first of the class, *Izumo*, was commissioned in March 2015. The second, *Kaga*, will be commissioned in 2017. The MSDF has also acquired two P-1s, which is modelled on the P-3C patrol aircraft, but wields increased detection/discrimination capability, flight performance, information-processing capability, and strike capability. For 2016 and beyond, the MSDF is improving the capabilities of its P-3C patrol aircraft, acquiring 17 SH-60K patrol helicopters, and developing a variable depth sonar system, thereby enhancing capabilities of destroyers to detect and classify submarines.

Given the spike in Chinese activity in the waters and air around the Senkaku/ Diaoyu Islands by both military and paramilitary forces, and the persistent threat China may one day attempt enforcement of its East China Sea ADIZ, Tokyo has made a concerted effort to strengthen its island defences through more mobile equipment and development of amphibious capabilities for the Ground Self-Defence Force's (GSDF) Western Army Infantry Regiment into an Amphibious Rapid Deployment Brigade. With plans to acquire 52 amphibious assault vehicles, 36 light mobile combat vehicles, and 17 V-22 Osprey tilt-rotor aircraft (operable from the new DDH), augmented by recent acquisitions of CH-47JA helicopters

Framing Sino-Japan competition   37

and mobile missile batteries and a plan to station a patrol unit on Miyako, the GSDF is making a dedicated effort to protect its far-flung islands.

All of this is supported by acquisitions of enhanced firepower, such as additional *Aegis* destroyers and *Soryu*-class submarines with enhanced X-band satellite communications capabilities and torpedo countermeasures, new ship-to-ship missiles with improved guidance precision and extended range, additional stealth F-35A fighters, and improved air-to-air combat capabilities of existing F-15s and F-2s, respectively. Taken together, this supports the Abe administration's policy of "developing defense capabilities adequate both in quantity and quality that underpin various activities to realize a more robust defense force".[77]

Japan's China-focused defence mobilization extends to its management of its primary security relationship as well. Tokyo has worked in recent years to better leverage its alliance with the US while also developing new, complementary partnerships in East Asia. Turning first to its relationship with the US, Japan worked to strengthen the alliance as a means of reinforcing its deterrence capabilities and the alliance's contingency response capabilities.[78] Towards this end, the allies revised their bilateral Guidelines for Defense Cooperation (hereafter Guidelines), the first revision since 1997.[79] An objective was to ensure "seamless, robust, flexible, and effective" bilateral cooperation to meet fresh challenges to the international order, such as "state actions that undermine respect for sovereignty and territorial integrity by attempting to unilaterally change the status quo by force or coercion", a coded but clear reference to China.[80] Washington and Tokyo's shared concerns about managing a growing China are also evident in the declaratory language in the Guidelines,[81] and comments made by senior officials.[82] The functional areas identified for enhanced US–Japan cooperation all enable Japan to better operate in contested air and sea spaces. They include air and missile defence, ISR, asset protection, logistic support, use of facilities, maritime security, and partner capacity building. The revised Guidelines also support continued efforts to enhance the alliance's Ballistic Missile Defence capabilities and position more advanced US assets in Japan, including the P-8 maritime patrol aircraft, F-35B fighters, and the Global Hawk.[83] Each of these shifts reflects a shared US–Japan threat perception that a near-peer ally will put increasing pressure on Japanese territory and naval mobility. While China is not explicitly named, the Chinese military remains Japan's only near-peer competitor in the region. Though Japan continues to face territorial and maritime disputes with other neighbours (like Russia and South Korea), only China pursues its disputes with Japan through direct and regular use of its naval, air, and paramilitary assets. Within that context, many of the changes to capability investments in the US–Japan alliance should be interpreted as direct responses to a growing and more active China.[84]

In addition to leveraging the US alliance in new ways, Japan has sought out new security partnerships to strengthen its regional position vis-à-vis an increasingly active China. In particular, in 2014, the Abe administration made legislative changes to allow Japan to provide military support to developing states. The new authorities permit arms transfers under development funding, if they contribute to the "active promotion of peace contribution and international cooperation, or to

Japan's security".[85] Moreover, Japan's new Acquisitions, Technology, and Logistics Agency in the MOD is expected to streamline the process for Japan to provide military equipment and technology to like-minded partners. Writing in support of changes to Japan's Official Development Assistance (ODA), Prime Minister Abe confirmed that he views them as enabling Japan to "now offer rescue, transport, surveillance, and minesweeping equipment" to those working to ensure the security and free navigation of Asian waters and skies.[86] Mobilizing ODA in support of the freedom of navigation (FON) is not only evidence of Japan's increasing securitization of development assistance, but also part of its response to China's Anti-Access/Aerial Denial (A2/AD) strategy, which aims to limit navigational freedoms in areas China deems its own. More is written on the development of Japan's FON diplomacy and its role in expanding security partnerships throughout Asian seas in subsequent chapters, but from within an investigation of Japan's changing calculus with respect to China, it is enough to note that under the Abe administration, Japan is poised to embark on more Strategic Partnerships with more Asian states now than at any time in the post-Second World War period. Tokyo is clearly prepared to mobilize its considerable whole-of-government resources in service of its perceived national security needs, which it believes are growing more urgent.

Diplomatic policies

Just as the Abe administration has worked to bolster Japan's defence capabilities to counter Chinese assertiveness, it has advanced new diplomacy as well. According to Abe's national security adviser Yachi Shotaro, these efforts have targeted countries that share concerns regarding China, primarily maritime countries and sea powers.[87] Towards this end, the Abe administration has developed closer "Strategic Partnerships" with countries throughout the region.[88] This follows the Abe administration's desire to cooperate with "countries that share interests in responding to shared security challenges . . . and actively respond to maintain regional and global stability".[89] These efforts have focused predominately on Southeast Asia, where Tokyo is leveraging ties to gain influence in the management of the South China Sea disputes and make a contribution to defending the existing rules regulating the maritime domain.[90]

Prime Minister Abe has used regional forums to advance its agenda to support for FON and those ASEAN member states that seek to do the same. Delivering the keynote address at the 2014 Shangri La Dialogue, Abe explicitly offered "utmost support for the efforts of the countries of ASEAN as they work to ensure the security of the seas and the skies, and thoroughly maintain freedom of navigation and freedom of overflight".[91] Towards this end, Japan has worked to deepen existing Strategic Partnerships in the region, intending to "play an even greater and more proactive role than it has until now in making peace in Asia", while enjoying "the explicit and enthusiastic support of the leaders of [Japan's] allies and other friendly nations, including every leader of ASEAN member countries."[92] The result has been a proliferation of new working-level consultations, security

Framing Sino-Japan competition 39

dialogues, and maritime cooperation between Japan and new partners in Southeast Asia, including the Philippines, Vietnam, Indonesia, Singapore, and Malaysia. The Abe administration has begun to make inroads with states traditionally seen as Chinese allies, establishing Strategic Partnerships with Cambodia and Laos[93] and moving quickly to engage Myanmar as it democratizes.[94] Today, Japan has Strategic Partnerships with all ASEAN members except Singapore, Myanmar, and Brunei.

Importantly, the Abe administration has boosted Japan's profile in multilateral forums throughout the region. In ASEAN and the East Asia Summit, the Abe administration has actively advocated for maritime issues, even over Chinese opposition. As a case in point, Japan successfully overrode China's opposition to adding explicit references to the deteriorating security situation in the South China Sea in the Chairman's Statement of the November 2015 East Asia Summit. The final text underlined "the importance of maintaining peace, stability, security and upholding freedom of navigation in and over-flight above the South China Sea" and "ongoing developments in the area, which have resulted in the erosion of trust and confidence amongst parties [which] may undermine peace, security and stability in the region."[95]

The Abe administration has also made concerted efforts to strengthen relations with Australia. It values Canberra's partnership as another US ally, and as a willing and capable partner that shares Japan's democratic values. In a 2014 speech to the Australian parliament, Abe invoked Japan's "special relationship" with Australia, calling on Canberra to join Tokyo "in order to make the vast seas from the Pacific Ocean to the Indian and those skies open and free . . .[to] follow the law and never fall back onto force or coercion".[96] These overtures are welcomed in Australia, where anxiety regarding China has been on the rise since the mid-2000s. This was first seen in Australia's 2007 Defense Update, which states that the pace and scope of China's military expansion risks regional instability.[97] The theme continued in the 2009 White Paper, which warns "the pace, scope and structure of China's military modernization have the potential to give its neighbors cause for concern".[98] These strategic views have been put into practice in Japan–Australia bilateral diplomacy and military agreements. The two countries conduct a 2+2 Dialogue between their foreign and defence ministers (Japan's first non-US 2+2), enjoy an Information Security Agreement and an Acquisition and Cross-Servicing Agreement, making Australia Japan's first logistic partner beyond the US. Importantly, the two have agreed to collaborate on issues surrounding the South China Sea.[99] Australia now stands as Japan's closest security partner after the US.[100]

Perhaps the most understudied aspect of the Abe administration's diplomatic activities vis-à-vis China has been its efforts to promote legal interpretations of maritime law based on Japan's interpretation of the UN Convention on the Law of the Sea. In a regional environment increasingly characterized by China's A2/AD strategy, Japan's legal diplomacy can only be understood as a means to counter China's attempts to legitimate its limits on navigational freedoms in Chinese waters. In an implicit critique of China, Abe stated in his 2014 Shangri La Keynote Address that "the least desirable state of affairs is having to fear that coercion and

40   *Jeffrey Reeves and Jeffrey Hornung*

threats will take the place of rules and laws".[101] In a declaration of regional solidarity, Abe declared: "Japan for the rule of law. Asia for the rule of law. And the rule of law for all of us."[102] To operationalize this belief, Abe has utilized its growing list of Strategic Partnerships to vigorously promote its legal interpretations of maritime law, which stand in stark contrast to those promoted by China.[103]

Economic policies

Similar to the security and diplomatic spheres, Japanese competition with China is increasingly visible in the economic realm. Even as China remains a vital partner for Japan, there are a growing number of arenas in which their economic rivalry is apparent in the region. This includes in development assistance, FTAs, and infrastructure investments. This section will consider each in turn. With respect to the latter, as discussed above, competition over high-value, high-end infrastructure technologies is particularly acute. Just as China seeks to expand its reputation as a high-technology partner, Japan is sensitive to China's emergence in this field because it threatens to undermine Japan's own comparative advantage in that area. For that reason, this section will deal specifically with competition for high-speed rail contracts as an area viewed with special sensitivity in Tokyo.

Japan has been a major player in ODA since it first began providing aid six decades ago. The focus was always non-military in nature and on the recipient country, with investments in infrastructure, public health, and education. Abe's new Development Cooperation Charter (hereafter Charter) released in February 2015 expands Japan's traditional focus towards one that is more "strategic" in nature.[104] Contemporary Japanese commentary takes for granted that the pre-eminent consideration behind this shift has been China.[105] Unlike the past, the Charter explicitly declares that ODA is meant to ensure Japan's national interests.[106] As such, the Charter focuses on regional and international cooperation, with Southeast Asia listed first.[107] Additionally, new efforts are seen as means by which to counter China's influence in Asia. One is that Japan "will provide assistance so as to share universal values such as freedom, democracy, respect for basic human rights and the rule of law as well as to realize a peaceful, stable and secure society."[108] The other is Japan's providing assistance to "the capacity of law enforcement authorities including capabilities to ensure maritime safety . . . and the capacity of developing countries in relation to global commons such as seas, outer space, and cyberspace."[109] Importantly, as discussed above, the Charter now allows Japan to provide assistance to foreign militaries for non-combat uses, which will enable Japan to build military partnerships with regional countries through capacity-building programmes.

Related is the bilateral competition over regional development institutions. Although the Abe administration does not disagree in principle with President Xi Jinping's announcement of the AIIB initiative, like the US, Japan refrained from signing the agreement in June 2015, citing specific concerns.[110] Japanese leadership has raised questions over transparency in the AIIB's governance, operations, and lending rules; the membership of a permanent board of governors; and China's

Framing Sino-Japan competition 41

track record on human rights, debt sustainability, and environmental protection.[111] Tokyo is concerned that Beijing may use the AIIB to bend regional lending patterns to conform with its own economic policies and national interests, for example, to implement its OBOR initiative.[112] Fears that China seeks to distort the AIIB by overwhelming its funding base are supported by data trends. Despite an initial capitalization of US$50 billion, as the number of AIIB member countries rose, China doubled its investment to US$100 billion.[113] More importantly, given that China is set to occupy a dominant presence in the AIIB, headquartered in Beijing, Japan sees it as a competitor to the ADB, which is headed by a Japanese. The AIIB's growth means that the ADB will lose significant regional influence as it is forced to compete for regional projects.

Faced with this prospect, Japan mounted its own response. Prime Minister Abe announced US$110 billion (¥13 trillion) in aid for "high-quality" infrastructure development in Asia over the course of five years in collaboration with the ADB. The amount represents a 30 per cent increase in Japan's infrastructure funding over the previous five years. Under this initiative, about US$53 billion will be financed through the ADB, US$33.5 billion will be loaned through the Japan International Cooperation Agency, and roughly US$20 billion will be funded through agencies including the government-affiliated Japan Bank for International Cooperation.[114] The sum of these investments promise continued Japanese leadership of regional development projects, countering China's bid to expand its financial influence in the region.

While Japan's moves to counter Chinese development financing initiatives are reasonably clear, it is harder to discern in the ongoing negotiations over the Trans-Pacific Trade Partnership (TPP). While commentators argue that Japan's main objective in the TPP negotiation is to exclude China,[115] this is not the government's stated objective. There are more subtle indications, however, that Japanese policy makers intend to use the TPP as an avenue to strengthen the US–Japan alliance. In Abe's speech to Congress, speaking about the TPP, he stated that the rule of law, democracy, and freedom are "exactly what the TPP is all about."[116] He noted that his government is focused on spreading these US–Japan shared values around the world, implying that TPP would be a tool to that end. Japanese policy makers see the TPP as a chance to write the rules that will set trading patterns favourable to Japan at a time when China remains unable to join the negotiation.[117] It is a means to shape China's rise in a regional order defined by Japan and like-minded others, and under which Japan prospers.[118] Seen as such, Japan's interest lies in crafting the strategic economic environment in which China exists and forcing China to abide by the rules Japan helps craft, if it wishes to join.

The economic rivalry has even played out in large-scale, high-technology infrastructure projects. As mentioned above, these cover a range of areas, from dam building to airport construction to port development. Yet, the most politicized has been the bilateral competition in the region over high-speed and medium-speed rail development contracts. Over the past years, Premier Li Keqiang has led a drive to promote China's high-speed technology in Thailand, Britain, and Russia.[119] Prime Minister Abe has actively promoted Japan's *shinkansen* technology, which the Japanese officials market as the best, safest, most established technology

42 *Jeffrey Reeves and Jeffrey Hornung*

available. While a primary objective is certainly economic, it can also be seen as a competition for regional influence through infrastructure funding.

The first two sites of this emerging competition are Indonesia and Thailand. In Indonesia, though Japan was considered a frontrunner to build a 150-kilometre high-speed railway connecting Jakarta to Bandung, China undercut Japan's bid to win the contract. Reports attribute China's bid to the fact that it forewent Indonesian spending and a sovereign debt guarantee.[120] Japan responded by modifying its own bid, lessening the responsibility of the Indonesian sovereign guarantee, shortening completion time, and including a knowledge transfer. In the end, Beijing's bid was accepted, successfully challenging Japan's traditional influence in Indonesia. In direct response to this loss, in November 2015 Japan eased conditions on yen loans for emerging Asian economies.[121] This enhanced its competitiveness in a bid for a 505-kilometre high-speed rail deal linking Mumbai with Ahmedabad in India shortly thereafter. The contract impacted China's OBOR initiative, which actively positioned itself as it stands as an alternative development source for Indian infrastructure.[122] A pattern of rivalry in the rail sector seems established. With proposed railways linking Kuala Lumpur with Singapore, and Bangkok with Pattaya currently under examination, this rivalry will have room to grow.[123]

Conclusion

This chapter outlines areas of competition between China and Japan that shape the countries' respective military, economic, and diplomatic strategies and that influence and shape Asia's regional security dynamics. The authors have provided strategic and operational accounts of Sino-Japanese security relations, avoiding discussion of more issue-specific engagements. The authors have similarly adhered to the volume's geographical focus on Asia – to include the Northeast and Southeast Asian sub-regions – rather than examining Sino-Japanese competition at an extra-regional or global level. As such, the chapter is an appropriate analytical primer for the volume's subsequent case studies, not an isolated discussion on the depth and scope of the security outcomes resulting from Sino-Japanese competition.

The volume's subsequent case studies address the issue areas in more specific detail. These investigations will answer the many questions the chapter raises but does not adequately answer. These case studies provide greater clarity to the volume's central contention: that competition between China and Japan stands as a central driver of Asia's regional security complex. Their bilateral relations generate interconnectivity, strengthen patterns of amity and/or enmity between third states, and underlie regional balancing and friendships. Understanding the ways in which Sino-Japanese relations are manifest across the region is a prerequisite to understanding contemporary Asia and its possible futures.

Notes

1 Although both China and Japan have pursued improvements in relations with India in the military, economic, and diplomatic fields, India falls outside the scope of the regional security complex examined here. As such, India is not included in this study.

Framing Sino-Japan competition 43

2 Liang Haiming, "Should China also Rebalance to Asia?" (Zhongguo ye yao chongfan yazhou ma?), *Sina Economic*, January 5, 2015.

3 Yan Xuetong, "Zhengti de zhoubian bi meiguo geng zhongyao" (The entire periphery is more important that the United States), *Global Times*, January 13, 2015.

4 Embassy of the People's Republic of China in the Republic of Korea "Xi Jinping zai zhoubian waijiao gongzuo zuotanhui shang fabiao zhongyao jianghua" (Xi Jinping's Important Speech at a Peripheral Working Group Published), www.fmprc.gov.cn/ce/cekor/chn/xwxx/t1093366.htm, accessed January 22, 2016.

5 Xinhua, "Xi Jinping chuxi zhongyang waishi gongzuo huiyi bing fabiao zhongyao jianghua" (Xi Jingping Attends a Central Foreign Affairs Working Group and Gives an Important Speech), *Xinhua*, November 29, 2014.

6 "Li Keqiang Speaks about Peripheral Diplomacy: Chinese People Emphasise Reciprocity (Li Keqiang tan zhoubian waijiao: Zhongguo ren jiangqiu "yide baode"), *Cankao Xiaoxi*, April 11, 2014, http://china.cankaoxiaoxi.com/2014/0411/373988.shtml.

7 National Development and Reform Commission, *Push Forward the Silk Road Economic Belt and the 21st Century Maritime Economic Road's Common Vision and Operation* (Tuidong gong jian sichou zhilu jingji dai he 21 shiji haishang sichou zhilu de yuanjing yu xingdong). Beijing, March 28, 2015.

8 Su Xiaohui, "Why Does China Attach More and More Importance to Periphery Diplomacy?" (Zhongguo weihe yuelaiyue zhongshi zhoubian waijiao), *Communist Party of China News (Zhongguo Gongchandang xinwen)*, December 22, 2014.

9 Yang Rui, "China's Periphery Diplomacy's New Expedition: Director General of China's Department of Asia Affairs, Ministry of Foreign Affairs, Luo Zhaohui gives a 'Foreign Policy Expert' Interview" (Zhongguo zhoubian waijiao zhengcheng – waijiaobu Yazhousi sizhang Luo Zhaohui jieshou "waijiao dajia tan" wei fangtan), Ministry of Foreign Affairs, www.fmprc.gov.cn/web/wjb_673085/zzjg_673183/t111 2423.shtml, last modified December 26, 2013, accessed February 11, 2016.

10 Central Compilation and Translation Bureau, "Sino-Japan Relations: Cooperative Partnership or Competitive Opponents" (Zhong-Ri guangxi: hezuo huoban he jingzheng duishou?), July 6, 2010, www.cctb.gov.cn/llyj/lldt/hwzg/201007/t20100706_247955.htm.

11 Liu Jiangyong, "China's Peripheral Diplomacy: Continuity and Innovative Development" (Zhongguo zhoubian waijiao: zai jicheng zhong fazhan chuangxin), *Contemporary International Relations (xiandai guoji guanxi jiqi sikao)*, 10 (2013).

12 Liu Xinmin, "Reflection on United Nations Security Council Reform and China/Japan/US Relations" (An Lihui gaige shijiao xia de Zong Ri Mei guanxi), *Theory Horizon (Lilun jie)*, 8 (2014); Liu Juntao, "The US State Department Welcomes Japan's Continued Strengthening Within the US–Japan Alliance" (Meiguo guowuyuan chen huanying Riben chixu qianghua yu Meiguo de tongmeng guanxi), *Renmin Ribao*, July 16, 2015; Shen Yamei, "Japan Responds to and Influences US Strategy to Shift East" (Riben yinying meiguo zhanlue Dong yi de jucuo jiqi yingxiang), China Institute of International Studies, November 26, 2013, www.ciis.org.cn/chinese/2013-11/26/content_6489909.htm.

13 Richard Bush, *The Perils of Proximity: China–Japan Security Relations* (Washington, DC: Brookings Institute Press, 2013), 57.

14 Ibid, 50–51.

15 Lu Ningsi, "China's Restructuring of its Military Regions is a Response to Japan's Hidden Threat" (Zhongguo jiang zhongxin hua junqu yingdui riben qianzai duikang), *Phoenix TV*, http://phtv.ifeng.com/a/20150107/40934023_0.shtml, last modified January 7, 2015, accessed February 11, 2016; *Sina*, "American Media Announce that China's Military Reforms are Primarily Concerned with Restricting Military Districts to Resist Japan" (Meimei pilu Zhongguo jundui gaige hexin: chonghua junqu duifang Riben), *Sina*, May 26, 2014.

44 *Jeffrey Reeves and Jeffrey Hornung*

16 Tan Boya, "What are Xi Jinping's Five Points Regarding Sino-Japan Relations?" (Xi Jinping dui Zhong-Ri guanxi de wuci biaotai du shuo le shenme?), *Renmin Ribao*, May 25, 2015.

17 Xing Xiaojing, "Chinese State Media Notes that Japan has Followed a 70 Year Pacifist Period of Flogging" (Zhongguo guan mei gei Riben fengxing 70 nian de heping zhuyi zhiming yi bian).

18 Ministry of National Defense of the People's Republic of China, "National Defense White Paper: Mission Diversification of China's Armed Forces" (Guofang baipishu: Zhongguo wuzhuang liliang de duoyanghua yunyong), www.mod.gov.cn/affair/2013-04/16/content_4442839.htm, last modified April 2013, accessed February 11, 2016.

19 Ministry of National Defense, People's Republic of China, "National Security Situation", May 26, 2015, http://eng.mod.gov.cn/Database/WhitePapers/2015-05/26/content_4586688.htm.

20 Tao Ran, "Japan's Government Fiercely Protests the Contents of China's Defense Whitepaper" (Riben zhengfu xiang Zhongfang qianglie kangyi Zhongguo guofang baipishu neirong), *Xinhua*, April 17, 2013.

21 *Global Times*, "Foreign Press: Japan's Arming of the Philippines Challenges China's Desire to Avoid Conflict" (Riben yu wuzhuang Feilubin tiaozhan Zhongguo buyuan qinzi shangzhen), *Global Times*, November 17, 2015; Zhang Jie and Liu Zhang, "Japanese Media: Japanese Warships Will Dock at Cam Ranh Bay in Vietnam, Cooperating with the US to Contain China" (Rimei: Ri zhanjian jiang tingkao Yuenan jinlan wan peihe mei qianzhi Zhongguo), *Global Times*, November 9, 2015.

22 Lin Hai, "Analysis of Why China is Modernizing its Military: It Appears it Really isn't About War with Japan" (Jiexi Zhongguo weihe junshi xiandaihjua: sihu bingfei wei Riben kaihan), *Sina*, February 17, 2014.

23 Anthony H. Cordesman, *Chinese Strategy and Modernization in 2015: A Comparative Analysis* (Washington, DC: CSIS, 2015), 558–559.

24 Wendell Minnick, "White Paper Outlines China's Ambitions", *Defense News*, May 27, 2015, www.defensenews.com/story/defense/policy-budget/warfare/2015/05/26/china-us-pentagon-taiwan-report-south-east-sea-islands-reefs-s400-su35-missiles-satellite-space-deterrence/27957131.

25 Ryan Martinson, "Deciphering China's Armed Intrusion Near the Senkaku Islands", *The Diplomat*, January 11, 2016.

26 Shiloh Rainwater, "Race to the North: China's Arctic Strategy and Its Implications", *Naval War College Review*, 66:2 (2013), 62–82.

27 Christopher Carlson, "Inside the Design of China's Yuan-class Submarine", *UNSI News*, http://news.usni.org/2015/08/31/essay-inside-the-design-of-chinas-yuan-class-submarine, last modified August 31, 2015, accessed February 11, 2016.

28 Alexander Martin, "Tokyo Issues Warning After Submarines are Spotted", *Wall Street Journal*, May 14, 2013.

29 Zhang Yun, "Sino-Japanese Economic Diplomacy Should Not be Zero Sum" (Zhong-Ri jingji waijiao jingzheng bu ying shi linghe youxi), *Lianhe zaobao*, August 1, 2015.

30 Yuan Keyan, "Global Competitiveness: Japan 6, China 28" (Quanqiu jingzhengli: Riben Di 6, Zhongguo di 28), *Nikkei*, September 30, 2015; Qiu Yu, "China and South Korea Overtake Japan in International Competitive Strength as Japan's Economic Dynamism Slows" (Quanqiu jingzhengli paiming Riben bei Zhong Han ganchao Riben jingji zengsu fanghuan), *Global Times*, May 28, 2015.

31 Houze Song and Arthur R. Kroeber, "How Far have China's Economic Reforms Come Over the Year?", *China File*, November 2, 2015, www.chinafile.com/conversation/how-far-have-chinas-economic-reforms-come-over-past-year; Gabriel Wildau, "China's State-Owned Enterprise Reform Plans Face Compromise", *Financial Times*, September 14, 2015.

32 Wei Jianguo "'One Belt, One Road' is Inseparable from Financial Innovation" ("Yidai, yilu" libukai jinrong chuangxin), *Study Times*, August 6, 2015; National Development and Reform Commission, "Push Forward the Silk Road Economic Belt and the

Framing Sino-Japan competition 45

21st Century Maritime Economic Road's Common Vision and Operation" (Tuidong gong jian sichou zhilu jingji dai he 21 shiji haishang sichou zhilu de yuanjing yu xingdong), March 28, 2015; Ministry of Foreign Affairs of the People's Republic of China "To Dream of Wings: 'One Belt, One Road' Toward a Better Future (Gei mengxiang chashang chibang, rang "yidai, yilu" tongxiang meihao weilai), April 30, 2015.

33 ASEAN, "Top Ten ASEAN Trade Partner Countries/Regions, 2014", www.asean.org/storage/2016/01/statistic/table20_asof121Dec15.pdf, last modified December 21, 2015, accessed February 13, 2016.

34 Observatory of Economic Complexity, "Indonesia: Trade", http://atlas.media.mit.edu/en/profile/country/idn/#Imports, last updated in January 2016, accessed February 11, 2016.

35 Observatory of Economic Complexity, "Vietnam: Trade" http://atlas.media.mit.edu/en/profile/country/vnm, last updated in January 2016, accessed February 11, 2016.

36 Zhang Yan, "Asian Development Bank: China Leads Japan as Asia's High-tech Exporter but Falls Short of South Korea" (Ya hang: Zhongguo cheng Yazhou gaokeji chukou zhudao Riben buji Hanguo), *Global Times*, January 4, 2016.

37 Michael Holtz, "China-Japan Rivalry: Who Will be Asia's Master Builder?", *Christian Science Monitor*, January 18, 2016.

38 He Ping, "Could Sino-Japanese Competition Benefit Asia?", *East Asian Forum*, www.eastasiaforum.org/2015/11/09/could-sino-japanese-competition-benefit-asia, last modified November 9, 2015, accessed February 11, 2016.

39 Zhou Zhangfei, "The 'One Belt, One Road' Will Develop Taiwan's Advantage" (Canyu "yidai, yilu" fahui Taiwan youshi), Shanghai Institutes for International Studies, May 6, 2015, www.siis.org.cn/index.php?m=content&c=index&a=show&catid=22&id=638.

40 Xie Ban, "Future High-Speed Rail Could Directly Connect Kunming with Singapore" (Weilai ke cong Kunming zuo gaotie zhida xinjiapo), *Guanxi News*, August 5, 2014.

41 Ben Bland, "Chinese $5.5bn High-Speed Rail Project Held Up in Indonesia", *Financial Times*, January 28, 2016.

42 Jong-Wha Lee and Warwick McKibbin, "Service Sector Productivity and Economic Growth in Asia", International Monetary Fund, www.imf.org/external/np/seminars/eng/2012/korea/pdf/lee.pdf, last modified September 2013, accessed February 11, 2016.

43 Ministry of Foreign Affairs of Japan, "Announcement of 'Partnership for Quality Infrastructure': Investment for Asia's Future", www.mofa.go.jp/policy/oda/page18_000076.html, last modified May 21, 2015, accessed February 13, 2016.

44 Anna Andrianova, Zulfugar Agayev, and Karl Lester M. Yap, "Japan-Led ADB Starts Feeling Competitive Heat From AIIB", Bloomberg, May 4, 2015.

45 Jeff Smith, "Beware China's Strategy: How Obama Can Set the Right Red Lines", *Foreign Affairs*, May 20, 2015.

46 Evan A. Feigenbaum, "The New Asian Order: And How the United States Fits In", *Foreign Affairs*, February 2, 2015.

47 Lu Yaodong, "We Must Beware the Japanese Variable as China and the US Establish a 'New Type Great Power Relationship'" (Zhongmei goujian "xinxing daguo guanxi" yao jingti Riben bianliang), *Xinhua*, June 6, 2015; "Successfully Solving the Japan Problem is the Key to Establishing a Sino-US New Type of Great Power Relationship" (Riben wenti youwang cheng goujian Zhongmei xinxing daguo guanxi de hexin wenti), China.com.

48 Zhou Yang, "Ministry of Foreign Affairs: Japan–US alliance is a Cold War Construct; It Must Not Harm China" (Waijiaobu: Rimei tongmeng shi lengzhan chanwu buying sunahi Zhongguo zhuquan), *Global Times*, http://mil.huanqiu.com/china/2014-04/4979514.html, last modified April 24, 2014, accessed February 17, 2016.

49 Chen Jimin, "Back to Cold-War Mentality", *China US Focus*, www.chinausfocus.com/foreign-policy/back-to-cold-war-mentality, last modified August 11, 2015, accessed February 17, 2016.

46 *Jeffrey Reeves and Jeffrey Hornung*

50 Feng Zhongping and Huang Jing, *China's Strategic Partnership Diplomacy: Engaging with a Changing World* (Brussels: European Strategic Partnership Observatory, 2014).
51 Wang Ruifan, "Diplomats View the 'One Belt, One Road': Increase Political Coordination and Connection" (Waijiaoguan yanzhong de "yidai, yilu': jiaqiang zhengce goutong yu xietiao) Cri.cn, June 19, 2015, http://gb.cri.cn/42071/2015/06/19/882s5002865.htm.
52 Chen Xiaochen, "Elaboration of Chinese Foreign Partnership: High-level Strategic Cooperation" (Xishuo Zhongguo duiwai huoban guanxi: zhanlue xie zuowei zuigao cengji), *Sina*, November 24, 2014.
53 Yan Xuetong, "Inside the China–U.S. Competition for Strategic Partners", *Huffington Post*, November 2, 2015, www.huffingtonpost.com/yan-xuetong/china-us-competition-allies_b_8449178.html.
54 Zhang Liwei, "Diplomatic Competition with Japan May Make China's Diplomacy More Flexible" (Yu Riben de waijiao jingzheng huo shi Zhongguo waijiao geng linghuo), *Sohu*, January 12, 2014, http://news.sohu.com/20140112/n393356036.shtml.
55 The Central People's Government of the People's Republic of China, "China and Asia: Strategic Stability and Prosperous Symbiosis" (Zhongguo yu Yazhou: zhanlue wending yu fanrong gongsheng), www.gov.cn/zhengce/2014-04/11/content_2657191.htm, last modified April 11, 2015, accessed February 17, 2016.
56 *Sina*, "Japan or the Philippines Upgraded the Nearest Military Base in Nansha" (Riben huo zizhu Feilubin shengji ju Nansha zuijin junshi jidi), *Sina*, March 12, 2015, http://mil.news.sina.com.cn/2015-03-12/0935824128.html.
57 Li Xiguang, *Soft Power and the China Dream* (*ranshili yu Zhongguo meng*) (Beijing: Falu Chubanshe, 2014).
58 Sun Cunliang "'One Belt, One Road" Cultural Exchanges: Significance, Practice, and Mechanisms" ("Yidai, yilu" renwen jiaoliu: zhongda yiyi, shijian lujing he jiangou jizhi), *International Aid* (2015), 14–20.
59 Liang Yunxiang and Wang Xiuli, "Japanese Social Study on China's Soft Power and Its Influence on Sino-Japanese Relations" (Cong Riben shehui diao chakan Zhongguo de ruanshili jiqi dui Zhong-Ri guanxi de yingxiang), Central Compilation and Translation Bureau, December 16, 2012, www.cctb.net/llyj/lldt/hwzg/201210/t20121015_248099.htm.
60 *China News*, "Japanese speculates of China Threat to Shale Gas Energy Diplomacy in its Diplomacy Blue Book" (Riben waijiao lanpishu chaozuo "Zhongguo weixie" kaizhan yeyanqi nengyuan waijiao), *China News*, March 28, 2013.
61 Central Government Portal "Japan's Defense White Paper's 'China Threat Theory' Absurd" (Haiwai yulun pi Riben fangwei baipishu xuanran "Zhongguo weixie lun" huangmiu), July 22, 2015, www.gov.cn/xinwen/2015-07/22/content_2900349.htm.
62 Huang Rui, "The Japanese Government's Ulterior Motives in Speculating on the "China Threat Theory" (Jiama chaozuo "Zhongguo weixie lun" Riben zhengfu bieyou yongxin), *Xinhua* July 22, 2015.
63 Feng Zhaokui, "Errors in Japan's Periphery Foreign Policy are the Greatest Hidden Threat to its Energy Security" (Cuowu de zhoubian waijiao zhengce shi Riben nengyuan anquan zuida qianzai fengxian), *Fengzhaokui*, August 22, 2015, http://blog.ifeng.com/article/37081266.html.
64 Cabinet Secretariat (CAS), "National Security Strategy", December 17, 2013, 2–3, www.cas.go.jp/jp/siryou/131217anzenhoshou/nss-e.pdf.
65 Ministry of Foreign Affairs (MOFA), "Statement by the Press Secretary, Ministry of Foreign Affairs of Japan, on an Issue Concerning the South China Sea (Arbitral Proceedings by the Philippines under the United Nations Convention on the Law of the Sea)", March 31, 2014, www.mofa.go.jp/press/release/press4e_000257.html.
66 Japan does not refer to its armed forces as a military; instead, it is called the Self-Defense Forces. In this book, the term military is utilized for comparative purposes.
67 CAS, "National Security Strategy".
68 Ibid., 8.

Framing Sino-Japan competition   47

69 Ibid., 12.
70 "Naze Ima Heiwa Anzen Hosei ka" (Why the Peace Security Legislation Now?), February 12, 2016, www.kantei.go.jp/jp/headline/heiwa_anzen.html.
71 Ministry of Defense (MOD), "Security Environment Surrounding Japan", White Paper, 2015, 3, www.mod.go.jp/e/publ/w_paper/pdf/2015/DOJ2015_1-1-0_web.pdf.
72 "Kishida Gaimu Daijin Kaiken Kiroku" (Record of Foreign Minister Kishida Press Conference), January 4, 2016, www.mofa.go.jp/mofaj/press/kaiken/kaiken4_000281.html.
73 MOD, "National Defense Program Guidelines for FY 2014 and Beyond", December 17, 2013, 5, www.mod.go.jp/j/approach/agenda/guideline/2014/pdf/20131217_e2.pdf.
74 This policy is a continuation of efforts first put forward by the Democratic Party of Japan (DPJ) in 2010 to revise Japan's National Defense Program Guidelines (NDPG). For comparisons between the two, see MOD, "National Defense Program Guidelines for FY2011 and Beyond", December 17, 2010, 7, www.mod.go.jp/e/d_act/d_policy/pdf/guidelinesFY2011.pdf and "National Defense Program Guidelines for FY2014 and Beyond", 7–8.
75 MOD, "Defense Programs and Budget of Japan, Fiscal Year 2016", 46, www.mod.go.jp/e/d_budget/pdf/271016.pdf.
76 MOD, "Defense Programs and Budget of Japan, Fiscal Years 2012–16", www.mod.go.jp/e/d_budget. Also see MOD, "Chuuki Boueiryouku Seibi Keikaku (Heisei
26 nendo-Heisei 30 nendo) ni tsuite" (Mid-Term Defense Program (FY2014–FY2018)), December 17, 2013, www.mod.go.jp/j/approach/agenda/guideline/2014/pdf/chuki_seibi26-30.pdf
77 MOD, "National Defense Program Guidelines for FY2014 and Beyond", 7–8.
78 Ibid., 9.
79 MOFA, "The Guidelines for Japan–U.S. Defense Cooperation", April 27, 2015, www.mod.go.jp/e/d_act/anpo/pdf/shishin_20150427e.pdf. An important prior action enabling these revisions was Abe's July 2014 reinterpretation of Article 9 of Japan's constitution, making the (limited) exercise of collective self-defense constitutional. CAS, "Cabinet Decision on Development of Seamless Security Legislation to Ensure Japan's Survival and Protect its People", July 1, 2014, www.cas.go.jp/jp/gaiyou/jimu/pdf/anpohosei_eng.pdf.
80 White House, "U.S.–Japan Joint Vision Statement", April 28, 2015, www.whitehouse.gov/the-press-office/2015/04/28/us-japan-joint-vision-statement.
81 For example, Washington states its continued willingness "to extend deterrence to Japan through the full range of capabilities, including U.S. nuclear forces." MOFA, *The Guidelines for Japan–U.S. Defense Cooperation*, 1.
82 Examples include President Barack Obama's reiteration of the "absolute" US commitment to Japan's security that covers all territories under Japan's administration, including the Senkaku Islands, and Secretary of State John Kerry's proclamation that the US commitment to Japan's security remains "iron-clad and covers all territories under Japan's administration". For the former, see White House, "Remarks by President Obama and Prime Minister Abe of Japan in Joint Press Conference", April 28, 2015, www.whitehouse.gov/the-press-office/2015/04/28/remarks-president-obama-and-prime-minister-abe-japan-joint-press-confere. For the latter, see Arshad Mohammed, "U.S., Japan Unveil New Defense Guidelines for Global Japanese Role", *Reuters*, April 28, 2015, www.reuters.com/article/us-usa-japan-defense-idUSKBN0NI08O20150428.
83 MOFA, "Joint Statement of the Security Consultative Committee, Toward a More Robust Alliance and Greater Shared Responsibilities", October 3, 2013, 2, www.mofa.go.jp/files/000016028.pdf.
84 One notable exception to this are investments directed at countering the missile threat from North Korea. With no changes to North Korea's air and naval capability, investments made in those realms cannot reasonably be argued to be responses to Pyongyang, but are likely intended to counter China instead.

85 MOD, "Three Principles on Transfer of Defense Equipment and Technology", April 1, 2014, www.mod.go.jp/e/pressrele/2014/140401_02.pdf.
86 Shinzo Abe, "Military Transparency and Asian Security", Project Syndicate, June 23, 2014,www.project-syndicate.org/commentary/shinzo-abe-calls-on-the-region-s-governments-to-make-their-defense-budgets-public.
87 Yachi Shotaro, personal interview by Jeffrey Hornung, January 15, 2013.
88 There is no strict meaning of the term. The term refers to a cooperative relationship in wide fields such as politics, security, and economics with countries that have an influence on global or regional stability and peace or have close connected influence on realizing Japan's national interests. In the case of ASEAN, it is more of the latter. Such partnerships signal a willingness to cooperate towards common strategic interests of maintaining and enhancing regional peace, stability, and prosperity.
89 "National Defense Program Guidelines for FY2014 and Beyond", 5.
90 Here again, much of the important groundwork for these Strategic Partnerships was set in place during the Noda administration. For example, Noda elevated predominately economic ties with the Philippines and Thailand to that of Strategic Partnerships, enjoyed low-level security discussions with Thailand and Singapore (Strategic Dialogue; Defense Ministers' Dialogue with Thailand; Maritime Security Dialogue with Singapore), and agreed to strengthen strategic dialogues with Vietnam. See Jeffrey Hornung, "Japan's Growing Hard Edge Against China", *Asian Security*, 10:2 (2014).
91 Shinzō Abe, "Shangri La Dialogue 2014 Keynote Address", May 30, 2014, www.iiss.org/en/events/shangri%20la%20dialogue/archive/2014-c20c/opening-remarks-and-keynote-address-b0b2/keynote-address-shinzo-abe-a787.
92 Ibid.
93 Japan's relationships with these two were traditionally relegated to development assistance and economic ties. Under Abe, discussions now include security issues. With Laos, for example, Japan has agreed to promote security and defense cooperation in various areas. With Cambodia, the two agreed not only to coordinate and cooperate more closely on security issues, they signed a Memorandum on Defense Cooperation and Exchanges, which includes high-level and working-level defense meetings; military–military consultations; unit–unit exchanges of militaries, capacity building to Cambodia; and multilateral cooperation in multilateral frameworks like ASEAN Regional Forum, ASEAN Defense Minister's Meeting Plus, and the Western Pacific Naval Symposium.
94 Despite the first visit by a Japanese premier in 36 years, one of the elements Abe secured was cooperation to enhance dialogue on security issues and exchanges between defence authorities. MOFA, "Joint Statement Between Japan and the Republic of the Union of Myanmar: New Foundation for Mutual Friendship", May 26, 2013, www.mofa.go.jp/files/000006671.pdf. Also, MOFA, "Tai Myanma- Purojekuto" (Project List for Myanmar), www.mofa.go.jp/files/000006668.pdf.
95 Chairman's Statement of the 10th East Asia Summit, November 22, 2015, www.asean.org/storage/images/2015/November/10th-EAS-Outcome/Chairmans%20Statement%20of%20the%2010th%20East%20Asia%20Summit%20Final.pdf.
96 Kantei, "Remarks by Prime Minister Abe to the Australian Parliament", July 8, 2014, http://japan.kantei.go.jp/96_abe/statement/201407/0708article1.html.
97 Ministry of Defence (Australia), "Australia's National Security: A Defence Update 2007", 2007, 19, www.defence.gov.au/oscdf/ans/2007/contents_pdf.htm.
98 Ministry of Defence (Australia), "Defending Australia in the Asia Pacific Century: Force 2030", 2009, 34, www.defence.gov.au/whitepaper2009/docs/defence_white_paper_2009.pdf.
99 MOFA, "Japan–Australia Foreign Ministers' Meeting", July 1, 2013, www.mofa.go.jp/region/page6e_000103.html.
100 Previous PM Tony Abbott even referred to Japan as its "best friend in Asia" "Tony Abbott Invites Shinzo Abe, Saying Japan is Australia's 'Best Friend in Asia'",

Framing Sino-Japan competition 49

Guardian, October 9, 2013, www.theguardian.com/world/2013/oct/10/aboott-invites-abe-japan-friend.

101 Abe, "Shangri La Dialogue 2014 Keynote Address".

102 Ibid.

103 A lot of the language that has been used first appeared in a September 2011 Joint Statement with the Philippines, where the peace and stability of the South China Sea is said to be vital to both. In it, the two countries agreed on the importance of protecting "freedom of navigation. . . and compliance with established international law including the UNCLOS". A month later, Japan and Vietnam used language verbatim to the Japan–Philippine Joint Statement but, going one step further, added a welcoming of "the adoption of the Guidelines for the Implementation of the Declaration on the Conduct of Parties in the South China Sea" and called for its full implementation and "the early formulation of a Code of Conduct in accordance with established international law". This sort of language becomes standard in subsequent bilateral statements with other ASEAN countries.

104 MOFA, "Cabinet Decision on the Development Cooperation Charter", February 10, 2015, www.mofa.go.jp/mofaj/gaiko/oda/files/000067701.pdf. For discussion on strategy, see pages 9–10.

105 "Japan Likely to Channel ODA to Southeast Asia, Middle East Under New Charter", *Asahi Shimbun*, January 9, 2015, http://ajw.asahi.com/article/behind_news/politics/AJ201501090067.

106 MOFA, "Cabinet decision on the Development Cooperation Charter", 3.

107 Ibid., 8.

108 Ibid., 6.

109 Ibid.

110 This contrasts with delegates from 57 countries signing the agreement.

111 Finance Minister Taro Aso has publicly spoken on many of these issues, including his admission that Tokyo has pressed Beijing repeatedly on these issues but fails to get a response. Atsushi Kodera, "Is China-led Bank a Lost Opportunity?" *Japan Times*, April 15, 2015, www.japantimes.co.jp/news/2015/04/15/reference/is-china-led-bank-a-lost-opportunity/#.VoGXMEorKc0. Similarly, Abe's spokesman, Yasuhisa Kawamura, spoke to reporters at the 2015 G-7 summit on a number of these issues. See "Corruption, Environment, Governance Issues Must be Addressed Before Japan Weighs AIIB Entry: Abe", *Japan Times*, June 8, 2015, www.japantimes.co.jp/news/2015/06/08/business/corruption-environment-governance-issues-must-addressed-japan-weighs-aiib-entry-abe/#.VoGWzEorKc0. Even Abe's ruling Liberal Democratic Party drafted a recommendation calling for a "cautious response", citing many of these concerns. "Abe's Ruling Party Calls for Cautious Approach to AIIB", *Japan Times*, June 4, 2015, www.japantimes.co.jp/news/2015/06/04/business/abes-ruling-party-calls-cautious-approach-aiib/#.VoGW3korKc0.

112 This refers to the maritime Silk Road that links China with Southeast Asia, the Middle East and Europe, and the overland Silk Road that connects China with Europe. Critics point out that the infrastructure being developed, such as railways, ports, and airports, is often dual-use in nature, thereby able to be used by China to project power throughout the region.

113 This made the AIIB nearly two-thirds the size of the Japan-led ADB.

114 Ministry of Economics, Trade and Industry (METI), "Partnership for Quality Infrastructure: Investment for Asia's Future", May 21, 2015, www.meti.go.jp/english/press/2015/pdf/0521_01a.pdf. See also Masaaki Kameda, "Abe Announces $110 Billion in Aid for 'High-Quality' Infrastructure in Asia", *Japan Times*, May 22, 2015, www.japantimes.co.jp/news/2015/05/22/business/abe-announces-110-billion-in-aid-for-high-quality-infrastructure-in-asia/#.VoGW8EorKc0.

115 David Pilling, "It Won't be Easy to Build an 'Anyone But China' Club", *Financial Times*, May 22, 2013, www.ft.com/intl/cms/s/0/08cf74f6-c216-11e2-8992-00144feab7de.html#axzz40vjWdUDk.

50   *Jeffrey Reeves and Jeffrey Hornung*

116 Prime Minister Shinzō Abe, "Toward an Alliance of Hope", Address to a Joint Meeting of the US Congress, April 29, 2015, http://japan.kantei.go.jp/97_abe/statement/201504/uscongress.html.
117 Shotaro Yachi, personal interview, January 15, 2013.
118 Anonymous former MOFA official, personal interview, January 15, 2013.
119 Brenda Goh, "China Wants to Sell High-Speed Trains to California", *Business Insider*, October 21, 2014, www.businessinsider.com/r-china-to-pitch-high-speed-trains-to-california-2014-10.
120 Also included were development of local manufacturing industries and promising completion by 2019 to enable President Joko Widodo to claim success when he will likely run for a second term.
121 "Japan to Win Contract for India's First High-Speed Railway", *Japan Times*, December 8, 2015, www.japantimes.co.jp/news/2015/12/08/business/japan-win-contract-indias-first-high-speed-railway/#.VoF8_korKc0.
122 The new conditions enabled him to offer a $12 billion package of financing and technical assistance – for the project's $14.6 billion cost – at an interest rate of 0.1 per cent to be repaid over 50 years (with a 15-year moratorium), on condition that India buys 30 per cent of the equipment, including the coaches and locomotives, from Japanese firms. "Japan Offers India Soft Loan for $15 Bln Bullet Train in Edge over China", *Reuters*, October 22, 2015, www.reuters.com/article/india-trains-idUSL3N 12L3HW20151022; Tien Sze Fang, "Warning for Beijing", *Indian Express*, December 17, 2015, http://indianexpress.com/article/opinion/columns/warning-for-beijing; "Japan to Help Set Up Mumbai–Ahmedabad High Speed Rail Link", *Business Standard*, December 12, 2015, www.business-standard.com/article/news-ians/japan-to-help-set-up-mumbai-ahmedabad-high-speed-rail-link-115121200606_1.html.
123 Robin Harding and Tom Mitchell, "Rail Battle Between China and Japan Rushes Ahead at High Speed", *Financial Times*, December 20, 2015, www.ft.com/cms/s/0/c28fe2e8-a6fe-11e5-9700-2b669a5aeb83.html#axzz3v4LStzZ9.

Part I
Security institutions

3 Sino-Japanese competition over regional institutions in Asia

Mie Oba

Historically, Asia has few longstanding regional institutions, and regionalism has not been a primary factor in shaping its regional circumstances. Since the end of the 1980s, however, regionalism has advanced rapidly in Asia, and led to the establishment of various regional institutions. Regionalism and regional institutions are now important aspects of Asia's regional politics.

Regionalism describes a "state-led or states-led project designed to reorganize a particular regional space along defined economic and political lines".[1] Most regionalism conducted by a state and states is intended to establish a specific regional institution. Such attempts have failed in some cases, but succeeded in others. The extent to which a regional institution evolves after its establishment depends on the extent to which member countries are cooperatively engaged in its activities. Having one or more countries undertake initiatives that promote regional cooperation is also critical for the further development of a regional institution.

The development of regionalism in Asia has been shaped primarily by the dynamic relationship between Japan and the US, which is characterized by both competition and coordination. Japan was one of the important actors that proposed some ideas for regional cooperation, and influenced the establishment of regional institutions. When Japan promoted regionalism, it always had to address the serious question of how to demarcate the boundary of a "region" in a way that would promote regional cooperation. Conflicts sometimes occurred within Japan and/or with people in other countries as to whether or not a region should include the US.

The US, on the other hand, was a relatively passive actor in the development of regionalism in Asia. However, it was anxious about the formation of a regional bloc that would exclude the US, and had tried to preclude Asian countries from creating one. Consequently, Asian countries always had to take into account the likely reaction from the US when they promoted regional projects. Regionalism in Asia was largely characterized by the competition between Japan and the US on how to shape the regional order.

Now, however, in addition to Japan and the US, China has become another main actor involved in shaping regionalism in Asia. Moreover, Sino-Japanese competition to expand or preserve each country's leverage in East Asia has had a significant influence on the characteristics of the regional institutions that have

54   *Mie Oba*

been developed, and the levels of cooperation evident in these institutions. How these two countries promote regionalism and the development of regional institutions has been intertwined with competition over how and to what extent they should each take a leading role in constructing and maintaining a new order in this region. Since China's attitude towards regional institutions in Asia became positive at the end of the 1990s, these two countries have competed with each other in their attempts to expand their roles in promoting regionalism and regional institutions.

The dynamic ongoing confrontations that continue to occur between these two countries as a result of the changing power balance between them has strongly influenced the Sino-Japanese competition over regionalism in Asia. China and Japan are neighbouring countries, yet they are rivals when taking initiatives in the region, since each wants to outperform the other. In previous decades, Japan maintained its "special" position as the only advanced industrial country in Asia, the region's biggest economic power, and the only country in Asia with imperial experience.

Relations between Japan and other Asian countries – including China – used to be vertical, and Japan held a prominent position in regional politics, even though its political influence was sometimes limited by its prohibition on using military power and the negative legacy of its history. However, both the rapid rise of China and the longstanding recession of the Japanese economy brought about a drastic change in the power balance in East Asia, and relations between China and Japan became horizontal. Now, China has economically surpassed Japan, becoming the second largest economic power in the world. Chinese people have strong feelings about the historical experiences inflicted on their country by past Japanese imperialism. Such feelings, deeply related to nationalism, are responsible for their tough stance towards Japan. On the other hand, Japanese people are feeling increasingly impatient, partly as a result of the fact that they are losing their special position, due to the changing power balance between China and Japan. The trend towards China's ascendancy and Japan's relative decline will not stop or reverse direction, so their confrontations will become more intransigent, and easing their underlying tensions will be difficult.

To better understand the emerging structural confrontations between China and Japan, this chapter tries to describe both countries' involvement in various regional institutions in East Asia, and to discuss how these two countries' promotion of regionalism have been intertwined with their competition for leadership in establishing and maintaining a regional order in East Asia. Furthermore, this chapter attempts to clarify the changing dynamics that are evident in the trends that characterize the competition between China and Japan.

The beginning of the competition over regionalism

Japan's involvement in regionalism in Asia following the Second World War began in the 1950s, when it joined the Economic Commission of Asia and the Far East and the Colombo Plan in 1954.[2] In the 1960s, Japan took a leading role in

Competition over regional institutions 55

establishing the Asian Development Bank (ADB) and the Ministerial Conference for the Economic Development of Southeast Asia (MCEDSEA), and joined the Asia-Pacific Commission led by the Republic of Korea (ROK). In addition, some politicians and intellectuals in Japan had been proposing various ideas such as the Pacific Free Trade Area for Pacific cooperation since the mid-1960s. At the end of the 1970s, Prime Minister Masayoshi Ohira proposed a Pacific community concept, and this proposal led to the establishment of the Pacific Economic Cooperation Conference. At the end of the 1980s, Japan undertook an initiative with Australia to establish an Asia-Pacific framework for economic consultation and cooperation. Initiatives undertaken by these two countries led to the establishment of the Asia-Pacific Economic Cooperation (APEC) in 1989. Japan also took a leading role in establishing the ASEAN Regional Forum (ARF) in 1994, against the backdrop left by the end of the Cold War.

Although Japan sometimes assumed substantial roles in promoting regionalism in Asia, Japanese attitudes were tempered by a wish to avoid criticisms that might originate from neighbouring countries as a result of the negative historical legacy left by the "Greater East Asian Co-Prosperity Sphere" during the Second World War. Besides, Japan's vigorous efforts to promote regionalism sometimes failed – as for example the MCEDSEA, which became deadlocked in the early 1970s. Even when Japan promoted the establishment of APEC, it tried to collaborate with Australia and maintain the appearance that Australia was the main "entrepreneur".

On the other hand, China, from the end of the 1980s and the early 1990s, did not contribute positively to these processes. China joined APEC in 1991, with Taiwan and Hong Kong, but the Tiananmen Square incident in July 1989 prevented China from participating in APEC as a founding member. China's affiliation with APEC, from the Chinese perspective, was derived from a strategy intended to find a way out of its isolation from international society in the wake of that incident. Furthermore, China was reluctant to join the ARF, while China's affiliation was primarily important for the other founding members. China was worried that its room for manoeuvre would be limited in this new framework, constrained by members' expectations for cooperation and dialogue on matters of politics and security.

China's reluctant and cautious attitude towards regionalism changed at the end of the 1990s. Chinese Foreign Minister Qian Qichen gave a speech at the Fourth Meeting of the ARF in July 1997, in which he evaluated the ARF approach very positively,[3] and China hosted the ARF intersessional meeting on confidence-building that year.[4] China's changing attitude was derived from its strategy for mitigating "the China threat chorus" voiced by neighbouring countries, including Japan and Southeast Asian nations.

The Asian financial crisis, triggered by the collapse of the Thai baht in the summer of 1997, gave China an opportunity to further promote this strategy, to dispel neighbouring countries' anxieties about the rise of China, and to improve China's relations with them. During the crisis, China could have devalued the Chinese yuan, placing China's exports in a more favourable position relative to other Asian economies. Instead, Beijing announced that it would not adopt this

56   *Mie Oba*

policy. This decision was based on its own national interests, but intended to assist Asia's damaged economies as well.[5] Beijing also gave US$4 billion in financial assistance to Indonesia, South Korea, and Thailand. This included a US$1 billion pledge to the International Monetary Fund (IMF) for that organization's aid package to Thailand.[6] These policies were appreciated in the region.

China's contribution to the damaged neighbouring economies was impressive. However, Japan also took the initiative to address the financial crisis, leading to a new phase of regionalism in Asia, the activation of East Asian regionalism, and regional cooperation. A typical example of Japan's positive commitment was its encouragement of East Asian financial cooperation. Japan's proposal for the Asian Monetary Fund failed because of strong opposition from the US and lack of support from China. After this failure, in October 1998, Japan announced the US$30 billion New Miyazawa Plan intended to provide financial assistance to Thailand, Indonesia, South Korea, Malaysia, and the Philippines in the form of traditional bilateral assistance. The New Miyazawa Plan became the template for the Chiang Mai Initiative (CMI), formally agreed to in the Second Association of Southeast Asian Nations Plus Three (ASEAN+3) financial ministers' meeting in May 2000.

The first ASEAN+3 Summit was held at the end of 1997 as it had been scheduled before the occurrence of the crisis, but this framework functioned as a forum in which East Asian countries could demonstrate their will to resolve the crisis, and promote specific regional cooperation initiatives for the future of East Asia. Japan, under the Obuchi Keizo administration, used the ASEAN+3 Summits to announce its various assistance programmes for neighbouring countries, and generally tried to encourage the development of East Asian regional cooperation under ASEAN+3. Unlike its previous position, Japan actively encouraged East Asian regionalism from the end of the 1990s to the early 2000s.

During this period, competition in Chinese- and Japanese-led institution-building began to focus on ASEAN. The Japan–ASEAN relationship has a long history, going back to the early 1970s, when this group held informal dialogues to resolve trade conflicts over synthetic rubber. Japan had become one of ASEAN's Dialogue Partners in the 1970s, and also became a member of the ASEAN Post-Ministerial Conference. In 1977, Prime Minister Fukuda Takeo's landmark speech, containing the well-known Fukuda Doctrine, emphasized the importance of ASEAN in Japan's diplomatic relations with Southeast Asia.

Against a backdrop of changing strategic situations in the Asia-Pacific as a result of the end of the Cold War, Japan's Ministry of Foreign Affairs encouraged the establishment of an ASEAN-centred framework to foster security dialogue in the Asia-Pacific, and the ARF was subsequently formed. Furthermore, in the 1990s Japan's Ministry of International Trade and Industry attempted to promote industrial cooperation with ASEAN, as well as to provide assistance to mitigate the economic and social gaps between ASEAN's advanced members and the CLMV (Cambodia, Laos, Myanmar, and Vietnam), prior to ASEAN enlargement.

The China–ASEAN relationship was more complex. In the Cold War era, China had been deeply involved in wars and political turmoil in Indochina, in some cases involving the use of its armed forces. The strong suspicion of the "Communist threat" among ASEAN's founding members was a serious obstacle to improving Sino-ASEAN relations. The end of the Cold War gave China the opportunity to begin building a relationship with ASEAN on new, less ideological foundations. China restored diplomatic relations with Indonesia in July 1990, and officially initiated relations with Singapore in October. Qian Qichen, China's foreign minister, attended the opening session of the 24th ASEAN Ministerial Meeting in July 1991 in Kuala Lumpur. This event marked the commencement of China–ASEAN relations, and China became a full ASEAN Dialogue Partner in July 1996. Since 1997, China, as well as Japan and the ROK, have respectively hosted the ASEAN+1 Summit.

China, however, has had conflicts over territorial and maritime issues in the South China Sea with some ASEAN countries, and these conflicts have led to serious anxieties and doubts in Southeast Asia about the negative impacts of China's behaviour on peace and stability. The dispute over China's claims in the South China Sea has been obvious since the 1970s. China seized the Paracel Islands from Vietnam in 1974, passed a Chinese Territorial Sea Law in 1992 to establish its territorial rights in the South China Sea, and in 1995 occupied Mischief Reef. These actions have caused ASEAN countries to question the probability of peace and stability in the region.

At the beginning of the 2000s, Japan enjoyed stronger ties with ASEAN than did China. The same Japanese advantage could be noted with respect to their relative economies. The GDP of Japan in 2000 was about US$5.5 trillion.[7] China's GDP in 2000 was about US$1.2 trillion.[8] The "China threat" argument had already appeared among East Asian countries in the 1990s due to China's rapid economic development and the expansion of its military budget. However, according to the above data, the size of China's economy was only about one-quarter that of Japan's.

Putting these facts together, prior to the competition between China and Japan that began in the early 2000s, Japan retained some advantage over China in terms of its leverage in East Asia.

The three dimensions of the escalating competition in the 2000s

In the 2000s, the Sino-Japanese competition to expand countries' roles in regionalism and regional institutions began to escalate in three dimensions: strengthening ASEAN+1 ties, promoting a new regional vision for East Asia, and expanding their roles as they related to regional cooperation.

The direct trigger for intensifying Sino-Japanese competition to develop stronger ties with ASEAN was the agreement between China and ASEAN to conclude the ASEAN–China free trade agreement (FTA) within ten years of November 2001. Japanese government officials in charge of Asian affairs were shocked by this decision, and their anxiety about enhanced China–ASEAN ties under an FTA prompted Tokyo to develop an extended East Asian Community concept, and the idea of a Japan–ASEAN Comprehensive Economic Partnership. Both were raised

58 *Mie Oba*

by Prime Minister Koizumi Junichiro in a speech he gave during his visit to Singapore in January 2002.[9]

China and ASEAN signed the Framework Agreement on Comprehensive Economic Co-Operation Between ASEAN and the People's Republic of China on November 4, 2002, and the ASEAN–China Free Trade Agreement (ACFTA) came into effect in July 2005. ACFTA reduced tariffs on 96 per cent of items traded, the goal agreed by China and ASEAN. China became the first external party to sign the ASEAN Treaty of Amity and Cooperation (TAC) in October 2003.

In addition, China and ASEAN adopted the Declaration on Conduct of Parties in the South China Sea (DOC) in Phnom Penh on November 4, 2002.[10] Adoption of the DOC in 2002, from China's perspective, was a measure taken to ease ASEAN countries' anxieties about China's activities in the South China Sea. The DOC stipulated that a legally binding Code of Conduct should be pursued, and demonstrated that relations between China and ASEAN were improving.

In 2004, China also began hosting the annual China–ASEAN Expo (CAEXPO) in Nanning, the capital city of Guangxi Zhang Autonomous Region, which it has continued to host. Nanning, as well as Kunming, represents China's strategic foothold for its political and economic leverage in Southeast Asia. Hosting the CAEXPO in Nanning annually is an expression of China's strong desire to enhance and deepen ties with ASEAN.

The CAEXPO is both a political show that demonstrates the good relationship and deepening economic interdependence between China and ASEAN, and an exhibition in which enterprises that are mainly from China and ASEAN countries exhibit various goods and items. As a political show, the CAEXPO has succeeded in displaying a good relationship between China and ASEAN. For example, Chinese Prime Minister Wen Jiabao, the Minister of Commerce Bo Xilai, and the Secretary General of ASEAN Ong Keng Yong, as well as all ASEAN leaders, attended the opening ceremony of the third CAEXPO in October 2006. Over time, the scale of the exhibition and the number of participants has increased.[11]

On the other hand, Japan and ASEAN agreed to conclude the FTA as much as ten years earlier at the Japan–ASEAN Summit in November 2002, but negotiations made slow progress, mainly because of conflicts over the liberalization of agricultural trade. At the same time, Japan promoted negotiations of bilateral FTAs with some ASEAN member countries. The Japan–Singapore FTA came into effect in November 2002, and FTAs with Malaysia (in July 2006), Brunei and Indonesia (in July 2007), Thailand (in November 2007), the Philippines (in July 2008), and Vietnam (in October 2009) followed. The ASEAN–Japan Comprehensive Economic Partnership came into effect in December 2008, and Japan signed the TAC in July 2004.

The second aspect of the Sino-Japanese competition, namely their visions of East Asia, took shape in the formation of the East Asian Summit (EAS). During this process, China and Japan managed to draft a regional framework for East Asia that would be favourable for each of them. In 2001, the idea of the EAS, apart from the existing ASEAN+3, was proposed in the final report prepared by the East Asian Vision Group. This summit was originally conceived as a genuine

East Asian framework in which all member countries had the same status. In this case, "East Asia" was defined by ASEAN+3 members.

However, Prime Minister Koizumi proposed an extended East Asian Community idea. In a speech in January 2002 while visiting Singapore, Koizumi said that the community should be based on the Japan–ASEAN partnership, and it should include Australia and New Zealand in addition to ASEAN+3 members. This proposal for a new type of East Asia was derived from Japanese decision-makers' intention to dilute China's increasing leverage in the region, and the desire to construct an East Asia based on global norms and rules compatible with a special relationship with the US, such as those associated with democracy, human rights, and the rule of law. On the other hand, China promoted its own idea of an EAS. These two directions apparently clashed in the sequence of discussions from 2002 to 2005. Malaysia supported the Chinese position, and Singapore and Indonesia supported Japan's. The EAS that was finally established in December 2005 was based on Japan's suggested membership, which included Australia, New Zealand, India, and ASEAN+3 members.[12]

The clash between China and Japan over what form the EAS would take continued after the establishment of the EAS. The final report also proposed the idea of an East Asian Free Trade Area (EAFTA), which was a framework for the economic integration of East Asia that included ASEAN+3 members. China and the ROK supported this idea. The Japanese government, on the other hand, proposed the Comprehensive Economic Partnership for East Asia (CEPEA) in 2005. Members of CEPEA, according to the Japanese government, should include all members of the EAS. Because China and Japan could not reach a compromise, both ideas remained under consideration for several years. Then, in 2011, they were unified under the Regional Comprehensive Economic Partnership (RCEP).

There is a third aspect of Sino-Japanese institutional competition that underlies competition to establish forums. Once established, China and Japan also compete over their relative contributions to existing frameworks. The most visible example of this is the process that led to the realization of the Chiang Mai Initiative Multilateralization (CMIM). CMIM is a multilateral currency-swap arrangement that replaces a network of bilateral swap arrangements initially led by Japan under the CMI. When the CMIM agreement was signed in 2009, it had access to US$120 billion.[13] During the negotiations that led to the establishment of the CMIM, China and Japan competed with each other as to the size of their individual financial contributions. Neither side wanted to contribute less than the other. Finally, both China and Japan agreed to provide the same financial contribution, US$38.4 billion dollars, or 32 per cent each of the total CMIM foreign exchange reserves pool.[14]

In the 2000s, China and Japan attempted to expand their leverage in all three areas: ASEAN engagement, East Asian regionalism and relative contributions to functional mechanisms. Meanwhile, their bilateral diplomatic relations with one another became progressively worse. The direct reason for this was Prime Minister Koizumi's repeated visits to the Yasukuni Shrine between 2001 and 2006. However, the Sino-Japanese tensions had a more fundamental origin, namely an emerging

60 *Mie Oba*

structural tension precipitated by a rapid shift in the power balance. China's development in the 2000s was more remarkable than that of the previous decade, and it was rapidly catching up to Japan's economy.

After Koizumi's term, relations between the two countries improved. In 2008, the bilateral accord between China and Japan on joint gas development in the East China Sea indicated a détente in their relations. However, the structural tension between China and Japan made this détente temporary. Against the backdrop of its economic development, as well as its success in hosting the Beijing 2008 Summer Olympics, some of China's elite citizens and leaders developed greater confidence in their country. In addition, China's political voice on the international scene became stronger after the global financial crisis damaged the US and European economies. By contrast, the Japanese economy did not achieve the intended gains from Koizumi's deregulation of the economic and social welfare system. After Koizumi's term ended, domestic politics in Japan remained unstable, with prime ministers changing every year.

A comparison of Chinese and Japanese GDPs for 2000 and 2010 clearly shows a change in their relative position during the 2000s. Japan's GDP in 2000 was US$4.7 trillion, while China's was US$1.2 trillion. Japan's GDP represented 14.6 per cent of the total world GDP, while China's was only 3.7 per cent. However, comparing these figures in 2010, Japan's GDP was about US$5.5 trillion, and China's was US$6 trillion, therefore surpassing Japan's GDP.[15] Moreover, in 2010, Japan and China's respective shares of the world's GDP was 8.6 per cent and 9.4 per cent.

The shifting power balance between China and Japan led to increasing structural tensions, and their Sino-Japanese competition to expand their roles in regionalism and regional institutions in Asia in the 2000s was reflected in an increasing number of confrontations during this decade. In this phase, attempts to lead regional institution-building played out mainly within the existing ASEAN-centred regional institutional architecture. Both countries respected ASEAN's centrality and unity, and both tried to enhance their ties with, and expand their own role in existing ASEAN-centred regional institutions. The EAS that was newly established in 2005 eventually became the ASEAN-centred regional institution.

Prime Minister Hatoyama Yukio's East Asian Community concept in 2009 was unique in the trend of Sino-Japanese competition over regionalism in this decade. The idea of community-building in East Asia was not new, and the substance of this idea was vague. However, at the beginning, it seemed to apply diplomacy independent of US leverage and the diplomacy based on "fraternity" towards China and the ROK, in order to lead the new order in East Asia.[16] It had a different flavour from the trend of Sino-Japanese competition in the 2000s. The uniqueness of this concept derived from Hatoyama's private eagerness for independent diplomacy and the intention of the new Democratic Party of Japan's administration to exhibit different policy directions from those of the longstanding Liberal Democratic Party.

The concept eventually failed to provide any substantial results because of its own vagueness and strong criticism by the domestic government officials and specialists on the US–Japan alliance. Additionally, this concept was proposed just when the power balance between China and Japan had reversed, and China's attitudes towards its neighbour were becoming more strict. Hatoyama's East Asian Community concept was characterized as the old-fashioned "friendly relationship between China and Japan" in the 1970s and 1980s, and was proposed at an inappropriate moment. The Chinese government officially welcomed this concept, but did not appear to seriously consider it.

Entering the new phase of Sino-Japanese competition

Sino-Japanese competition over regionalism and regional institutions is ongoing, but it seems to have entered a new phase. This has occurred for several reasons. First, China's economic growth has continued since the end of the 2000s, so the change in the power balance between the two countries is more obvious in the 2010s than it was in the previous decade. As mentioned before, China's GDP overtook Japan's GDP in 2010, and China became the world's second largest economic power. In 2015, China's GDP reached US$10.8 trillion, while Japan's was US$4.1 trillion. China's share of the world's GDP reached 14.8 per cent; Japan's was only 5.6 per cent.

In addition to the rise of China, the growing economies of ASEAN countries should not be ignored. In 2000, the total GDP of all ASEAN member countries was US$606 billion, and their share of the total world GDP was 1.9 per cent. In 2010, the GDPs of ASEAN countries totalled US$1.9 trillion, and their share of the total world GDP was 3.01 per cent. In 2015, ASEAN countries' total GDPs amounted to US$2.44 trillion, and their share of the world's GDP was 3.3 per cent. ASEAN's latest GDP figures and world share are still small, but they have undoubtedly grown. On the whole, Japan's economic power is in relative decline, while China's and ASEAN countries' economies are growing.

The recent and obvious shift in the balance of power between Japan and China sharply increased tensions between the two countries. The deterioration of the Sino-Japanese relationship after the short détente that followed the Koizumi era was directly derived from the conflict over the Senkaku/Diaoyu Islands. China began to take an assertive stance with regard to territorial issues in both the East China Sea and the South China Sea in the late Hu Jintao era. Since 2008, China has regularly sent government ships to the waters off of the Japan-administered Senkaku/Diaoyu Islands. The so-called "Senkaku boat collision incident" occurred in this context in September 2010, and strained Sino-Japan relations. Shortly thereafter, the Noda Yoshihiko administration's decision to purchase three islets in the island chain from their private Japanese owner had a disastrous effect on the Sino-Japanese relationship. The disagreement over competing territorial claims on both sides is very much related to their different views of history. The "Senkaku incident" and historical perceptions are serious wedges between China and Japan. However, the structural confrontation between the two countries due to the changing power balance is fundamental to the China–Japan relationship. Growing tensions and freezing relations between China and Japan have intensified their competition for expanding and maintaining leverage in the region and need to be understood in light of the changing balance of power.

62 Mie Oba

Second, the US began to adopt a positive attitude towards regionalism and regional institutions in the East Asian/Asia-Pacific region. US engagement in Asian regionalism has gradually become regarded by Chinese and Japanese elites as measures to contain China in the context of its remarkable rise. The US decision to join the Trans-Pacific Partnership (TPP) towards the end of George W. Bush's term in office indicated that the US was searching for new measures that would allow it to maintain its interests and leverage in East Asia. The TPP and its effects on regional circumstances will be examined in the next section. The Barack Obama administration, which took office in 2009, made further changes to US engagement in regionalism and regional institutions in East Asia. It signed the TAC in 2009, and joined the EAS in 2011. In addition, the US became a founding member of the ASEAN Defense Ministers' Meeting Plus (ADMM+), which was established in 2010.

Obama's approach to regional institutions in East Asia derived from its "pivot" or "rebalancing policy". Whether the Bush administration actually neglected Asia and "just had took aside from the development of regional organizations and meetings" needs to be examined carefully.[17] However, there is an apparent difference between Bush's approach and Obama's approach. The former allowed East Asian countries to develop new regionalism, such as through the EAS, and to have discussions about an East Asian Community and regional integration, such as the EAFTA and CEPEA. The US is, however, sometimes observing and sometimes concerned about the development of East Asia as a regional group, and its attempts at regional economic integration. In particular, anxiety about the possibility of a US-excluded East Asian economy by means of the EAFTA or CEPEA led to US enthusiasm for joining and expanding the TPP.

When the US joined East Asia's central regional institutions under Obama's "rebalance to the Pacific", the EAS and ADMM+ became the most important regional forums in which all key stakeholders could meet regularly to discuss regional issues. With growing US engagement in Asia's regional architecture, Japan attempted to unite with the US to present a unified front against China with regard to regional issues – such as the South China Sea – at recent EAS and ADMM+ gatherings. China reacted negatively to this approach. As a result, these forums became arenas in which countries came into disagreement with each other with regard to their own claims.

Third, after Xi Jinping became China's president, China began to elucidate its regional vision. At first, it described its new regional vision in terms of security. Xi proposed a New Asian Security concept at the Fourth Summit of the Conference on Interaction and Confidence Building Measures in Asia (CICA) in May 2014. During his speech at this conference, Xi emphasized the importance of cooperative security in Asia, the importance of enhancing the CICA's capacity- and institution-building capabilities, China's intention to engage in security arrangements and discussions in Asia, and the need for a new regional architecture for Asian security. He also said: "It is for the people of Asia to run the affairs of Asia, solve the problems of Asia and uphold the security of Asia."[18]

China hosted the Fourth Summit of the CICA, and effectively used this event as an opportunity to demonstrate China's active intention to be embedded in Asian affairs, and to aggressively promote security cooperation. Xi's words in his speech implied China's preference that the New Asian Security architecture should be built by Asian countries alone. These remarks were interpreted as a vocal criticism of the existing US-centred hub-and-spoke system in the Asia-Pacific, and reflecting China's desire to exclude the US from Asia's future security frameworks.

The other Asian participants at the summit did not demonstrate enthusiastic support for China's New Asian Security concept, while participants from several countries, including the US and Japan, expressed their anxiety about China's real intentions. At least at the current stage, the new concept seems to lack sufficient attractiveness and feasibility to be accepted. China's assertive diplomacy over territorial issues in recent years has increased the anxieties of neighbouring countries regarding China's expanding role in Asia's security field.

However, China's regional vision, in terms of the economy and economic assistance, received support from Asian countries. One Belt One Road (OBOR) and the Asian Infrastructure Investment Bank (AIIB) are China's proposals for new economic development schemes in Central Asia, Southeast Asia, South Asia, and elsewhere. In his speech at Kazakhstan's Nazarbayev University in September 2013, President Xi proposed "a Silk Road economic belt" that would be created by enhancing cooperation with Central Asian countries.[19] In the following month, he also proposed "build[ing] the Maritime Silk Road of the 21st Century" and "the establishment of the AIIB" in his speech to the Parliament of Indonesia.[20] The Silk Road Fund, which mainly aims to provide investment and financial support for trade and economic cooperation under the OBOR framework, comprising the two Silk Roads mentioned above, was established in December 2014.[21]

Although the entire picture and details of the OBOR are still unclear, China's influential news network Xinhua has reported that the land portion of the Silk Road originates in Xi'an, runs through the main cities of Central Asia – including Urumqi, Huoerguosi, Almaty, Bishkek, and Samarkand – and passes through the Middle East to Istanbul, and then Moscow, from where it runs through Eastern Europe, Rotterdam, and Dulsburg, before reaching Venice. The Maritime Silk Road strategic initiative would open the route from Fuzhou, other cities on the southern coast of China, Hanoi, Kuala Lumpur, Jakarta, Kolkata, Colombo, and Nairobi on the east coast of the African continent, after which it would cross the Red Sea and the Suez Canal, and finally reach Athens and Venice. The OBOR covers a huge area composed of several sub-regions, and includes attempts to expand the amount of China's investment in, and economic assistance to Central Asia, Southeast Asia, South Asia, and the Middle East.[22] If realized, China's economic leverage would expand exponentially, and Chinese businesses and financial investors will easily be able to maintain and extend their access to these sub-regions. This economic leverage can then be mobilized as a strengthening political influence in a huge area of the Eurasian continent.

The AIIB, first proposed in Jakarta in October 2013, was officially launched in December 2015, when the AIIB's Articles of Agreement entered into force. There were 57 founding members, including all ASEAN member countries. The AIIB's Board of Directors approved loans to finance six projects until

64 *Mie Oba*

September 2016, and the total amount of financing stands, at the time of writing, at US$910 billion.[23]

These Chinese proposals now lead to a new phase in the history of regionalism in Asia. First, these proposals were not consistent with existing ASEAN-centred regional institutions in East Asia/Asia-Pacific. Non-ASEAN-centred regional institutions such as the Shanghai Cooperation Organization, Trilateral Cooperation between China, Japan, and South Korea, and the South Asian Association for Regional Cooperation already existed, but none included any Southeast Asian countries. The Asia Cooperation Dialogue organization, which was established by the strong leadership of Thailand's Prime Minister Thaksin Shinawatra in 2002, covers various sub-regions, much like OBOR, from Northeast Asia to West Asia. However, it has not actually demonstrated any regional cooperation, and has instead only provided a forum for foreign ministers of Asian countries to discuss regional issues.

The intensification of confrontations between China and Japan in the 2010s reflects Japan's reaction to China's proposals for these regional initiatives. The Japanese government has shown itself to be sceptical regarding the feasibility of China's ideas for the AIIB and OBOR, and thought that advanced Western countries shared its understanding. Consequently, it came as a shock when the United Kingdom joined the AIIB in March 2015, and when the other European countries followed suit. The question of whether Japan should join the AIIB was raised, but the Japanese government decided in June 2015 that it would not join as a founding member. This decision indicated not only Japan's scepticism about the AIIB's governance system, but also its serious anxiety about China's apparent ambition to replace the region's existing financial system of governance – led by Japan and the US – with one led by China.

Are the TPP, RCEP, and AIIB in conflict with each other?

In addition to the establishment of the AIIB, the conclusion of the TPP and negotiations for the RCEP revealed various attempts to construct a new economic order in East Asia/Asia-Pacific. During the latter part of the George W. Bush administration, the US had begun to show an interest in joining the TPP, originally conceived as a high-level and comprehensive FTA between Singapore, Brunei, Chile, and New Zealand. Since 2009, the Obama administration positioned the TPP in the context of its own "rebalance to the Pacific". US interest in the TPP was a strong impetus to expand TPP negotiations in March 2010. In Japan, controversy emerged over whether Japan should join the TPP or not, and in July 2013 it did join the negotiating process for the TPP. After a lengthy and rough negotiation process, 12 member countries concluded their negotiations in October 2015, and signed the new TPP in February 2016.

The TPP is sometimes framed as a US tool to "contain" the expansion of China's power, while the AIIB and RCEP are sometimes understood as China's tool to "counter" US intent to construct a new economic order by means of the TPP. From such a geo-economics point of view, Japan, a member of both the TPP and the

Competition over regional institutions 65

RCEP, is also engaged in the attempt to "counter" or "contain" China. However, the reality of the emerging economic order in Asia evidenced by the TPP, AIIB, and RCEP cannot be reduced to Sino-US confrontation. Considering the characteristics of international politics and the economic structure in the Asia-Pacific at the current stage, arguments such as "TPP vs. AIIB" and "TPP vs. RCEP" are oversimplifications.[24]

First, even though the US and China are in significant opposition to each other over some issues, their relationship is obviously interdependent. The US–China Strategic and Economic Dialogues have continued, despite intensifying differences of opinions concerning the South China Sea issue and other common issues including cyberterrorism. The two countries have also maintained their military exchanges and cooperative relations. The US and China are developing a complex, nuanced relationship as they confront one another while also seeking ways to co-exist. It is undeniable that the US and China are in a competitive relationship regarding the shape the regional order should take, and regarding leadership in this respect. However, the view that US–China relations are deterministically regulated solely by confrontation is too one-dimensional. The TPP in particular should not be understood as an intrinsically exclusive grouping against China.[25]

Sino-Japanese relations are similarly nuanced and complex, but the aspect of competition is a crucial factor. In the context of the growing structural tension, territorial and historical issues between these two countries are becoming more serious.

The second observation regarding attempts to create a new economic order is related to the first. Namely, the Chinese economy is deeply embedded in the regional and global economy, so China's containment is economically unrealistic. China–Japan trade amounted to about US$270 billion in 2015, and China is Japan's largest trading partner. Japan's exports to China in 2015 accounted for 17.5 per cent of Japan's total exports, and Japan's imports from China represented 24.8 per cent of Japan's imports in the same year. The number of Chinese visitors to Japan is increasing, and in 2015 reached five million. Chinese tourists and their purchases led to the expansion of benefits for Japan's tourism industry, as well as its retail industry. For China, Japan is its third-largest trading partner, and the US is its second. Japan's foreign investments in China amounted to US$3.2 billion in 2015, which is the third-largest investment figure for China.[26] The China–ASEAN economic relationship is also deepening. Today, China is ASEAN's largest single trading partner, and it accounted for 15.2 per cent of all ASEAN trade in 2015.[27] The inflow of foreign direct investment (FDI) from China comprised 6.8 per cent of its total inflow with ASEAN in 2015, but the amount of FDI inflow from China to ASEAN economies is increasing,[28] and is expected to expand in the future.

Third, the member countries of the TPP, AIIB, and RCEP overlap, calling into question their value as tools of containment. China, India, South Korea, Australia, New Zealand, and all ASEAN members have joined both the RCEP and AIIB. Australia's decision to join the AIIB is very interesting because it is a US ally, and, much like Japan, its security policy is based on its alliance with the US. Australia is also a member of the TPP. Canada, a member of the TPP and an ally and

66 *Mie Oba*

neighbour of the US, decided to apply to join the AIIB in August 2016.[29] Now the TPP includes only four ASEAN member countries – Brunei, Malaysia, Singapore, and Vietnam. Anxieties about the division of the ASEAN Economic Community (AEC) by the TPP have influenced Indonesia, the Philippines, and Thailand – advanced countries of ASEAN and non-members of the TPP – to issue statements regarding their positive stances on joining the TPP in the near future. In short, the leading roles played by the US and Japan in TPP negotiations and their non-participation in the AIIB are impressive, but many countries in the Asia-Pacific are joining all three: the TPP, AIIB, and RCEP. This indicates that they are using a hedging strategy by being engaged in several regional frameworks.

Finally, one should be careful when evaluating the extent to which the governance of the AIIB will be out of step with the existing standards for international institutions led by Western countries, as has been suggested by many critics. Some have said that the decision-making process in the AIIB is unclear and too China-centred, because China is the largest shareholder of the AIIB. Beijing contributed US$29 billion to the fund, 33.4 per cent of the total amount contributed by all member countries, and has 28.8 per cent of the voting rights.[30] Critics argue that China has a virtual veto over the decision-making of the AIIB. This might be theoretically true.

However, the AIIB is a multilateral regional bank, and many Western countries, including European countries and Australia, are members. In general, these powers are unlikely to support governance that lacks a consideration for transparency, human rights, or the environment, and it is likely that they will influence Chinese behaviour from the inside. Moreover, recipient countries that are mainly in Asia, to various degrees, do not want to deepen their reliance on Chinese investments, so they have not always welcomed China's investment approach due to its lack of transparency. Consequently, China will face difficulties if it tries to ignore these voices. China already has bilateral ties and unilateral agencies to aid and assist the building of infrastructure overseas, but it has also proposed a few regional and multilateral frameworks. China's proposal of the AIIB derived from its consideration of the demand of domestic private sectors to invest abroad, and its intention to expand its leverage in the region.

Simultaneously, however, it might indicate the intention of at least some of the Chinese elite to contribute to regional economic development by collaborating with neighbouring countries, beyond unilaterally obtaining economic benefits. China might have some regrets about the assistance it has provided to developing countries, as these efforts were sometimes strongly criticized due to their lack of transparency and consideration of environmental and human rights protection, effectiveness, and efficiency.

In addition, early management decisions taken by the AIIB already suggest that the institution seeks to be integrated with existing finance institutions and prevailing governance norms. It has invited many experts with rich experience in international organizations to become involved. For example, Jin Liqun, the AIIB president, was the executive director for China at the World Bank, and also the vice-president and ranking vice-president of the ADB from 2003 to 2008.

Moreover, among six projects already approved by the AIIB, three projects are co-financed with another international institution such as the World Bank, the European Bank for Reconstruction and Development, and the ADB. Co-financing arrangements will surely be managed according to the accepted practices of conduct used by existing international banks, and the AIIB seems satisfied with that reality.

Furthermore, many countries, including Southeast Asian nations, welcome China's positive attitude with regard to its assistance and investments via the AIIB and the OBOR initiative. From their perspective, China's new approach to regionalism meets the demands of neighbouring countries in Southeast Asia, even while China's assertive stance on territorial issues has led to the rise of tensions between China and neighbouring countries at the same time.

The AIIB aims to produce actual results by financing specific projects that mainly involve constructing the hard infrastructure that many Asian countries need. A joint study by the ADB and the ADB Institute (ADBI) released in 2009 focuses on the importance of creating an infrastructure for a "seamless Asia" to achieve sustainable prosperity for the region as a whole.

The study estimates that total investments in the order of US$8 trillion in national infrastructure would be needed from 2010 through 2020 to achieve this objective.[31] Extrapolating from this estimate, Asian countries require about US$750 billion in infrastructure investment each year. The ADB, the regional bank long led by Japan, cannot meet such huge demand. The ADB's operations totalled US$27.17 billion each year.[32] Even though this figure was the highest in ADB history, infrastructure development in Asia needs more financing. In other words, the AIIB has the potential to provide the resources that Asian countries want at a time when existing institutions cannot. This is the main reason all ASEAN countries joined the AIIB, even though it is not an ASEAN-centred framework, even despite the fact that some ASEAN countries have serious conflicts with China over the South China Sea.

The capacity of the AIIB should not be overestimated, although most Asian countries expect a great deal from it. However, it should also not be underestimated and concluded that it cannot operate effectively. The relationship between the AIIB and ADB is not merely competitive. The promotion of co-financing projects between them indicates room for cooperative relations between China- and Japan-led financial initiatives.

China's assertive stance on the South China Sea issue became obvious around 2009, during the latter part of Hu's tenure. China occupied Scarborough Shoal in 2012. China's stance on the South China Sea became more assertive after Xi Jinping became China's president in 2013. In May 2014, China's national company set up an oil rig in Vietnam's Exclusive Economic Zone (EEZ), and thereby provoked sharp antagonism and criticism among Vietnamese people against China, and led to anti-China demonstrations in several Vietnamese cities, in which several people died. Thereafter, China's rapid reclamation efforts and its construction of facilities on the eight Spratly Island maritime features that it had already seized came to light. Vietnam and the Philippines adopted very critical attitudes towards China's

68 *Mie Oba*

activities, and almost all ASEAN countries became anxious about the negative repercussions of China's activities for the region's peace and stability. Brunei, Malaysia, the Philippines, and Vietnam are the only claimants among ASEAN countries, but for these two years, non-claimant countries such as Indonesia and Singapore seem to have also become more anxious about peace and stability in the South China Sea.

In spite of these recent developments, all ASEAN countries – including the Philippines – have joined the AIIB and been supportive of OBOR. This fact indicates that even though the South China Sea issue causes deep concerns about China's strict stance on sovereignty-related issues, it is only one part of the overall China–ASEAN relationship.

Conclusion: Asian regionalism and co-existence in conflicts

There are many competing perspectives regarding the construction or reconstruction of a new regional order in East Asia. Such competing views are deeply related to differing interpretations of China and Japan's respective attempts to expand or maintain their leverage in regional politics. Many regional institutions are impacted, making the Sino-Japanese competition an important factor shaping the regional order of the future. Unfortunately, the structural confrontation between China and Japan seems to have become more serious, but nonetheless the two countries have to cooperate, even in regional institutions.

Second, as mentioned before, with a deepening Sino-Japanese structural confrontation, Japan relies on the US–Japan alliance in an attempt to form a united front against China, and to some extent the Southeast Asian countries that seem to share that threat perception. Japan's position on this matter is obvious in its regional institutional behaviour, and especially in the EAS and ADMM+. However, it should be pointed out that the US and Southeast Asian countries do not always vote against China. China and the US disagree sharply on several issues, and compete over rule-setting for economies in the region via the TPP and the AIIB. At the same time, they search for opportunities to cooperate in various fields. Even though Vietnam and the Philippines are in conflict with China over the South China Sea, they too try to keep and even enhance their ties with China.

The Sino-Japanese relationship is thus becoming more complex. It is a mixture of confrontation and cooperation. Currently, Sino-Japanese structural confrontation is increasing, even though this causes disharmony to the promotion of regionalism and regional cooperation in the short term. However, regional institutions in East Asia surely provide member countries with critical opportunities for communicating with each other, even though they have serious conflicts. As a result, even though regional institutions are now an arena in which China and Japan compete with each other, they will also, at least partly, function to regulate the structural confrontation between them.

Notes

1 Andrew Gamble and Anthony Payne, eds, *Regionalism and World Order* (London: Macmillan, 1996), 2.
2 Mie Oba, *Ajia-Taiheiyo Chiiki Keisei Heno Dotei: Nichi-go no Aidentiti mosaku to Chiikishugi* (The Formation of Asia Pacific: The Journeys of Australia and Japan to Search Their Identity and Their Region) (Kyoto: Minerva Shobo, 2004), ch. 2, Mie Oba, "Japan's Entry into ECAFE", in, Junko Tomaru, Makoto Iokibe, and Caroline Rose, eds, *Japanese Diplomacy in the 1950s* (London: Routledge, 2007).
3 Qichen Qian, "Opening Statement at the Fourth ARF Ministerial Meeting", Kuala Lumpur, July 27, 1997.
4 Thomas J. Christensen, "China, the U.S.–Japan Alliance and the Security Dilemma in East Asia", *International Security*, 23:4 (1999), 72.
5 Marc Lanteigne, *China and International Institutions: Alternate Paths to Global Power* (London: Routledge, 2005), 69–70.
6 Lanteigne, *China and International Institutions*, 71.
7 "Japan", World DataBank. http://databank.worldbank.org/data/reports.aspx?source=2&series=NY.GDP.MKTP.CD&country=JPN
8 "China", World DataBank. http://databank.worldbank.org/data/reports.aspx?source=2&series=NY.GDP.MKTP.CD&country=CHN
9 Junichiro Koizumi, "Japan and ASEAN in East Asia: A Sincere and Open Partnership", Singapore, January 14, 2002.
10 Declaration on the Conduct of Parties in the South China Sea, Phnom Penh, Cambodia, November 4, 2002. Wang Yi, who has shown an assertive attitude over the South China Sea issue since he assumed the position of the foreign minister of China, signed the Declaration for China.
11 There were about 18,000 participants at the first CAEXPO, but at the third CAEXPO there were 38,900, and at the ninth CAEXPO there were 42,000. Suehiro Akira, "Nanshin suru Chugoku to Chuugoku ASEAN Hakuran-kai" (China's Southern Advance and CAEXPO), in Suehiro Akira, *Nanshin-suru Chugoku to Tounan-Ajia: Chiiki no "Chugoku-ka"* (Is China's Southern Advance Sinicizing Southeast Asia?) (Institute of Social Science, 2014), 52. In addition, according to the author's field research, during in the ninth and tenth CAEXPOs (2009 and 2010), enterprises from outside Southeast Asia and China participated in the exhibition.
12 For details of the Sino-Japanese conflicts that occurred in the process of establishing the EAS, see Mie Oba, "Regional Arrangement for Trade in Northeast Asia", in Vinod Aggarwal and Min Gyo Koo, eds, *Asia's New Institutional Architecture: Evolving Structures for Managing Trade, Financial and Security Relations* (Dordrecht: Springer, 2007).
13 The CMIM agreement was amended in July 2014 to enhance its function and expand its size. The total size of the CMIM is now US$240 billion.
14 China's financial contribution includes those of China and Hong Kong.
15 The figures for the GDPs of these two countries were found in DataBank at the World Bank homepage: http://data.worldbank.org/indicator/NY.GDP.MKTP.CD
16 For details of Hatoyama's East Asian Community concept in the early days of the Hatoyama administration, see Yukio Hatoyama "Watashi-no Seiji Tetsugaku" (My Political Philosophy), *Voice*, September 2009; Yukio Hatoyama, "A New Path for Japan", *New York Times*, August 26, 2009.
17 Jeffrey A. Bader, *Obama and China's Rise: An Insider's Account of America's Asia Strategy* (Washington, DC: Brookings Institution Press, 2012), 4.
18 Xi Jinping, "New Asian Security Concept for New Progress in Security Cooperation", speech given at the Fourth Summit of the CICA, Shanghai, May 2014. www.china.org.cn/world/2014-05/28/content_32511846_2.htm, accessed October 20, 2016.
19 "President Xi Jinping Delivers Important Speech and Proposes to Build a Silk Road Economic Belt with Central Asian Countries", Ministry of Foreign Affairs of the

70 *Mie Oba*

People's Republic of China, September 7, 2013, www.fmprc.gov.cn/mfa_eng/topics_665678/xjpfwzysiesgjtfhshzzfh_665686/t1076334.shtml, accessed October 20, 2016.

20 Xi Jinping, "Speech by Chinese President Xi Jinping to Indonesian Parliament", Jakarta, Indonesia, October 3, 2013, www.asean-china-center.org/english/2013-10/03/c_133062675.htm, accessed October 20, 2016.

21 www.silkroadfund.com.cn/enweb/23775/23767/index.html, accessed October 20, 2016.

22 "Chronology of China's Belt and Road Initiative", *Xinhuanet*, June 24, 2016, http://news.xinhuanet.com/english/2016-06/24/c_135464233.htm, accessed October 20, 2016.

23 The AIIB homepage has links to each project:, accessed October 20, 2016.

24 The author has already referenced the oversimplification of the argument as "TPP vs. RCEP" in Mie Oba, "TPP, RCEP, and FTAAP: Multilayered Regional Economic Integration and International Relations", *Asia-Pacific Review*, 23:1 (2016).

25 Oba, "TPP, RCEP, and FTAAP".

26 China–Mongol Division, MOFA, *Nichu-keizai kankei to Chugoku no keizai-josei* (Economic Relations Between China and Japan and Condition of Chinese Economy), www.mofa.go.jp/mofaj/files/000007735.pdf, accessed October 20, 2016.

27 ASEAN Secretariat, "Top Ten ASEAN Trade Partner Countries/Regions, 2015", ASEAN Statistics, http://asean.org/storage/2016/06/table20_as-of-30-Aug-2016-2.pdf, accessed October 20, 2016.

28 ASEAN Secretariat, "Foreign Direct Investment Net Inflows in ASEAN from Selected Partner Countries/Regions", ASEAN Statistics, http://asean.org/storage/2015/09/Table-26_oct2016.pdf, accessed October 20, 2016.

29 "Canada Applies to Join AIIB", *Wall Street Journal*, August 31, 2016, www.wsj.com/articles/canada-applies-to-join-aiib-1472642406, accessed October 20, 2016.

30 "Asian Infrastructure Development Bank, "Subscriptions and Voting Power of Member Countries", www.aiib.org/uploadfile/2016/0930/20160930035841674.pdf, accessed October 20, 2016.

31 Asian Development Bank and Asian Development Bank Institute, *Infrastructure for a Seamless Asia* (Metro Manila: Asian Development Bank, 2009), 167.

32 Asian Development Bank, *Annual Report 2015* (Mandaluyong: ADB, 2015), 6.

4 China, Japan, and economic security competition (and cooperation) in the Asia-Pacific

Ramon Pacheco Pardo

Economic security has arguably become the top priority across the Asia-Pacific region. Territorial and maritime disputes, North Korea's nuclear programme, or cyber-attacks, among others, might make the headlines. Yet, the risk of a full-blown conflict in the Asia-Pacific has dramatically decreased since the end of the Cold War. Simply put, it seems highly unlikely for two or more countries in the region to escalate tensions to the extent that war becomes inevitable. Security, in its traditional sense, is becoming a defining characteristic of the Asia-Pacific.

In sharp contrast, economic security – here defined as the ability of a government to guarantee access to a stable income for its population – is far from guaranteed.[1] As the global financial crisis (GFC) has painfully demonstrated, even highly developed Western economies can suffer from a recession, high or even mass unemployment, and associated political instability. Brexit and the Donald Trump and Marine Le Pen phenomena are vivid examples of the potential for a lack of economic security to result in political dislocation. The Arab Spring shows that neither are authoritarian regimes immune to the effects of economic insecurity.

The Asia-Pacific is home to some of the fastest-growing economies in the world. This was also the case in the 1990s, when the Asian financial crisis (AFC) wreaked havoc across the region. It withstood the GFC relatively unscathed. Yet the slow-down in the US and Europe – large export destinations for Asian goods – resulted in impaired growth and even recession in several Asia-Pacific countries. And the fate of then-Indonesian President Mohammad Suharto in 1998 or Japan's Liberal Democratic Party in 1993–1994 and 2009–2012, as well as the electoral victories of Thaksin Shinawatra in Thailand three times and Rodrigo Duterte in the Philippines in 2016, are telling proof that economics affects politics in the Asia-Pacific as well. Hence why economic security can be considered the top priority for any government wishing to retain power, whether democratic or authoritarian.

The question then becomes how to achieve and maintain economic security. With economic nationalism having been discredited across most of the Asia-Pacific – even North Korea has enacted economic reforms starting from 2002 – East Asian tiger-style liberalism and openness coupled with government interventionism has become common.[2] This has led to strong and well-developed trade regionalization and, increasingly, regionalism, a wariness towards uncontrolled free capital flows that many blame for the AFC, and the use of official development assistance (ODA) and infrastructure investment to promote economic growth.

72 *Ramon Pacheco Pardo*

The result has been the quasi-organic development of an economic regional security complex (RSC) characterized by a commitment to openness, growing interconnectedness and interdependence, at least in theory if not always in practice. The three just-mentioned characteristics of this RSC, however, do not necessarily result in Sino-Japanese cooperation. Starting from the 1930s, a "flying-geese" model with Japanese companies as the top goose and other Asian countries as following geese dominated the economic structure of the region.[3] Following China's accession to the World Trade Organization (WTO), this model was replaced by Sino-centric trade and production networks.[4] Regardless of whether it was Japan or China at the centre of Asia-Pacific economic links, openness defined the system. However, Tokyo seems not to have come to terms with its decreasing centrality to Asia-Pacific economic flows. Beijing, meanwhile, is clearly satisfied with having once again become the key country in regional economic links.

The scene is therefore set for Sino-Japanese competition and enmity in the Asia-Pacific economic RSC. As this chapter will illustrate, China and Japan compete in a number of areas – namely trade agreements, development aid, and infrastructure development. However, memories of the AFC and a shared belief in government interventionism mean that the RSC affords opportunities for cooperation between the two economic giants. This is the case in the areas of finance and development banks – despite the apparent competition in the latter brought by the launch of the Asian Infrastructure Investment Bank (AIIB).

This chapter is organized as follows. In the next section, I will analyse three areas of economic activity in which the Asia-Pacific RSC is characterized by enmity and rivalry between China and Japan. In the section following, I will focus on finance, and the extent to which amity and an undeclared alliance characterize the RSC in this area. In the subsequent section, I will explain how China and Japan are moving towards amity and agreement in the areas of development banks. I will summarize my argument in the concluding chapter.

China against Japan: trade agreements, development aid, and infrastructure construction

The Sino-Japanese rivalry takes many different forms and economic competition is among the most important. As two of the three largest national economies in the world, and the top two holders of international reserves, China and Japan have the necessary tools to engage in economic statecraft: capital, and a willingness to use it for political purposes. Considering that the regional economic structure in the Asia-Pacific combines a high level of trade interdependence, decreasing but still-important ODA flows, big infrastructure development needs, and a relatively low level of intraregional investment flow, it is unsurprising that the first three areas afford great scope for competition between Beijing and Tokyo.

Certainly, the securitization of the RSC in the areas of trade, ODA, and infrastructure has led to enmity between China and Japan. Rival webs of trade agreements, a lack of any meaningful cooperation in the provision of ODA, and competition to win infrastructure development contracts is both explained by and helps to

Economic security competition 73

explain this enmity. As a result, rivalry defines the relationship between both powers in these areas of the economic RSC. It is unlikely that rivalry will be replaced by any other form of power relations any time soon, considering that neither Beijing nor Tokyo seems to be willing to reach a grand bargain with the other to diffuse tensions – even though, as we will see later, regional development banks could help to diffuse this rivalry in the areas of ODA and infrastructure.

Trade agreements

The Asia-Pacific region is often associated with trade. It can be said that exports made the region what it is today.[5] Japan first, the East Asian tigers afterwards, and China today are all assumed to have launched their development paths with a focus on trade.[6] Today, the Asia-Pacific is the second most integrated region in the world in terms of trade. As much as 50–55 per cent of commercial flows in Asia are intraregional – the second highest figure in the world behind the EU.[7] Yet, this has been the result of regionalization rather than regionalism. In other words, intraregional trade flows have developed due to market forces rather than the implementation of a regional trade agreement, which the Asia-Pacific still lacks. This is a crucial difference from the two other well-integrated regions – the EU and North America – in which regional trade agreements laid the ground for markets to follow.[8]

In the absence of a regional trade agreement, Beijing and Tokyo have engaged in a two-tier competition to shape trade in the region. The first tier involves the network of bilateral trade agreements that each of them has established with different Asia-Pacific countries. The second tier includes the competing regional trade agreements that each of the two powers promotes. This competition has only intensified with the decision by the US Obama administration to take the lead in Trans-Pacific Partnership (TPP) negotiations, which Japan supported. Even though ratification of the TPP seems unlikely at the time of writing, Tokyo's support throughout a negotiation process that excluded China proves the competitive aspect of trade agreements in the region.

Asia is home to over 200 trade agreements involving two or more countries in the region. China has signed four already, with Singapore, South Korea, Thailand, and the Association of Southeast Asian Nations (ASEAN). Japan, meanwhile, has agreements signed and in effect with ASEAN, Brunei, Indonesia, Malaysia, Mongolia, the Philippines, Singapore, Thailand, and Vietnam. Both of them also have agreements that have entered into force with Australia, and China has another with New Zealand.[9] This suggests that Japan has been more successful in luring ASEAN member states with bilateral trade incentives. China, in contrast, has been more skilful in dealing with the two big Oceanian economies, as well as with the biggest prize for both China and Japan in the Asia-Pacific – South Korea, the fourth-largest Asian economy.

Each country's network of trade agreements reflects the economic security concerns of the rest of the region, particularly Southeast Asian countries. Many ASEAN member states consider China a destination for their exports – particularly intermediate goods – but they also see themselves as competitors to China's

74 *Ramon Pacheco Pardo*

manufacturing base.[10] Vietnam has already become a strong textile and shoe-making production location, and Indonesia and Malaysia have long held ambitions to diversify their economies and attract factories in a range of industries. Trade agreements with China would make it harder to compete as a manufacturing base, while agreements with Japan are more naturally complementary.

But aside from bilateral frameworks, it is the two regional trade agreements currently on the table in the Asia-Pacific where the rivalry between China and Japan is clearest. Free trade agreements (FTAs) promote commercial exchanges, but they also set the norms and rules governing trade. With the Doha round of trade negotiations long-stalled, bilateral and regional trade have become the de facto main conduit for shaping these norms and rules.[11] This is the case with the competing views offered by the Regional Comprehensive Economic Partnership (RCEP) and the TPP.

Dating back to 2005, TPP negotiations gained new impetus when the US joined in January 2008. Signed in February 2016, the TPP sets out an ambitious agenda addressing barriers to trade in goods and services, environmental and rights standards, intellectual property rights, investor–state arbitration, and regulatory cooperation.[12] In short, it is much more than a traditional trade agreement only focusing on barriers to trade. The agreement seeks to define standards for a new generation of FTAs.

Japan only joined TPP negotiations in May 2013. However, it was seen by the other parties as the key country in the negotiation process, along with the US. Not only is Japan the second-largest economy among TPP signatories, but it has also traditionally been reluctant to discuss any trade provision encroaching on its sovereignty.[13] The TPP does exactly that. Thus, Prime Minister Abe Shinzō's acquiescence to TPP provisions sends a clear political signal to the Asia-Pacific region. Japan no longer sees economic security through the lens of protecting its domestic economy, but increasingly understands it in terms of growing interdependence, openness, and mutual concessions.

Differently, the RCEP favoured by China is a less ambitious trade agreement. Negotiations were only formally launched in November 2012, to a large extent as a reaction to TPP discussions.[14] From the outset, it became clear that the focus was going to be on lowering barriers to trade in goods. Trade in services is part of the negotiation process, but the goal is to reach an agreement consistent with WTO rules – not going beyond them. Similarly, investment facilitation measures would also be part of any RCEP agreement but would not impinge on any country's sovereignty, a clear contrast with the TPP's investor–state arbitration provision.[15] In terms of economic security, it seems clear that China still considers non-negotiable the protection of one's sovereignty to make its own policy choices on issues such as government procurement, environmental, labour, or food security standards. These and other areas do not feature in the RCEP as currently conceived.

The differences between the TPP and RCEP with regards to the complexion of the Asia-Pacific economic RSC extend to the geographic definition of the region itself. Simply put, the TPP included, at least until the Trump administration decided to withdraw, the US and the RCEP excludes it. For Japan, ensuring that Washington remains committed to the Asia-Pacific is one of the cornerstones of foreign policy.[16]

Economic security competition 75

As other chapters in this volume show, the US is very much part of the Asia-Pacific's RSC. Tokyo – the US's closest ally in the region – wants this to be the case in the economic RSC as well. Economic security is closely connected with military security in the eyes of the Abe administration.[17]

Through the RCEP, meanwhile, China promotes the view that the US is not part of the economic RSC in the Asia-Pacific.[18] The RCEP includes all ASEAN+6 countries. This means that Australia, India, and New Zealand are included. Thus, geography does not necessarily exclude the US from the agreement. Politics rather than economics dictate Washington's absence from RCEP negotiations.

Development aid

ODA remains an important feature of the political economy of the Asia-Pacific. Even though ODA is decreasing as a percentage of GDP, several countries in the region remain net ODA recipients. Top among them is Vietnam, the world's second-largest recipient of international aid. Most ASEAN countries are also net recipients of aid, including middle-income Malaysia and Thailand.[19] This implies that aid has a clear economic rationale – to support development – but also a politico-diplomatic component, a signal suggesting the securitization of ODA. Indeed, the politico-diplomatic component is compounded by the fact that almost two-thirds of Japanese – and incidentally, South Korean – bilateral ODA goes to Asia, essentially ASEAN and India.[20] Were Japanese aid to be genuinely needs-based, a much higher percentage would in all likelihood go to poorer regions such as sub-Saharan Africa or countries such as Bangladesh and Sri Lanka. Chinese bilateral aid figures are not easily accessible, but it is generally agreed that well over half of Beijing's ODA goes to Southeast Asia.[21] In other words, both China and Japan make use of ODA to strengthen their position in the Asia-Pacific's RSC.

The sectors targeted by Chinese and Japanese ODA further illustrate the extent to which ODA is securitized and part of the economic RSC. Most notably, Japan is the only Organization of Economic Cooperation and Development (OECD) Development Assistance Committee (DAC) member using over half of its ODA in Asia for economic rather than social projects – essentially for transport, communications, and energy schemes. By way of comparison, social projects including education, health, or water supply and sanitation are the largest recipients of South Korean ODA – in common with all other DAC members.[22] Similarly to the case of Japan, it is estimated that some figure between half and two-thirds of Chinese aid is used for economic projects.[23] Since cooperation between Chinese and Japanese officials and firms when implementing ODA projects is uncommon, enmity and rivalry define Sino-Japanese relations in this field. Incidentally, rivalry among donors is common beyond the case of Beijing and Tokyo.[24]

The focus on economic-type ODA highlights two aspects of the competition between Beijing and Tokyo. To begin with, it suggests a long-term and mutually beneficial relationship between the donor and the recipient. China and Japan engage in the construction of roads, ports, pipelines, and other infrastructure that will strengthen the economy of the recipient country. But this will also support

76   Ramon Pacheco Pardo

long-term trade between the recipient and China or Japan, as the case may be.[25] Beijing and Tokyo are unlikely to build infrastructure that will not be helpful in developing bilateral economic links with the recipient. As an example, China has been busy building ports, roads, and bridges in Myanmar – at least partly funded with ODA – that can give it access to the Indian Ocean.

In addition, China and Japan compete in terms of supporting their companies in winning infrastructure development contracts in third countries (of which more below). Economic-type ODA is normally implemented by the donor's companies and, not uncommonly, their workforce too – whether by themselves or in cooperation with local labour in the recipient country. ODA provision is a great means for a company to gain a foothold in a particular area, and may bring synergies in the form of the award of further contracts. For Japan – whose projects are often more expensive – ODA provision allows the state to support private company expansion overseas.[26]

Another component of the enmity and rivalry between China and Japan has already been teased out and relates to the fact that the latter is part of the OECD's DAC and the former is not. Comprised of 29 members, the DAC serves as a forum to coordinate aid policy with the aim of supporting sustainable development.[27] Even though its effectiveness has been called into question,[28] membership of the DAC indicates a commitment to provide ODA for the benefit of the recipient rather than the donor, by coordinating with other donors to reduce waste and duplication. Japan and South Korea are members of the DAC, which indicates their willingness to work together with other developed countries to streamline aid for more impact, even at some cost to themselves in terms of administrative burden or lost opportunities to promote national firms.

China, in sharp contrast, is often portrayed as a challenger to the DAC's ODA regime.[29] Beijing has attended the Committee's meetings since 2011. Yet, China has been accused of providing aid according to the interests of governments rather than the needs of the general population.[30] Regardless of whether Beijing is challenging the prevailing ODA regime, it is true that its emergence as a donor has upended the development world. Combined, Beijing's China Development Bank and Export–Import Bank of China provide more aid than the World Bank and the five major regional development banks put together.[31] Conditionality, a key component of multilateral bank and developed country aid, is not a feature of Chinese ODA.[32] In common with their counterparts in other regions, many Asia-Pacific recipients prefer aid without strings, and China delivers. This can be detrimental to Japan, whose aid in theory is subject to conditionality requirements, and therefore less attractive.

Notwithstanding the above, it seems that a modicum of agreement between China and Japan could emerge in the area of ODA provision. As a promising sign, the Beijing-dominated AIIB and Tokyo-led Asian Development Bank (ADB) have started to work together. As explained below, a more developed Asia-Pacific benefits both Beijing and Tokyo. The prospects of mutual benefit could just as well be the driver behind a modicum of agreement between Chinese and Japanese ODA programmes, in so far as both nations' companies could benefit from easier access to producers and markets across the Asia-Pacific.

Economic security competition 77

Infrastructure-building

Short- to mid-term infrastructure investment needs in the Asia-Pacific region are estimated to be in the trillions of US dollars. Studies by the ADB, for example, indicate that developing economies in Asia needs infrastructure investment of US$8.2 trillion between 2011 and 2020 – with the bulk of the demand coming from China, India, and Southeast Asia.[33] In particular, energy and transport infrastructure require most of the investment. Yet, there is a deficit in infrastructure investment running into the tens – if not hundreds – of billions of US dollars per year in the region.[34] Furthermore, there is no regional institution or fund with the financial power to plug this gap. The ADB, for example, has an agreed capital base of only US$165 billion. In this context, China and Japan are engaged in a competition to develop the infrastructure that the Asia-Pacific needs. For decades, Tokyo was the dominant player in this area. Japanese industrial heavyweights were key in the development of the infrastructure of East Asia's tigers and ASEAN emerging economies. Often supported by the Japanese government through its diplomatic corps and cheap financing, Japanese companies helped to build the roads, ports, factories, and other infrastructure that propelled high rates of economic growth across the Asia-Pacific.[35] As of 2015, Japan remained the largest single national source of foreign direct investment (FDI) in ASEAN, with an annual flow of US$17.5 billion.[36] The bulk of this investment is in infrastructure.

China is a recent newcomer to this area and still lags behind Japan. At US$8.2 billion in 2015, Chinese investment in ASEAN is less than half of Japan's.[37] However, this difference masks the huge increase in Chinese investment over the past decade. Prior to joining the WTO, China's annual *global* FDI outflows were only US$2 billion.[38] In the aftermath of the GFC and facing overcapacity at home, Chinese companies are very actively seeking investment opportunities overseas. Infrastructure-building in the Asia-Pacific region is one of their clearest targets.

Rivalry between Beijing and Tokyo in the area of infrastructure developments is visible in three primary dimensions. To start with, Chinese and Japanese companies directly compete for contracts. High-speed railways are a case in point. Chinese and Japanese companies and consortiums have bid or are bidding for the same project contracts in Indonesia, Thailand, and the Malaysia–Singapore link. Their competitive bids reflect different industrial strengths. Japan typically offers more advanced technology, but China is more cost-competitive. This competition is replicated in areas such as metro systems, power generation and supply, ports, roads, and telecommunications.[39] Direct competition over project contracts will only intensify as China moves up the value-added chain.

The two other areas of rivalry between Beijing and Tokyo are politico-economic. Infrastructure-building entails a long-term commitment. Bidding for a contract, building a project, and maintenance implies a multi-year if not multi-decade relationship between the builder and the client. In that light, contract awards are a diplomatic and political prize, not just an economic one. For example, the Indonesian government's decision to award its first high-speed railway contract to China Railway Group in October 2015 instead of a Japanese consortium was seen as a sign of closer Sino-Indonesian relations.[40] Tellingly, infrastructure-building is

78 *Ramon Pacheco Pardo*

the main basis of One Belt, One Road (OBOR), unveiled by the Xi Jinping government in October 2013. Roads, railways, ports, or pipelines are all part of an infrastructure network seeking to connect the Eurasian landmass and the Indo-Pacific ocean.[41] OBOR would serve China to position itself as a centre for long-term infrastructure development across both regions.

Meanwhile, infrastructure-building can be seen as a proxy for state-supported economic competition between Beijing and Tokyo. China's infrastructure giants are state-owned; Japan's receive much political support from their government, as discussed above. Successful bidding for overseas infrastructure construction projects confers prestige on the winner and its home country, and showcases and even expands one's technology.[42] For the Chinese government, showing that it is moving up the value-added chain and able to win contracts against Japanese competitors is useful to slowly move away from its image as a producer of cheap, low-end goods. For Tokyo, it is essential to maintain its image as a producer of cutting-edge technology as Japanese companies are overtaken by South Korean, Taiwanese and other Asian companies in mobile, semiconductor, flat-screen TV, or shipping technologies. As economic competition in the Asia-Pacific intensifies, rivalry between the Chinese and Japanese governments over reputation and national brand is likely to intensify due to the ancillary politico-economic benefits that infrastructure contracts bring to the winner.

China with Japan: finance

The Asia-Pacific's economic RSC includes many issue-areas in which enmity and competition are dominant, as seen in the previous section. Nonetheless, the regional economic structure in the Asia-Pacific also leaves scope for other types of securitization to co-exist. This is the case in the area of finance, where Sino-Japanese amity reigns. Indeed, there seems to be an undeclared alliance between Beijing and Tokyo in this realm. Together with other Asia-Pacific countries – most notably South Korea – China and Japan are setting up an institutional network with a clear shared objective: to tame the financial sector, avoiding financial crises while creating stable financial flows supportive of sustainable economic growth.

There are three key reasons behind the amity and de facto alliance in this area. To begin with, intraregional portfolio investment flows in the Asia-Pacific are low, that is, there is an overreliance on flows from outside the region. Data from the International Monetary Fund (IMF) indicate that intraregional portfolio investment flows make around 10–15 per cent of the Asia-Pacific's total in any given year.[43] In other words, there is limited regionalization in the financial sector. This reduces the scope for competition between Chinese and Japanese banks and other financial firms, as well as between both governments. Concurrently, there are more opportunities for cooperation to protect against extraregional portfolio investment.

In addition, memories of the AFC in 1997–1998 run deep in the region.[44] The crisis was blamed on the sudden withdrawal of portfolio investment from Thailand first, but extending to other countries across the region, including Malaysia, Indonesia, and South Korea. In the case of Indonesia, international capital flight

Economic security competition 79

was the main reason behind the collapse of Suharto's regime. Ever since the AFC, avoiding a new financial crisis has been a key motivation underpinning economic policy making across the Asia-Pacific.[45] Even though China and Japan were less affected by the AFC than other countries in the region, both of them suffered in terms of lower economic growth. Furthermore, Beijing, Tokyo, and other governments across the region realized that national-level self-protection mechanisms such as foreign exchange reserves and central bank swap arrangements could be insufficient to stop the cross-border spread of a crisis.

The GFC of 2007–2008 reinforced these views. Of course, the Asia-Pacific region was not as affected as the US or the EU, and the activation of self-protection mechanisms was an important reason for this. Yet, the development of a comprehensive institutional network in the aftermath of the AFC – detailed below – was very important as well.[46] It made the region's governments less reliant on extraregional portfolio flows, thus reducing the impact of the GFC and providing more leeway to governments to use self-protection mechanisms to support the private sector as the crisis unfolded. Both China and Japan benefited from this more resilient regional institutional framework.

The final main reason why amity and a de facto alliance underpin the finance sector within the Asia-Pacific economic RSC is the widespread support for state interventionism in the economy. China, Japan, and other countries in the region have decades-old policies of supporting economic growth through targeted state intervention. In the case of finance, this policy was abandoned by most countries in the region throughout the 1990s.[47] The Washington Consensus – including capital account liberalization – diffused across the Asia-Pacific, resulting in the AFC. Since then, state intervention in the form of capital controls, stimulus packages, and other measures has once again become common.[48] At the regional level, shared state interventionism has legitimized financial regionalization.

The creation of an Asia-Pacific institutional financial network to tame this sector rests upon three pillars: crisis prevention, crisis resolution, and market strengthening. In the area of crisis prevention and resolution, the Chiang Mai Initiative (CMI) was launched in 2000 and CMI Multilateralization (CMIM) in 2009.[49] In other words, it was launched following the AFC and upgraded right after the GFC. As of 2017, the CMIM is a US$240 billion fund that can be activated by any country for precautionary or stability purposes.[50] This means that it can be used for crisis prevention or resolution. China – including Hong Kong – and Japan are the largest financial contributors. Each of them contributes 32 per cent of the total signed up capital.[51] In tangible terms, then, Beijing and Tokyo have agreed to make an equal financial contribution to the stability of the Asia-Pacific.

In relation to crisis prevention specifically, the ASEAN+3 Macroeconomic Research Office (AMRO) was established in 2011. It has a surveillance role, and regularly monitors the state of the ASEAN+3 and Hong Kong economies. It became the first legally established international organization under ASEAN+3 in 2016.[52] This means that AMRO has been granted legal independence from ASEAN+3 member states to pursue its mandate. Thus, the Chinese and Japanese governments have agreed to allow an independent regional institution to monitor their economies – in common with the other countries in ASEAN+3. This signals that in the area of financial governance at least, Beijing and Tokyo are willing to cooperate with each other and with other countries in the Asia-Pacific.

Less talked about, but of great relevance, is the Asian Bond Markets Initiative (ABMI). Launched in 2003, the ABMI has the goal of facilitating development of local-currency-denominated debt markets in the region. The ultimate objective is to avoid one of the underlying drivers of the AFC – the fact that most borrowing was denominated in US dollars and had short-term maturity, while lending was denominated in local currency and had long-term maturity. The asymmetry resulted in a decline of local currencies against the US dollar, which meant that debt-matured governments and companies found it very difficult to fulfil their contracts. By facilitating the use of the pool of reserves and savings accumulated in ASEAN+3 countries to buy bonds issued in the region, the ABMI seeks to facilitate the issuance of debt denominated in local currencies. Indeed, the ABMI has helped foster rapid growth of local-currency-denominated bonds.[53] This was helpful in providing stability in the region throughout the GFC and avoiding the problems experienced by Asia-Pacific countries during the AFC. Japan has been a key supporter of the ABMI, and its investors have benefited from the initiative.

The above suggests that amity dominates Sino-Japanese financial interactions. However, there is also a modicum of enmity and competition. Most notably, China has launched several initiatives to internationalize the renminbi.[54] If successful, this could make it the dominant currency across the Asia-Pacific region and thus undermine Japan's position. Bilateral swap arrangements between the People's Bank of China and other central banks, seeking to denominate cross-border trade in renminbi, establishing offshore currency centres in several East Asian cities, or successfully lobbying for inclusion of the renminbi in the IMF's currency basket point to the importance that Beijing places on internationalization.[55] Thus, while a great degree of harmonization of interest and activity characterizes their financial relations today, it is not unimaginable that the economic RSC could be home to a new area of Sino-Japanese enmity in the future.

China and Japan: development banks

Securitization of the Asia-Pacific economic RSC mixes Sino-Japanese enmity with amity and competition with a de facto alliance, as explained above. Yet, great power relations in specific issue-areas are not fixed. They can fluctuate from enmity to amity, as has been the case with regional development banks. The establishment of the AIIB in 2015 was portrayed as a direct Chinese challenge to the ADB – formed in 1966 and long seen as Japan-dominated – as well as to the World Bank.[56] However, the first steps taken by the AIIB and its early interactions with the ADB and World Bank suggest that a degree of amity rather than much-touted enmity will be the main feature of the interaction of regional development banks. Sino-Japanese power relations in this area seem to be heading towards concert rather than much-feared competition or straightforward cooperation.

Economic security competition 81

The gradual move towards amity and concert can be explained by the potential benefits of a successful AIIB and ADB, the needs of the Asia-Pacific region and how to serve them, and Chinese behaviour with regards to the AIIB. In this light, it is worth noting the main goal of development banks, that is, to foster development. This is not to deny that promoting specific economic ideas, creating goodwill towards the donor, or supporting other politico-economic goals might be sought.[57] But development remains the key objective. The AIIB and ADB are not exceptions to this. Economic and social development of the Asia-Pacific region has been supported by the work of the ADB over the decades.[58] The AIIB has a mandate to foster both as well. For Japan over the past few decades and China more recently, a more developed Asia-Pacific is beneficial for trade. Both of the two largest regional economies gain clear advantages through the success of both the AIIB and ADB.

The needs of Asia-Pacific countries and how to best serve them also serves to define Sino-Japanese relations in the area of development banks. As already explained, the financing requirements of the region for only short- and mid-term infrastructure projects run into the trillions of US dollars. Adding the estimated demand for social projects, an additional tens of millions of US dollars is needed in the region in the coming decades. Simply put, no single source of financing can meet these requirements. There is ample scope for the private sector and multilateral development banks and other institutions to find suitable projects starved of the necessary funding.[59] The ADB's capital base of US$165 billion and the AIIB's own authorized capital stock of US$100 billion will serve to plug some of the financing needs in the Asia-Pacific without necessarily regularly competing against each other for new projects.

Notwithstanding the above, Chinese behaviour regarding the AIIB could undermine the move towards amity with Japan. Beijing could take a confrontational approach, undercutting the ADB – as well as the World Bank – and aggressively pursuing new projects.[60] The reputational risks of taking such an approach, however, are very high, and thus far the Xi Jinping government has not shown any willingness to bear them. Beijing is aware that the mere fact that the AIIB has been established is seen as a challenge to existing institutions. Accordingly, the AIIB's first steps following its launch have clearly been intended to reassure its critics. The Beijing-headquartered institution has emphasized that it will move towards compliance with existing development project granting, implementation, and monitoring standards. Moreover, it has launched jointly financed projects with the ADB, and signed agreements with the World Bank, European Investment Bank, and European Bank for Reconstruction and Development to do the same.[61] These steps facilitate a move towards Sino-Japanese concert.

Equally relevant, Beijing expects a return on its investment. A significant number of Beijing's soft loans offered to countries in Africa and Latin America have been wasted, yielding little to no return.[62] The Xi Jinping government does not want the same to happen with AIIB funding. To mitigate this risk, the AIIB requires that potential borrowers meet the same requirements that the ADB and other multilateral development banks demand. Moreover, presumably, other signatories

82 *Ramon Pacheco Pardo*

to the AIIB do not want to lose their capital in politically motivated, ill-conceived projects either. This includes Australia, New Zealand, Singapore, South Korea, and several European countries that joined the AIIB prior to its launch. These members also have a role in ensuring that the AIIB is a legitimate regional financier rather than a tool of Chinese foreign policy.

The move towards amity and concert is further compounded by internal debates in Japan. Along with the US, Japan was one of the few large, developed economies declining to join the AIIB. This is now seen as a political miscalculation. Led by large infrastructure companies, there is a constituency in Japan lobbying for the Japanese government to sign on to the AIIB.[63] It is not unconceivable that their efforts will persuade Japan to eventually join the AIIB, or that ADB–AIIB joint projects will become the norm. Either result, would strengthen relations between Beijing and Tokyo.

Nonetheless, and similarly to Sino-Japanese financial relations, securitization of development institutions could include elements of competition. There is an obvious degree of competition between the AIIB and ADB in that potential recipients of multilateral development bank financing now have a variety of potential sources. In an interesting change from the 1980s, many borrowers have the power to decide which source of capital to use and thus some ability to shape their relationship with the donor.[64] Nevertheless, these phenomena are not specific to AIIB–ADB interactions and can be mitigated through their cooperation.

Arguably a bigger source of potential competition between China and Japan is the Silk Road Fund. Launched in 2014 with an initial capital base of US$40 billion, the fund has been set up to support OBOR-related projects. The AIIB is also meant to support development of this initiative.[65] Considering that infrastructure-building is an area in which Beijing and Tokyo compete directly, there is a possibility that this competition could spill over to the area of development banks, were the AIIB to focus too heavily on infrastructure construction projects along proposed OBOR routes. This might undermine the emerging concert among Chinese- and Japanese-preferred development banks.

Conclusions

Economic security is a top concern across the Asia-Pacific. Developments in the region have resulted in an economic RSC characterized by a commitment to openness, growing interconnectedness, and interdependence. However, this has not been translated into cooperative great power relations in the region. On the contrary, China and Japan are engaged in a competitive relationship in the economic domain. Their respective power and wealth means that the enmity between them is not just another feature of, but is a defining characteristic of, the Asia-Pacific's economic RSC.

Enmity and competition are most notable in the areas of trade agreements, development aid, and infrastructure-building. Trade regionalization and concomitant regionalism, a clear development need across the region, and infrastructure shortcomings suggest that amity and cooperation could be possible. The example

Economic security competition   83

of the RSC in the EU is telling. Following the end of the Second World War, the common market and growing intra-EU trade, a huge demand for reconstruction investment, and post-war infrastructure deficits eventually fostered a stable economic RSC. Accordingly, relations between Germany and France improved swiftly. This is yet to happen in the Asia-Pacific in the case of Sino-Japanese relations. This is not to deny that relations between the two Asian powers could improve as they did in the case of Germany and France. But more than 40 years after they normalized bilateral relations, Beijing and Tokyo are yet to get anywhere close to the level of trust and friendship that characterizes relations between Berlin and Paris.

Nevertheless, there are clear signs that amity and cooperation between Beijing and Tokyo could prevail. Finance and development banks are two areas in which amity already defines the relationship. Cooperation in the former and concert in the latter are the norm. Even though there are issues that could push China and Japan towards greater enmity and competition, this is not yet the case. Tensions are subdued under the realization that their goals and approaches do not differ. As openness, interconnectedness and interdependence continue in the region, and even grow, it is not unthinkable that great power amity could spill over into areas of present enmity between the two great powers of the Asia-Pacific.

Notes

1 For an in-depth discussion of economic security, see Vincent Cable, "What is International Economic Security", *International Affairs*, 71:2 (1995), 305–324.
2 Kevin G. Cai, *The Political Economy of East Asia: Regional and National Dimensions* (Basingstoke: Palgrave Macmillan, 2008).
3 Kiyoshi Kojima, "The 'Flying Geese' Model of Asian Economic Development: Origin, Theoretical Extensions, and Regional Policy Implications", *Journal of Asian Economics* 11:4 (2000), 375–401.
4 Prema-chandra Athukorala, "Production Networks and Trade Patterns in East Asia: Regionalization or Globalization", ADB Working Paper Series on Regional Economic Integration 56 (2010).
5 Masahiro Kawai and Ganeshan Wignaraja, "Trade Policy and Growth in Asia", ADBI Working Paper Series 495 (2014).
6 Cai, *The Political Economy of East Asia*.
7 World Trade Organization, *International Trade Statistics 2015* (Geneva: World Trade Organization, 2015).
8 Francoise Nicolas, "The Political Economy of Regional Integration in East Asia", *Economic Change and Restructuring*, 41:4 (2008), 345–367.
9 Asian Development Bank, *Asia Regional Integration Centre: Free Trade Agreements*, https://aric.adb.org/fta-country, accessed November 3, 2016.
10 Mohamed Aslam, "The Impact of ASEAN–China Free Trade Agreement on ASEAN's Manufacturing Industry", *International Journal of China Studies*, 3:1 (2012), 43–78.
11 Stephen Woolcock, *Trade and Investment Rule-making: The Role of Regional and Bilateral Agreements* (Tokyo: United Nations University Press, 2006).
12 Vinod K. Aggarwal, "Mega-FTAs and Trade–Security Nexus: The Trans-Pacific Partnership (TPP) and Regional Comprehensive Economic Partnership (RCEP)", *Asia Pacific Issues*, 123 (2016).

84   Ramon Pacheco Pardo

13 Mireya Solis and Saori N. Katada, "Unlikely Pivotal States in Competitive Free Trade Agreement Diffusion: The Effects of Japan's Trans-Pacific Partnership Participation on Asia-Pacific Regional Integration", *New Political Economy*, 20:2 (2015), 155–177.

14 Aggarwal, "Mega-FTAs and Trade–Security Nexus".

15 Ibid.

16 Solis and Katada, "Unlikely Pivotal States".

17 Sebastian Maslow, "A Blueprint for a Strong Japan? Abe Shinzo and Japan's Evolving Security System", *Asian Survey*, 55:4 (2015), 739–765.

18 Aggarwal, "Mega-FTAs and Trade–Security Nexus".

19 OECD, Development Assistance Committee, *Development Aid at a Glance: Statistics by Region – Asia*, www.oecd.org/dac/stats/documentupload/4%20Asia%20-%20 Development%20Aid%20at%20a%20Glance%202016.pdf, accessed November 3, 2016.

20 Ibid.

21 Naohiro Kitano, "China's Foreign Aid at a Transitional Stage", *Asian Economic Policy Review*, 9:2 (2014), 301–317.

22 OECD, Development Assistance Committee, *Development Aid at a Glance*.

23 Kitano, "China's Foreign Aid".

24 Andreas Fuchs, Peter Nunnekamp, and Hannes Ohler, "Why Donors of Foreign Aid do not Coordinate: The Role of Competition for Export Markets and Political Support", *The World Economy*, 38:2 (2015), 255–285.

25 See Hyo-sook Kim and David M. Potter, eds, *Foreign Aid Competition in Northeast Asia* (Boulder: Lynne Rienner Publishers, 2012).

26 Ibid.

27 OECD, *Development Co-operation Directorate (DCD-DAC)*, www.oecd.org/dac, accessed November 3, 2016.

28 Joren Verschaeve and Jan Orbie, "The DAC is Dead, Long Live the DCF? A Comparative Analysis of the OECD Development Assistance Committee and the UN Development Cooperation Forum", *The European Journal of Development Research*, 28:4 (2016), 571–587.

29 Deborah Brautigam, "Aid 'With Chinese Characteristics': Chinese Foreign Aid and Development Finance Meet the OECD-DAC Aid Regime", *Journal of International Development*, 23:5 (2011), 752–764.

30 Ibid.

31 Kevin P. Gallagher, Rohini Kamal, and Yongzhong Wang, "Fueling Growth and Financing Risk: The Benefits and Risks of China's Development Finance in the Global Energy Sector", GEGI Working Paper 2 (2016).

32 Ngaire Woods, "Whose Aid? Whose Influence? China, Emerging Donors and the Silent Revolution in Development Assistance", *International Affairs*, 84:6 (2008), 1205–1221.

33 Georg Inderst, "Infrastructure Investment, Private Finance, and Institutional Investors: Asia from a Global Perspective", ADBI Working Paper Series 555 (2016).

34 Ibid.

35 Purnendra Jain, "Japan's Foreign Aid: Old and New Contests", *The Pacific Review*, 29:1 (2016), 93–113.

36 ASEAN, *Foreign Direct Investment Statistics*, http://asean.org/?static_post=foreign-direct-investment-statistics, accessed November 3, 2016.

37 Ibid.

38 IMF, *Foreign Direct Investment Statistics*, http://data.imf.org, accessed November 3, 2016.

39 Economist Intelligence Unit, "Japan and China Vie for Infrastructure Deals in Asia", February 17, 2016.

40 Rieka Rahadiana, "China to Build $5 Billion High-Speed Rail in Indonesia", Bloomberg, October 16, 2015.

Economic security competition 85

41 Zhiqun Zhu, "China's AIIB and OBOR: Ambitions and Challenges", *The Diplomat*, October 9, 2015.
42 Economist Intelligence Unit, "Japan and China".
43 IMF, *Coordinated Portfolio Investment Survey*, http://data.imf.org, accessed November 3, 2016.
44 Cai, *The Political Economy of East Asia*.
45 Ramon Pacheco Pardo and Pradumna B. Rana, "Complementarity Between Regional and Global Financial Institutions: The Case of ASEAN+3 and the Global Financial Safety Net", *Global Governance: A Review of Multilateralism and International Organizations*, 21:3 (2015), 413–433.
46 Ibid.
47 Cai, *The Political Economy of East Asia*.
48 Ramon Pacheco Pardo, "The Quest for Economic Security in East Asia", in Ramon Pacheco Pardo and Jeffrey Reeves, eds, *Non-traditional Security in East Asia: A Regime Approach* (London: Imperial College Press, 2015), pp. 119–141.
49 Pacheco Pardo and Rana, "Complementarity Between Regional and Global Financial Institutions".
50 Masahiro Kawai, "From the Chiang Mai Initiative to an Asian Monetary Fund", ADBI Working Paper Series 527 (2015).
51 Ibid.
52 AMRO, "Opening Ceremony of AMRO as an International Organization", February 19, 2016.
53 Kawai, "From the Chiang Mai Initiative"; Yohei Kitano, "Development of Asian Local Currency Bond Markets and Remaining Challenges", *Nomura Journal of Capital Markets*, 6:3 (2015), 1–16.
54 See Barry Eichengreen and Masahiro Kawai, eds, *Renminbi Internationalization: Achievements, Prospects, and Challenges* (Tokyo: Asian Development Bank Institute, 2015).
55 Ibid.
56 Gregory T. Chin, "Asian Infrastructure Investment Bank: Governance Innovation and Prospects", *Global Governance: A Review of Multilateralism in International Organizations*, 22:1 (2016), 11–25.
57 See Susan Park and Jonathan R. Strand, eds, *Global Economic Governance and the Development Practices of the Multilateral Development Banks* (London: Routledge, 2016).
58 Chin, "Asian Infrastructure Investment Bank".
59 Inderst, "Infrastructure Investment".
60 Xiao Ren, "China as an Institution-Builder: The Case of the AIIB", *The Pacific Review*, 29:3 (2016), 435–442.
61 Economist Intelligence Unit, "China's AIIB: A Surprisingly Normal Bank", October 28, 2016.
62 FT Reporters, "China Rethinks Developing World Largesse as Deals Sour", *Financial Times*, October 13, 2016.
63 Saori N. Katada, "At the Crossroads: The TTP, AIIB, and Japan's Foreign Economic Strategy", *Asia Pacific Issues*, 125 (2016).
64 Chris Humphrey and Katharina Michaelowa, "Shopping for Development: Multilateral Lending, Shareholder Composition and Borrower Preferences", *World Development*, 44 (2013), 142–155.
65 James Kynge, "How the Silk Road Plans will be Financed", *Financial Times*, May 9, 2016.

5 Sino-Japanese competition and energy security

Vlado Vivoda

The spectacular economic growth of China and other developing Asian economies has spurred a vast expansion in the need for energy services, and an expansion in the demand for the fuels that help to supply these services. Asian energy demand has doubled since 2001, with the region's share in global energy demand increasing from 29 per cent to 42 per cent. Most projections suggest that Asia's voracious thirst for energy will further expand in the coming decades. Moreover, regional states are becoming increasingly reliant on imported fossil fuels. For example, the region hosts four of the world's five largest oil importers and the top three liquefied natural gas (LNG) and coal importers, respectively.[1] Finally, the increased fossil fuel demand has had a significant carbon impact, with the region's CO_2 emissions doubling since 2001, mainly caused by China's rapidly growing coal demand.[2]

Energy security has become both a national priority for Asian states and an important regional-level security consideration. Energy security is a primary contributor to regional tensions as it contributes to territorial disputes and environmental security. For example, a key facet of East China Sea and South China Sea maritime disputes is the belief that the seas hold large underwater reserves of hydrocarbons.[3] Growing regional coal demand contributes to poor transnational air quality within Asia. Growing salience of the issue of energy security in the regional has led to engagement between states, such as the 2007 Cebu Declaration on East Asian Energy Security and the Asia-Pacific Economic Cooperation (APEC) Energy Security Initiative.[4]

Three major energy challenges affect all Asian states to varying degrees: (1) continued, or in some cases increasing, dependence on non-renewable energy sources to meet demand; (2) the environmental impact of energy use, as seen by the environmental repercussions of heavy coal use; and (3) underdeveloped energy infrastructure and transportation networks both within and between Asian states. With the epicentre of global energy demand moving from industrialized western economies to East Asia, regional energy security attitudes and approaches carry major consequences for global energy geopolitics, markets, and efforts to tackle climate change.

As discussed in Chapter 1 of this volume, regional security complexes are home to regional powers that act as poles, creating either a bilateral or multilateral overlay to the region's security regimes. Nowhere is this pattern of state competition

Competition and energy security 87

in Asia clearer than between China and Japan. Both states exert significant influence and leverage over regional energy developments through their energy security approaches. While global in their economic outreach, both states primarily focus on the Asian region for energy relations. Thus, the two states are central to the region's energy security regime complex. Their engagement, often with competing goals, shapes the regional energy security context.

Against this background, this chapter examines how Japanese and Chinese competition over access to energy resources in Asia is influencing regional energy security. The chapter examines patterns in regional energy trade and transportation, bilateral energy diplomacy, and sustainability of energy use related to the Sino-Japanese relationship. The chapter demonstrates how competition between the two largest Asian economies shapes the Asia-Pacific energy security environment and leads to diffusion of policy priorities and competitive approaches across the region.

The concept of energy security

As an analytical concept, energy security has been established since the 1970s, when two oil crises shocked the major industrialized nations. The heavy external energy dependence and supply risks threatened their economic interests and national security, and shaped energy security thinking and behaviour. A traditional energy security approach characterized by a supply-side, primarily oil-oriented strategic thinking, as well as a foreign policy response to safeguard energy security, has remained the mainstream until the end of the century. Most early studies conceptualized energy security in terms of security of oil supplies.[5]

Over the past two decades, energy security has become an emerging area of policy focus, with high energy prices, the increased demand and competition for geographically concentrated resources, the fear of resource scarcity, and concerns over the economic, environmental, social, and geopolitical effects of climate change. According to Victor and Yueh, the extraordinary shift in energy security concerns has challenged hitherto dominant policy orthodoxies.[6] Accordingly, with a broader set of issues, the concept has been expanded to include many new factors and challenges.[7] With increasingly global, diverse energy markets and increasingly global problems resulting from energy transformation and use, issues such as climate change have become increasingly salient. In the academic literature, the substance of emerging challenges has been incorporated into a new concept of energy security, commonly defined as the availability of energy at all times in various forms, in sufficient quantities and at affordable prices, without unacceptable or irreversible impacts on the economy and the environment.[8]

Energy policy approaches and trends

National energy policy frameworks summarize existing policies and formulate strategies to support delivery of the core objectives. Traditionally, the main objective was to secure access to reliable energy supplies at affordable or competitive prices.

88 *Vlado Vivoda*

Increasingly, in addition to availability and affordability, policies are aimed at improving environmental sustainability of energy choices. Looking for simultaneous progress towards the energy availability, affordability, and sustainability objectives, policy makers face complex and sometimes contradictory choices.[9] The challenge of concurrently meeting these three objectives is referred to as the "energy trilemma", a term coined by the World Energy Council.

The three objectives are regularly in tension, and difficult trade-offs are often required. For example, improved sustainability requires a trade-off with affordability when significant capital expenditure is directed at reducing greenhouse gas emissions. Alternatively, improved supply security requires a trade-off with affordability when an importing state decides to diversify supply sources and transportation routes. Ideally, policies should be framed so that the three objectives are tackled concurrently with none (explicitly) given precedence over the others. However, political reality dictates otherwise and one objective is often privileged over the other two. Most often policy outcomes involve compromises among interested parties.

The relative significance of the three objectives is influenced by the national and international policy setting in which states and markets interact. This also includes the national views towards the teleology of the markets and the degree of optimal state intervention. In state capitalist systems, such as China and Japan, the extent of government intervention in energy markets is greater than in countries with a market capitalist tradition, such as the US, UK, and Australia.[10] National governments also vary greatly in the importance they attach to environmental sustainability of energy choices relative to supply security and affordability.

Two ideal-type policy approaches are based on a diametrically opposing view of the role of the state in energy markets: strategic and market-based. In reality, there is always a degree of intervention even by the most market-oriented governments.[11] The strategic approach posits that leaving energy to market forces does not provide optimal outcomes. Government intervention in energy-related activities is necessary in order to steer the market towards the state's best interests. The thrust is that energy is too important strategically to be left to market forces alone. Governments use a range of strategies and regulatory instruments to steer the market towards desired objectives. For example, subsidies and taxes can promote or curb the use of a specific energy source; state ownership of energy companies and infrastructure may lead to greater control across the value chain; diplomatic activity and provision of foreign assistance to resource-rich governments can improve access to energy resources.[12]

In contrast, according to the market-based approach, energy markets should be exposed to the same conditions as other commodity markets. The belief is that open and competitive markets deliver energy at the best prices and ensure adequate and reliable supplies. Government interference is only needed in times of market failure.[13] The market approach is characterized by agnosticism regarding the source of energy imports; eschewal of policies that seek to promote the interests of national over foreign firms; liberalization of domestic resource sectors and integration with international markets through open trade and investment policies;

Competition and energy security 89

and foreign policy cooperation with other states to improve the functioning of international markets on a multilateral basis.[14]

During the 1970s and the early 1980s the energy sector was heavily politicized and security of supply was at the top of the political agenda. The involvement of major consuming governments in energy markets reflected the prevailing interventionist approach to economic management, as well as concerns over security of supply. In industrialized economies, state-owned companies held statutory monopolies as importers and wholesale traders. Long-term contracts between well-established parties, with secure prices, were essential to protect both the supplier and buyer. The suppliers regarded the powerful position of state-owned monopolies as a guarantee that the purchase obligations under long-term contracts would be fulfilled.[15]

The 1986 oil price collapse contributed to a changed government attitude towards energy. This began in the early 1980s, as a consequence of Ronald Reagan's and Margaret Thatcher's crusades in favour of politically unhampered market solutions and competition. As the decade evolved, there was increasing disillusion with the far-reaching energy policies implemented in the preceding years. The oil price collapse was seen as a confirmation that energy supplies were ample and that public interventions to assure supply security – for example in the form of national monopolies – were costly and unnecessary. Prevailing attitudes, values, and beliefs during the 1990s were based on the idea that the markets were more efficient than governments.[16]

Since the turn of the century, intensified competition, high and volatile prices, and ambitious renewable energy targets have motivated governments to adopt a proactive approach to energy issues. This is reflected in the policy trend to consider energy increasingly as a strategic issue in both exporting and import-dependent countries. As a consequence, energy supply and demand are increasingly shaped by geopolitical developments and government intervention. This policy trend is particularly pronounced in Asia's two major economies, China and Japan.

Perceptions and competitive approaches to energy security

Independent self-interested behaviour can result in undesirable or suboptimal outcomes, referred to as dilemmas of common interests and dilemmas of common aversions.[17] According to this "security dilemma", many of the means by which a state tries to increase its security will decrease the security of others.[18] When one state pursues a market interventionist strategy to secure sufficient energy supplies, this may result in enhanced national energy security, but may simultaneously deteriorate energy security of its regional neighbours.

Regional energy security remains dominated by strategic approaches due to continued prevalence of nationalism, political tensions, and distrust among major powers, most notably China and Japan. Policy measures included in China's and Japan's energy security approaches embody elements of a strategic approach. These measures include governmental assistance to national firms to acquire ownership and control of international energy projects, energy diplomacy initiatives,

90 Vlado Vivoda

and energy-related bilateral free trade agreements.[19] Since China and Japan are the region's largest economies and energy importers, their energy security approaches are both indicative of and the drivers of broader regional trends.

Since the mid-1990s, China's government has been particularly alert to the country's growing energy deficit and demand for imported supplies. As a rapidly growing economy that has been a net energy importer since only 1996, examining the nexus of energy and national security has become an urgent task for scholars and policy makers alike. Mainstream thinking on energy security in China shares characteristics of the traditional energy security approach.[20] Chinese scholars and policy makers largely equate energy security to the security of external energy supply, often referring to oil imports transported through key sea lines of communication, such as the Malacca Strait. Government-supported research has concluded that energy security is more accurately depicted as oil security. Therefore, a common perception in China is that the country's energy security problem is its growing oil deficit.[21] The possibility of a deliberate interruption to oil supplies by a potential adversary poses one of the biggest threats to China's energy security.[22] In response to threat perceptions, China has adopted an energy security approach emphasizing the security of imported supplies, particularly oil. As early as 1993, Premier Li Peng set the stage for this approach by defining the objectives of the country's energy policy as to secure the long-term and stable supply of oil to China.[23] This fundamental objective continues to guide China's energy strategy.[24]

In Japan, the state is an active participant in the energy markets. The government regularly sets the overarching energy strategy, including specific targets, with the aim of ensuring access to reliable and affordable energy supplies for Japanese consumers. The oil crises of the 1970s marked a major shift towards government intervention in the energy markets. The perceived need to reduce Japan's external dependency played an important role in Japanese policy makers' move to more active government management of Japan's energy supply and demand mix. The surge in energy prices since the turn of the century associated with the perceived competition with China for energy supplies has given further impetus to government intervention. A general view among Japanese energy policy makers is that a "leave it to the market" approach is not a solution since this could render oil and gas security more vulnerable.[25] Instead, energy in Japan remains conceptualized as a national security issue.[26] The Fukushima disaster and the ensuing energy crisis have cemented this view.[27]

The rapid economic growth in the region has intensified competition for increasingly scarce energy resources, elevating energy security to the top of the regional agenda. China and Japan maintained a cooperative energy relationship before China became a net oil importer in the early 1990s. The past two decades have witnessed an increasingly intensive competition between the two countries over oil and gas supplies. When China became a net oil importer, Sino-Japanese energy cooperation weakened dramatically.[28] China's transformation to a net oil importer and its growing economic potential turned the two countries into competitors over oil and gas supplies and also rendered cooperation less likely because of their increasing concerns over relative gains. The end of the Cold War

Competition and energy security 91

not only weakened their shared strategic and political interests, but also positioned China as one of the major threats in Japan's security agenda. The trend towards energy "securitization" has aggravated tensions among China and Japan.[29] China and Japan have no concrete form of policy adjustment towards energy suppliers at the bilateral level.[30] The competitive nature of China's and Japan's mercantilist strategies has intensified political and economic competition for energy among Asia's major powers.[31]

Bilateralism, strategic competition, and energy affordability

Bilateralism is a historically developed practice of realizing the security of supplies.[32] China and Japan use strategic partnerships and bilateral agreements with energy exporters in order to lock-in future supplies.[33] Most notably, China and Japan have implemented strategies aimed at enhancing energy security by promoting bilateral cooperation with major suppliers.[34] Both countries have targeted their free trade agreement initiatives at a common group of key energy suppliers that reflect their import needs, including the Gulf Cooperation Council for oil and gas and Australia for coal and gas.[35] There is also evidence that patterns of Sino-Japanese competition have driven these initiatives. Both countries have engaged in the practice of promoting overseas investment in order to secure equity in, or self-developed, oil and gas stakes guided by the perception that this enhances their energy security and provides protection against supply disruptions.[36] With a distrust of the international energy market, both Beijing and Tokyo believe that special diplomatic relationships with energy producers guarantee reliable access to energy imports.[37] Aggressive diplomatic efforts by both states in recent years reveal that the objective is to groom special and preferred energy suppliers instead of looking to open and transparent international energy markets.[38]

In Japan's case, the first national target of securing self-developed oil supplies was set during the 1970s and revised downward several times; however, none of the targets were achieved. Historically, self-developed overseas ventures never generated more than 15 per cent of Japan's oil imports.[39] Supported by the government, Chinese national oil companies (NOCs) commenced their quest to acquire overseas oil and gas assets in the mid-1990s. While China's aggressive pursuit of self-developed oil has been much more successful than Japan's, oil produced by China's NOCs is neither cheaper nor more available to the Chinese customers in a supply crisis.[40] Both governments have justified financial assistance policies for their companies as necessary to support national firms in a globally competitive environment for energy projects.[41]

There is ample evidence that regional states routinely pay higher prices for energy because of the hoarding practices of their regional neighbours.[42] At minimum, the Sino-Japanese competition has raised the costs of oil imports for both countries by delaying the development of domestic and regional energy infrastructure. For example, Tokyo's original impetus for participation in the Azedegan project in Iran was to regain a foothold in the Middle East following initial Chinese gains; the loss of the stake was seen in zero-sum terms.[43] Similarly,

92   *Vlado Vivoda*

the competition over the preferential route of Russia's ESPO pipeline developed a soap opera-like quality.[44] Japan's involvement in influencing Russia to preference the longer pipeline route to the Pacific Ocean strengthened Beijing's perception that security of the energy supply is an important aspect of strategic competition. The ever-shifting pipeline route delayed the final investment decision and raised import costs through expensive stop-gap measures, such as China's oil imports by rail and shipment by rail to the Pacific. The dispute over gas and oil exploration rights in the East China Sea has delayed full production at Chunxiao field.[45] Japan contested China's right to produce resources in the area and on several occasions China has halted development of the fields for diplomatic purposes, which has delayed full production.

The tussle between China and Japan over oil and gas reserves in the East China Sea demonstrates that rigorous competition over energy sources can result in diplomatic disputes and deepen mutual mistrust between countries. Despite the compelling common interest in developing energy resources for mutual benefit, energy concerns have emerged as a significant source of friction in the Sino-Japanese relationship. Both parties have conceptualized energy as a security issue and have approached it in the context of an already tense and deteriorating bilateral relationship. While Japan's tendency to conceptualize energy as a national security issue is not a recent development, Tokyo's increasingly assertive regional energy diplomacy constitutes a significant departure from Cold War precedents. China's newly found dependence on energy imports has seen it follow Japan's longstanding example in securitizing energy as a policy issue.[46]

The recent escalation of the South China Sea dispute indicates that resource nationalism extends beyond the two major regional powers. Maritime disputes elsewhere in Asia have historically stemmed from unsettled territorial and maritime claims. However, in recent years, energy security concerns have increasingly inflamed these disputes. Rising energy prices, fears of supply scarcity and rapid increases in import dependence have perpetuated resource nationalism.[47] The South China Sea dispute illustrates that resource nationalism increasingly drives the involvement of the more "institutionalized" member states of the Association of Southeast Asian Nations (ASEAN). Growing energy security concerns, historical and political tensions that continue to fuel nationalism and distrust, and the diversity in political, economic, and social conditions among ASEAN member states continue to hinder progress towards mutually beneficial outcomes.

Regional geography and energy market fragmentation

Asian oil and gas markets are fragmented. Unlike their European and North American counterparts, Asian markets are not well connected by pipelines, and are dominated by seaborne trade. For example, in 2015 Asian states imported 70.5 per cent of internationally traded LNG, but only 8.7 per cent of piped gas.[48] Due to its geographical isolation and strained relations with its closest neighbours, Japan is not connected to international gas pipelines and only imports LNG. Japan accounts for half of Asian LNG demand and remains the world's largest LNG importer by a significant margin.

Competition and energy security 93

In contrast, China is the only major regional oil and gas importer that has significant domestic pipeline connections to major exporters. In addition to several international gas pipelines in Southeast Asia, regional gas pipeline infrastructure includes China's import pipelines from Myanmar and the former Soviet Union.[49] China's pipeline gas imports from Turkmenistan and Myanmar commenced in 2010 and 2013, respectively.[50] In addition, in May 2014, China and Russia signed a US$400 billion natural gas deal with Russia to supply 38 billion cubic metres of natural gas per annum via pipeline for 30 years.[51] Chinese oil imports via the Kazakhstan–China oil pipeline, from Russia (via the Eastern Siberia–Pacific Ocean (ESPO) oil pipeline), and in transit via the Sino-Myanmar crude oil pipeline, commenced in 2006, 2011, and 2014, respectively.

The Chinese government's concern about the security of seaborne energy imports and a desire to diversify oil supplies away from the Middle East, as well as diversify the energy transport routes away from the Malacca Strait, have triggered long-term supply agreements with Russia and Central Asian countries in parallel with Chinese-financed construction of long-distance oil and gas pipelines from the former Soviet Union and Myanmar. Most Chinese analysts regard participation in the development of Russian and Central Asian energy resources as an important source of energy security, as oil and gas imported by pipeline is perceived as less vulnerable to disruption than seaborne imports.[52]

With the exception of Chinese pipelines, due to geographic separation and long distances between major producers and between major producers and consumers, there are limited prospects for establishing greater regional connectivity through cross-border oil and gas pipeline infrastructure. Where geography does not present an insurmountable obstacle, politics have prevented pipeline projects from materializing. The most notable examples include the Sakhalin–Hokkaido gas pipeline (from Russia to Japan), the trans-Korean gas pipeline, and three proposed gas pipelines to India – from Myanmar (via Bangladesh), Turkmenistan (via Afghanistan and Pakistan), and Iran (via Pakistan).[53]

Fossil fuel subsidies and environmental sustainability

Developing Asia is home to a majority of the world's energy poor, with about 615 million people having no electricity and 1.8 billion burning firewood, charcoal, and crop waste to meet their basic needs.[54] Energy is essential for economic growth and human progress and the region's energy demand will continue to rise as economies grow and living conditions improve. The continued growth in demand for affordable energy underlies the widespread use of subsidies on fossil fuels (oil, gas, and coal) and electricity across Asia. Ten of the top 25 countries in the world that subsidize fossil fuel are located in Asia. Developing Asian countries also account for close to one-third of global subsidies on fossil fuel consumption, equivalent to about 2.5 per cent of gross domestic product (GDP). Fossil fuel subsidies in India, Indonesia, and Thailand stand at 2.7 per cent, 4.1 per cent, and 1.9 per cent of GDP, respectively.[55] Low-priced petroleum products account for over half of these subsidies in each country.

94 *Vlado Vivoda*

In 2009, the Group of Twenty (G20) and APEC committed to rationalizing and phasing out inefficient fossil fuel subsidies. Unfortunately, there has been little progress on subsidy reforms. As people get used to low prices and powerful beneficiaries oppose reforms, governments are unable to push their reform agendas for fear of social unrest and political upheaval when prices rise. In some Asian countries, government expenditure on fossil fuel subsidies, which covers the gap between global and domestic prices, exceeds public spending on education or health. High fossil fuel subsidies also reduce incentives for investment in renewable energy and energy efficiency. Moreover, fossil fuels (coal, oil, and gas) are major carbon emitters, and burning coal, the most carbon-intensive energy source, has serious climate change implications.[56] Consequently, energy subsidy reform remains as one of the most important policy challenges for China and other developing Asian economies.

Although the global energy system showed a decarbonizing trend before the turn of this century, in recent years this trend has been reversed mainly because of growing coal use in Asia.[57] The carbonization of the global energy system poses a severe challenge for efforts to reduce carbon emissions. The increase in the carbon intensity of global energy use is caused mainly by the increased use of coal, primarily in China. The relatively low price and widespread resource abundance are key drivers of increased coal use in China and elsewhere in the region. This underlines the importance of cheaply available energy for economic growth and suggests that viable alternatives to cheap coal are required to ensure the participation of developing countries in global climate change mitigation.[58]

The low price of coal relative to gas and oil has played an important role in accelerating coal consumption since the turn of the century. The Intergovernmental Panel on Climate Change (IPCC) Fifth Assessment Report identified the replacement of coal-fired power plants by less carbon-intensive energy technologies as one of the most cost-efficient options to reduce global greenhouse gas emissions.[59] The fact that China and other emerging Asian economies mainly meet their growing energy appetite with coal raises serious doubts about whether current development trajectories are compatible with climate change mitigation. If future economic growth in Asia is fuelled mainly by coal, ambitious mitigation targets will become unfeasible. Building new coal-fired power plants will lead to lock-in effects for the next several decades. If that lock-in is to be avoided, international climate policy must find ways to offer viable alternatives to coal for developing countries.[60] Without government intervention, it is highly unlikely that coal use will decline drastically in the near future.

Focusing on synergies between climate policy and other policies, McCollum *et al.* point out that ambitious climate measures would reduce the costs of clean air policies and energy security measures by US$100–600 billion (0.1–0.7 per cent of GDP) annually by 2030.[61] However, China and most other major Asian governments consider energy in isolation from climate policy. According to Jakob *et al.*, the best incentive for switching to alternative sources of energy lies in policy objectives other than climate policy, such as those addressing energy security, localized air pollution, and energy access.[62] Measures that would discourage coal

Competition and energy security   95

use and encourage the use of low-carbon technologies as a co-benefit of other policies require identifying country-specific policy goals and opportunities. A salient example of a policy that serves objectives that are not national security or climate related but that nevertheless could reduce coal use is China's implementation of the "Action Plan for Air Pollution Prevention and Control". Even though it is aimed at improving ambient air quality, this policy could lead to declining CO_2 emissions from 2020 onwards.[63] Other examples include Vietnam's recent Green Growth policies that include a reform of implicit fossil fuel subsidies in the power sector and India's climate discourse, which largely revolves around energy security.[64]

Conclusion

Christensen argued that Asia is characterized by skewed distributions of economic and political power within and between countries, political and cultural heterogeneity, anaemic security institutionalization, and widespread territorial disputes that combine natural resource issues with nationalism. He suggested that if security dilemma theory is applied to the region, the chance for spirals of tension in the area seems great.[65] Similarly, Calder warned that energy competition in Asia will lead to strategic rivalry and represents a recipe for conflict.[66]

Reducing competition for fossil fuels and mitigating the climate change risks posed by greenhouse gas emissions are desirable regional (and global) outcomes. Security of energy supply and climate change mitigation are inherently cross-border concepts – trade behaviour of, and emissions in, one state affects others – and many important influences (e.g. transnational business cooperation and broader relations between states) are situated at the transnational and international level.

While China and Japan remain highly dependent on uninterrupted supplies of energy, and share common interests as major energy consumers, regional cooperative mechanisms remain underdeveloped. Indeed, since the turn of the century, regional security dynamics have deteriorated both in terms of prospects for energy and environmental security and broader regional cooperation. While the importance of regional energy security cooperation has been consistently emphasized as a means to cope with uncertainties in the global energy market, and to avert potential conflicts regarding energy supply among major consumers, the lack of progress is reflective of the competitive nature of China's and Japan's energy security strategies.

As a consequence, regional energy cooperation remains limited to information sharing, confidence-building measures, and the setting of aspirational targets.[67] China, Japan, and other regional powers are unwilling to commit to mutually binding multilateral rules and principles that effectively constrain state sovereignty. Nationalism and political tensions remain the major obstacles for deeper regional cooperation. China and Japan perceive that their interests in the energy sector are best served by national rather than collective action and that cooperative arrangements fail to provide sufficient incentives to prevent states from succumbing to opportunistic behaviour in the event of a short-term clash of interests. The absence of deep trust is an additional constraint to deeper forms of regional

96 *Vlado Vivoda*

cooperation.[68] As illustrated in this chapter, in the case of China and Japan, the absence of trust reinforces a more deeply rooted and continuing preference for state autonomy.

Competitive energy security approaches adopted by China and Japan are not conducive to addressing the urgent and complex energy challenges and promoting transformation to alternative and sustainable energy systems. Energy cooperation in Asia is essential for the prevention of potential conflicts stemming from competitive energy procurement.[69] Given that China, Japan, and other major Asian economies share common concerns with regards to energy security, it is in their interests that they pool their resources and jointly strive for collective energy security. For that reason, multilateral initiatives are preferable to bilateral efforts.

How can regional states improve mutual cooperation in light of common energy and climate challenges? Potential areas for cooperation include energy efficiency and renewable energy technology, energy poverty reduction strategies, regional natural gas market integration, cross-border electricity grid interconnections, reform of domestic markets (including fossil fuel subsidies), nuclear energy cooperation, and the management of nuclear waste.

For example, industrialized countries, such as Japan, could assist developing economies in improving energy efficiency, conservation, and fuel-switching. Particularly appealing in this context is Japan's experience in energy conservation, efficiency, and fuel substitution following the oil crises and, more recently, the Fukushima disaster.[70] According to Prantl, one of the most promising issue areas for collective action is research and development investment in clean-energy technologies.[71] Japan's advanced coal-fired power plant efficiency technology and China's low-cost solar and wind energy technologies are particularly appealing. In this context, it is crucial that any newly constructed coal-fired power plants are "capture-ready", that is that they can be retrofitted with carbon capture and storage (CCS) technology to avoid emissions. In the longer term, such a scheme could be complemented with subsidies for CCS.[72]

Importantly, it is crucial that China, Japan, and other regional governments broaden their perception of energy security risks, moving away from traditional approaches, which focus on reducing risks associated with supply security. In addition to diverting more attention to demand management, governments should divert their attention to environmental and social sustainability of energy use when devising energy policies and energy security strategies.

Acknowledgements

Research for this chapter was supported by the National Research Foundation of Korea Grant, funded by the Korean government (NRF-2015S1A3A2046684).

Notes

1 BP, *Statistical Review of World Energy 2016*. London: BP, 2016. www.bp.com/content/dam/bp/pdf/energy-economics/statistical-review-2016/bp-statistical-review-of-world-energy-2016-full-report.pdf.

Competition and energy security 97

2 Ibid.

3 J. Manicom, *Bridging Troubled Waters: China, Japan, and Maritime Order in the East China Sea* (Washington, DC: Georgetown University Press, 2014); S. Wu and H. Nong, *Recent Developments in the South China Sea Dispute: The Prospect of a Joint Development Regime* (London: Routledge, 2014).

4 B. Kong and J.H. Ku, *Energy Security Cooperation in Northeast Asia* (London: Routledge, 2015).

5 E.R. Fried and P.H. Trezise, *Oil Security. Retrospect and Prospect* (Washington, DC: The Brookings Institution, 1993), www.brookings.edu/book/oil-security; K.D. Stringer, "Energy Security: Applying a Portfolio Approach", *Baltic Security & Defence Review*, 10 (2008).

6 D.G. Victor and L. Yueh, "The New Energy Order: Managing Insecurities in the Twenty-First Century", *Foreign Affairs*, 89:1 (2010), 61–73.

7 D. Yergin, "Ensuring Energy Security", *Foreign Affairs* 85:2 (2006), 69–82.

8 V. Vivoda, "Evaluating Energy Security in the Asia-Pacific Region: A Novel Methodological Approach", *Energy Policy*, 38:9 (2010), 5258–5263.

9 C. Maurin and V. Vivoda, "Shale Gas and the Energy Policy 'Trilemma'", in T. Hunter ed., *Handbook of Shale Gas Law and Policy* (Cambridge: Intersentia, 2016), 369–382.

10 V. Vivoda, "State–Market Interaction in Hydrocarbon Sector: The Cases of Australia and Japan", in A.V. Belyi and K. Talus, eds, *States and Markets in Hydrocarbon Sectors* (Basingstoke: Palgrave Macmillan, 2015), 240–265.

11 Roman Sidortsov and Benjamin Sovacool, "Left out in the Cold: Energy Justice and Arctic Energy Research", *Journal of Environmental Studies and Sciences*, 5:3 (2015): 302–307.

12 V. Vivoda and J. Manicom, "Oil Import Diversification in Northeast Asia: A Comparison Between China and Japan", *Journal of East Asian Studies*, 11:2 (2011), 223–254; E. Stoddard, "Reconsidering the Ontological Foundations of International Energy Affairs: Realist Geopolitics, Market Liberalism and a Politico-Economic Alternative", *European Security*, 22:4 (2013), 437–463; K.J. Hancock and V. Vivoda, "International Political Economy: A Field Born of the OPEC Crisis Returns to its Energy Roots", *Energy Research & Social Science*, 1 (2014), 206–216.

13 Vivoda and Manicom, "Oil Import Diversification".

14 Hancock and Vivoda, "International Political Economy"; J.D. Wilson, "Northeast Asian Resource Security Strategies and International Resource Politics in Asia", *Asian Studies Review*, 38:1 (2014), 15–32.

15 M. Radetzki, "European Natural Gas: Market Forces Will Bring about Competition in Any Case", *Energy Policy*, 27:1 (1999), 17–24.

16 D. Helm, *Energy, the State, and the Market: British Energy Policy since 1979* (Oxford: Oxford University Press, 2004).

17 Arthur A. Stein, "Coordination and Collaboration: Regimes in an Anarchic World", *International Organization*, 36:2 (1982): 299–324.

18 J.H. Herz, *Political Realism and Political Idealism: A Study in Theories and Realities* (Chicago: University of Chicago Press, 1951); R. Jervis, "Cooperation under the Security Dilemma", *World Politics*, 30:2 (1978), 167–174; K. Booth and N.J. Wheeler, *The Security Dilemma: Fear, Cooperation and Trust in World Politics* (Basingstoke: Palgrave Macmillan, 2007).

19 Wilson, "Northeast Asian Resource Security Strategies".

20 E.S. Downs, "The Chinese Energy Security Debate", *The China Quarterly*, 177 (2004), 21–41.

21 V. Vivoda, "Energy Security in East Asia", in J. Reeves and R. Pacheco Pardo, eds, *Non-Traditional Security in East Asia: A Regime Approach* (London: Imperial College Press, 2015), 143–165.

22 B. Kong, "Governing China's Energy in the Context of Global Governance", *Global Policy*, 2:1 (2011), 51–65.

98 *Vlado Vivoda*

23 F.K. Chang, "Chinese Energy and Asian Security", *Orbis*, 45:2 (2001), 211–240.
24 Vivoda "Energy Security in East Asia".
25 V. Vivoda, *Energy Security in Japan: Challenges after Fukushima* (Abingdon: Routledge, 2014); K. Nakatani, "Energy Security and Japan Energy Security and Japan: The Role of International Law, Domestic Law, and Diplomacy", in B. Barton, C. Redgwell, A. Rønne, and D.N. Zillman, eds, *Energy Security: Managing Risk in a Dynamic Legal and Regulatory Environment* (Oxford: Oxford University Press, 2004), 413–427.
26 A. Phillips, "A Dangerous Synergy: Energy Securitization, Great Power Rivalry and Strategic Stability in the Asian Century", *The Pacific Review*, 26:1 (2013), 17–38.
27 V. Vivoda, "Japan's Energy Security Predicament Post-Fukushima", *Energy Policy*, 46 (2012), 135–143.
28 J.P. Dorian, *Energy in China: Foreign Investment Opportunities, Trends and Legislation* (London: Financial Times Energy Publishing, 1995).
29 H. Lai, ed., *Asian Energy Security: The Maritime Dimension* (New York: Palgrave Macmillan, 2009); Phillips, "A Dangerous Synergy".
30 S. Itoh, "Russia's Energy Policy Towards Asia: Opportunities and Uncertainties", in C. Len and E. Chew, eds, *Energy and Security Cooperation in Asia: Challenges and Prospects* (Stockholm: Institute for Security and Development Policy, 2009), 143–166.
31 J.D. Wilson, "Northeast Asian Resource Security".
32 P. Aalto and D. Korkmaz Temel, "European Energy Security: Natural Gas and the Integration Process", *Journal of Common Market Studies*, 52:4 (2014), 758–774.
33 J.D. Wilson, "Resource Security: A New Motivation for Free Trade Agreements in the Asia-Pacific Region", *The Pacific Review*, 25:4 (2012), 429–453.
34 B.K. Sovacool and V. Vivoda, "A Comparison of Chinese, Indian, and Japanese Perceptions of Energy Security", *Asian Survey*, 52:5 (2012), 949–969.
35 Wilson, "Northeast Asian Resource Security Strategies".
36 Z. Zhang, "The Overseas Acquisitions and Equity Oil Shares of Chinese National Oil Companies: A Threat to the West but a Boost to China's Energy Security?" *Energy Policy*, 48 (2012), 698–701. doi:10.1016/j.enpol.2012.05.077; Vivoda, *Energy Security in Japan*.
37 Vivoda, "Energy Security in East Asia".
38 Wilson, "Northeast Asian Resource Security Strategies".
39 R. Drifte, "Japan's Energy Policy in Asia: Cooperation, Competition, Territorial Disputes", *Oil, Gas & Energy Law*, 4 (2005); M. Koike, G. Mogi, and W.H. Albedaiwi, "Overseas Oil-Development Policy of Resource-Poor Countries: A Case Study from Japan", *Energy Policy*, 36:5 (2008), 1764–1775; Vivoda, *Energy Security in Japan*.
40 A.B. Kennedy, "China's New Energy Security Debate", *Survival*, 52:3 (2010), 137–158; Zhang, "The Overseas Acquisitions".
41 Wilson, "Northeast Asian Resource Security Strategies".
42 Vivoda and Manicom, "Oil Import Diversification in Northeast Asia".
43 R. Shaoul, "An Evaluation of Japan's Current Energy Policy in the Context of the Azadegan Oil Field Agreement Signed in 2004", *Japanese Journal of Political Science*, 6:3 (2005), 411–437.
44 Vivoda and Manicom, "Oil Import Diversification in Northeast Asia".
45 Ibid.; Manicom, *Bridging Troubled Waters*.
46 Phillips, "A Dangerous Synergy".
47 G. Collins and A.S. Erickson, "Energy Nationalism Goes to Sea in Asia", The National Bureau of Asian Research, NBR Special Report 31, September 2011.
48 BP, *Statistical Review of World Energy 2016*.
49 V. Vivoda, "Natural Gas in Asia: Trade, Markets and Regional Institutions", *Energy Policy*, 74 (2014), 80–90.
50 V. Vivoda, "LNG Import Diversification in Asia", *Energy Strategy Reviews*, 2:3/4 (2014), 289–297.

Competition and energy security 99

51 C. Russell, "Cheaper Asian LNG Depends on Coal, Japan Nuclear", *Reuters*, March 25, 2014.
52 Vivoda, "Energy Security in East Asia".
53 Vivoda, "Natural Gas in Asia".
54 Asian Development Bank, *Fossil Fuel Subsidies in Asia: Trends, Impacts, and Reforms: Integrative Report* (Mandaluyong City: Asian Development Bank, 2016).
55 Asian Development Bank. *Fossil Fuel Subsidies in Asia*.
56 Ibid.
57 Intergovernmental Panel on Climate Change, *Climate Change 2014: Mitigation of Climate Change. Contribution of Working Group III to the Fifth Assessment Report of the Intergovernmental Panel on Climate Change* (Cambridge: Cambridge University Press, 2014).
58 J.C. Steckel, O. Edenhofer, and M. Jakob, "Drivers for the Renaissance of Coal", *Proceedings of the National Academy of Sciences of the United States of America*, 112:29 (2015).
59 Intergovernmental Panel on Climate Change, *Climate Change 2014*.
60 Steckel et al., "Drivers for the Renaissance of Coal".
61 D.L. McCollum, V. Krey, K. Riahi, P. Kolp, A. Grübler, M. Makowski, and N. Nakićenović, "Climate Policies Can Help Resolve Energy Security and Air Pollution Challenges", *Climatic Change*, 119:2 (2013).
62 M. Jakob, J.C. Steckel, S. Klasen, J. Lay, N. Grunewald, I. Martínez-Zarzoso, S. Renner, and O. Edenhofer, "Feasible Mitigation Actions in Developing Countries", *Nature Climate Change*, 4:11 (2014), 961–968.
63 P. Sheehan, E. Cheng, A. English, and F. Sun, "China's Response to the Air Pollution Shock", *Nature Climate Change*, 4:5 (2014), 306–309.
64 A. Zimmer, M. Jakob, and J.C. Steckel, "What Motivates Vietnam to Strive for a Low-Carbon Economy? On the Drivers of Climate Policy in a Developing Country", *Energy for Sustainable Development*, 24 (2015), 19–32; N.K. Dubash, "The Politics of Climate Change in India: Narratives of Equity and Co-benefits", *Wiley Interdisciplinary Review of Climate Change*, 4:3 (2013), 191–201.
65 T.J. Christensen, "China, the U.S.–Japan Alliance, and the Security Dilemma in East Asia", *International Security*, 23:4 (1999), 49–80.
66 K.E. Calder, *The New Continentalism: Energy and Twenty-First-Century Eurasian Geopolitics* (New Haven: Yale University Press, 2012).
67 J. Ravenhill, "Resource Insecurity and International Institutions in the Asia-Pacific Region", *The Pacific Review*, 26:1 (2013), 39–64.
68 R. Foot, "Asia's Cooperation and Governance: The Role of East Asian Regional Organizations in Regional Governance – Constraints and Contributions", *Japanese Journal of Political Science*, 13:1 (2012), 133–142.
69 J.-S. Lee, "Energy Security and Cooperation in Northeast Asia", *Korean Journal of Defense Analysis*, 22:2 (2010), 217–233.
70 K.E. Calder, *Asia's Deadly Triangle: How Arms, Energy and Growth Threaten to Destabilize Asia-Pacific* (London: Nicholas Brealey Publishing, 1997); Vivoda, *Energy Security in Japan*.
71 J. Prantl, "Crafting Energy Security Cooperation in East Asia", S. Rajaratnam School of International Studies, Centre for Non-Traditional Security Studies, Policy Brief 9, April 2011.
72 M. Kalkuhl, O. Edenhofer, and K. Lessmann, "The Role of Carbon Capture and Sequestration Policies for Climate Change Mitigation", *Environmental and Resource Economics*, 60:1 (2015), 55–80.

Part II
Security issues

6 Sino-Japan relations in Asia's maritime worlds

Rivalry in the East and South China Seas

Kerry Lynn Nankivell

The purpose of this volume is to shed light on the under-examined effects of Sino-Japanese rivalry on the Asian region. Working from the theoretical framework established in Chapter 1, this chapter evaluates the extent to which this bilateral relationship has observable effects in the maritime and territorial disputes in the South China Sea. Such an examination enhances the existing literature on Asian regional security, which oftentimes privileges great power politics at the expense of understanding the important relationships that are endogenous to Asia. Taking the kind of perspective offered in this volume holds out the promise of achieving two ends: first, to tell us a bit more about the ways in which Asian regional relations operate in the contemporary context, apart from the role of external great powers like the US (which is an important, but well-examined consideration); and second, to uncover the effects of endogenous relationships on the evolution of security partnerships and multilateral security issues of common concern. This chapter will endeavour to do both in some measure with reference to the operation of Sino-Japanese rivalry in the politics of the South China Sea disputes.

This exploration will conclude that while it is premature to say that the South China Sea disputes are a primary site of Sino-Japanese rivalry, there are good reasons to anticipate this eventuality in the future. Currently, the East China Sea is the most pronounced area of maritime tension between Tokyo and Beijing. The Sino-Japanese competition over sovereignty of the Senkaku/Diaoyu Islands in the East China Sea remains both central to Japan–China relations, and distinct from the disputes between Beijing and its rival claimants farther south. To borrow the terminology that frames this volume, these disputes currently represent separate maritime regional security orders (RSOs).[1] But steady Chinese assertiveness in both regional seas is providing powerful incentive for Tokyo to widen its scope of strategic interests to include the disputed waters of the South China Sea: a change in aperture would both open up opportunities for new coalitions at sea and aim to outflank (or at least substantially distract) China's maritime forces in the East China Sea. This kind of direct instrumentalization of the South China Sea to secure the East China Sea is possible (and logical), but, as of late 2016, only observable in small but significant ways. Japan increasingly perceives its interests vis-à-vis China in the East China Sea as linked to developments in the South China Sea. Japanese leaders have begun to draw direct parallels between Chinese behaviour

104 *Kerry Lynn Nankivell*

at sea in these separate disputes. They seem to identify Chinese expansionism as a single threat looming over both maritime sub-regions. Moreover, the July 2016 ruling of the Arbitral Tribunal at the Permanent Court of Arbitration at the Hague inevitably impacts the legal status of the disputed islands in the East China Sea, and the negotiating positions of the rival claimants. Tokyo has taken a more active role in the South China Sea disputes, positioning itself in increasingly open opposition to China there as an important corollary to its island defence strategy in the East China Sea.

Thus far, Japan's approach to the South China Sea has inspired angry rhetoric from Beijing, but little else. As of 2016, there is little evidence to suggest that Beijing is responding to Japanese engagement with the South China Sea with any deliberate policy of its own designed to limit Tokyo's operational options in Southeast Asian waters. Ironically, to the extent that Beijing links the two seas, it has done so by using the legal findings of the Philippine arbitration to cast doubt on the integrity of Japanese maritime claims. But even this development remains primarily rhetorical. To date, China has stayed the course in the East China Sea, neither adapting its longstanding opposition to Japan's East China Sea claims to reflect new developments in international law, nor pursuing them in radically new ways. China does not seem to have linked its East China Sea and South China Sea strategies in any tangible way. That said, though the disputes remain distinct RSOs today, Japan's growing tendency to conceive policy from within a perception of Chinese expansionism suggests that these two RSOs will interact in ever-more important ways in the medium term. They may one day form what Amitav Acharya terms a "multiplex": a single security order in which different sub-plots to the main drama run in parallel in different sub-regions.[2] Today, Japan's South China Sea engagements are tentative when compared against Tokyo's available resources. This may not always be the case. And so far, Beijing's response is more rhetorical than real. This will likely change if a more active Japan constrains its strategic options in the South China Sea. Investigation of Sino-Japanese rivalry in the South China Sea gives us hints about the possible futures of maritime Asia, even as it has limited explanatory power with respect to the present.

The proposition that the first signs of Sino-Japanese rivalry are observable in the South China Sea, and may portend the eventual development of an East Asian maritime multiplex, will require three moves to substantiate. First, tracing Japan and China's historical engagement with the South China Sea disputes and their more recent trajectories vis-à-vis one another will apply the broad parameters of the "multiplex" argument to these maritime worlds. Second, investigating changes to these parameters in more empirical detail, we will consider Japan's engagement with the South China Sea disputes since the 1990s along three planes: support to multilateralism in maritime Southeast Asia (1993–2009), use of freedom of navigation (FON) diplomacy (2010–present), and operational engagement with non-Chinese claimants to South China Sea features (2012–present). This section will also consider China's reaction to changes in Japanese South China Sea-related activities. The chapter will close with some conclusions about the increasing extension of Sino-Japanese rivalry from the East China Sea into the South China Sea, and what that might portend for the East Asian seascape.

Post-war approaches to the South China Sea: resident China, reluctant Japan

For much of the history of the People's Republic of China, Japan remained very cautious about engaging with issues related to Southeast Asia's maritime spaces due to its unpleasant Second World War history.[3] Imperial Japan is still the only power to have successfully established exclusive administrative control over the Spratly Islands, the only one to operate submarines from a base on South China Sea features, and the first to apply sea control to military ends in mainland Southeast Asia.[4] From within that context, Japan has worked over many decades to ease Southeast Asian fears of Japanese adventurism at sea. This policy continues to be prudent. Even today, Japan's occupation of the South China Sea likely informs Southeast Asian concerns about foreign encroachment on sovereign maritime jurisdictions. As Southeast Asian claimants in the South China Sea consider the strategic implications of foreign occupation and regional hegemony, they can (rightly or wrongly) draw on Japanese colonialism as a cautionary tale. Of course, Japan's occupation of the Spratly Islands during the Second World War ultimately proved of little value in either establishing sea command in the South China Sea or providing a shield for its landward holdings. Nonetheless, it is natural for Southeast Asia to take the need to prevent foreign domination of the South China Sea as the lesson of history. Operating from within that historical and political context, Japan's approach to engagement with the South China Sea since 1945 has been cognizant of the sensitivities that it might provoke.

China, on the other hand, occupies the inverse position in the politics of the South China Sea. Beijing is a resident littoral power and always has been. While there is much controversy over the administrative history of the South China Sea and its features,[5] there is little debate about the fact that coastal populations occupying what is today a part of China (including Hainan) have enjoyed a long association with that sea, though probably primarily in private commercial terms rather than as an affair of the state.[6] But the merits of China's current controversial claims aside, its interests in the sea are an inevitable fact of the region, where Japan's are contingent on its economic and strategic goals. This asymmetry of interest between them is geographically determined and fundamental. In the post-Second World War period, China's pursuit of its claims have been limited only by its material and political capabilities vis-à-vis its rival claimants; Japan's engagement has been limited by the lingering effects of its Second World War defeat and naval disarmament. As a result, though Chinese activities in the South China Sea have been an active driver of events, Sino-Japan relations in the South China Sea were simply not an empirical consideration for either policy makers or scholars.

Japan's development as a regional centre of gravity for shipping and trade in the 1960s and 1970s provides a caveat to that assertion. Tokyo's increasing economic reliance on Southeast Asian sea lanes in the middle of the twentieth century prompted a strategic drift to consideration of its lifelines in the South China Sea. In 1977, Japanese Prime Minister Fukuda Takeo cemented Tokyo's commitment to making a positive contribution to regional maritime stability in a

106 *Kerry Lynn Nankivell*

speech delivered in Manila. The Fukuda Doctrine marked an important milestone in the development of Japan's post-Second World War relations with maritime Southeast Asia. Prior to that time, Japan explicitly pursued a division of labour in its Asia policy, furthering trade relations with its neighbours under security guarantees provided by the US. After 1977, Japan assumed some of the burden of underwriting regional sea lane security, in limited but path-breaking ways.[7] This role mostly took shape as sustained capacity-building assistance to littoral states. For the period of 1970 to around 2010, these activities were focused on safety, not security. That is, they were non-military, development-centric, and directed at safeguarding uncontroversial public goods, like aids to navigation and the administrative machinery of pollution control.[8] Even when carried out by paramilitary organizations, Japanese policy was only obliquely paramilitary: capacity-building programmes aimed at improving safety of navigation were administered by the Japan Coast Guard (JCG), but funded through Overseas Development Assistance (ODA), not the JCG's main operating budget.[9]

As a regional supporter of safety of navigation, Japanese activities in maritime Southeast Asia during this period generated little interest in Beijing, whose comparative commercial interest in the sea lanes from 1970 to the mid-1990s was negligible. At that time, Beijing's interests in the South China Sea were primarily political and military in nature, embedded within a narrative of national unity, not commercial access. As a result, China's approach to the South China Sea disputes was somewhat unrelated to Japanese activity in the same space, which was focused on the safety of commerce. This co-existence presented a stark contrast to Sino-Japanese maritime rivalry in the East China Sea, which was robust during the same period. Beijing officially laid claim to the Senkaku/Diaoyu Islands in 1971, extending its struggle for national unity into the East China Sea. Sino-Japanese rivalry over those territories and their claimed jurisdictions opened almost immediately after they reverted from US to Japanese control in 1972,[10] ending a long period in which the dispute was latent but probably well-understood by the primary stakeholders.[11] From reversion, Japan's maritime policies became increasingly explicitly defined by two relatively exclusive geographies, each operating under a different logic. Maritime policy in the East China Sea was security-driven and China-focused. A separate South China Sea policy remained safety-driven, aimed at minimizing non-state risks to commercial navigation. As a result of their distinct interests in each regional sea, Beijing and Tokyo operated uncontroversially alongside one another in the South China Sea even as they managed delicate strategic relations in the East China Sea. This remained the case even during the most tense circumstances. As a case in point, neither Chinese military operations to oust Vietnam from the Paracel Islands in 1974 nor those that pushed Hanoi from parts of the Spratly Islands in 1988 generated any response in Tokyo, despite its cooperative activities with maritime partners in Southeast Asia.[12]

In the last decade, however, Japanese and Chinese interests in the South China Sea have begun to interact in important ways. This is the natural result of the expanding maritime interests of each into the established sphere of the other, that

Rivalry in the East and South China Seas   107

is, Japan's military "normalization" and China's economic rise. In the last two decades, China's commercial interests in regional sea lanes have rivalled Japan's. China has become the world's most important seafaring nation by every important measure: total volume of seaborne trade, total merchant fleet tonnage, mega-port throughput, and shipbuilding orders and output.[13] Meanwhile, in the same period, Japan has taken some significant first steps in evolving its defence and security posture to reflect wider, more "normal" articulation of its interests.[14] This re-definition of its interests and legitimate area of operation has particularly important effects on the missions undertaken by its Maritime Self-Defense Force (MSDF).[15] The result of this simultaneous broadening of Chinese and Japanese interests at sea has been increased interaction of their once-parallel engagement trajectories in the South China Sea. Japan has begun to see security interests in the South China Sea, particularly with respect to what it sees as Chinese expansionism throughout its near seas. Meanwhile, Beijing has become increasingly wary of Japan's engagement with maritime affairs in the South China Sea, even those ostensibly falling under the "safety-driven" commercial agenda.

While it is premature to conclude that the regional security order in the South China Sea has been subsumed by the rivalrous politics of the East China Sea, in recent years they have become harder to consider in isolation. The Sino-Japanese politics of the East China Sea bear unique characteristics, including competing claims, disputed maritime resources, strategic competition for control of the water-ways, and bilateral regional diplomacy to manage all three. These are quite distinct from Sino-Japanese relations in the South China Sea, an arena dominated by the relations among littoral powers and, increasingly, ASEAN-centric diplomatic processes. But they also have begun to share important characteristics: China's anti-access/aerial denial (A2/AD) strategies in both seas are fundamentally the same, though they are more easily applied against the smaller claimants in the South China Sea than they are against Japan.[16] China's deft operation in the "grey zone" between civilian, paramilitary, and military realms is another important similarity tying the two regions together, even though it has not yielded similar results.[17] Considering Japan, its ongoing re-evaluation of its security posture has prompted a tangible shift in its maritime engagements around the world outward from supporting sea lane safety to sea lane security. The increasing interaction of developments in the East and South China Seas is an incontrovertible fact of the region, and has drivers originating in both Tokyo and Beijing.

The next section will more closely examine layered changes in Japan's engagement with the South China Sea and Chinese responses. But before considering the evidence, we should consider what the above discussion means in theoretical terms. The extension of Sino-Japanese rivalry into the politics of the South China Sea suggests that the regional security complex theory (RSCT) framework requires some extension for this case. While RSCT advocates for the explanatory power of regional investigations, Sino-Japanese rivalry in the South China Sea does not fit easily into this mould. In fact, Sino-Japanese competition in the South China Sea falls somewhere between the regional and global levels of analysis as it involves the expansion of one sub-regional phenomenon into another. This sub-regional cross-over goes beyond that for which RSCT is meant to account. Amitav Acharya offers a theoretical extension that provides a useful supplement to RSCT, introducing the notion of a"security multiplex". The multiplex is characterized by the intermingling of two sub-regional security complexes in important ways that nonetheless fall short of full integration. The concept accepts Barry Buzan's idea that the useful unit of analysis of international relations is not the global system, but its regional manifestation.[18] Like Buzan, Acharya starts by challenging the discipline to consider that international relations (IR) theory assumes greater explanatory weight if developed from within "regional worlds", rather than from a "global" perspective, which is too often a Western view dressed up in universalist claims.[19] But if we take as given that a regional approach carries the promise of a more precise account of sub-systemic developments than global IR constructs can support, we are still left with the rather important question of where to draw boundaries around the RSOs that are the object of study. In terms of the subject of this case study, do we draw boundaries around the East and South China Seas as separate sites of competition, or is it fair to say that the entire East Asian littoral now forms a single RSO?

This chapter will not provide an easy final answer to that question, but will make an important contribution to the discussion. In the context of the above broad historical sketch, it seems clear that the East and South China Seas have operated as separate security orders for most of the post-Second World War period. While China and the Southeast Asian claimants to the features of the South China Sea have been locked in a strategic rivalry for several decades, Japan is only recently re-entering this strategic space in any significant way. But in the last decade,the two security complexes have become undeniably intertwined as Japan has added important new layers to its South China Sea policy, and China has seen Japan's safety-driven engagements in Southeast Asia as newly relevant to its own interests. Judging these changes, it seems likely that the East and South China Seas will undergo deepening enmeshment in the years to come. This has already been borne out by events: Tokyo's cooperative activities with the Philippines have drawn official reprimand from Beijing's Foreign Ministry.[20] Prime Minister Abe Shinzō denounced Chinese "attempts to change unilaterally the *status quo* in the East and South China Sea", drawing explicit attention to the linkage between the two seas at the 2016 ASEAN Summit, capitalizing on Philippine revelations of stepped-up activity by Chinese vessels around the disputed Scarborough Shoal.[21] Tokyo's disinterest in operational activities in the South China Sea in 1974 and 1988 is clearly a relic of the past. Today, contemporary Sino-Japanese relations in the South China Sea are an excellent case study of the proposition that sub-regional RSOs may interact with one another to eventually create a regional security "multiplex" falling somewhere between the global and regional levels of analysis. This study is an investigation of the early formation of the kind of security multiplex that Acharya's theorizing posits.

Intermingled seas: Japanese engagement with the South China Sea and Chinese response

An analysis in support of the proposition that the Sino-Japanese rivalry has become a feature of the South China Sea disputes has to demonstrate three things: first, that Japan is active in the politics of the disputes (versus the South China Sea as a geographic entity); second, that Japan's engagement with the disputes is linked to its China policy; and third, that China's South China Sea policy is targeted, at least in part, at countering Japan. At the time of writing, it is possible to establish the first two developments, but not the third. It is premature then to conclude that Sino-Japan relations are a primary consideration in understanding the South China Sea disputes, or that the East Asian littoral is a single security order governed by a prevailing logic. China continues to pursue its interests in the South China Sea exclusive of its rivalry with Japan. At the same time, it does seem clear that the first two parts of the argument are observable: as of late 2016, Japan is unquestionably developing a strong South China Sea policy and there is evidence to suggest that it is directed primarily at securing Japan's territories and disputed waters in the East China Sea by countering an expansionist maritime China farther abroad. There is evidence of a nascent security multiplex linking the East and South China Seas disputes. This analysis will focus on outlining the evidence for those two propositions.

Recent developments provide support to the claim that Japan's engagement with the South China Sea disputes has become increasingly activist. Published strategic documents confirm that the Abe administration in particular is devising maritime policies from within a paradigm that links Japan's interests in the East China Sea with events in the South China Sea. The 2015 Japanese Defence White Paper suggests this, noting "grave concern" over Chinese activities in both the East and South China Seas, without distinguishing clearly between the two. The document does not make an important distinction between frequent Chinese intrusions into what it perceives to be Tokyo's territorial seas around the Senkaku/Diaoyu Islands and the massive land reclamation activities of 2014–2016 in the Spratly Islands. Both sets of activities are treated under a single heading in the text.[22] Prime Minister Abe has made more explicit linkages between the East and South China Seas before. Writing in 2013, and referring to China's 2012 seizure of the Scarborough Shoal from the Philippines, Abe declared: "Japan must not yield to the Chinese government's daily exercises in coercion around the Senkaku Islands . . . . If Japan were to yield, the South China Sea would become even more fortified."[23] This is the clearest expression to date that the Abe government perceives itself to be functioning within an interactive regional multiplex stretching from Japanese to Singaporean waters.

But Prime Minister Abe's explicit statements reflect a longer-term evolution of Japanese approaches to the South China Sea since the end of the Cold War. Over that period, Japan has furthered its policy of engagement with the disputes in three progressively proactive layers. Starting in the 1990s, Japan sought to maintain some influence over the prevailing discourse and direction of events in the South

110　*Kerry Lynn Nankivell*

China Sea through the creation and use of multilateral diplomatic forums. From 1993, Japan played a key role in realizing meaningful multilateralism in Asia, particularly with respect to the maritime domain. Having succeeded in creating standing multilateral processes and organizations, Japan then used these venues to raise its concerns about the outcome of the disputes in the Paracels and Spratlys, and to influence events in limited ways. Its influence in the South China Sea was primarily manifest in rising regional awareness about threats to sea lane security, and emergent norms in Southeast Asia to address common maritime challenges by cooperative means.[24]

In 2010, Tokyo's South China Sea policy added a new layer of diplomatic effort centred on FON as a result of two catalysing events. The 2010 ASEAN Regional Forum (ARF) Summit in Hanoi in July that year and the September JCG violent confrontation with a Chinese fishing trawler prompted Japan to advance a diplomatic agenda focused on FON in regional seas. This shift from *safety* of navigation to *freedom* of navigation brought Japan into more direct diplomatic confrontation with Beijing than in preceding years. Last, following the demonstration of new capabilities by both Japan's MSDF and the People's Liberation Army (Navy) (PLA(N)) around 2012/2013, Japan's South China Sea policy assumed a new layer characterized by direct operational involvement with China's rival claimants in the South China Sea. The overall trend has been a thickening of Japan's South China Sea policy to become more confrontational to Beijing. This thickening is reasonably evaluated as the result of increased concern over China's intentions over Japanese-administered territory in the East China Sea. We shall examine each layer in turn.

Creation of institutional linkages through talk-shop diplomacy

Japanese engagement with the South China Sea maintains a primary focus on the promotion and use of multilateral diplomacy to protect national interests, even as the environment around Japan continues to be challenged by an increasingly active China. In the 2015 Defence White Paper, in the Outline of the National Security Strategy, the Abe government lists "[a]dvance vibrant diplomacy" first under the heading of "Strengthening and Expanding Japan's Capabilities and Roles".[25] Japan's diplomatic role in fostering an international order "favorable for Japan" is noted even before more conventional capabilities are listed – jointness, maritime surveillance, territorial patrols, and assistance to like-minded partners in maritime security. The ordering of these priorities is a signal that Japan's traditional reliance on diplomacy will continue even as new policy layers overlay this approach.

Japanese diplomacy has long been used as a tool to internationalize the South China Sea disputes and put a degree of regional pressure on Beijing. Japan has been a key player in establishing multilateral diplomatic forums for some decades, a leadership role which is perhaps under-emphasized by current scholarship.[26] Certainly after the financial crisis in 1997, Tokyo has deliberately pursued the creation of an East Asian community with the goal of improving the regional security environment for Japan.[27] This includes balancing against China. The creation of

Rivalry in the East and South China Seas   111

the ARF in 1994 is often described as the most prominent success in this policy – a body that has been consistently used by Tokyo as a vehicle to raise maritime security issues. Under Japanese initiative, the ARF was established to bring China into dialogue with more of Japan's like-minded partners than was permitted under the ASEAN+3 process. This 27-member body widened the scope for security dialogue in Asia, inviting Australia, New Zealand, India, Canada, and the US into the conversation. Japanese Foreign Minister Nakayama Taro in particular has been credited with playing a "significant role" in the establishment of this forum as a security-focused body,[28] introducing maritime issues to its Senior Officials Meeting (SOM) in the early years. Paul Midford credits Japanese pressure at the 1995 ARF SOM with Beijing's first agreement to discuss South China Sea issues multilaterally, after years of stone-walling ASEAN on that point.[29] A similar logic of "soft balancing" led Prime Minister Koizumi Junichiro to ensure that Australia, New Zealand,[30] and the US were included the East Asia Summit (EAS) when it was formed, arguing that "U.S. participation [in the EAS] would do some good for the promotion of solidarity among the East Asian community."[31] Today's multilateral Asia is, in part, the result of Japanese initiative.

Since 2000, Japan has also played a leadership role more specific to the maritime domain. Japan was the initiator of the North Pacific Coast Guard Forum (NPCGF) in 2000. This six-nation forum brings together the Coast Guards of Canada, China, Japan, Russia, South Korea, and the US to share information and coordinate operations to counter transnational maritime crimes like illegal fishing, drugs trafficking, and irregular migration.[32] Supported by Tokyo and Washington, this unlikely coalition has been so successful that the NPCGF was used as the model to establish counterparts in the North Atlantic (2007) and the Arctic (2015).[33] With similar success, both Japanese Prime Ministers Obuchi Keizo and Koizumi pursued information-sharing cooperation to facilitate counter-piracy operations in Southeast Asia. Their efforts paid dividends in 2004 when negotiations held under Japan's leadership resulted in the establishment of the Regional Cooperation Agreement on Combating Piracy and Armed Robbery against Ships in Asia (ReCAAP).[34] ReCAAP has significant shortcomings, not least of which are that neither Malaysia nor Indonesia are members, and it serves no direct operational function (though it holds that as an eventual possibility). Nevertheless, ReCAAP's Information Sharing Center (ISC) does play a role as a regional clearing house for incident reporting and information sharing, and its interaction with the better-established Information Fusion Center (IFC) of the Republic of Singapore Navy gives operational effect to its information-gathering. ReCAAP also remains a favourite vehicle for non-resident stakeholders of maritime trade,[35] including the US and Australia, supporting capacity-building programming and coordination among those interested members.[36] Japan continues to nurture ReCAAP, providing the second-largest tranche of funds for its operations, and often providing its executive director.[37] It was also a Japanese proposal in late 2012 to widen the Track 1.5 ASEAN Maritime Forum to include the ARF dialogue partners in an Expanded ASEAN Maritime Forum (EAMF). The EAMF was established by ASEAN in October 2012 with the objective of "conflict management and harmonisation" of views on maritime security.[38] It has since become an annual fixture of the ASEAN

112 *Kerry Lynn Nankivell*

calendar and, at the time of writing, members were exploring ways to formalize a more authoritative EAMF role.[39]

All four multilateral bodies – the ARF, NPCGF, ReCAAP, and EAMF – are instruments of Japan's South China Sea engagement. They accomplish two important aims. First, they engage China in maritime-focused multilateral processes and contribute to efforts to socialize Beijing to the responsible use of maritime power.[40] Second, they bring Japanese maritime agencies in operational proximity of other maritime powers, many of which harbour similar concerns about China's maritime rise. These include Australia, South Korea, Singapore, and India, as well as others in Southeast Asia like Vietnam and the Philippines, all of whom are both members of the EAMF and participating members in the ReCAAP ISC. Absent these multilateral venues, Japan would be almost completely isolated from the regional maritime community due to self-imposed constitutional limits on military-to-military relations. As the centrepiece of Japan's South China Sea policy, development and use of multilateral diplomacy has been effective at achieving these limited ends within current constraints.

It is in this diplomatic realm that China has moved most directly against Japanese efforts. Japanese efforts to expand ASEAN+3 into the ARF format were resisted by Beijing, especially with respect to the inclusion of the US or its partners like Australia.[41] Japan's support to functionally focused multilateral organizations was similarly lambasted by China. In 2004, shortly after China signed ReCAAP's founding agreement, China's Foreign Broadcast Information Service claimed that Tokyo was "using the fight against piracy as an excuse to cover Malacca with its military attack power".[42] In more recent years, as the South China Sea disputes have heated up, China has reacted strongly to even smaller maritime forums or meetings led by Japan. Reacting to a "maritime countries conference" hosted by Japan's Foreign Ministry in 2013, China News Agency called Japan a "troublemaker", accusing it of "establishing a strategy against China to encircle it".[43] Following the July 12, 2016 tribunal ruling in favour of the Philippines in the South China Sea case, China's condemnation of Japan's "manipulation" of the disputes became more pronounced. Vice-Minister for Foreign Affairs Liu Zhenmin accused Japan of tainting "the entire proceedings", accusing tribunal member and former Japanese president of the International Tribunal for the Law of the Sea of anti-China bias in his deliberations.[44] Nevertheless, it is interesting to note that beyond government statements and inflamed media commentary, China does not seem to have mounted any specific campaign to diminish Japanese standing in Southeast Asia. Indeed, despite angry statements, China is party to all of the multilateral organizations initiated by Japan (ARF, NPCGF, ReCAAP, and EAMF). For now, Beijing has limited its responses to rhetoric rather than diplomatic manoeuvre or punitive action.

2010–2014: establishing normative linkages and identifying a common threat

Japan's engagement with the South China Sea disputes assumed a new layer of activity around 2010. This new approach to Southeast Asian maritime affairs was coincident with a sharp deterioration in Sino-Japanese relations in Northeast Asian seas, suggesting that Tokyo came to see actual or potential strategic links between developments in the East and South China Seas around this time. In September 2010, a confrontation between a Chinese fishing trawler and the JCG around the Senkaku/Diaoyu Islands resulted in a ramming incident and a regional political scandal. Though Tokyo did what it could to limit the political damage throughout its handling of the sensitive case, its approach to charging, processing, and eventually extraditing the captain of the Chinese trawler under pressure from Beijing was widely interpreted as a strategic loss of face for Japan.[45] Analysing subsequent developments in Sino-Japanese relations in disputed seas, Sheila Smith avers that the 2010 ramming incident "fundamentally altered the status of [the Senkaku/ Diaoyu] dispute, and has created a new basis for understanding the potential consequences of a future incident."[46]

Part of that "new understanding" is an increasing tendency in Tokyo to see common strains in China's assertive maritime posture across its sub-regional disputes. The National Security Strategy implemented in December 2013 lists anti-piracy activities in cooperation with countries concerned, and capacity-building assistance of coastal states in waters "other than those surrounding the nation" under the heading of "all possible measures" to maintain "open and stable seas", a coded reference to China.[47] Ahead of change to official strategy, the National Institute for Defense Studies (NIDS, a Ministry of Defense-affiliated think tank) anticipated the linkage. NIDS's annual *East Asian Strategic Review* of 2010 draws explicit parallels between Chinese behaviour in all the semi-enclosed seas on its littoral, implying that China presents a common challenge to the whole of East Asia. Citing "China's steadily increasing military power", the report notes frictions between China and many others in the maritime domain, including the US, over the "*new* issue of 'freedom of navigation'" and Beijing's "more stringent monitoring of foreign fishing operations and intensified maneuvers by its navy and maritime law enforcement agencies" in the South China Sea.[48] Interestingly, Japan's own difficulties in managing China's "extremely antagonistic posture" in the East China Sea are cited last, not first, in this string of Chinese challenges to the maritime order. The use of the adjective "new" to describe the issue of FON in Sino-American relations is also interesting. As FON has in fact been a preeminent national interest of the US for some decades, the "newness" referred to is not the issue of FON, but the US commitment to engage in the South China Sea disputes to preserve FON against Beijing's creeping assumption of maritime jurisdiction. In 2011, the always China-centric *East Asian Strategic Review* was noticeably more focused on the South China Sea than the East China Sea, despite the fishing trawler crisis of 2010.

This reference to the "new" issue of FON reflects another seminal event in the politics of the South China Sea in 2010. A fraught ARF Summit in Hanoi in November resulted in the first US statement of its "national interest" in the outcome of the South China Sea disputes. Secretary of State Hillary Clinton expressed US concern with rising tensions in the South China Sea, noting the US Navy's longstanding commitment to preserve FON around the world. Secretary Clinton's

114 *Kerry Lynn Nankivell*

statement was interpreted as a direct challenge to Beijing; indeed, China's Foreign Minister Yang Jiechi immediately called it an "attack on China".[49] It became the single story of the summit's media coverage that year, and raised the stakes of South China Sea diplomacy within ASEAN. Anecdotal reports from the Summit suggest that Clinton's strong South China Sea statement prompted 11 other ARF members to make South China Sea statements as well, though they had initially hoped to avert official commentary.[50] Japan made no statement in defence of FON at that time. Japan's Ministry of Foreign Affairs' official record of the summit is limited to the Chairman's Statement released by Vietnam; Japan's contribution to the meeting appears to have been focused on regional coordination for civilian disaster relief.[51]

Interestingly, prior to 2010, Japan took a rather reserved view of FON despite its obvious interest in commercial navigation. Writing after both the ARF Summit and the JCG ramming incident, Kotani Tetsuo noted that Japan should clarify its position on FON, which some believed remained ambiguous. Kotani went on to recommend that the US–Japan alliance should be used to provide regional leadership to promote a "universal interpretation" of the FON principles enshrined in the UN Convention on the Law of the Sea (UNCLOS) as a response to the "threat of [China's] legal warfare".[52] The Abe administration took this approach beginning in 2013, introducing a newly normative component, based on FON, to Japan's maritime diplomacy. Abe thus staked a new Japanese position within regional maritime politics, pitting a strengthened assertion of FON against China's expansion of its exclusive jurisdiction in new and very clear terms.

Japan's use of key leader statements in ASEAN Forums and elsewhere to re-inforce this view of the primacy of the FON stood in stark contrast to Chinese statements of the same period. China's ambiguous claims in the South China Sea seem aimed at eliminating FON for both rival claimants and user states. Chinese statements at the ASEAN Summit in Hanoi in 2010 illustrate the point that China's understanding of the way forward in its multilateral disputes with rival claimants is unavoidably opposed to the acknowledgement of the FON interests of outside stakeholders. Beijing argues that FON is merely a wedge intended to drive Southeast Asia's rival claimants out of Beijing's orbit and justify the protective presence of non-claimant others (namely the US).[53] Japan's entry into this deeply politicized regional discourse on FON has normative overtones, implying that Japan views itself not only as willing but also *entitled* to play an important role in the South China Sea in defence of FON. This normative approach is quite different than previous decades of Japanese engagement with South China Sea issues. While previous Tokyo administrations focused maritime engagements on less-sensitive non-traditional threats to the *safety* of navigation,[54] Japan's FON diplomacy after 2010 emphasized the politically loaded *freedom* of navigation instead.

The trend became most pronounced with the election of Abe Shinzō as Japan's prime minister in December 2012. Elected on a platform that included a stronger approach to a rising China, the Abe administration quickly moved to leverage Japanese influence to include references to FON in official ASEAN statements at every opportunity. Senior leader statements throughout 2013 confirm a decisive shift in Japanese policy from one that focused on safety of sea lanes to the more normatively charged principle of FON. Abe emphasized Japan's role in defence of those freedoms for all states with maritime interests. In a January 2013 address outlining the "Abe Doctrine", the new prime minister declared a five-pillar Japanese foreign policy that included "ensur[ing] that the maritime domain remained 'governed by laws and rules, not might'".[55] Cabinet secretaries echoed and strengthened the theme: Foreign Minister Kishida Fumio linked Japan's traditional concern with safety of navigation and broadened it to include "free navigation" in a speech in Tokyo in May of that year. Defence Minister Onodera Itsunori proclaimed at the regional Defence Minister's Summit at Shangri-La a month later that Japan "intended to play a greater role" in upholding both FON and adherence to UNCLOS in Asia.[56] An Abe speech during a visit to Singapore in July 2013 declared that ASEAN and Japan had "gone beyond their economic relations to forge a relationship that takes responsibility for the security of the region, particularly freedom of navigation on the seas".[57] In a more coded reference to assertive Chinese behaviour, Abe noted in the same speech that Asia is not linked by "coercion through force" but through "maritime trade" fuelled by the "blessings of the seas".[58]

Abe also worked to embed FON language in ASEAN joint statements. Media reporting of the 2013 ASEAN Summit in Brunei in October and the Japan–ASEAN commemorative summit to follow describe Abe's determination to "use whatever means necessary to ensure that 'Freedom of Navigation' appears in the text" of both the ASEAN Chairman's statement and the Joint Japan–ASEAN Communiqué.[59] Prime Minister Abe's keynote address at the 2014 Shangri-La Dialogue in Singapore offered perhaps the most forceful and detailed articulation of Japan's hardening position on FON with respect to its maritime relations. In that speech, Abe not only encouraged legal measures taken by the Philippines and Vietnam to resolve their disputes in the South China Sea, but moreover drew a straight line from Manila and Hanoi's approach to managing China to Japan's own experience.[60] His remarks noted China's unwillingness to return either to the ASEAN 2002 Declaration on a Code of Conduct or the stalled Sino-Japanese Communication Mechanism in the East China Sea. By referring to the two moribund agreements in tandem, Abe strongly suggested that Beijing's intransigent approach to its maritime disputes presents a common threat to Japan and Southeast Asia.[61] Last, in case there was any question about Japan's commitment to meet that common threat, Prime Minister Abe used the Shangri-La speech to announce a new "strategic use" of Japan's ODA to "seamlessly support the capacity of ASEAN countries in safeguarding the seas", including through provision of patrol vessels and the dispatch of technical experts.[62] By June 2014, the Abe government was signalling its belief that its own concerns vis-à-vis Chinese restrictions on FON in the East China Sea were mirrored in the South China Sea disputes, and that Japan intended to offer material and technical assistance to South China Sea partners in support of the rules-based maritime order in Asia.

FON diplomacy was an important addition to Japan's approach to the South China Sea issues, which had previously assumed a much more benign view of China's engagement with ASEAN.[63] After 2010, Tokyo shifted its focus from

116 *Kerry Lynn Nankivell*

supporting inclusive multilateralism aimed at socializing Chinese maritime power to encouraging exclusive multilateralism in support of the mainstream interpretation of UNCLOS and, by extension, in opposition to Beijing. This was significant in two ways: first, it meant that Tokyo's approach to the South China Sea became more normative than functional, a major departure from decades of Japanese engagement with South China Sea issues. Second, it positioned Tokyo in direct rhetorical opposition to China in Southeast Asia. Throughout the Abe period, Tokyo's embrace of FON diplomacy eschewed functionality for normative posturing. Putting forward regional FON diplomacy was the first clear indication that Tokyo was carrying its East China Sea rivalry with China into Southeast Asian waters.

2011–2015: expanding operational presence into the South China Sea

Japan's expanding operational presence in the South China Sea and Chinese reactions to it provide the strongest evidence of the centrality of Sino-Japanese rivalry to the nature of Japan's engagement with the South China Sea. Beijing itself has acknowledged this reality. In November 2015, a Foreign Ministry spokesperson told *Xinhua* that Beijing was on "high alert" for Japanese "intervention" in the South China Sea.[64] The remark was a reaction to reports that Prime Minister Abe and US President Barack Obama had discussed the possibility of MSDF patrols in unspecified areas of the South China Sea. In return, Prime Minister Abe confirmed that though his government had no current plans to operate in that area, such activity would be dependent on his judgement of how developments in that area "affect Japan's security".[65] Beijing's sensitivity to Japanese operational involvement in disputed waters was no doubt fuelled in part by Japan's growing proclivity for sharpened military-to-military engagements with China's rivals, demonstrated throughout 2015. In turn, Japanese maritime engagement further from its home islands can also be read as a reaction to Chinese behaviour. Wherever one chooses to mark the "source" of Japan's and China's tit-for-tat game at sea, it seems in little doubt that there is in fact such a two-player game underway and that its boundaries are widening from the East China Sea to the South China Sea.

Examination of patterns of naval exercising in East Asia from 2011 to 2015 support the assertion. During that period, there was a clear escalation of rivalry as both navies demonstrated increased potential to expand their reach at sea in important ways, driven by new capabilities (in Beijing) and newfound political will (in Tokyo). In July 2011, Japan conducted its first exercise in the South China Sea, alongside the US and Australia. Designed to enhance communication and interoperability among the trilateral formation, the exercise was not "large scale". But strategic analysis in Japan noted at the time that as the exercise was synchronized to fall between US exercises with the Philippines and Vietnam, Washington achieved a "synergy effect" to the string of engagements which made it "an effective means of sending a message to neighbouring countries".[66] So less than one year after the 2010 Sino-Japanese crisis over the ship-ramming in the East China Sea, Japan's MSDF was operating in the disputed waters of the South China Sea.

Rivalry in the East and South China Seas 117

This first foray occurred in a multilateral context, with Japan operating alongside other navies, and marked an important milestone in what proved to be a steadily increasing willingness to send naval assets into the South China Sea.

In late 2013, the PLA(N) launched Maneouver-5, its largest ever exercise at sea. The complex multi-fleet exercise was notable for several reasons: ten surface vessels from each of the PLA(N)'s three fleets simultaneously transited two choke-points in the first-island chain, the Bashi and Miyako Straits. This achievement alone prompted Senior Colonel Du Wenlong to proclaim that the PLA(N) had successfully "cut up the first island chain" so that the "so-called island chains are no longer existent".[67] Once they entered the Western Pacific, the fleet engaged in an unscripted confrontation exercise intended to simulate combat. The confront-ation involved surface vessels including shipboard helicopters, submarines, and use of the Beidou-2 satellite for communication and tracking. An exercise of this scale and complexity was confirmation that China's capabilities and range for large-scale multi-asset deployment had grown in impressive ways. Colonel Du's overconfident assertion that the island chain no longer exists is clearly misplaced, but the successful exercise does call into question the extent to which Japan maintains its geographical naval advantage vis-à-vis China.

This point was not lost on the MSDF, which conducted extensive surveillance and monitoring of the Chinese manoeuvres throughout. The Chinese spokesperson for the Ministry of Defence accused Japan of producing a "war-like atmosphere" by collecting intelligence on Chinese movements. Responding to official Chinese protests about the legality of Japanese surveillance, Prime Minister Abe told media that Japan "would not be bullied" and that his government was prepared to conduct any surveillance and intelligence collection necessary to ensure that there is no "change to the *status quo* by force".[68] In addition to close monitoring of the Chinese exercise, as the PLA(N) headed back to their ports in China, Japan itself launched an 18-day amphibious landing exercise south of Okinawa that simulated a solo response to a hostile landing on a remote island. The exercise, involving 34,000 Japanese personnel, was clearly built off of a US–Japan joint exercise held in California earlier in the year on the same theme. The fact that Japan was exercising this capability without US armed forces was an important signal to Beijing that Japan will not be constrained by Washington's strategic choices when it comes to its own territorial defence.[69]

That demonstration of both capability and resolve, as well as Japan's ability to track the PLA(N)'s movements, suggest that while China's maritime capabilities are growing in impressive ways, it is premature to conclude that Beijing enjoys the advantage. That said, Beijing's ability to deploy widely, and coordinate the simulta-neous movement of several flotillas through multiple chokepoints in the first-island chain, have no doubt caused Japanese defence strategists to rethink their posture, which has been historically limited to the near seas of the Japanese home islands. The prospect that Japan might allow itself to be "encircled" by a nuclear-capable rival is clearly not a strategically acceptable proposition.[70] Japan has mitigated the threat of encirclement by updating its monitoring, surveillance, and control infra-structure in the East China Sea.[71] But the combination of lack of strategic depth and

118 *Kerry Lynn Nankivell*

intense reliance on sea lanes for economic existence make mobility at sea an existential matter for Tokyo. Faced with this reality, it is only logical that Tokyo should seek to expand its own reach at sea, both to demonstrate operational capability as well as to strengthen maritime partnerships in other ocean areas.

It should not be surprising, then, that Japan took advantage of Beijing's deteriorating relationships with its South China Sea rivals to expand its activities in China's southern backyard. In 2014, as China engaged in large-scale land reclamation projects in the Spratly Islands and alarmed its neighbours, Japan took on newly active engagement with China's most active rivals. In so doing, Japan takes on additional risk: both the strategic risk associated with the potential deterioration of Sino-Japanese relations, and also the operational risk of unintended confrontation. This assumption of risk is only explained as an expansion of the East China Sea rivalry as Japan came under threat from newly demonstrated Chinese capabilities. After 2010, diplomatic incidents at the ARF and in the JCG ramming prompted Tokyo to layer its South China Sea engagement with FON diplomacy. After 2013, the demonstration of new Chinese operational capabilities in both seas prompted an additional layer of naval operational response by Tokyo. These operations were foreshadowed in the Japanese National Defence Program Guidelines in 2010, in which Tokyo committed to strengthening ties with other US-allied forces.[72] They were not put into practice, however, until new and impressive capabilities were put on display by the Chinese in both the East and South China Seas.

In the most evident manifestation of that claim, Japan–Philippines relations hit new highs in 2015–2016. In May 2015, the MSDF sent two frigates to exercise with the Philippine Navy in waters near the Scarborough Shoal; in June, Tokyo deployed a single maritime patrol aircraft to exercise search-and-rescue techniques with the armed forces of the Philippines. Immediately complementing these two exercises, during a state visit to Tokyo by Filipino President Benigno Aquino III, Japanese officials confirmed that the two governments would start negotiations for the transfer of military equipment. At the same time, President Aquino indicated that he and Prime Minister Abe had further agreed to negotiation of a Status of Forces Agreement (SOFA), an instrument that would allow Japan access to Filipino military facilities for refuelling and joint exercises. While no further progress appears to have yet been made on the SOFA, the equipment transfers have been confirmed. In mid-2015, Tokyo announced the provision of ten new patrol vessels for the Philippine Coast Guard. The 44-foot ships are suited to high-seas patrol, a new capability for Philippine law enforcement. The package, funded by low-interest loans provided by the Japan International Cooperation Agency,[73] complements the increased tempo of joint exercising that JCG already conducts with its Philippine counterpart.[74] By mid-2016, the commitment was expanded to include two additional larger patrol ships and up to five TC-90 surveillance aircraft.[75] There seems no doubt that, as Renato Cruz De Castro notes, "both countries are determined to pursue strategic partnership".[76] Of course, the impact that this new partnership will have on China's strategic options in the disputes will depend in large part on how fruitful it proves to be. The long history of US–Philippines partnership seems neither to have constrained China's active pursuit of its claims vis-à-vis Manila,

Rivalry in the East and South China Seas 119

nor to have resulted in a strong maritime capability in the Philippines. Whether Japan will have more success at achieving one of these two goals remains an open question, but that it is pursuing that goal is becoming more obvious.

Cooperation at sea between Japan and Vietnam has moved more cautiously, but maintains steady momentum in the wake of China's rejection of the tribunal ruling in 2016. As with the Philippines, the first signal of closer ties came during a visit by Prime Minister Kan Naoto in October 2010 and the announcement of a "strategic partnership" between the two countries. One should not overestimate the relative significance of this development. Vietnam enjoys many "strategic partnerships" around Asia, and reserves its highest designation, the "comprehensive strategic partnership", for Russia and China.[77] Inclusion of Japan as a strategic partner signals the intent to deepen Japan–Vietnam relations as a means of mitigating their relations with Beijing, especially vis-à-vis maritime issues. This partnership will no doubt be used in specific and limited ways, like capacity-building and facilitating Japan's South China Sea presence. This already includes new patrol ships sold to Vietnam through Japanese low-interest financing,[78] adding to the transfer of six used patrol vessels in 2015.[79] The partnership has already facilitated increased Japanese presence in the South China Sea, including through joint exercises,[80] planned port calls by MSDF vessels, and refuelling stops for Japanese maritime patrol aircraft at Cam Ranh Bay.[81] The latter two moves position Japan to conduct FON operations in either the Spratly or Paracel Islands. This kind of operational assertion would make good on the Abe administration's FON diplomacy and leverage the Japan–Vietnam partnership to counter China's South China Sea claims. Safeguarding FON, compliance with UNCLOS, and the peaceful resolution of disputes are all listed among the common interests underpinning the Japan–Vietnam partnership.[82]

Thus far, there is no evidence to suggest that China is directly countering Japan's operational activities in the South China Sea. There are no open reports of Chinese approaching or issuing warnings to any Japanese platforms operating there, though this is a common occurrence in the East China Sea. Moreover, though there is surely a lot of diplomacy happening behind closed doors, there are no accounts that suggest that Beijing has explicitly sought to curtail or counter Japan's ongoing ODA assistance to rival claimants. As with the other two strands of Japan's emerging South China Sea policy, Beijing has thus far limited itself to government statements warning Japan to avoid interfering or "creating tension" in the South China Sea through military presence.[83] Direct operational confrontation between Chinese and Japanese vessels or aircraft in the South China Sea would be an important milestone in the incorporation of Sino-Japanese rivalry into the South China Sea disputes and the establishment of a robust East Asian multiplex. At the time of writing, this remains a milestone not yet crossed.

Collapsing regional worlds: Sino-Japan relations and the South China Sea disputes

The policy conclusions that result from an interlinkage between the East and South China Seas are substantively different than those that assume that Sino-Japanese

120 *Kerry Lynn Nankivell*

rivalry is contained to the East China Sea. While both might induce Tokyo to make increased investments in its national defence, only the former circumstance impels the more activist Japan outside of Northeast Asia that has been on display in recent years.[84] The strength of this volume's central argument, that Sino-Japanese rivalry is an important driver of regional security dynamics, stands or falls in the maritime context on whether or not one can demonstrate that Tokyo has taken on a deliberately activist engagement with the South China Sea disputes to mitigate the risk presented by China in the East China Sea. As this chapter uncovered, the balance of evidence suggests that this is increasingly true. Working from within a tradition of functionally based diplomatic engagement, Japan has layered normative FON diplomacy and operational cooperation onto its South China Sea policy. In making the case that the Sino-Japanese rivalry plays an important role in the South China Sea, the most significant of these layers is Japan's increased willingness to insert itself operationally into the South China Sea. Beyond the empirical fact of increased Japanese military and paramilitary engagement with these contested waters and its rivals, this development is notable for two reasons. In the first instance, they have happened rather more quickly than most would have projected only a short decade ago. Recall the difficult debates that the popular Prime Minister Koizumi Junichiro had to endure over the MSDF refuelling mission to the Indian Ocean. Indeed, the Japanese public's distaste for the expeditionary role that the MSDF played in that mission foreshadowed things to come: the resignation of Prime Minister Fukuda Yasuo less than a year later was in part attributed to intense controversy over his party's "global diplomatic and security ambitions".[85] True, the Japanese public continues to be uneasy about conventional military roles, but that uneasiness has not precluded any of the South China Sea activities already discussed from moving forward. Large-scale protests held in Tokyo throughout the summer of 2015 are perhaps misleading. Despite the public protests, a survey conducted by *Asahi* in November of that year suggests that 58 per cent of the Japanese public "welcomed passage of the change [enacted by the new security law]", while only 27 per cent did not.[86] Fast-moving changes to Japan's behaviour as a stakeholder and security provider in Southeast Asia can be anticipated.

Japan's increasingly confident engagement with the South China Sea disputes is also notable because it represents an important evolution in Japan's approach to security cooperation. While in the past Tokyo has preferred to stay in the background, choosing most often to act as an enabler of regional coast guards and maritime authorities, today Tokyo is shifting course to become a "normal" security partner. The 2015 modifications to Japan's ODA Charter to allow "strategic use" of development funding for military organizations are an indication of this trend, and prospective deals with Vietnam and Malaysia were already being discussed by mid-2016.[87] In Malaysia's case, Japan confirmed the transfer of two patrol vessels to Malaysia Maritime Enforcement Agency (MMEA) in November 2016.[88] Adding joint exercises and periodic patrol of disputed areas to Japan's traditional capacity-building activities is also a significant change in government policy. Theoretically, in determining how best to exert influence on developments in the South China

Sea, Tokyo has many options. Scaling up its development assistance to regional coast guards, for example, or providing more training opportunities in Japan to those organizations, might have been less notable. Instead, Japan has signalled that it intends to offer direct military assistance and Japanese presence to China's rivals in the South China Sea. Demonstrating willingness to "show up" in the South China Sea will bring a certain measure of regional confidence in Japan, where before there was uncertainty about its role. This is a qualitative shift in the strategic environment and will no doubt eventually attract stronger reactions from Beijing. Indeed, China's muted reactions to Japan's increased South China Sea involvement are the primary bulwark against full integration of the East and South China Seas' RSOs. A continued permissive approach to Japanese presence in South China Sea is the best means Beijing has to segregate these two maritime regions and will likely remain Beijing's preference for as long as the policy remains tenable. For now, Beijing seems to prefer to confine its assertive approaches to Japan to the East China Sea. For example, following the Arbitral Tribunal award in 2016, China did not stiffen its opposition to Japanese activities in Southeast Asia, but did challenge Japan's administration of the Senkaku/Diaoyu Islands by sailing more than 230 fishing vessels and seven China Coast Guard ships to disputed waters. Japanese sources also reported China's installation of a radar system on one of its oil platforms near the median line between Japan and China.[89] Conversely, diffusion of tensions in the South China Sea as a result of a rapprochement led by Philippine President Rodrigo Duterte in October was coincident with the resumption of bilateral maritime talks between Japan and China in December.[90] Whether positive or negative, the emerging trend appears to be that China responds to Japanese behaviour in Southeast Asia by applying more pressure in the East China Sea. This strategy enables Beijing to undertake assertive action in the face of a changing Japanese approach to regional maritime security, while also maintaining a degree of operational segregation between the two spaces. Segregation, of course, works to Beijing's advantage. Enmeshment of the two might invite coalition-building among China's many rival claimants.

All this taken into account, it would be remiss to consider the extension of the Sino-Japanese rivalry into the waters of the South China Sea without acknowledging the role of the US. Since 2010, the US has made its "core interest" in FON in the South China Sea very clear. It has continued to exert influence on China and the other claimants in its own right. It also has sought to influence the South China Sea through its alliance with Japan, including through coordination of senior leader statements at important regional forums[91] and staging exercises, as noted above. But at the same time, relegating Japan to an instrument of Washington's China policy is a vast oversimplification. Indeed, there is a reasonable case to be made that this kind of behaviour cuts both ways: one might also say that Japanese policy instrumentalizes the US–Japan alliance to achieve its own regional aims.[92] Japan has its own strategic relationship with Beijing and, as this analysis has shown, works quite independently to advance its interests in that relationship into the waters of the South China Sea. But there is some interesting work to be done to answer the question of how Japan's management of its rivalry with China both impacts and is

122   Kerry Lynn Nankivell

impacted by its alliance with the US. That work is beyond the scope of this chapter, but will be an important element of any eventual East Asian security multiplex.

We can conclude, with all caveats made, that Sino-Japanese rivalry is already observable in the South China Sea disputes in important ways, and that many indicators suggest that it will grow over time in line with Chinese maritime capabilities. If Japan continues to use its considerable seapower – which includes not only the MSDF but its JCG and ODA funding too – to exert influence over the security environment in the South China Sea, it will mean the end of China's position as the central fulcrum of the East Asian littoral. For much of the post- Second World War period, China operated in both the East and South China Seas against its rival claimants, which were themselves isolated from one another. The entry of Japan into the South China Sea and the collapsing of the two regional RSOs into a single East Asian multiplex will come at China's expense. Beijing will no longer be able to drive strategic dynamics in each sub-regional ocean basin without taking sober account of what opportunities its actions might provide to Japan's engagement with Southeast Asian rival claimants. Given the complexities already at play in China's South China Sea policies, Japan's increasing presence on its southern shore will be a difficult reality for Beijing. For Japan, increased involvement in the South China Sea disputes will come at some risk: as a stakeholder without a direct claim, it has more to lose than to gain through violent encounters with the PLA(N) in the South China Sea. But so long as Tokyo sees China's East and South China Sea strategies as two parts of a whole, it may prefer to assume those risks at some distance from its home turf. If so, Japan will likely work to make Sino-Japanese rivalry more pronounced in the South China Sea. This approach will make life more difficult for Beijing, while also insulating Japan's own disputed territories and jurisdictions from Beijing's exclusive focus. And of course, robust Sino-Japanese rivalry will make the South China Sea more dangerous than ever before, raising the stakes of regional confrontation between China and those that seek to limit its ambitions at sea.

Notes

1 See Chapter 1, p. 2.
2 Amitav Acharya, "Global International Relations (IR) and Regional Worlds: A New Agenda for International Studies", *International Studies Quarterly*, 58:4 (2014), 653. Acharya suggests that the emergence of a security "multiplex" for IR requires scholars to "give more play to regions, regional powers, and regionalisms than the American-led order". This volume answers that suggestion. See also Amitav Acharya, *The End of American World Order* (Cambridge: Polity Press, 2014).
3 Paul Midford argues that Japan "refrained from even discussing security with Southeast Asian nations, multilaterally as well as bilaterally" until the end of the Cold War. See Paul Midford, "Japan's Approach to Maritime Security in the South China Sea", *Asian Survey*, 55:3 (2015), 529.
4 European powers largely ignored the features of the South China Sea, documenting them as navigational hazards, not strategic assets. Kerry Lynn Nankivell, "The Stories Nations Tell: In Three Voices", *Asian Security*, 11:1 (2015), 93.
5 For one treatment of this controversial history, see Bill Hayton, *The South China Sea: The Struggle for Power in Asia* (New Haven: Yale University Press, 2014), ch. 1.

Rivalry in the East and South China Seas 123

6 Leonard Blusse, "Gang Zhao: The Qing Opening to the Ocean – Chinese Maritime Policies, 1684–1757", *The American Historical Review*, 119:3 (2014), 868.
7 For a good discussion of the origins of the Fukuda doctrine and its implications for contemporary Japan–ASEAN relations, see Lam Peng Er, *Japan's Relations with Southeast Asia: The Fukuda Doctrine and Beyond* (Abingdon: Routledge, 2013).
8 Euan Graham, *Japan's Sea Lane Security, 1940–2004: A Matter of Life and Death?* [e-book] (Taylor & Francis: 2005), 149. Chapter 6 in Graham's volume considers the evolution of this non-military approach to securing commercial access to Southeast Asia's sea lanes.
9 Midford, "Japan's Approach", 528.
10 For a full consideration of China and Japan's joint management of their strategic rivalry in the East China Sea, see James Manicom, *Bridging Troubled Waters: China, Japan and the Maritime Order in the East China Sea* (Washington, DC: Georgetown University Press, 2014).
11 The conclusion that US and Japanese governments understood the latency of the Senkaku disputes, including its legal, military, and political implications, at least from 1895 is strongly suggested, but not entirely substantiated in Robert D. Eldridge, *The Origins of U.S. Policy in the East China Sea Islands Dispute: Okinawa's Reversion and the Senkaku Islands* (New York: Routledge, 2014).
12 Writing in 1996, Lam Peng Er explained Japan's quiet acceptance of Chinese aggression in the South China Sea in 1974 and 1988, noting that Tokyo viewed both incidents as symptomatic of the Hanoi–Beijing Cold War-era rivalry, not as Chinese "expansionism", and therefore unrelated to its own disputes with China in the East China Sea. Lam Peng Er, "Japan and the Spratlys Dispute: Aspirations and Limitations", *Asian Survey*, 36:10 (1996), 1000.
13 In 2015, China's overseas trade in all sectors placed it first in global rankings. WTOStat, "China", 2014, http://stat.wto.org/CountryProfile/WSDBCountryPFView.aspx?Country=CN&. Beijing's shipping registry (including Hong Kong) accounts for approximately 13 per cent of the global fleet, and China is the site of six of the world's top ten container ports. Altogether, Chinese ports handle almost six times as many containers as the second-ranked national handler (more than 181 million TEUs to Singapore's 34 million). UNCTADStat, "Merchant Fleet by Flag of Registration and by Type of Ship, 1990–2015", http://unctadstat.unctad.org/wds/TableViewer/tableView.aspx; UNCTAD Review of Maritime Transport, 2014, 67–69, http://unctad.org/en/PublicationsLibrary/rmt2015_en.pdf. As of 2015, China still takes the most orders for new builds in the shipping market, despite large year-on-year declines since 2013. "China's Shipbuilding Sector Sees 26% Decline in New Orders in 2015: Bancosta", *Platts*, February 2, 2016, www.platts.com/latest-news/shipping/london/chinas-shipbuilding-sector-sees-26 -decline-in-26356173.
14 Whether these changes are "evolution" or "revolution" remains the subject of some discussion. For the "evolution" view, see, *inter alia*, Jeffrey W. Hornung, "Japan's Security Policies as Pragmatic Response to Changing Asia", *World Politics Review*, October 3, 2013, www.worldpoliticsreview.com/articles/13268/japan-s-security-policies-a-pragmatic-response-to-changing-asia; Brendan Howe and Joel Campbell, "Continuity and Change: Evolution, Not Revolution, in Japan's Foreign and Security Policy Under the DPJ", *Asian Perspectives*, 37:1 (2013), 99–123; and with specific reference to the South China Sea, Midford, "Japan's Approach". For a recent analysis that argues that Japanese policy has undergone "quick" and "significant transformation", see Ji Young Kim, "Dismantling the Final Barrier: Transforming Japan into a 'Normal' Country in the Post-Cold War Era", *Pacific Focus*, 16:3 (2015), 223–248. Earlier works discussing Japan's transformation in revolutionary terms include Kenneth B. Pyle, *Japan Rising: The Resurgence of Japanese Power and Purpose* (New York: The Century Foundation, 2007) and Christopher W. Hughes, *Japan's Remilitarization* (Abingdon: Routledge, 2009).

124 *Kerry Lynn Nankivell*

15 The most prominent include Prime Minister Koizumi's authorization of refuelling missions in the Indian Ocean in support of coalition operations in Afghanistan and Iraq, and ongoing support for anti-piracy efforts in the Gulf of Aden. Expeditionary missions undertaken by the MSDF were deeply politicized in Japan, and eventually contributed to the defeat of the Aso government in legislative elections in August 2009. Michael J. Green, "U.S.–Japan Relations: Traversing a Rough Patch", *Comparative Connections*, 10:4 (2009).

16 It is common for Western analysts to make no geographical distinction between the East and South China Seas in Chinese strategy, applying the blanket characterization of A2/AD to the area "within the first-island chain", which encompasses both semi-enclosed seas. See Lowell Dittmer, "China's New Asia Policy", *China: An International Journal*, 12:2 (2014), 116–117.

17 Denny Roy, "China Wins the Gray Zone by Default", *PacNet*, 60, September 17, 2015, www.csis.org/analysis/pacnet-60-china-wins-gray-zone-default.

18 Barry Buzan and Ole Wæver, *Regions and Powers: The Structure of International Security* (Cambridge: Cambridge University Press, 2003). Buzan and Wæver do discuss super-power penetration of regional complexes here, but remain stuck on the relationship between the regional and the global so evident during the Cold War. Acharya's suggestion that two sub-regional complexes might mingle or eventually converge is a related but distinct observation.

19 Acharya. "Global International Relations", 649.

20 Zachary Keck, "China Warns Japan to Stay out of South China Sea", *The National Interest*, June 12, 2015, http://nationalinterest.org/blog/the-buzz/china-warns-japan-stay-out-south-china-sea-13102.

21 "Beijing's South China Sea Claims Scrutinized at Summit", *Al Jazeera*, September 8, 2016, www.aljazeera.com/news/2016/09/south-china-sea-row-overshadows-asean-summit-160907051502873.html.

22 "Overview", Defense White Paper 2015, Ministry of Defence, Japan, December 22, 2015, 5, www.mod.go.jp/e/publ/w_paper/pdf/2015/DOJ2015_1-1-0_web.pdf.

23 H.E. Mr. Shinzo Abe, Prime Minister of Japan, cited in Ian Storey, "Japan's Maritime Security Interests in Southeast Asia and the South China Sea Dispute", *Political Science* 65:2 (2013), 146.

24 Hiro Katsumara, "Establishment of the ASEAN Regional Forum: Constructing a 'Talking Shop' or a Norm Brewery?", *The Pacific Review*, 19:2 (2006), 181–198.

25 Fig. 2-1-3 in Part II, "Chapter 2: Japan's Security and Defense Policy and the Japan–U.S. Alliance", Defence White Paper 2015, 155, www.mod.go.jp/e/publ/w_paper/pdf/2015/DOJ2015_2-2-1_web.pdf.

26 See Seng Tan, "Asian Multilateralism in an Age of Japan's 'New Normal': Perils and Prospects", *Japanese Journal of Political Science*, 16:3 (2015), 296–314, particularly 301–306.

27 Japan Policy Report on the State of the Concept of the East Asian Community and Japan's Strategic Response, cited in Dinh Thi Hien Luong, "Vietnam–Japan Relations in the Context of Building an East Asian Community", *Asia-Pacific Review*, 16:1 (2009), 100, 106.

28 Tan, "Asian Multilateralism", 302.

29 Midford, "Japan's Approach", 530.

30 Tan, "Asian Multilateralism", 304.

31 H.E. Mr. Junichiro Koizumi cited in Dinh, "Vietnam–Japan Relations", 107.

32 Midford, "Japan's Approach", 533.

33 Ronald A. LaBrec, "U.S. Coast Guard Unveils a New Model for Cooperation Atop the World", *Defense in Depth*, November 2, 2015, http://blogs.cfr.org/davidson/2015/11/02/u-s-coast-guard-unveils-a-new-model-for-cooperation-on-top-of-the-world.

34 Midford, "Japan's Approach", 534.

35 Personal communications with US and Australian officials, 2016.

Rivalry in the East and South China Seas 125

36 Joshua Ho, "Combating Piracy and Armed Robbery in Asia: The ReCAAP Information Sharing Center (ISC)", *Marine Policy*, 33:2 (2009), 433.

37 Storey, "Japan's Maritime Security", 141.

38 Ibid., 151.

39 Author's notes, Expanded ASEAN Maritime Forum 2015, Manado, Indonesia, September 9–11, 2015.

40 This was reportedly one of Japan's intended outcomes in the creation of the ARF. Tan, "Asian Multilateralism", 302.

41 Ibid. Japanese officials went to great lengths to ensure that China agreed to participate in both the ARF and the ADMM+ processes, despite Chinese reluctance to multilateralize security issues.

42 Foreign Broadcast Information Service (FBIS), December 13, 2004 cited in Midford, "Japan's Approach", 535.

43 "Japan Arranged a Maritime Countries Conference", China News Review Agency, October 20, 2013, www.zhgpl.com/doc/1027/7/3/9/102773950.html?coluid=1&kindid =0&docid=102773950&mdate=1020000050

44 Isabel Reynolds, "Japan's Abe Meets China's Li as Maritime Tensions Flare", *Chicago Tribune*, July 15, 2016, www.chicagotribune.com/news/sns-wp-blm-china-sea-3a4b f072-4a76-11e6-8dac-0c6e4accc5b1-20160715-story.html.

45 Sheila Smith. "Japan and the East China Sea Dispute", *Orbis*, 56:3 (2012), 378.

46 Ibid., 373.

47 National Security Strategy (NSS) of Japan, 18, cited in Emi Mifune, "Impact of the American 'Re-Balance' Strategy on Japanese Naval Power", in Greg Kennedy and Harsh V. Pant, eds, *Assessing Maritime Power in the Asia-Pacific: The Impact of American Strategic Re-Balance* (Aldershot: Ashgate, 2015), 145.

48 *East Asian Strategic Review 2010*, chapter 4: "China: Toward a Less Cooperative, More Assertive Posture", 3, www.nids.go.jp/english/publication/east-asian/pdf/2011/east-asian_e2011_04.pdf. Emphasis added. Published in the first half of 2011, the use of the adjective "new" to describe the American interest in FON is undoubtedly a reaction to the Clinton statement at the ARF Summit. FON has in fact been a preeminent US national interest for decades.

49 Gordon Chang, "Hillary Clinton Changes America's China Policy", *Forbes*, July 28, 2010, www.forbes.com/ 2010/07/28/china-beijing-asia-hillary-clinton-opinions-columnists-gordon-g-chang.html.

50 Ibid.

51 Chairman's Statement, 17th ASEAN Regional Forum, July 23, 2013, http://aseanregional forum.asean.org/files/library/ARF%20Chairman's%20Statements%20and%20 Reports/The%20Seventeenth%20ASEAN%20Regional%20Forum,%202009-2010/ ARF%2017%20Chairmans%20Statement%20-%20Final%20(rev.%20on%20 title%20year).pdf.

52 Tetsuo Kotani, "Freedom of Navigation and the US–Japan Alliance: Addressing the Threat of Legal Warfare", US–Japan Papers, Japan Center for International Exchange, December 2011, 4, www.jcie.org/researchpdfs/USJapanPapers/Kotani.pdf .

53 For a fuller discussion of the statements made at the 2010 ASEAN Summit in Hanoi and ensuing diplomacy, see "Stirring Up the South China Sea (I)", Crisis Group Asia Report No. 233, April 23, 2012, 3–7, www.crisisgroup.org/~/media/Files/asia/north-east-asia/223-stirring-up-the-south-china-sea-i.pdf.

54 For example, use of ODA to provide training and/or technical expertise through ASEAN to improve Southeast Asia's capacity for environmental stewardship and safety of sea lanes. See Dinh, "Vietnam–Japan Relations", 110.

55 H.E. Mr. Shinzo Abe, cited in Storey, "Japan's Maritime Security", 150.

56 Ibid., 150.

57 H.E. Mr. Shinzo Abe, Prime Minister of Japan, "Japan and ASEAN, Always in Tandem: Towards a More Advantageous Win–Win Relationship Through My 'Three Arrows'",

126 *Kerry Lynn Nankivell*

33rd Singapore Lecture (Provisional Translation), July 26, 2013, 5, www.mofa.go.jp/mofaj/press/enzetsu/25/pdfs/pm_ja_130726_en.pdf.

58 Ibid.

59 "Freedom of Navigation Pits Japan, U.S. Against China", *Asahi Shimbun*, December 26, 2013, http://ajw.asahi.com/article/behind_news/politics/AJ201312260024.

60 H.E. Mr. Shinzo Abe, Prime Minister of Japan, "Peace and Prosperity in Asia, Forever More: Japan for the Rule of Law, Asia for the Rule of Law, And the Rule of Law for All of Us", Keynote Address to the 13th IISS Asian Security Summit – the Shangri-La Dialogue, May 30, 2014, www.mofa.go.jp/fp/nsp/page4e_000086.html.

61 The Communication Mechanism was conceived as a Sino-Japanese crisis communication link to mitigate the risk of escalation of an unintended encounter at sea. It has been under negotiation in some form since 2008, but has not been operationalized. For a fuller discussion, see James Przystup, John Bradford, and James Manicom, "Japan–China Maritime Confidence Building and Communication Mechanisms", *PacNet*, 67, August 20, 2013, http://csis.org/files/publication/Pac1367.pdf. Also Mina Pollman, "Can Japan and China Ever Finish Their Maritime Communications Negotiation?", *The Diplomat*, November 12, 2015, http://thediplomat.com/2015/11/can-japan-and-china-ever-finish-their-maritime-communication-negotiations.

62 Abe, "Peace and Prosperity".

63 Citing the *East Asia Strategic Review* (2007), Ian Storey concludes that state-affiliated Japanese analysts took a "benign, even positive, view of China–Southeast Asia relations". This period marked the late stages of Beijing's "charm offensive" in Southeast Asia. Storey, "Japan's Maritime Security", 143.

64 Franz Stephan-Gady, "China is on 'High Alert' for Japan's 'Intervention' in South China Sea", *The Diplomat*, November 21, 2015, http://thediplomat.com/2015/11/china-is-on-high-alert-for-japans-intervention-in-south-china-sea.

65 Ibid.

66 *East Asian Strategic Review* (2013), National Institute for Defense Studies, 116, www.nids.go.jp/english/publication/east-asian/pdf/2013/east-asian_e2013_03.pdf.

67 Andrew Bergland, "'Maneuver-5' Exercise Focuses on Improving Distant Seas Capability", U.S.–China Economic and Security Review Commission, Staff Report, December 16, 2013, 3.

68 David Lague, "Special Report: China's Navy Breaks Out to the High Seas", *Reuters*, November 28, 2013, www.reuters.com/article/us-china-navy-specialreport-idUSBRE9AQ04220131128.

69 David Lague, "Japan Pivots to Counter Chinese Navy", *Reuters*, November 26, 2013, www.reuters.com/article/us-china-navy-japan-idUSBRE9AQ04820131127?mod=related&channelName=asia.

70 US Pacific Command Commander, ADM Samuel Locklear testified to Congress that US naval intelligence estimates that China currently operates three *Jin*-class submarines already, capable of carrying the JL-2 submarine-launched ballistic missiles (SLBMs). He reported that US PACOM expected nuclear deterrent patrols to begin in late 2015, giving China an at-sea nuclear strike capability. Richard D. Fisher, "US Upgrades Assessment of China's Type 094 SSBN Fleet", *IHS Jane's 360*, April 19, 2015, www.janes.com/article/50761/us-upgrades-assessment-of-china-s-type-094-ssbn-fleet.

71 "Japan, U.S. Running Undersea Listening Post to Detect Chinese Subs", *The Japan Times*, September 15, 2015, www.japantimes.co.jp/news/2015/09/10/national/japan-u-s-running-undersea-listening-post-detect-chinese-subs/#.V9CjCZjr17g.

72 "National Defense Program Guidelines", Ministry of Defense, December 17, 2010, 8, www.mod.go.jp/e/d_act/d_policy/pdf/guidelinesFY2011.pdf.

73 Sekiguchi Toko, "Japan to Provide Patrol Vessels to Philippines", *Wall Street Journal*, June 4, 2015, www.wsj.com/articles/japan-to-provide-patrol-vessels-to-philippines-1433424771.

Rivalry in the East and South China Seas 127

74 The Philippines announced the acquisition of 100 new vessels, 27 of which are expected to be capable of high-seas operation in mid-2015. This would vastly increase the Philippines' Coast Guard capability, whose current fleet stands at 20 vessels. See Praseth Parameswaran, "Philippines Buys 100 New Vessels for War on Poaching", *The Diplomat*, June 24, 2015, http://thediplomat.com/2015/06/philippines-buys-100-new-patrol-boats-for-war-on-poaching.

75 "Japan to Provide Planes, Ships for Philippines Amid Sea Dispute with China", *Reuters*, September 6, 2016, http://af.reuters.com/article/energyOilNews/idAFL3N1BI2OE.

76 Renato Cruz De Castro, "Philippines and Japan Strengthen a Twenty-First Century Security Partnership", *Asia Maritime Transparency Initiative*, December 17, 2015, http://amti.csis.org/philippines-and-japan-strengthen-a-twenty-first-century-security-partnership.

77 Bill Hayton, *Vietnam and the United States: An Emerging Security Partnership* (Sydney: The United States Studies Center at the University of Sydney, 2015), http://ussc.edu.au/ussc/assets/media/docs/publications/Emerging-Asia-Reports/MacArthur-Vietnam-ONLINE.pdf

78 "Japan to Provide Patrol Ships to Vietnam Amid Maritime row with China", *Reuters*, September 7, 2016, www.reuters.com/article/us-asean-summit-japan-vietnam-idUSK CN11D2CB.

79 Murray Hiebert and Phuong Nguyen, "Vietnam Ramps Up Defence Spending, but its Challenges Remain", *Asia Maritime Transparency Initiative*, March 18, 2015, https://amti.csis.org/vietnam-ramps-up-defense-spending-but-its-challenges-remain.

80 "Japan's Maritime Force Conducts Joint Drills with Vietnam's Navy in South China Sea Base", *South China Morning Post*, February 18, 2016, www.scmp.com/news/asia/east-asia/article/1913923/japans-maritime-force-conducts-joint-drills-vietnams-navy-south.

81 Prasanth Parameswaran, "Japan Eyes Bigger South China Sea Presence in 2016", *The Diplomat*, January 12, 2016, http://thediplomat.com/2016/01/japan-eyes-bigger-south-china-sea-presence-in-2016.

82 Storey, "Japan's Maritime Security", 155.

83 "China Urges U.S., Japan not to Flex Military Muscle on South China Sea", *Xinhua*, November 26, 2015, http://english.chinamil.com.cn/news-channels/china-military-news/2015-11/26/content_6787705.htm.

84 For one consideration of what such a strategy and posture would look like, see Captain Takuya Shimodaira, "The Japan Maritime Self Defense Force in the Age of Multilateral Cooperation", *Naval War College Review*, 67:2 (2014), 52–68.

85 David Pilling and Michiyo Nakamoto, "Fukuda Stuns Own party with his Resignation", *Financial Times*, September 2, 2008, www.ft.com/cms/s/0/92469e96-7886-11dd-acc3-0000779fd18c.html#axzz3x9ziYqWg.

86 "Japan PM's Support Rebounds After Difficult Debate over Security Laws", *Asia Times*, November 29, 2015, http://atimes.com/2015/11/japan-pms-support-rebounds-after-difficult-debate-over-security-laws.

87 "Japan to Provide Patrol Ships to Vietnam".

88 "Japan giving two coast guard boats to Malaysia", *Straits Times*, 15 November, 2016, http://www.straitstimes.com/asia/east-asia/japan-giving-two-coast-guard-boats-to-malaysia.

89 "Over the Line: Tracking Energy Competition in the East China Sea", *Asia Maritime Transparency Initiative*, October 14, 2016, https://amti.csis.org/energy-competition-east-china-sea.

90 Oki Nagai, "Japan, China Rekindle Defense Talks, Seek Maritime Security", *Nikkei Asian Review*, November 29, 2016, http://asia.nikkei.com/Politics-Economy/International-Relations/Japan-China-rekindle-defense-talks-seek-maritime-security.

91 Storey, "Japan's Maritime Security", 155.

92 For a discussion of the importance of the alliance to the achievement of Japan's aims in East Asia, particularly vis-à-vis China, see Shimodaira, "Age of Multilateral Cooperation".

7 From backdoor to bridge

Japan as a Western power in cyberspace

Lora Saalman

Japan represents a geographic paradox within China. It is an Asian power that has similar linguistic and cultural roots. And yet, Japan's political system, economic ascent, and military actions during the Second World War have bound it within Chinese consciousness as a power marked by behaviour and norms historically attributed to Western powers.[1] While decades old, Chinese views on Tokyo as a Western capital are reemerging in one of the most modern domains, namely cyberspace.

In cyber security parlance, Chinese analyses indicate that Japan effectively creates a backdoor for Western countries to engage in regional intrusion, establishing network persistence in both lawfare and warfare. They see Tokyo's adherence to Western-centric cyber legal frameworks and military cyber umbrella as the basis for capitals like Washington to dominate the region. This trend complicates Beijing's efforts to solidify deterrence by denial in cyberspace. According to this view, cyberspace is not an amorphous domain, but a territory to be defended.

So while regional security complex theory postulates that Tokyo adds to the complexity of Beijing's environment beyond the US–China paradigm, Chinese narratives interpret Tokyo as a pawn of, or even appendage to, Washington in cyberspace. Facing external intrusions into its networks, more than one-third of Chinese analyses surveyed advocate cyber control (*zhiwang quan*), reflecting a concept often applied in the maritime domain.[2] To better understand this phenomenon, this chapter delves into Chinese perceptions of Japan as both an Asian and Western power and how they shape Sino-Japanese dynamics in cyberspace.

Cyber lawfare

The term "lawfare" is much debated, and yet since the publication of *Unrestricted Warfare* by Chinese People's Liberation Army (PLA) officers in 1999, it has gained currency in describing Beijing's actions from the maritime to the space domain.[3] Today it has crossed into cyberspace. Despite its seeming origin in the East, one of the oft-cited definitions for lawfare comes from a 2001 paper from a Western military scholar, who defines it as "the use or misuse of law as a substitute for traditional military means to accomplish an operational objective".[4] In the past decade, this definition has taken on a more aggressive information warfare-oriented

From backdoor to bridge   129

form. Lawfare is "a weapon designed to destroy the enemy by using, misusing, and abusing the legal system and the media in order to raise a public outcry against that enemy".[5]

Despite the lack of a common definition of lawfare in the West,[6] much less the East, Chinese writings on Japan and cyberspace continue to emphasize the inherent Western nature of Tokyo's cyber legal framework. When referring to Japan's adherence to the Convention on Cybercrime, one Chinese analyst emphasizes that

> the convention primarily reflects the aspirations and interests of developed countries. In many ways, it embodies the values of the European Union and does not take into account the demands and interests of the vast number of developing countries. As such, it suffers significant limitations in the context of a global and diversified Internet.[7]

Through its emphasis on the rights of the individual, protection of personal information, non-intervention, and freedom of speech, Chinese analysts frame Japan as building upon a legal foundation in cyberspace laid by such powers as the US, Canada, and the UK.[8] While these Chinese descriptions do not vilify Japan for its Western approach, they create a paradigm within which Tokyo is once again seen as an anomaly among Asian capitals. To concretize this point, Chinese sources highlight a range of Japanese cyber laws and organizations developed with attention to Western structures between 2000 and 2016. Among these, they emphasize Japan's pursuit of the Unauthorized Computer Access Law in 2000 and Comprehensive Strategy on Information Security in 2003 as indications of its early commitment to the rights of the individual over those of the state.[9]

While some of Japan's laws are contrary to China's domestic cyber governance structure, Chinese analysts do note the value of Japan's success in establishing inclusive governance institutions, like the Information Security Policy Council in 2005. In doing so, they advocate emulating Tokyo's articulation of its (1) national information security strategy; (2) basic principles, national objectives; (3) public–private partnership regulations; (4) public opinion formulation; (5) information security standardization; (6) advanced technology dissemination; (7) central and local government harmonization; and (8) media outreach.[10] However, Beijing's interest is in using the Japanese structure as an example, rather than leveraging it as a normative coordinating mechanism between the two capitals.

Instead, a number of Japan's structures and strategies receive critique within Chinese discourse, in particular for their contents. When it comes to Japan's National Information Security Center's release of its Cyber Security Strategy to lead the world in the active use of cyberspace, Chinese analysts express discomfort at how such documents target Beijing.[11] This widespread view reveals two central insights about Beijing's approach to international cyber governance. The first is that Japan and Washington share a desire to maintain dominance of the cyber domain, at Beijing's expense. The second is that China continues to self-identify as a developing country. Chinese experts argue that despite Beijing's best efforts, it remains a recipient of norms, rather than a shaper of norms, in cyberspace.

130 *Lora Saalman*

As one Chinese analyst observes,

> Recently, the Japanese government has made it clear that [its] goal is to achieve the goal of information technology, to surpass to the United States and the European Union, to again become the most technologically powerful country . . . if we only imitate and borrow other's technology, lack self-driven awareness and efforts, then we will always be in a passive and backward state.[12]

China's perceived gap with Japan and the West drives its demand to keep indigenous capacity growth apace.[13]

Despite these assertions, Chinese perceptions do not appear to reflect reality. External coverage suggests that Tokyo's policy shifts and developments in cyberspace have emerged relatively late and at times after those of Beijing. Formulation and implementation of a legal structure that governs cyberspace has only recently entered the Japanese consciousness. It was only in November 2014 that Japan's Parliament passed the Cyber Security Basic Act, which formalized the National Center of Incident Readiness and Strategy for Cyber Security (NISC).[14] So while the NISC may have been established a decade earlier, its website, cyber security strategy, and incomplete authority over other ministries and agencies indicate that it has only just begun to come into its own.[15]

Moreover, such developments in Japan are dwarfed by the consolidation that has occurred in China since 2013. While in the Japanese case such organizations as the NISC have evolved through layers of rotating and often disinterested government bureaucracy,[16] within China the consolidation of cyberspace and information security since 2013 has been swift and decisive. The Cyberspace Administration of China (CAC) that formed in 2014 is the central internet governance body in China and oversees all dimensions of cyberspace, from economic to military, suggesting a much broader mandate than that of Japan's NISC. So while there is a tendency on the part of Chinese analysts to view Japan as a competitive player in cyberspace, this is far from reality.

China's CAC is not only an institutional departure from the Japanese approach, but has been instrumental in promotion of another key arena in which Beijing and Tokyo seemingly differ, namely cyber sovereignty. Though cyber sovereignty reportedly first appeared in China's 2010 white paper "The Status of China's Internet" and in Chairman Xi Jinping's remarks at the sixth BRICS summit in 2014, it was the Wuzhen World Internet Conference in 2015 that launched the concept into the mainstream.[17] Cyber sovereignty equates with a view that the internet is a reflection of physical space and, hence, a state's sovereign territory. Thus, the internet should not be subject to foreign interference. Each country should have the right to control its domestic cyberspace. In other words, any internet regulation, such as state control over internet content, is justified to defend national territory and sovereignty.

To cement this norm, China is working to establish regulatory institutions and mechanisms to strengthen cyber governance both domestically and abroad.

From backdoor to bridge 131

Beijing's promotion of cyber sovereignty in tandem with its promulgation of the joint Code of Conduct for Information Security at the United Nations in 2011 and 2015 demonstrates Beijing's emphasis on norm creation in cyberspace.[18] The election of Zhao Houlin as Secretary General of the International Telecommunication Union (ITU) at the 2014 ITU Plenipotentiary Conference further facilitates the entrance of Chinese standards into the international sphere. Also, the Cyber Security Association of China formed in 2016 – while seemingly only nationally oriented – has also been tasked with international cyber diplomacy.

In spite of Tokyo's reticence to accept its principles, Beijing has not been alone in its views relating to cyber sovereignty. Trends resonant with the Chinese perspective are emerging in increasingly wide swathes of Asia, including Russia, Thailand, Malaysia, Tajikistan, and Uzbekistan, each of which have their own concerns over internal stability and external interference via information flows in cyberspace. As cyber sovereignty and related trends of territoriality spread throughout the region, it is likely to marginalize Japan even further as a Western power that pursues cyber freedoms over cyber sovereignty. However, there are signs that this trajectory may be shifting. This is occurring not simply at the regional, but also at the international level.

In terms of norms, there are some new mechanisms in cyberspace to which both China and Japan are parties, though even within these, suspicion and important points of disagreement persist. The United Nations Group of Governmental Experts (UNGGE) is one of the more integral of these. It is representative of not just East and West, but also North and South. In their fourth report in 2015, 20 participating countries that represent all regions of the globe have agreed upon new norms and principles.[19] While still generalized in coverage, this UNGGE report and its follow-on iterations have the potential to contribute to both strategic restraint and best practices, including prohibitions on the use of information communication technologies (ICTs) to damage critical infrastructure or other states' emergency response teams.

Though both Japan and China support the UNGGE's work, divisions between them shape its work as it moves from broad policy to tactical, implementable provisions. Indeed, the 2015 UNGGE report is noteworthy in that it makes specific provisions for supply chain security, prevention of the proliferation of malicious ICTs, human rights on the internet, rights to privacy, as well as information exchange and assistance to prosecute terrorist and criminal use of ICTs. These provisions raise important questions about the best means to determine instances when states "conduct or knowingly support" seditious activities. This attribution dilemma, which points to the limitations of forensics and verification, remains paramount in Chinese discussions, and again highlights the state-centric versus individual-centric approaches to cyber governance promoted by China and Japan, respectively.[20] It also further highlights the US role as a dominant cyber ally to such countries as Japan. As long as Japan, in the Chinese view, is co-opted into a larger US-dominated network structure, Tokyo will be viewed as a tool of Washington in future virtual and real conflict scenarios. China believes that the US can conduct intrusions and attacks in cyberspace with impunity, and understands Tokyo's role in global and regional governance frameworks as facilitating that fact.

132   Lora Saalman

Cyber warfare

Much as with the term "lawfare", there remains no internationally accepted definition for "cyber warfare". The closest approximation of a multilateral consensus comes from the Tallinn Manual released in 2013 and its follow-on 2.0 version, to be released in late 2016. It defines a cyberattack as "a cyber operation, whether offensive or defensive, that is reasonably expected to cause injury or death to persons or damage or destruction to objects".[21] Given its Western origin under North Atlantic Treaty Organization (NATO) auspices, however, Chinese analysts often criticize the limitations of the Tallinn Manual.[22] In doing so, their emphasis on cyber sovereignty and information warfare is much more in line with that of Russia and their neighbours.

Still, Beijing and Tokyo are not as conceptually far apart on warfare in cyberspace as they are on its legal foundations. Instead, Chinese analyses reveal viewpoints that tend towards greater complementarity than competition. Rather than stabilizing Sino-Japanese interaction, this trend suggests that similar postures and capabilities may lead to a greater chance of future collision. Chinese writings cite an information warfare policy for Japan that seeks to achieve a multiplier effect by undermining an opponent's situational awareness and information dependence, namely "paralysis warfare" (*tanhuan zhan*).[23] The focus is on destruction of information, rather than lives. When it comes to critical infrastructure, whether civilian or military, the distinction becomes murkier. Chinese descriptions refer to Japan's cyber capabilities as an "assassin's mace" (*shashoujian*), mirroring Chinese descriptions of Beijing's pursuits in advanced technologies and C4ISR.[24] Both countries are driven by a concern over how military operations other than war can be leveraged for advantage beyond the battlefield and into the boardroom.

Beyond the larger strategic level, at the tactical level Chinese discussions of Japan's 2011 Defence White Paper focus on the potential threats of Japan's development of military capabilities for defensive and offensive aims.[25] Similarly, China's official 2015 Defence White Paper emphasizes its own need for a cyber army, stating

> as cyberspace weighs more in military security, China will expedite the development of a cyber force, and enhance its capabilities of cyberspace situational awareness, cyber defense, support for the country's endeavors in cyberspace and participation in international cyber cooperation, so as to stem major cyber crises, ensure national network and information security, and maintain national security and social stability.[26]

While Japan does have some cyber capabilities that give China pause, Beijing remains fixated on the role of Washington.[27] Chinese analysts denounce the level of US influence, under which Japan, Russia, Germany, the UK, France, and India have strengthened their technical research and development in cyberspace, bringing cyber combat and confrontation to new heights. When describing Japan's reportedly 5,000-strong cyberspace defence force (*wangluo kongjian fangwei dui*), these experts describe these troops as an extension of Washington that benefits

From backdoor to bridge   133

from US training and tools.[28] From Duqu to Flame malware, these cyber intrusions and attacks link such capitals as Washington, London, Tel Aviv, and Tokyo, again orienting Japan towards the West, rather than towards the East.[29]

As one Chinese analyst notes,

> In recent years, some western countries, especially the United States and Japan, have used their advanced information network technology to propagandize the so-called "Yellow Peril," "China Threat" and "China Crash," constantly "demonizing" China.[30]

At the political level, this quote typifies an Asian power co-opted by the West to engage in information warfare against Beijing. It also feeds the cyber sovereignty narrative, justifying the argument to close off the Chinese internet and eliminate any possibility that Tokyo might serve as a backdoor to extraregional interference. At the technical level, it explains the pace with which China has been pursuing quantum communications to thwart surveillance. For China, control of its "cyberspace border frontier" (*wangluo bianjie*) is paramount, particularly with the "monopoly" (*longduan*) of the US, Japan, and Australia in internet root servers that field global network traffic flows.[31]

Again contrasting perceptions with reality, Japan's enhanced cooperation with the West in cyberspace stem from some very real concerns. Among the more notable of these hacking incidents, in 2011 Mitsubishi Heavy Industries[32] saw a reported 80 servers connected to various Japanese military programmes breached. More recently, in 2015, Advanced Persistent Threat 30 was discovered to have lasted an estimated ten years in 17 countries. In doing so, it allegedly penetrated the Japanese government, industry, and media to uncover information on such issues as the South China Sea.[33] As the latest in this series, reports emerged in 2016 on Operation Dust Storm that uses spear phishing, waterholes, unique backdoors, and zero-day variants to breach corporate networks and Android-based mobile devices associated with critical infrastructure and resources in Japan.[34]

While Chinese analyses do not tend to provide coverage of the aforementioned cyber incidents, they offer overviews of a variety of other lower-level cyber intrusions that belie their stance on Japan and cyberspace. These discussions emphasize the non-state origins of these cyber intrusions and attacks. Some argue that Japan's own foreign policies and activities, which draw ire from citizenry across the Asian region, are fundamental in eliciting such cyber acts. Among these, Chinese analysts point to the role of patriotic hackers incensed by Japanese prime ministers' visits to the Yasukuni Shrine and Japan's activities in the East China Sea as motivating cyber-attacks against the Japanese National Police Agency, National Defense Agency, and the Ministry of Foreign Affairs, as well as websites considered to support right-wing forces.[35]

These writings condemn the Japanese non-proportional response via the Self-Defense Force reliance on the US military to counter network attacks. They highlight how the US government seeks to integrate network warfare with sea, air, and space as a new field of operations to strengthen the network defence

134　*Lora Saalman*

capabilities of such allies as Japan. And in citing the US–Japan Review Conference decision to expand cooperation on military intelligence networks, some of these Chinese reports focus on both parties' joint exercises to counter simulated cyber-attacks, as with the Yama Sakura 69.[36] When taken in combination with Japan's formation of its "water and land mobile mission" (*shuilu jidongtuan*) in 2014 to establish monitoring bases in the East China Sea, these activities are seen as being worrisome developments for China's own security.[37] In essence, they confirm China's worst-case scenario linkage between Japanese and US threats in the maritime domain and the cyberspace domain.

Most recently and perhaps most tellingly for long-term relations in cyberspace, Chinese analyses are increasingly trained on the 2015 declaration at the US–Japan Cyber Defense Policy Working Group that the US would extend its cyber defence umbrella over Japan, effectively employing a form of extended deterrence. This conceptual framework, analogous to the US–Japan nuclear umbrella, further concretizes a defence relationship that is already viewed as emboldening Tokyo to engage in provocative behaviour under security guarantees from Washington. In light of these shifts and greater tactical and strategic Japan–US collaboration in cyberspace, Chinese analyses advocate enhancement of Beijing's own naval battlefield cyber warfare capability, with the development of advanced combat power network weapons, a variety of hardware and software tools and equipment, and combat command-and-control systems to counter paralysis or destruction.

Throughout these analyses of China's countermeasures, a premium is placed on Beijing's ability to engage in both cyberspace control (*zhiwang quan*) and maritime control (*zhihai quan*).[38] The interplay between these two arenas marks Beijing's own pursuit of deterrence by denial, through (1) its great firewall and quantum communications pursuits in cyberspace, and (2) its anti-access area denial advances and efforts to shape maritime law. In making their case for these cyber lawfare and cyber warfare improvements, Chinese analysts continually cite the ways in which Tokyo has been bolstered by Washington to challenge Beijing's aims in the cyberspace and maritime domains.[39] As long as these perceptions dominate Chinese discourse, Japan will continue to occupy a peripheral and often isolated position as a Western power in Asia.

Conclusion

While complicating Japan's interactions with China, its position between East and West may not be entirely negative. Within Asia, the Japan Computer Emergency Response Team has played a formative role in the secretariat of the Asia-Pacific Computer Emergency Response Team (APCERT). Within Europe and the US, Japan serves as a partner on such initiatives as the Protected Repository for the Defense of Infrastructure Against Cyber Threats project, the Proactive Response Against Cyber-Attacks Through International Collaborative Exchange project implemented by the US Department of Homeland Security and Japan's Ministry of Internal Affairs and Communications, as well as the EU–Japan Cyber Dialogue and EU–Japan ICT Dialogue.[40]

From backdoor to bridge 135

Despite its prominence in both Eastern and Western mechanisms, Chinese analyses continue to portray Japan as out of sync with Asia. They relegate Tokyo to a Western role in cyberspace, particularly in terms of norms, security, and development. Chinese analysts maintain that Washington and Tokyo have the highest level of "information power" (*xinxi shili*), while lamenting China's low level of network development.[41] Yet, perception and reality are once again mismatched. China has its own substantial experience and advances in cyberspace. Beijing's cyber security training and experience in hosting such events as the Olympics in Beijing and the G20 in Hangzhou are enviable in Tokyo, as it ramps up for the 2020 Olympic and Paralympic Games.[42] Indeed, Chinese best practices would also benefit Japan as it develops such government agencies as the Industrial Cyber Security Promotion Agency to protect critical infrastructure from cyber-attacks.[43] Despite this, there is no evidence that China sees itself as the more experienced player in the Sino-Japanese dyad, and this self-perception plays an important role in feeding a competitive dynamic in cyber affairs between Asia's two leading powers.

Should perceptions shift, cooperative exchange of best practices in the cyber domain would expand upon the tactical work already conducted under the China–Japan–Korea trilateral framework, laying the groundwork for more substantive strategic and normative discussions on cyberspace within Asia. Within their latest meetings in 2015, the three capitals have been at the forefront of recommending confidence-building measures, cyber strategies and policies, international norms, as well as possible areas of trilateral cooperation that expand beyond computer emergency response team meetings and cybercrime director workshops. The triumvirate has also expressed support for the 2015 UNGGE consensus report on rules and norms of state behaviour, application of international laws, and confidence- and capacity-building in cyberspace.[44]

Such integrative efforts suggest that while Japan is still largely isolated from Asia within Chinese discourse, at the substantive level it is being increasingly drawn into the fold. Within this process of norm synthesis and synchronization, Tokyo is not the only capital likely to be integrated. Beijing's and Moscow's promotion of state sovereignty, sovereign equality, and non-intervention appear in the most recent UNGGE report, suggesting that their influence on cyberspace norms is already increasing.[45]

Growing comity at the UNGGE level has the real potential to mitigate the marginalization of Japan and to narrow the currently wide gap between East and West on normative issues in cyberspace. Tokyo's already prominent role in the regional structure APCERT and in the global Forum for Incident Response and Security Teams indicates that Tokyo has increasing technological and political gravitas both regionally and abroad. Japan is well-placed to identify common points for further exchange, whether in terms of mapping the legal structure in cyberspace or even the very definition of cyber warfare that, heretofore, has been guided by NATO-driven structures like the Tallinn Manual process.

Tokyo's enhanced participation as a member of both Asian trilateral dialogues and Western multilateral groupings places it in a unique position. It has the ability

136 *Lora Saalman*

to traverse and interpret differences in how cyberspace is defined in legal and warfare terms in the East and West. Given the West's current tensions with China and Russia on cyberspace issues, Japan could provide a voice at the table that can better interpret how cyberspace is evolving in Asia. Rather than serving as a Western backdoor into Asia, Japan could thereby use its liminal position to serve as a bridge between East and West. This would create a new pathway for more inclusive and connected global exchanges on the evolution of tactical cooperation and strategic norms in cyberspace. Yet, as long as there remains a tendency to isolate Tokyo within Asia, as indicated by the seeming postponement of the 2016 China–Japan–South Korea trilateral cyber talks, its role as a bridge will remain an aspiration rather than a reality.

Notes

1 The prevalence of Chinese serial programmes and education on the War of Resistance against Japan continue this narrative of Japan as inherently Western, cruel, and barbaric. While Chinese use of the term "Japanese devils" (*riben guizi*) has become less common over the past decade, this label continues to lurk behind perceptions of Japan's inherent ties to "foreign devils" (*yang guizi*) from the West.

2 Han Songyang is affiliated with the Training and Research Center of the Liaison Office of the Central People's Government in the Hong Kong Special Administrative Region. Han Songyang, "Cong zhihai quan dao zhiwang quan: Tanxi dashuju shidai zhengzhi wangluo yingxiao de zhongyaoxing" (From Sea Control Rights to Network Control Rights: An Analysis of the Importance of Political Network Markets in the Big Data Era), *Nanfang lunkan* (*Southern Journal*), 9 (2014), 34–35.

3 Qiao Liang and Wang Xiangsui, *Unrestricted Warfare: China's Master Plan to Destroy America* (Beijing: PLA Literature and Arts Publishing House, 1999).

4 Colonel Charles J. Dunlap, Jr., "Law and Military Interventions: Preserving Humanitarian Values in 21st Century Conflicts", unpublished paper presented at Harvard University, Carr Center, Humanitarian Challenges in Military Intervention Conference, November 29, 2001.

5 Susan W. Tiefenbrun, "Semiotic Definition of Lawfare", School of Law, Case Western Reserve University (2010), http://scholarlycommons.law.case.edu/cgi/viewcontent. cgi?article=1142&context=jil.

6 Mark Scott, "U.S. and Europe in 'Safe Harbor' Data Deal, but Legal Fight May Await", *New York Times*, February 2, 2016, www.nytimes.com/2016/02/03/technology/us-europe-safe-harbor-data-deal.html.

7 Wang Kongxiang is affiliated with the Southeast University Law School, where he heads a National Social Sciences Foundation project on "International Law under Internet Governance". Wang Kongxiang, "Wangluo anquan de guoji hezuo jizhi tanxi" (Analysis on International Cooperative Mechanisms on Cyber Security), *Guoji luntan* (*International Forum*), 5 (2013), 1–7.

8 Dong Aixian is affiliated with PLA Unit 91635. "Guoji wangluo kongjian zhili de zhuyao jucuo, tedian ji fazhan qushi" (Major Initiatives, Characteristics, and Development Trends in International Cyberspace Governance), *Xinxi anquan yu tongxin baomi* (*Information Security and Communication Confidential*), 1 (2014), 36–41.

9 Ibid.

10 "2003–2013 nian quanqiu wangluo he xinxi anquan fazhan dongtai" (2003–2013 Global Network and Information Security Development Dynamics), *Xinxi anquan yu tongxun baomi* (*Information Security and Communication Confidential*), 12 (2013), 48–56.

From backdoor to bridge 137

11 "Mei ri zhendui zhong e gao wangluo junyan" (The United States and Japan Engage in Military Cyber Exercises Against China and Russia), *Guofang shibao* (*Defense Times*), August 22, 2011, 3.

12 Wang Zhuangdong, "Wangluo anquan guanxi guojia mingyun" (Cyber Security Relations and National Fate), *Jisuanji anquan* (*Computer Security*), 3 (2004), 3–4.

13 Yuan Yi is affiliated with the Chinese Academy of Military Sciences. Yuan Yi, "Zhihui chengshi de wangluo anquan yinhuan ji duice" (Hidden Dangers and Countermeasures of Network Security in Smart Cities), *Wangluo kongjian zhanlue luntan* (*Cyberspace Strategy Forum*), 7 (2016), 30–32.

14 Liu Yuqing and Gong Yanli are affiliated with the Xi'an Jiaotong University Military Department. Liu Yuqing and Gong Yanli, "Wangluo zhan shidai de anquan weixie ji duice yanjiu" (Study on Security Threats and Countermeasures in an Era of Cyber warfare), *Qingbao tansuo* (*Intelligence Exploration*), 11 (2014), 61–64.

15 Government of Japan, "Cybersecurity Strategy", National Center of Incident Readiness and Strategy for Cybersecurity, September 4, 2015. www.nisc.go.jp/eng/pdf/cs-strategy-en.pdf, accessed October 7, 2016.

16 Based on discussions with Japanese cyber security expert at the Pacific Telecommunications Council Conference PTC 2015 in Honolulu, Hawaii.

17 Ye Zheng and Zhao Baoxian, "Guanyu wangluo zhuquan, wangluo bianjiang, wangluo guofang de sikao" (Thoughts on Cyber Sovereignty, Cyber Borders, and Cyber Defense), *Wangluo kongjian zhanlue luntan* (*Cyberspace Strategy Forum*), 1 (2014), 28. Wei Yuxi, "China–Russia Cybersecurity Cooperation: Working Towards Cyber-Sovereignty", Jackson School of International Studies, University of Washington, June 21, 2016, https://jsis.washington.edu/news/china-russia-cybersecurity-cooperation-working-towards-cyber-sovereignty, accessed October 7, 2016.

18 Russia and Central Asian states also promoted the Code of Conduct on Information Security. "Letter Dated 12 September 2011 from the Permanent Representatives of China, the Russian Federation, Tajikistan and Uzbekistan to the United Nations Addressed to the Secretary-General", United Nations General Assembly, A/66/359, September 14, 2011, https://ccdcoe.org/sites/default/files/documents/UN-110912-CodeOfConduct_0.pdf; "Letter Dated 9 January 2015 from the Permanent Representatives of China, Kazakhstan, Kyrgyzstan, the Russian Federation, Tajikistan and Uzbekistan to the United Nations Addressed to the Secretary-General", United Nations General Assembly, A/69/723, January 13, 2015, https://ccdcoe.org/sites/default/files/documents/UN-150113-CodeOfConduct.pdf.

19 "Group of Governmental Experts on Developments in the Field of Information and Telecommunications in the Context of International Security", United Nations General Assembly, A/70/174, July 22, 2015, www.un.org/ga/search/view_doc.asp?symbol=A/70/174.

20 Based on talks and discussions at a range of think tanks in Beijing and Shanghai in 2014, 2015, and 2016.

21 NATO Cooperative Cyber Defence Centre of Excellence, *Tallinn Manual on the International Law Applicable to Cyber warfare* (Cambridge: Cambridge University Press 2013), https://ccdcoe.org/research.html.

22 Cui Wenbo is affiliated with the School of International Studies of Peking University. Cui Wenbo, "'Talin shouce' dui wo guo wangluo anquan liyu de yingxiang" (The Impact on Chinese Cyber Security Interest [sic] Tallinn Manual), *Jiangnan shehui kexueyuan xuebao* (*Journal of Jiangnan Social University*), 3 (2013), 23–26; Huang Zhixiong, "Guojifa shijiao xia de 'wangluo zhan' ji zhongguo de duice – yixizhe wuliquan wei zhongxin" (International Legal Issues Concerning "Cyber Warfare" and Strategies for China: Focusing on the Field of Jus Ad Bellum), *Xiandai faxue* (*Modern Law Science*), 5 (2015), 145–158.

23 Tan Xueping and Yu Feng, "Ri ziweidui zengjia yusuan zhaobing maima: Yusuan zengjia 0.6% youxian goumai hai, kong zhuangbei, bing sida wangluo tanhuanzhan"

138 *Lora Saalman*

(Japan Self-Defense Forces to Increase Budget for Recruiting: Budget Increased by 0.6%, Giving Priority to the Purchase of Sea and Air Equipment, Intended for Paralyzing War), *Waijun liaowang* (*Foreign Military Lookout*), October 11, 2011, 5; Du Chaoping, "Riben ziweidui luezhan 'diwu zhanchang'" (Japan's Self-Defense Forces Prepare for the "Fifth Battlefield"), *Zhongguo guofang bao* (*China's Defense Newspaper*), February 18, 2014, 17.

24 C4ISR stands for Command, Control, Communications, Computers, Intelligence, Surveillance, and Reconnaissance. Ren Jianzhong is affiliated with the Tianjin Public Security Bureau and Zhang Xin is affiliated with the National Computer Virus Emergency Response Center. Ren Jianzhong and Zhang Xin, "2012 nian jisuanji bingdu fazhan qingkuang ji fan bingdu jishu fazhan qushi" (2012 Developments of Computer Viruses and Anti-Virus Technology Development Trends), 10 (2013), 211–214.

25 Zhou Yongsheng is affiliated with the International Relations Institute of the China Foreign Affairs University. Zhou Yongsheng, "Riben weihe xuanran zhongguo wangluo weixie" (Why Japan Poses a Threat to China's Networks), *Renmin Luntan* (*People's Tribune*), 8 (2011), 27; "2011 nian shijie zhuyao guojia he diqu xinxi anquan jianshe zhuangkuang" (2011 Condition of Cyber Security Formation in the World's Primary Countries and Regions), *Zhongguo xinxi anquan* (*China's Information Security*), 1 (2012), 68.

26 "2015 Zhongguo guofang baipishu 'Zhongguo de junshi zhanlue' (quanwen)" (2015 China's Defense White Paper "China's Military Strategy"), *Zhongguo ribao* (*China Daily*), May 26, 2015, http://world.chinadaily.com.cn/2015-05/26/content_20821000.htm, accessed October 7 2016.

27 Wang Haiping and Zhu Jie are affiliated with the Xi'an Institute of Political Science, Department of Military Law and the Graduate Management Brigade of Shaanxi. Wang Haiping and Zhu Jie, "2013 nian wuzhuang chongtu fa yanjiu zongshu" (A Summary of Studies on Armed Conflict Law), *Xian zhengzhi xueyuan xuebao* (*Journal of Xi'an Politics Institute*), 3 (2014), 98–102.

28 Ma Linli, "'Zhaobing maima' qiangzhan 'zhiwang quan' – Jinnian guowai bufen ji zuzhi wangjun jianshe zuixin dongtai" (Recruitment "To Seize the Network" – Some Foreign Countries in Recent Years and Their New Developments in Building Their Cyber Armies", *Wangjun jianshe* (*Building a Cyber Army*), *Zhonggyo xinxi anquan* (*China's Information Security*), 8 (2012), 42; Tang Lu is affiliated with the College of Humanities and Social Sciences at the National University of Defense Technology. Tang Lu, "Qianxi yi falv xingshi kongzhi wangluo junbei jingsai de biyaoxing" (An Analysis on the Necessity of Controlling Cyber Arm- [sic] Race Juristically [sic]), *Guofang keji* (*Defense Technology*), 3 (2010), 33–36; Xin Qi, Yuan Yi, and Zhu Danlong, "Chu meiguo wai, e, ri, yin, han, fa, ying deng guo ye bugan luohou – fazhan wangluo zhan, geguo you zhaoshu" (Aside from the United States, Russia, Japan, India, Korea, France, Britain and Other Countries Are Not Far Behind: The Development of Cyber Warfare, Each Country Has its Tricks), *Jiefangjun bao* (*People's Liberation Army Daily*), April 17, 2015.

29 Xiao Dan, "Jiyu kekong yu de wangluo gongji zhuizong jishu yanjiu" (Research on Techniques of Intrusion Traceback Based on Controlled Network), (Master's dissertation, PLA Information Engineering University, 2007).

30 Zhang Xianlong, "Hulianwang shidai weihu guojia anquan de zhanlue sikao" (Strategic Thinking on Safeguarding National Security in the Internet Age), *Zhongguo xinxi anquan* (*China Information Security*), 7 (2013), 78.

31 Jia Zhe and Zhang Linjie are affiliated with the Science and Technology on Information Transmission and Dissemination in Communication Networks Laboratory in Shijiazhuang. Jia Zhe and Zhang Linjie, "Zizhu wangluo kongjian anquan jishu yanjiu" (Research on Independent and Controllable Cyberspace Security Technology), *Jisuanji yu wangluo* (*Computers and Networks*), 6 (2015), 59–61.

From backdoor to bridge 139

32 "Japan's Defense Industry Hit by its First Cyber Attack", *Reuters*, September 19, 2011, www.reuters.com/article/us-mitsubishiheavy-computer-idUSTRE78I0EL20110919, accessed October 7, 2016.

33 "APT30 and the Mechanics of a Long-Running Cyber Espionage Operation: How a Cyber Threat Group Exploited Governments and Commercial Entities across Southeast Asia and India for Over a Decade", *FireEye*, April 2015, www2.fireeye.com/rs/fireye/images/rpt-apt30.pdf, accessed October 7, 2016.; Bryan Krekel, Patton Adams, and George Bakos, "Occupying the Information High Ground: Chinese Capabilities for Computer Network Operations and Cyber Espionage", prepared for the U.S.–China Economic and Security Review Commission by Northrop Grumman Corporation, March 7, 2012, http://nsarchive.gwu.edu/NSAEBB/NSAEBB424/docs/Cyber-066. pdf, accessed October 7, 2016.

34 Jon Gross and Cylance SPEAR Team, "Operation Dust Storm", Cylance, February, 23, 2016, www.cylance.com/hubfs/2015_cylance_website/assets/operation-dust-storm/Op_Dust_Storm_Report.pdf?t=1456259131512, accessed October 7, 2016.

35 Sun Jianhe, "Zhong ri wangluo duihua chenggong de jushi" (Revelations from the Successful China–Japan Dialogues), *Duiwai da chuanbo* (*External Communication*), 6 (2007), 41–43; Mao Libing, "Xinxi anquan ma? Quanqiu daxiang xinxi anquan baowei zhan" (Is Information Secure? The Global War for Information Security Protection), *Zhishi jingji* (*Information Economy*), 6 (2013), 38–42.

36 "Mei ri zhendui zhong e gao wangluo junyan" (The United States and Japan Engage in Military Cyber Exercises Against China and Russia), *Guofang shibao* (*Defense Times*), August 22, 2011, 3; Eliverto Larios, "Yama Sakura 69 Enhances Relationship Between US and Japan", *PACOM News*, December 11, 2015, www.pacom.mil/Media/News/Article/633886/yama-sakura-69-enhances-relationship-between-us-and-japan.

37 Liu Yuqing and Gong Yanli are affiliated with the Xi'an Jiaotong University Military Department. Liu Yuqing and Gong Yanli, "Wangluo zhan shidai de anquan weixie ji duice yanjiu" (Study on Security Threats and Countermeasures in Era of Cyber warfare), *Qingbao tansuo* (*Intelligence Exploration*), 11 (2014), 61–64.

38 Wang Wenyan, Zhao Yan, Lu Shan, and Zhao Meng are affiliated with PLA Unit 91469. Wang Wenyan, Zhao Yan, Lu Shan, and Zhao Meng, "Hai zhanchang wangdian kongjian zuozhan xitong yanjiu (Research on Marine Battlefield Network Space Warfare Systems), *Xin Jujiao* (*New Focus*), issue unavailable, date unavailable, 9–10.

39 Liu Yuqing and Gong Yanli, "Wangluo zhan shidai".

40 Japan Ministry of Internal Affairs and Communications, "Joint Press Statement for the U.S.–Japan Policy Cooperation Dialogue on the Internet Economy", Fifth Director General-Level Meeting, March 13, 2014, www.soumu.go.jp/main_content/000279477. pdf, accessed October 8, 2016; European Commission, "21st EU–Japan ICT Dialogue: Strengthening Cooperation", *Digital Economy and Society*, March 24, 2015, https://ec.europa.eu/digital-single-market/en/news/21st-eu-japan-ict-dialogue-strengthening-cooperation, accessed October 8, 2016; "Japan and EU Shake Hands on Cyber Security Agreement", *Infosecurity Magazine*, May 8, 2014, www.infosecurity-magazine.com/news/japan-and-eu-shake-hands-on-cyber-security, accessed October 8, 2016.

41 Liao Danzi is affiliated with the School of Finance and Public Administration at the Zhejiang University of Finance and Economics. Liao Danzi, "'Duoyuanxing' feichuantong anquan weixie: Wangluo anquan tiaozhan yu zhili" ("Pluralism" Non-Traditional Security Threats: Cyber Security Challenges and Governance), *Guoji anquan yanjiu* (*International Security Research*), 3 (2014), 26, 35.

42 "Guoji wangluo he xinxi anquan fazhan dongtai" (Development Dynamics in International Cyber and Information Security), *Xinxi anquan yu tongxin baomi* (*Information Security and Communication Confidential*), 6 (2015), 10–11.

43 Catalin Cimpanu, "Japan to Create Cyber-Defense Government Agency to Protect SCADA Infrastructures: Country Boosts Cyber-Security for 2020 Olympic Games",

Softpedia, May 20, 2016, http://news.softpedia.com/news/japan-to-create-cyber-defense-government-agency-to-protect-scada-infrastructures-504293.shtml, accessed October 7, 2016.

44 Ministry of Foreign Affairs, "The 2nd Korea–Japan–China Cyber Policy Consultation", Republic of Korea, October 15, 2015, www.mofat.go.kr/webmodule/htsboard/template/read/engreadboard.jsp?typeID=12&boardid=302&seqno=315774, accessed October 7, 2016.

45 "Group of Governmental Experts on Developments in the Field of Information and Telecommunications in the Context of International Security", United Nations General Assembly, A/70/174, July 22, 2015, www.un.org/ga/search/view_doc.asp?symbol=A/70/174.

Part III
Security relations

8 Australia navigates Sino-Japanese competition

Engaging, binding, and hedging

Nick Bisley

Contemporary debate about Australian security policy and its broader international engagement is dominated by Sino-American relations and their implications for the country's future. Since China overtook Japan as Australia's number-one trade partner in 2007,[1] scholars, analysts, and policy makers have sought to make sense of what it means for the country to have a non-democratic, non-ally of a different cultural heritage as its most important economic partner. But it is not just China's political system and cultural differences that are a cause for concern, it is that this vital economic partner appears to be entering into a period of extended rivalry with the US, Australia's most important security and strategic partner. Would Australia be faced with the awful situation of having to choose between its economic and its strategic interests? As this volume attests, fixating only on the Beijing–Washington axis of regional security tells at best a partial story of Australia's security and strategic outlook. Indeed, it omits perhaps the most important recent development in Australian security policy, the rapid growth of a rich array of defence ties to Japan. Equally, it is often forgotten that Japan remains Australia's second most important trading partner, with a long history of commercial and people-to-people links. Japan is a crucial factor in any assessment of Australia's evolving strategic policy.

The aim of this chapter is to explore the ways in which Sino-Japanese competition has shaped Australian security and defence policy and, through this, to show not only that this has been a significant factor in shaping Australian behaviour over recent years, but also to illustrate the need to explore the complex detail of strategic relations across the region to fully grasp the forces shaping Asian security. The region's dynamics entail a good deal more than just a bilateral great power rivalry. The chapter will begin with an examination of the dynamics shaping Australia's relations with China. How Canberra navigates a world in which, for the first time since the creation of the Commonwealth in 1901, its economic and security interests are not tightly aligned has become perhaps the most significant debate in Australian security policy. Here I will argue that Australia has adopted an "engage but hedge" approach to China. This section will explain what this entails and how this approach has prevailed. The chapter will then turn to the relationship that has developed with Japan. Over the past decade and a half, bilateral security ties between Tokyo and Canberra have become remarkably strong. Indeed, both now describe the security

144 *Nick Bisley*

relationship as their most important and developed in the region. The section will examine what this involves and why the two "anchors" of the US alliance system in Asia have developed such a strong security bond. The chapter will conclude with a broader reflection on the dynamics of regional competition and what it means for Australia's security policy. A key aim of successive Australian governments has been to have strong bilateral relationships with all of the region's major powers. Most middle-ranking powers in Asia share Australia's basic economic and security dilemmas. In that light, how Australia has sought to do this, given the obvious tensions in the region, provides an important set of insights for the Asian region.

Australia and China

Since 2007 China has been Australia's top trading partner, surpassing Japan, the country that had held that spot for around 40 years. Since that time, the share of Australian two-way trade accounted for by China has grown every year. Around one-third of Australian exports go to China and nearly one-quarter of imports do as well.[2] This is despite the fact that, in 2015, for the first time in decades, the total value of exports to China declined, largely a result of the significant drop in iron ore prices. China has also become a growing source of foreign direct investment, and while it is some way from the traditional major investors in the country – the US and several EU countries – the rate of investment has grown rapidly and is likely to continue.[3] There can be no doubt that, economically speaking, China is of huge importance to Australia. It was in part because demand for Australian exports was sustained following the global downturn that started in 2008 that Australia was one of the few economies of the Organisation for Economic Cooperation and Development to avoid a recession and indeed continues to enjoy the longest un-interrupted period of growth in the nation's history: Australia marked 100 straight quarters of growth in September 2016.[4]

It is this extraordinary economic relationship that has prompted the most signifi-cant debate in Australian defence and security circles since the Vietnam War: how should Australia respond to the fact that, for the first time since federation in 1901, the country's most important economic partner was a country with whom it did not share an alliance, a culture, language, or political system? But it was not only that China was not an ally, a democracy, or a partner of an ally, as all Australia's top economic partners to that point had been. The policy dilemma is sharpened by the fact that China is also developing a relationship with the US that is characterized by rivalry.[5]

Among this wide-ranging and at times quite personalized debate, the issues at stake for Australia seemed to turn on three interrelated points: the extent to which American power was in decline, and if so to what extent; the nature of Sino-American relations; and the character of the regional order. Although the idea that Australia might get caught-up in a contest between Washington and China tended to dominate much discussion of these, it was by no means the only issue.[6] Given the levels of dependence on the US for Australian security planning, any

Engaging, binding, and hedging 145

meaningful changes in Washington's standing in Asia would be of great significance. And perhaps most importantly, while the posture and relations of the two great powers were central to this discussion, a sometimes overlooked feature of the debate related to the broader regional circumstances Asia would enjoy as a result of the shifting power balance. Australia had benefited greatly from the long peace of the regional order that came into being following Sino-American rapprochement.[7] Would the shifting power balance and the changing behaviour of regional states transform Asia's international environment?

Arguments about what Australia ought to do in response to the rise of China and the disruptions this was causing to the region can be classified into four broad groups. The first, which I call the liberal optimists, are those that downplay both the prospects of Sino-American rivalry escalating further as well as the chances of there being meaningful change to the region's international order.[8] This liberal view is informed by the belief that the shared economic interests of the major powers will constrain their rivalry and contestation. Equally, it sees the broadly liberal international order as one that has benefited China and whose overturning or changing would not benefit that country. The second group shares the liberal sensibilities of the first, but has a less optimistic outlook. This pessimistic liberal position is one that sees shared interests as likely to ensure great power conflict is avoided, but which recognizes the need to develop policies and institutions to ensure that these interests prevail over less rational considerations.[9] This view sees rivalry and competition as plausible outcomes for which steps need to be taken to ensure they are avoided. Thus some adjustments to the regional order are necessary, particularly relating to institutions and the role they play in binding the countries of the region together.

The third group, optimistic realists, tend to take their optimism from the shared economic interests across the region but doubt the capacity of institutions to reduce the prospects of conflict. They believe that the shifting power balance is proving unsettling for the old ways of creating order and that this is an environment in which China is more likely to use force to advance its interests. As well as capitalizing on the economic opportunities presented by China's growth, this group argues that Australia, along with others, needs to take steps to hedge against a riskier strategic environment than has existed in the past.[10] The final group, the pessimistic realists, argue that change on all three dimensions – US power, Sino-American rivalry, and regional security order – is the inevitable consequence of China's rise. There are different prescriptions as to what should come next, with some arguing for a severance of the US alliance and the development of an independent Australian foreign policy,[11] while others argue that the region needs a concert of power to manage the new dispensation of power.[12]

Among these choices, the Australian government has opted for an approach that broadly falls within the optimistic realist camp. There has been considerable political volatility in Australia – since 2007 there have been five changes in prime minister – involving both shifts from right to left and back to right, as well as cleavages within parties. Yet in spite of this, Australian policy towards China has, in its larger orientations, remained fairly consistent. Canberra approaches Beijing

146   *Nick Bisley*

through what can best be described as an "engage but hedge" approach. That is, it seeks to have a strong and effective bilateral relationship with its most important economic partner and with the region's most important resident power more broadly. Yet it recognizes the reality that China's growing power is already disrupting the old strategic order and will continue to do so. Steps need to be taken to manage this. Given both Australia's relatively meagre resources as well as the belief that overt Cold War-style geopolitical competition is unlikely, the country has not taken a balance-of-power type posture or joined a coalition to contain China; rather, it is seeking to mitigate the risks that the changing security environment is likely to produce.

For almost a decade, Australian governments have argued that the country "doesn't have to choose between Beijing and Washington". This public diplomacy formulation represents an understandable desire to present a polite façade to a complex diplomatic reality, but it also helps obscure the fact that Australia has already made a series of important choices. Perhaps the most important of those has been the decision to bind the country very closely to the US. Engage but hedge is the reality behind the "not choosing" public façade in which the country seeks to manage the growing complexity of its relations not just with China and the US, but its ties to other middle-ranking powers, most obviously Japan.

Engaging China

The most obvious component of the engagement aspect of the strategy relates to the economic relationship. Plainly, the scale of relations has been a key driver in recent years; however, Canberra recognizes that notwithstanding their volume, Australian exports to China are very one-dimensional. Commodities dominate, with iron ore alone accounting for around half of exports by value.[13] The one exception to this is education and, more recently, tourism, with China now the biggest source country for inbound tourists to Australia. Yet these remain marginal in the overall scheme of the relationship and the Australian government's hope is to broaden and deepen the economic relationship beyond the heavy dependence on commodities. This entails strengthening service exports, particularly professional services, as well as increasing inbound investment. The coalition governments in place since 2013 have made economic diplomacy a key part of the country's overall foreign policy and have strongly emphasized trade agreements and other intergovernmental mechanisms as central elements of this approach. Perhaps the highest profile of these is the China–Australia Free Trade Agreement that was concluded in 2014, after around seven years of negotiation. The agreement provides some preferential access to China's growing services market as well as other areas such as agriculture.[14]

While it is far too early to determine the economic effect of the agreement, the speed with which it was concluded after the coalition came to government reflected a high political priority put on completing the deal. Its predecessor, the Labor government, had been negotiating for six years; the coalition finalized the agreement in a little over 12 months. It did so by compromising on issues such as investor–state dispute settlement, which Labor had been unwilling to do. The political aim was clear. The government wanted to bind Australia to China economically even if that meant an economically sub-optimal agreement. More importantly, it provided precisely the kind of political balance that the "engage but hedge" approach embodies. It sent a clear signal that Australia was not involved in anti-China coalition building and that the agreement represented the kind of "win–win" diplomacy regularly lauded by the People's Republic of China (PRC) officials.

Supplementing these economic ties has been an active diplomatic engagement. Under Prime Minister Julia Gillard the country established a comprehensive strategic partnership with China that entails a range of annual official dialogues culminating in an annual leaders' summit involving the Australian prime minister and the Chinese premier.[15] Australia has a large embassy as well as four consulates in Shanghai, Guangzhou, Hong Kong, and the recently established mission in Chengdu, as well as 11 Austrade offices. This diplomatic effort is matched by an active programme of military-to-military links that seek to improve communication between the two militaries and, more broadly, build confidence among the elites in Beijing and Canberra. This ranges from staff college exchange programmes and senior official dialogues, to a number of training exercises in humanitarian and disaster relief. These diplomatic and security efforts are functional – they serve specific operational purposes – but are also part of a larger signalling effort to show that although the country clearly has different views from China on many issues, it is not intent on containing China or being part of a larger effort to constrain Chinese potential.

The bilateral engagement is supplemented by the quintessential policy approach of middle-ranking powers: multilateralism. Like other similarly endowed countries, Australia sees multilateral institutions and processes as important means to shape the policies and preferences of the great powers. The country has been an enthusiastic multilateralist in the region – it is a member of every process and institution for which it is eligible[16] – though the motives for doing so are varied. Australia sees these mechanisms as important ways to have influence in the region, but it also sees them as an important way of binding the interests and actions of the major powers. And it is a key part of its strategy towards China whereby multilateral mechanisms are hoped to be an effective means through which to not only positively engage China, but also a means through which Chinese behaviour might be shaped.

This motivation is evident in the broad-ranging multilateral structures, such as the Asia-Pacific Economic Cooperation forum, the East Asian Summit, and the ASEAN Defence Ministers Meeting-Plus, but there is a recent development that sheds an interesting light on Australia's view of multilateralism as a means to engage China: the country's decision to join the China-led Asian Infrastructure Investment Bank (AIIB). Initially, Australia was divided about whether or not it should join the AIIB.[17] Senior ministers with an economic brief, notably the treasurer and trade minister, were supportive, while ministers of defence and foreign affairs, and the prime minister himself, were sceptical. The US actively

148 *Nick Bisley*

and very publicly lobbied its allies and friends not to join.[18] Australian thinking was split. On the one hand, there were those who saw participation as a means to drive infrastructure investment in the region, from which the country would indirectly benefit, as well as a further multilateral means through which to engage Beijing. On the other hand, the bank was seen as a potential means through which China could increase its strategic influence through soft loans and undermine existing multilateral lending institutions. After much prevarication, Australia ultimately joined as the reasons that had been put forward for remaining outside were rendered hollow by the flood of US allies joining, a trend prompted by the UK's decision to take part.[19] The debate and messy public diplomacy around the issue illustrated some of the practical difficulties of the "engage but hedge" approach, particularly as China started to take a more prominent international role and as Australia's economic ties to China became more complex.

Hedging its bets

Australia has done very well out of China's rise, but like many in the region and indeed the world, it is unsettled by the geopolitical consequences of China's growth. In its public statements, the Australian government has taken a positive outlook on the security and strategic consequences of China's rise.[20] With the exception of the 2009 Defence White Paper, which named the country as a possible source of conflict,[21] all formal government statements paint a broadly positive picture of the regional security outlook and China's role within it. This public facing policy is understandable, but the reality of Australian defence and strategic policy entails a much greater level of uncertainty about the region's future and scepticism about Chinese behaviour. This sentiment has strengthened since 2014 as China has acted more assertively in relation to its maritime disputes in the East and South China Seas. Even though official documents such as the 2016 Defence White Paper retain a broadly upbeat vision of China in the region,[22] public statements by politicians and senior officials have begun to articulate this scepticism.[23] This was vividly on display when, shortly after toppling Tony Abbott, Prime Minister Malcolm Turnbull described China's activities in the South China Sea as "pushing the envelope" and in need of "balancing" against.[24] But it is in Australia's actions much more than the statements of its senior officials that one can see the country taking steps to mitigate the growing sense of risk that it perceives to be evident in its security future.

The clearest statement about this is evident in its defence acquisition programme. For reasons largely to do with domestic politics there have been three Defence White Papers issued since 2009. Notwithstanding some differences in political messaging, there has been a consistent underlying strategic message in all three papers: the Australian military needs to be able to project more force further from home. There is bipartisan support to increase defence spending to pay for a new fleet of cutting-edge conventional submarines which would double the current number of vessels and significantly enhance Australia's distance and force projection capacity. There is also commitment to acquire 72 F-35s to ensure the country's edge in air warfare. Alongside the two recently commissioned helicopter landing dock ships – the largest ever commissioned by the Royal Australian Navy – this will strengthen Australia's capacity not only to protect its substantial air and maritime interests, but also to respond to military contingencies a long way from home. Plainly, Australia is not in a position to balance Chinese military power or act in ways that would constrain the PRC, but it is equipping itself to be able to assist its great power ally to do exactly that if necessary. And it is clear that the prospects of this happening have increased.

Related to its military modernization programme, indeed in many respects intimately bound up in that effort, has been Canberra's active efforts to tighten its strategic relationship with Washington. This process dates back to 2001, when Australia invoked the ANZUS Treaty (Australia, New Zealand, US Security Treaty) in response to the terrorist attacks of September that year.[25] This led to a decade of operational interaction between the two allies which provided the functional underpinning for a process of strategic binding in which Australia has committed itself not only to the alliance as the centrepiece of its international engagement, but to the broader US vision for Asia's future.[26] By tying itself closely to the US, Australia seeks the traditional security and political benefits of having the world's most powerful military as a guarantor. But it also sees close partnership with the US as a crucial part of its broader regional ambitions. A stable regional security order is a core interest to Australia, yet it is something to which it can, at best, contribute only marginally. Canberra's hope and belief is that the US-centred order is the optimal setting for the region's future. Yet it knows that some adjustments to that order will be necessary given China's emergence as a great power. Australia's ambition is to be able to contribute more, politically and militarily, in the region as an investment in the US commitment. Equally, and as will be discussed further below, it also recognizes that other allies, most importantly Japan, will also be required to do more and thus is taking steps to support that broader goal. In simple terms, Australia is binding itself to the US as part of an effort to hedge against the risks that China presents to the sustainability of Asia's security order.[27]

This is also evident in the way in which the idea of a "rules-based international order" has become an organizing feature of Australian strategic policy. It has featured prominently in the government's response to the South China Sea dispute and in particular in its reaction to the arbitral tribunal's findings in the case brought by the Philippines against China. The rules-based order is a concept that is used increasingly by the US and Japan to refer to the prevailing regional security order, and is being used to refer not just to the narrow international legal framework that Canberra wants to constrain Chinese behaviour, but to the overarching setting in which the legal framework operates. That is, the rules-based order is not just about the particularities of specific rules or the distribution of power and influence, but is the way in which the international environment operates. Thus it is a kind of diplomatic signalling that indicates Australia's, and other countries', disapproval of China, but in a relatively neutral way. But it is not only in this instrumental means that the concept has begun to be visible. It is also now a purposive concept in Australian defence policy. As set out in the 2016 Defence White Paper, it is now

150 *Nick Bisley*

an end to which Australian military force should be put.[28] The paper sets out a series of strategic goals that the country seeks to achieve, and one of these is the rules-based global order. The government clearly does not believe Australia can significantly achieve that lofty goal; nevertheless, it is striking that such a vast and indeed nebulous goal should appear in a document like the White Paper.[29] The intention is to lay down a purposive marker related directly to concerns that Australia has about the extent to which China could erode or indeed structurally damage the prevailing order.

Australia has invested greatly in an East Asian security order centred around the continuity of American primacy. Canberra is aware that some kind of adjustment to that order is needed to reflect China's economic revival and its international strategic consequences. Yet it is also deeply connected to that rise and is trying to takes steps to reconcile those attributes. In the past, managing these two ends through a policy of compartmentalization was relatively straightforward. But as China has become more internationally ambitious and as the two countries' economic relations have become more complex this is becoming more difficult. The AIIB debate was one example of this complexity, as has been decisions to prevent Chinese firms from investing in key infrastructure and agricultural programmes in 2015 and 2016. More recently, public opinion has begun to show some concerns about China, particularly as it has come to light that individuals and firms with close links to the Communist Party have sought to influence Australian politics and public debate in relation to China. Engage but hedge is becoming a much harder game to play.

Australia and Japan

Australia is fortunate, however, that it and its senior partner, the US, are by no means the only countries trying to reconcile a desire to maintain the strategic *status quo* while also benefiting from strong economic ties to China. Perhaps the most interesting development in Australian security policy over the past decade and a half has been the development of a very close relationship with Japan. Both countries now officially describe one another as their most important security partners after the US. In this section I will explore what this has entailed, why it has occurred, and what role it plays in shaping Australia's broader approach to the region.

Towards a special strategic partnership

In March 2007, Australia and Japan signed a joint security declaration.[30] The agreement was the first security agreement that Japan has signed with any country other than the US since 1945. The declaration was the culmination of many years in which the two countries had worked together on peacekeeping operations, and humanitarian and disaster relief exercises. But more than this it articulated a shared desire to collaborate on security policy in the future and provided a diplomatic foundation for this to occur. It also sent a signal, both

Engaging, binding, and hedging 151

between the two parties and to the international community more broadly, that the two shared a common sense of the regional security environment and the challenges they faced, and have a desire to work together to meet these concerns.[31] In the decade since inking the declaration the two countries have since signed three further agreements relating to information security, cross-servicing, and defence technology transfer.[32] At the time of writing, the two parties are finalizing negotiations on a service access agreement to clear the way for military training exercises. These formal documents are necessary legal instruments to facilitate cooperation in operational military matters, training, and information sharing, among others. As a capstone to these legal agreements, a statement signed by the two prime ministers in 2014 officially elevated the bilateral relationship to a strategic partnership.[33] While not necessary to facilitate the kind of security interaction the two intended to undertake, the statement was an important further signalling exercise. For Australia it meant adding Japan to the top tier of countries with whom it collaborates in the security domain, such as the UK and the US. For Japan, it was an important part of the Abe government's ambition to normalize the country's foreign and security policy. It demonstrated both a capacity to operate within legal and alliance frameworks while speaking to a larger ambition. Perhaps most importantly, it illustrated, both domestically and internationally, that Japan was prepared to take the necessary steps to play a role in supporting the prevailing regional security order in the face of a changing balance of power and security environment.

Beyond formal agreements, the two have also undertaken an increasingly broad-ranging set of security activities.[34] The links between Canberra and Tokyo were spurred by the experience of operational interaction in response to the 2004 Boxing Day tsunami and the post-conflict reconstruction effort in Iraq, where Australian defence force personnel provided security for Japanese Self-Defence Force engineers working in Samawah, among others. Since the signing of the various formal instruments the two have undertaken officer exchanges and military training exercises, including in trilateral format with the US. Planned bilateral exercises in Australia provide a very useful environment for Japan's ground forces, which lack strategic depth at home.

One of the most important features of the Australia–Japan security partnership has been the diplomatic role Australia sees for itself in helping to facilitate Japan's security reform. The efforts to move Japan beyond the post-1945 consensus about the kind of security role the country might play have been very contentious both at home and abroad.[35] Australia's strategic policy is predicated on a sustained regional status quo in East Asia for the medium-term future. Given China's rise, some changes will be necessary for this status quo to be retained. Crucially, such a future requires a Japan that has the strategic and security outlook of Britain or France, a major departure from the Japan of the post-1945 period. Thus, Australia can play a vital role as a buttress for that effort. Australia can help normalize Japan and send signals that a Japan that is doing more militarily is not necessarily reverting to a 1935 script. Rather, it is a country that operates within the constraints of the UN system, indeed is a crucial supporter of that system, has partnerships and

152   *Nick Bisley*

alliances with status quo powers, and is thus a player to be welcomed and not mistrusted. Australia is, in this sense, a vital support mechanism, diplomatically and politically speaking, in the efforts to make Japan a country that is not only politically in support of the status quo, but can take the necessary steps in concrete terms to help protect that order.

Finally, and as part of this, Australia saw that it could assist in Japan's efforts to begin to create a defence export business. This was an important part both of an economic reform programme – defence contracting is a lucrative business and Japan has some strong comparative advantage in the sector. For political reasons, Japan has not undertaken defence exports since 1945. Supporting the sector's renewal is part of Japan's larger security normalization programme. Here, Australia can continue to provide political support both in giving an international dimension to Japan's defence sector as well as helping to drain this move of its more controversial elements, both within and outside Japan. This was behind not just the technology transfer agreement of 2014 but the preference of the Abbott government to turn to Japan to supply Australia's next-generation submarines. Indeed, in many respects Prime Minister Abbott's strong preference for Australia's new fleet to be a variation of the Japanese *Soryu*-class submarine reflects the inter-section of these facets of relations.[36] Abbott saw the submarine as a high-quality vessel that could achieve desired operational ambitions at much lower cost than if Australia tried to build a submarine with the same capability. But that basic effi-ciency question was only one part. The government also saw this as an opportunity to cement the strategic relationship with Japan and through this strengthen trilateral strategic links between Tokyo, Washington, and Canberra so crucial to the government's larger strategic objective of being able to do more to support the prevailing regional order. Finally, it saw such a large contract as providing a help-ful first step into the competitive business of defence contracting. Unfortunately, with the fall of Tony Abbott's government this acceleration of the strategic ties between Japan and Australia came to an end. In hindsight it now appears that the two leaders had taken this too far too fast.[37] The eventual decision of the Turnbull government to award the contract to the French firm DCNS, and the manner in which the decision was leaked to the press,[38] was the most significant setback in what had been hitherto a story of an ever-closer security relationship.

Getting together

Japan and Australia have now become very close security partners. Indeed some have even described their security relationship as a quasi-alliance.[39] So why did the two countries, sometimes styled as the northern and southern anchors of Washington's Asian strategy, take these steps?

Perhaps the most important factor driving the development of the relationship is the convergence in interests between the two countries. Since 2001, Japan and Australia began to see regional and indeed global security threats in a similar way, both in terms of the kinds of threats they faced as well as the means necessary to combat them. Where in the past, Japan had a narrowly defensive approach to its

Engaging, binding, and hedging 153

security concerns and a development-focused "human security" framework for regional engagement, under the Koizumi government Tokyo began to see its external environment in ways that resonated with Canberra. This began in 2001 when both wanted to support the US in its response to the 9/11 attacks, and through their experiences they developed a shared broader outlook. This included a realization of what they could do collaboratively to strengthen the US alliance system in Asia in response to the region's changing geopolitics.[40] Although the unsettling actions of North Korea since its break out from the 1994 Agreed Framework were important, the primary driver of this was the rise of China and the disruption that this has caused to East Asian strategic balance.

If the first point relates to a convergence of interests then one must also recognize that individuals perceive these convergences and then take steps to act on them. It is by no means a coincidence that at the time of signing of the two most symbolically significant agreements, the 2007 Security Declaration and the 2014 Special Strategic Partnership agreement, Japan was under the leadership of Abe Shinzo. Abe has the ambition to make Japan a more normal member of international society in terms of foreign and security policy. This has been prompted both by his nationalist instincts but also his assessment of Japan's security environment. In Australia he sees a valuable ally in helping realize this ambition. Equally, the key foreign policy adviser to the Australian prime minister at both times was Andrew Shearer. While development of the relationship has been bipartisan with both Labor and coalition governments improving security relations, the key moves have come under Conservative governments. This is due not only to the close personal chemistry that Abe developed most obviously with Abbott, but also because of their shared outlook on the regional security setting and their misgivings about the impact China was having on that setting.

A third important force bringing the two together is the US. Washington has long wanted its regional allies and partners to begin to do more with one another.[41] This is intended as a load-sharing exercise in which allies working together help distribute the costs of the US regional order, and to help manage the wider array of security challenges in the region. But it is also about helping solidify the political foundations of US regional strategy. Getting partners to work together to advance a larger security goal commensurate with US ambitions ensures that those partners have a mutually reinforcing link to US ambitions. More importantly, their actions help signal to the region more generally that the security order has a wider political foundation. It is not based on dependent allies acting to placate their guarantor, but on autonomously acting regional residents choosing partnership with one another as well. The US has thus been encouraging Australia and Japan to do more together, in diplomatic and programmatic terms. It even provided clear incentives for the two to collaborate in the now defunct submarine deal through systems interoperability.

Finally, both countries are greatly invested in the larger US-centric regional security order. Each recognizes that the other needs to be able to contribute more to that order and to take on roles that they have not played in the past if that basic setting is to be sustained in the face of China's rise and other shifts. Most crucially,

154 *Nick Bisley*

it requires Japan to be able to take on a security role that is more active and more involved in defending the prevailing regional setting. Australia's limited resources and relatively isolated physical location mean that there is only so much that it can do. In contrast, Japan has the potential resource base and geographic platform to make a material difference to the regional security order, but faces considerable political and diplomatic challenges to a more assertive defence posture. And it is here where Australia feels it can play an important role.

Both Japan and Australia are dependent allies. They are dependent not only on the US for their core security guarantee, but for the underlying structure of East Asia's security order. Both need it to be sustained, yet both need to change their security policies to make this viable. And central to this dynamic has been Sino-Japanese competition. Indeed, in many respects the China factor has been the principal force motivating Japan's shifting security policy context, in which the development of the new relationship with Australia is perhaps the most significant feature.

Sino-Japanese competition and Australian security policy

For much of its history, Australia battled what came to be known as the tyranny of distance. As an outpost of imperial Britain it was 10,000 miles from the homeland, and its geographic isolation came at a high economic, strategic, and psychological cost. But as Britain declined and Asia rose, the costs and benefits of the country's geography have changed. Australia now has what some regard as "the promise of proximity".[42] Certainly the Gillard government's 2012 *Australia in the Asian Century* White Paper set out in detail the economic opportunities presented by the shift in global economic weight to Asia.[43] Yet the sense of possibility is also tempered by the realization that Australia's region is now beset with great power competition. As the chapters in this book attest, while much attention has focused on the very real consequences of US–China rivalry, there is a great deal more going on in East Asia. As a middle-ranking power dependent for its prosperity on integration into the global economy, Australia is acutely aware of the ways in which regional security has become increasingly unsettled. And a central component of that has been the growing number of major powers engaged in competitive behaviour in the region.

This chapter has shown the ways in which Australia has responded to the Sino-Japan dyad and in particular the trajectory of its security ties with each country. Like many in the region, China is Australia's top trade partner and the US its most significant strategic and security guarantor, but it is often overlooked that in 2015 Japan was the country's second most important trading partner and has become its most important security partner in Asia. Navigating increased Sino-Japanese competition, overlaid as it is by Sino-American rivalry, has been a significant influence on Australia's strategic outlook and its defence and security policy choices.

Although Australia's traditional concerns about geographic isolation have been replaced by a sense that the country is now closer to the world's centre of gravity,

Engaging, binding, and hedging 155

geography remains an important security advantage. Its distance from China and Japan has meant that Australia has not yet been dragged into the kind of zero-sum competitive dynamics that rivalry can create. Equally, it has allowed the country to manage its bilateral relationships in a compartmentalized manner. That is, Australia has been able to separate out its ties between each country and manage them individually. Australian politicians and policy elites have long claimed that the country does not have to choose between Washington and Beijing. While always a somewhat facile formulation, the underlying idea remains that Australia can develop productive bilateral relations with China, Japan, the US and indeed others, without third-party concerns such as Sino-Japanese rivalry having a negative impact on any one relationship.

This compartmentalization is not a viable long-term strategy, particularly in a region in which contestation is becoming more overt, spilling out from the security realm into other areas, and where economic interdependence is growing. The nature of Australia's economic ties to China in the past meant that although the volume of trade was great, there was little real leverage that China could exert over Australia.[44] But as trade is diversified away from commodities and as China becomes a significant investor in the country, that basic calculus changes. More importantly, the region is entering a period in which political and strategic concerns are beginning to influence economic relations. The side costs to Australia of its close relations with Japan and the US are beginning to be visible for the first time. For example, Australia has opted to cleave very closely to the diplomatic line taken by Japan and the US in relation to the South China Sea disputes. China has reacted strongly both officially, dressing down the foreign minister and the ambassador, and in unofficial state-owned media such as the *Global Times*.[45] Some have even speculated that the arrest of Australian casino executives for promoting casino-related travel in October 2016 was motivated, at least in part, by a Chinese desire to signal its displeasure with Australia. To this we must add the tensions in the relationship caused by repeated decisions by the government to turn down Chinese investment in key infrastructure and agriculture investments. Most recently, Canberra refused to approve the S. Kidman and Co. cattle station investment and the Ausgrid Energy part-privatization. It seems increasingly clear that the idea that Australia can endlessly manage its complex relationship with China on the basis that its third-party political and security relations can be isolated from those ties is fanciful.

East Asia has long been a region whose international politics are dominated by the interactions of the great powers. This is due to the presence of a small number of very large states and a large number of relatively small powers. The absence of a peer group of four to six major powers, the situation in eighteenth- and nineteenth-century Europe, has created what might be described as an oligopolistic tendency in the region's international order. For Australia, the principle challenge in managing its place in the emerging security order relates not just to the fact that there are now three major powers whose interactions are of vital importance – the US, China, and Japan – but that China seems increasingly to chafe against the prevailing regional order. This tension is going to increase over the coming years.

156 Nick Bisley

Australia and Japan have increased their bilateral security ties precisely because they want the underlying regional order to remain in place. Indeed, it has been a prime motivating force in their burgeoning security relationship. Washington, Tokyo, and Canberra all believe not only that China can be included within that order, but that it would be the optimal setting for the region as a whole. The problem is that China does not seem to have the same perception; indeed, there is a strong sense that under the current leadership, China perceives the international environment to be rigged against its interests. They seem to believe that crucial changes to the regional order will be necessary for the country to find an international environment most conducive to its interests.

In this sense, the Sino-Japanese competition examined in this book is a key component of what should be described as a contested regional order. Contested Asia involves not only competition among major powers for influence and advantage, but also contests about the form and function of Asia's emerging order. And it is this much more competitive regional security environment that presents Australia with the most demanding international environment that it has faced since 1945.

If the developments described in this chapter are any indication, then one should not expect Australia to begin to take a path in which it seeks to gain advantage by playing the great powers off against one another. Rather, it is likely to strengthen and deepen its existing ties to the US and Japan. The problem Canberra faces is how China responds not only to the specific decisions Australia makes, but to the nature of the competitive dynamics in contested Asia. It is this interaction that will determine the extent to which Asia's future will be as prosperous and stable as its recent past.

Notes

1 ABC, "China Unseats Japan as Australia's Largest Trade Partner", ABC News, August 31, 2007, www.abc.net.au/news/2007-08-31/china-unseats-japan-as-australias-largest-trade/656322.
2 Data from DFAT, *China Economic and Trade Fact Sheet*, June 2016, http://dfat.gov.au/trade/resources/Documents/chin.pdf.
3 KPMG, *Demystifying Chinese Investment in Australia* (Sydney: KPMG, 2016), http://demystifyingchina.com.au/reports/demystifying-chinese-investment-in-australia-april-2016.pdf.
4 Thy Ong, "GDP: Happy Birthday to Australia's Economic Growth" ABC News, September 7, 2016, www.abc.net.au/news/2016-09-07/gdp-australia-goes-25-years-without-recession/7823988; see also George Megalogenis, *Australia's Second Chance* (Sydney: Penguin, 2015).
5 For examples of this debate, see: William T. Tow and H.D.P. Envall, "Australia Debates American Primacy", in Yoichiro Sato and See Seng Tan, eds, *United States Engagement with the Asia-Pacific: Perspectives from Asia* (Amherst: Cambria Press, 2015); Carlyle Thayer, "China's Rise and the Passing of U.S. Primacy: Australia Debates its Future", *Asia Policy*, 12 (2011); Hugh White, "Power Shift: Australia's Future Between Beijing and Washington", *Quarterly Essay* 39 (2010); Nick Bisley, "Australia and Asia's Trilateral Dilemmas: Between Beijing and Washington?" *Asian Survey* 54:2 (2014).
6 On this, see Nick Bisley, "Never Having to Choose", in James Reilly and Jing-Dong Yuan, eds, *Australia and China at 40* (Sydney: New South Publishing, 2012).

Engaging, binding, and hedging 157

7 On the East Asian peace, see Timo Kivimaki, *The Long Peace of East Asia* (Farnham: Ashgate, 2014).
8 For example, Geoffrey Garett, "Cold War Talk is Hot Air", *Sydney Morning Herald*, July 15, 2011, www.smh.com.au/federal-politics/political-opinion/cold-war-talk-is-hot-air-20110714-1hfwb.html.
9 For example, Scott Dewar, *Australia and China and the United States: Responding to Great Power Dynamics* (ANU Centre for China in the World, 2011), http://ciw.anu.edu.au/publications/au_ch_and_us.pdf.
10 Rod Lyon, *Changing Asia, Rising China and Australia's Strategic Choices* (ASPI Policy Analysis, 2009), www.aspi.org.au/publications/changing-asia,-rising-china,-and-australias-strategic-choices/Policy_Analysis40.pdf.
11 Cain Roberts and Malcolm Fraser, *Dangerous Allies* (Melbourne: Melbourne University Press, 2014).
12 Hugh White, *The China Choice: Why the US Should Share Power* (Melbourne: Black Ink, 2012).
13 DFAT, *Composition of Trade Australia 2015* (Canberra: Commonwealth of Australia, 2016), 94, http://dfat.gov.au/about-us/publications/Documents/cot-cy-2015.pdf.
14 DFAT, "Free Trade Agreement Between the Government of Australia and the Government of People's Republic of China", http://dfat.gov.au/trade/agreements/chafta/official-documents/Documents/chafta-agreement-text.pdf.
15 Linda Jakobson, "Australia–China Strategic Partnership: Two Years of Fits and Starts", *Lowy Interpreter*, April 10, 2013, www.lowyinterpreter.org.au/the-interpreter/australia-china-strategic-partnership-two-years-fits-and-starts.
16 It is a member of: AIIB, ADB, ARF, ADMM+, APEC, East Asia Summit, and ASEM.
17 Michelle Grattan, "Division Over Bank as Australia Caught Between China and US", *The Conversation*, October 19, 2014, https://theconversation.com/division-over-bank-as-australia-caught-between-china-and-us-33153.
18 Jane Perlez, "US Opposing China's Answer to World Bank", *New York Times*, October 9, 2014, www.nytimes.com/2014/10/10/world/asia/chinas-plan-for-regional-development-bank-runs-into-us-opposition.html.
19 See Susan Harris Rimmer, "Why Australia Took so Long to join the AIIB", *Lowy Interpreter*, May 30, 2015.
20 For example, Matthew Franklin, "Julia Gillard Rejects Need to Contain China", *The Australian*, April 27, 2011, www.theaustralian.com.au/national-affairs/julia-gillard-rejects-need-to-contain-china/story-fn59niix-1226045266144.
21 Department of Defence, *Defending Australia in the Asia-Pacific Century: Force 2030* (Canberra: Commonwealth of Australia, 2009), www.defence.gov.au/whitepaper/2009/docs/defence_white_paper_2009.pdf.
22 Department of Defence, *2016 Defence White Paper* (Canberra: Commonwealth of Australia, 2016), www.defence.gov.au/whitepaper/Docs/2016-Defence-White-Paper.pdf.
23 John Garnaut and David Wroe, "China Not Fit for Global Leadership, Says Top Canberra Official Michael Thawley", *Sydney Morning Herald*, June 30, 2015, www.smh.com.au/federal-politics/political-news/china-not-fit-for-global-leadership-says-top-canberra-official-michael-thawley-20150630-gi1o1f.html.
24 Anna Henderson, "Malcolm Turnbull say China 'pushing the envelope' in South China Sea", ABC News, September 22, 2015, www.abc.net.au/news/2015-09-21/china-is-pushing-the-envelope-in-south-china-sea-turnbull/6793102.
25 Press Conference Transcript, Office of the Prime Minister, September 14, 2001, http://australianpolitics.com/2001/09/14/government-invokes-anzus-treaty.html.
26 See Nick Bisley, "'An Ally for All the Years to Come': Why Australia is Not a Conflicted Ally", *Australian Journal of International Affairs*, 67:3 (2013), 403–418.
27 The logic of Australian policy was vividly displayed in a cable published by wikileaks: Daniel Flitton "Rudd the Butt of Wikileaks Expose", *The Age*, December 6, 2010,

158 *Nick Bisley*

www.smh.com.au/technology/security/rudd-the-butt-of-wikileaks-expos-20101205-18lf2.html.

28 Department of Defence, *2016 Defence White Paper* (DOD, 2016), 68–69.

29 For a discussion of this, see Benjamin Zala, "The Australian *2016 Defence White Paper*, Great Power Rivalry and a 'Rules-Based Order'", *Australian Journal of International Affairs*, 70:5 (2016), 441–452.

30 MOFA, *Japan Australia Security Declaration*, March 13, 2007, www.mofa.go.jp/region/asia-paci/australia/joint0703.html.

31 See Nick Bisley, "'The Japan–Australia Security Declaration and the Changing Regional Setting: Wheels, Webs and Beyond?", *Australian Journal of International Affairs*, 62:1 (2008), 38–52.

32 The full agreements can be found here: Acquisition and Cross Servicing Agreement, www.mofa.go.jp/region/asia-paci/australia/pdfs/agree1005.pdf; Information Security Agreement, www.austlii.edu.au/au/other/dfat/treaties/ATS/2013/15.html; Transfer of Defence Equipment and Technology Agreement, www.mofa.go.jp/files/000044447.pdf.

33 MOFA, "Prime Minister Abbott and Prime Minister Abe Joint Statement: 'Special Strategic Partnership for the 21st Century'", July 2014, www.mofa.go.jp/files/000044543.pdf.

34 Thomas S. Wilkins, "From Strategic Partnership to Strategic Alliance? Australia–Japan Security Ties and the Asia-Pacific", *Asia Policy*, July 20, 2015, 81–111.

35 On the more recent efforts, see Christopher W. Hughes, *Japan's Foreign and Security Policy Under the "Abe Doctrine": New Dynamism or New Dead End?* (London: Palgrave, 2015).

36 See Graeme Dobell, "Tony Abbott and a Japanese Sub" *The Strategist*, May 25, 2015, www.aspistrategist.org.au/tony-abbott-and-a-japanese-sub.

37 See Nick Bisley and David Envall, "The Morning After: Australia, Japan and the Sub-Deal That Wasn't" *Asia-Pacific Bulletin*, 346 (2016), www.eastwestcenter.org/system/tdf/private/apb346.pdf?file=1&type=node&id=35662.

38 Jesse Johnson, "Canberra All but Rules out Japan Sub Bid: Report", *Japan Times*, April 20, 2016, www.japantimes.co.jp/news/2016/04/20/national/canberra-rules-japan-sub-bid-report/#.V_yyYJN97Vo.

39 John Garnaut, "Australia–Japan Military Ties are a 'quasi-alliance', Say Officials", *Sydney Morning Herald*, October 26, 2014, www.smh.com.au/national/australiajapan-military-ties-are-a-quasialliance-say-officials-20141026-11c4bi.html.

40 See Malcolm Cook and Thomas Wilkins, *The Quiet Achiever: Australia–Japan Security Relations* (Lowy Institute for International Policy, 2011).

41 For an early and influential articulation of this, see Dennis C. Blair and John T. Hanley, "From Wheels to Webs: Reconstructing Asia-Pacific Security Arrangements" *The Washington Quarterly*, 24:1 (2001), 7–17.

42 Tim Harcourt, "Power of Proximity in the Asian Century", *The Drum*, October 29, 2012.

43 Department of Prime Minister and Cabinet, *Australia in the Asian Century White Paper* (Canberra: Commonwealth of Australia, 2012), www.defence.gov.au/whitepaper/2013/docs/australia_in_the_asian_century_white_paper.pdf.

44 John Lee, "Divergence in Australia's Economic and Security Interests", in James Reilly and Jingdong Yuan, eds, *Australia and China at 40* (Sydney: UNSW Press, 2012), 142–161.

45 *Global Times* "'Paper cat' Australia Will Learn its Lesson", *Global Times*, July 30, 2016, www.globaltimes.cn/content/997320.shtml.

9 Vietnam between China and Japan in the Asian security complex

Alexander L. Vuving and Thuy T. Do

Located along Asia's lifeline, which runs through the South China Sea and the major land and sea routes connecting the north and the south of East Asia, Vietnam is of strategic importance for both China and Japan. Added to this critical location, Vietnam's growing market, fervent nationalism, and military tradition also have economic, security, and political implications that capture the attention of the two largest East Asian powers.

Its centrality, for better or worse, is reflected in both China and Japan's multi-dimensional approach to Vietnam. In 2008, Vietnam was the first to be formally declared China's "comprehensive strategic cooperative partner", an epithet meant to signify the highest level of commitment between Beijing and a foreign state. Vietnam is also the most important country in Southeast Asia for China in a different respect. It is China's main gateway into Southeast Asia, both on land and in the sea. In fact, Vietnam is the only Southeast Asian country with which China has engaged in war during the last 200 years. That said, Vietnam is considered a traditional sphere of influence that China does not want to lose to another power, as manifested in its 1979 "punitive" border war to "teach Vietnam a lesson" for acting, in Beijing's eyes, as a "regional hegemon" and for leaning towards the Soviet Union amid ongoing Sino-Soviet rivalry.

Japan's engagement of Vietnam is similarly important. Historically, Vietnam's strategic centrality made it a favourite destination of Japanese merchants since the seventeenth century and later a victim of Japanese militarism during the Second World War. Since the re-establishment of bilateral ties in 1992, twice Vietnam was the inaugural destination of a Japanese prime minister abroad. In November 2006, Prime Minister Abe Shinzō made his first foreign trip to Vietnam in conjunction with an Asia-Pacific Economic Cooperation (APEC) meeting in the country. He may be said to have had no choice at that time, but in January 2013, only a month after his re-election, Vietnam was once again his first visit. Judging from the commitment of Japanese leaders as expressed by their agreements of cooperation and leadership visits, Vietnam, as Japan's only "extensive strategic partner", is arguably Tokyo's fourth important partner in the Asia-Pacific region, after the US, Australia, and India, and on a par with the Philippines and Indonesia.[1] The strategic importance of Vietnam for Japan today appears to be derived from the country's location along the sea lanes of communication through the South China Sea and at the gateway between China and Southeast Asia.

160 *Alexander L. Vuving and Thuy T. Do*

If Vietnam is strategically important for both China and Japan, how are the two major powers influencing the smaller state? How is Vietnam responding to the influence of China and Japan? The next three sections of this chapter will address these questions. In the fourth section, we examine how the growing rivalry between China and Japan is played out in Vietnam and how this competition shapes Vietnam's strategic options. This analysis will provide the basis for us to draw, in the concluding section, a big picture of Vietnam between China and Japan in the Asian security complex.

China's influence in Vietnam

China has several advantages, some of which are unmatched, when it comes to its ability to influence Vietnam. A steep asymmetry of material capabilities, geographic proximity, cultural kinship, and regime affinity combine to provide the potential for China to be the most influential foreign power in Vietnam. The means by which China influences Vietnam's behaviour encompasses a full spectrum from military and politics, to economics and culture.

Military means have always been a key instrument with which China influences Vietnam. China invaded Vietnam in early 1979. The aim of the attack was, in the words of Chinese leaders, to "teach Vietnam a lesson". Although the invaders withdrew after a month, fighting continued along the land border throughout the next decade.[2] In addition to this border war, a naval clash in early 1988 at Johnson South Reef in the Spratly Islands, during which 70 Vietnamese troops were killed and the reef was taken by China, serves as a powerful reminder of China's willingness to use force against Vietnam. Preventing similar conflicts has subsequently been a key element of Vietnam's defence strategy. This naval clash also marked the shift of the major sites of Sino-Vietnamese conflict from the land border to the South China Sea. Since the renormalization of Sino-Vietnamese relations in 1991, China's use of military force against Vietnam has been reduced to a few occasions when the Chinese Navy was involved in chasing Vietnamese vessels out of areas China considered its own. More frequently in recent years, China uses paramilitary forces such as the Coast Guard (*haijing*), the Marine Surveillance (*haijian*), and the Fisheries Law Enforcement (*yuzheng*) as coercive tools against Vietnam in the South China Sea. Other use of military means to influence Vietnam include demonstrations of might through military exercises in the South China Sea and troop movements near the Sino-Vietnamese land border.

Military means can be used to generate both hard power and soft power, depending on the purpose of the action and its perception by the target audience. Japan's military cooperation with Vietnam is intended to bolster Hanoi's capability and position. As a result, the emphasis in the Japan–Vietnam relationship is on soft, not hard power. In contrast, Chinese military activities are generally perceived by the Vietnamese public as a threat because they target Vietnam's territorial and maritime claims in the South China Sea and reinforce Vietnam's sense of vulnerability vis-à-vis its giant neighbour in the north. However, this perception is complicated by the soft power effects of regime affinity, in which the military

Vietnam between China and Japan   161

plays a key role. The People's Liberation Army (PLA) of China and the People's Army of Vietnam share the same unusual characteristic as the military branches of their respective Communist Parties. Traumatized by the collapse of communism in Eastern Europe and the Tiananmen Square revolt in 1989, Vietnam and China found common ground to develop solidarity despite their territorial disputes. In fact, the Vietnamese military is the strongest advocate in Hanoi for close ties with China based on ideology. China employs military-to-military channels to directly influence the Vietnamese military and persuade Vietnam not to veer towards the US and the West. In 2015, less than a year after it caused the worst bilateral crisis since the renormalization by deploying a giant oil rig to waters Vietnam claims as an Exclusive Economic Zone (EEZ), China upgraded an annual border meeting between the two militaries to the ministerial level. Since the pro-China turn of the Vietnamese military in 1990, military-to-military relations have been a key force supporting friendship and cooperation between the two Communist regimes. It is notable that, in addition to deployment of military might as hard power, China also uses the military as soft power, as political communication rather than military operations. In this respect, the Chinese military is part of a larger political toolkit that China uses to influence Vietnam.

Besides the military-to-military relationship, ties between the two Communist Parties present another means to emphasize regime affinity. As such, they serve as another main channel through which China influences Vietnam. Like the ties between the two militaries, party-to-party relations strengthen the ideological bonds between the two ruling elites and it has been a primary conduit for bilateral relations in the renormalization period. It was through the separate but complementary military and party channels that the leaders of China and Vietnam negotiated their renormalization in the early 1990s, which sidelined the Vietnamese Ministry of Foreign Affairs and Embassy in Beijing.[3] As the Communist Party maintains exclusive and absolute leadership in the Vietnamese polity, military and party ties give China a huge advantage over the other major powers in influencing Vietnam.

Since the renormalization, Hanoi and Beijing have both been committed to frequent exchanges at all levels of the party-state, especially at the top. Perhaps more than any other country pair, China and Vietnam use bilateral diplomacy to advance relations. They conducted 29 bilateral visits at the top level of head of the Party, the state, and the government during the first 26 years after renormalization. These visits omitted only three years (2009, 2012, and 2014) but occurred twice per year in six others (1999, 2004, 2005, 2008, 2011, and 2015). The exchanges are meant to enhance mutual understanding and strengthen friendship, but they also provide an opportunity for influence. From the Vietnamese perspective, it is China that is better positioned to influence based on its greater power and larger capacity, but Vietnam also sees major benefits in the exchanges in terms of maintaining a positive relationship with Beijing and generating cooperation.

Agreements between successive generations of the two party-states' top leaders have served as fixtures of the relationship. These started with the secret agreements made on China's terms at the pre-normalization summit meeting at Chengdu in

162 *Alexander L. Vuving and Thuy T. Do*

1990 and reached new heights with those concluded at the visits of the General Secretaries of the Vietnam Communist Party (VCP) Le Kha Phieu in 1999 and Nong Duc Manh in 2008. On Phieu's visit in 1999, Chinese President and Party Chief Jiang Zemin offered a 16-word guideline for the Sino-Vietnamese relationship in the twenty-first century, which the Vietnamese readily accepted, although with a subtle twist. The guideline reads "long-term stability, future orientation, good-neighbourly friendship, comprehensive cooperation" in the Chinese version, but its Vietnamese version reverses the order and puts "friendly neighbours" first, followed by "comprehensive cooperation, long-term stability, future orientation". On Nong Duc Manh's visit in 2008, the two countries upgraded their relationship to a "comprehensive strategic cooperative partnership", placing each at the top tier in the hierarchy of the other's bilateral partnerships.[4] This epithet and the 16-word guideline serve as commitment devices that bind the two countries to a specific type of relationship. In the same spirit, during Chinese President and Party Chief Hu Jintao's visit to Vietnam in 2005, the Chinese gave their relationship a "four-good" motto that was to inspire them to be "good neighbours, good friends, good comrades, and good partners". Leaders' agreements made during the visits of VCP Chiefs Do Muoi and Le Kha Phieu to China in 1997 and 1999 were pivotal to the signing of the treaties delineating the Sino-Vietnamese land border and maritime border in the Gulf of Tonkin at the end of 1999 and 2000, respectively.

The settlement of the border disputes on land and in the Gulf of Tonkin and the adoption of the 16-word guideline at the end of the twentieth century raised Sino-Vietnamese relations to a new plateau characterized by unfettered bilateral engagement. An important effect of the enhanced partnership was a boom of economic exchanges, which had been insignificant as a means of influence in the 1990s. In 2001, two-way trade with China contributed 9.8 per cent of Vietnam's total foreign trade. This figure rose to 12.2 per cent in 2006, surged to 14.5 per cent in 2007, and steadily increased to 16.5 per cent in 2009 and 20 per cent in 2013. China replaced Japan as Vietnam's top trading partner in 2004 and has maintained its lead ever since, with a growing distance between the two. In 2013, Vietnam's trade with China was 1.67 times that with the US and 1.98 times that with Japan, the country's second and third largest trading partner.[5]

Sino-Vietnamese economic engagement has tightened Vietnam's economic dependence on its giant neighbour. The portion of Vietnam's imports from China in Vietnam's total imports grew rapidly from 9 per cent in 2000 to 16.4 per cent in 2006, surged to 20.3 per cent in 2007 and 23.6 per cent in 2011, peaked at 29.7 per cent in 2012 and stayed at 28.9 per cent in the first half of 2016.[6] During the same period, Vietnam's exports to China remained around the level of 10 per cent of Vietnam's total exports. As a result, Vietnam's China trade moved from surplus to deficit in 2001, and the balance of trade continued to tilt in China's favour. Vietnam's trade deficit with China rapidly deepened from US$190 million in 2001 to US$9 billion in 2007, US$23.7 billion in 2013, and US$32.3 billion in 2015.[7]

The trade deficit reflects the openness of Vietnam's economy combined with Vietnam's position relative to China in the geographic and technological landscapes. With its cheap consumer goods and equipment, China quickly gained the

Vietnam between China and Japan   163

dominant position in Vietnam's domestic market, locking its smaller neighbour in a structural disadvantage and tightening Vietnam's dependence on China. Vietnam's economic dependence on China rests primarily on Vietnam's imports, trade deficit, and the penetration of China's state-owned enterprises in Vietnam's construction, infrastructure, and energy sectors. As a tool of influence, foreign direct investment (FDI) from China plays an insignificant role, and official development assistance (ODA) that complies with the Organisation for Economic Cooperation and Development definition plays a minor role.[8] Much of Vietnam's imports from China and the domination of Chinese firms in the construction, infrastructure, and energy sectors are enabled not by ODA but by China's foreign aid, which is granted to Vietnam largely in the form of concessional loans procured by Chinese companies. These soft loans are relatively easy to obtain but are not without strings – the major conditions is the commitment to use Chinese contractors, equipment, and labour.[9] According to a report by the Finance and Budget Committee of the Vietnamese National Assembly, Chinese firms won the bids for about 90 per cent of the engineering, procurement, and construction projects in Vietnam, mostly in the energy, mining, and infrastructure sectors.[10]

China also influences Vietnam through cultural means. To signal Vietnam's commitment to friendship with China and also to meet Chinese leaders' requests, Vietnam is extremely accommodating of China with regard to domestic discourse on Sino-Vietnamese relations. History education in Vietnam after 1991 de-emphasized past conflicts with the People's Republic of China, and discussion of the 1979 war is reduced to less than half of a page in history textbooks, where at least 26 pages are devoted to the wars between 1961 and 1973 against the US.[11] By 2011, school textbooks in Vietnam also largely omitted discussion of the Paracel and Spratly Islands, with the result that most Vietnamese pupils were unaware of Vietnam's claims over these territories and Chinese occupation there. These self-binding measures began to be relaxed since 2009, with the rise of tension with China in the South China Sea. The public commemoration of the war with China in the 1970s and 1980s became normalized only after the 2014 oil rig crisis, which was triggered by China's deployment of the HYSY-981 oil platform to waters claimed by Vietnam as its EEZ.

On balance, political means appear to be China's most effective tool for influencing Vietnam. Beijing plays on the Vietnamese ruling elite's pervasive fear of regime change after the collapse of communism in Eastern Europe. Political influence has allowed China to gain advantage in Vietnam through economic, military, and cultural means. Economic means are highly effective in creating a structural dependence on China. In contrast, China's military-backed attempts to influence Vietnam have had mixed effects. They stoke fear and sometimes intimidation, but they also make the Vietnamese more suspicious and resentful of China. China's growing military power and assertive activities cause Vietnam to be accommodating and deferential to China, but they also cause Vietnam to seek means to resist.

Japan's influence in Vietnam

Unlike the complicated Vietnam–China relationship, the one between Vietnam and Japan is generally problem-free. Given the absence of the "tyranny of geography" and the strategic constraints imposed by its pacifist Constitution, Japan cannot influence Vietnam through military force. Tokyo's ability to use threat and intimidation to change Vietnam's behaviour is limited to the economic realm. The main pathways through which Japan exerts its influence on Vietnam are primarily soft power and secondarily the structural effects of Japan's engagement with Vietnam over time. Japan sometimes also acts as a bridge between Vietnam and the US and the West, and as a role model for "middle-power diplomacy". This is also an important aspect of Japan's soft power with Vietnam. With Japan's recent strategic resurgence amid growing Sino-Japanese rivalry and heightened territorial disputes in the East and South China Seas, Tokyo has attempted to strengthen its leverage over Hanoi through political and military means, making it an increasingly important factor in Vietnam's foreign policy.

Japan's influence on Vietnam is most obvious in the economic domain. Japan was among the first capitalist countries to reopen ties with Vietnam in the early 1990s. Later, Japan supported Vietnam's bid to join the World Trade Organization (WTO) in 2006 and was the second G-7 country (after Germany in 2008) to recognize Vietnam's full market economy status in 2011.[12] Being "the region's top trading partner and ODA provider, and a source of capital and technologies, Japan is of great significance to Vietnam's development".[13] Thus far, Japan is the only foreign country selected by Hanoi to support its long-term industrialization process, as manifest in "Vietnam's Industrialization Strategy in the framework of Vietnam–Japan cooperation towards 2020, vision to 2030". In recent years, Vietnamese leaders have repeatedly referred to Japan as their "first ranking economic partner" and "most important development partner", given that the latter has become their top ODA donor and the third largest investor and trading partner.[14] It is through such robust economic engagement that Japan has enjoyed structural and soft power effects on Vietnam.

Japanese investment in Vietnam is mostly private and primarily focuses on the processing and manufacturing industries. As of 2013, Japan was Vietnam's biggest foreign investor both in terms of registered and disbursed capital, with 1,990 valid projects capitalized at US$32.667 billion. By the end of 2015, Japan dropped to second place, with a cumulative US$39.176 billion of investment after South Korea's US$44.452 billion.[15] Among various industries, Japan has pledged to invest in six key sectors in Vietnam: consumer electrics/electronics, food processing, shipbuilding, agricultural machinery, environment and energy conservation, and automobile/spare part manufacturing. The programme, focusing on industries of strategic significance to Vietnam's future economic development, is tailored to enhance the competitiveness of Vietnamese enterprises when the tariff barrier in the Association of Southeast Asian Nations (ASEAN) Free Trade Area and other free trade agreements is lifted by 2018 and 2020, respectively.[16]

Japan was Vietnam's leading trading partner during the 1990s. This status was taken by China in 2004 and Japan now ranks third among Vietnam's biggest trading

Vietnam between China and Japan 165

partners (after China and the US). According to Vietnam Customs' statistics, two-way trade turnover has been growing steadily in the past ten years at an average annual rate of 13.9 per cent. In 2015, trade turnover reached US$28.49 billion, accounting for 8.7 per cent of Vietnam's total foreign trade. It is important to note that while Vietnam suffers from huge trade deficits with China, it enjoys trade surpluses with Japan (US$2.02 billion in 2013 and US$1.77 billion in 2014).[17]

Japanese ODA is significant as it primarily serves a two-fold objective: to help improve socioeconomic infrastructure, and to support the competitiveness of Vietnam's economy. Consistently Vietnam's top donor, Japan committed nearly US$20 billion for Vietnam between 1992 and 2011, accounting for about 30 per cent of the total ODA commitment from the international community. Since 2011, Vietnam has been Japan's largest ODA recipient country, making it "the most important ODA partner of Japan".[18] Recently, Japan also provided aid for Vietnam's maritime security forces amid Vietnam's heightened tensions with China in the South China Sea. This includes, among others, provision of patrol vessels and capacity-building assistance for the Vietnamese Coast Guard.

Overall, these economic means have exerted both structural and soft power effects on Vietnam. As the two economies are largely complementary, cooperation has been conducted on a win–win basis. There is little evidence of Japan trying to leverage its significant financial power to bribe Vietnam, whether at the state or individual levels. In addition, Japan's economic engagement has not generated similar vested interests among Vietnamese officials as China's does. Conversely, Japan's economic engagement has promoted positive structural change in Vietnam. For example, Vietnam has "effectively used Japan's ODA in accelerating economic restructuring, improving infrastructure, and in combating environmental pollution, infectious diseases, and in poverty reduction and hunger elimination, etc.".[19] This also helps increase Japan's soft power as trade and investment demonstrate the qualitative edge of Japan's technology, management, and people, while ODA sends a strong message about Japanese goodwill towards Vietnam. Although China has increased its aid and loans for Vietnam in recent years, the quality of Chinese suppliers is often not highly regarded, particularly when compared to their Japanese counterparts.[20] And while financial assistance from other Western donors often imposes strict requirements on Vietnam in terms of administrative reform and transparency, there are few political strings attached to Japanese capital, although lately Tokyo has conditioned its ODA on anti-corruption following several reports of bribery by Vietnamese officials in some Japanese-backed infrastructure projects.[21]

Other means for Japan to wield soft power in Vietnam include cultural and people-to-people exchanges. Japanese cultural products – such as movies, music, and games – are very popular in Vietnam, serving as mediums of information about Japan and Japanese people. Tourism, education and training, and immigration serve as other pathways for deepening the appeal of Japanese culture, society, and model of development. In 2015, Vietnam received 671,379 Japanese tourists (accounting for about 10 per cent of the total foreign visitors to the country in the year)[22] and there were about 185,395 Vietnamese tourists to Japan in 2015

166   *Alexander L. Vuving and Thuy T. Do*

(a two-fold increase from 2014).[23] Japan also provides generous non-returned aid for Vietnam in human capital development. Examples include the recent launch of the Japan–Vietnam University in Hanoi and Tokyo's pledge to help train 1,000 Vietnamese doctoral students in a 13-year-long project worth JPY20 billion, funded through ODA, starting from fiscal year 2008. Among the fields of study, Vietnam is placing priority on advanced technologies, such as information technology, mechanical engineering, materials, and nanotechnology, as well as agriculture, shipbuilding, and medicine.[24] As a result, the number of Vietnamese students in Japan has been growing steadily. In 2015, Vietnam had 38,882 students in Japan (a 47.1 per cent increase compared to 2014), making Vietnam the second-largest source of foreign students in Japan (after China).[25] Regarding labour exports, Vietnam sent about 31,000 workers and interns to Japan from 1992 to 2013.[26] As of 2015, there were 146,956 Vietnamese people studying and working in Japan (a 47.2 per cent increase from the previous year).[27] These Japan-trained human resources will serve as a bridge for technology and experience transfer from Japan to Vietnam, which in turn facilitates socioeconomic transformation in Vietnam.

Given these soft power effects, to date, the Vietnamese public holds a favourable image of Japan. According to a survey in 2004 by *Asia Barometer*, Japan ranks second in Vietnamese people's best images of foreign countries (only after Russia).[28] In another survey on public opinion on Japan in six ASEAN countries conducted by Japan's Ministry of Foreign Affairs in 2008, 98 per cent of the interviewees believe that Japan is a trustworthy friend to Vietnam and 100 per cent welcome Japanese companies to establish factories and facilities in their localities. Vietnamese people also chose Japan as the most important partner to their country both in the present and immediate future.[29] As Nghiem Vu Khai, Chairman of the Vietnam–Japan Friendship Association has noted,

> entering the life of the Vietnamese with the charm of sakura blossoms, practicality of numerous products like household utensils, motorbikes or at a more macro level, vital transport works, Japan has been closely associated to Vietnam in a very natural and close manner.[30]

The heart-felt support of Vietnamese people towards the victims of the tsunami and earthquake that hit Japan in 2011 and their admiration of how the Japanese people handled the hardship is one of the many examples to illustrate the solid ground of the empathy among the people.

Apart from economic and cultural means, political tools are also an increasingly significant component of Japan's influence. Japan was the first US ally to engage Vietnam after the Cold War and the Japanese (Asian) way of engagement is generally welcomed by Vietnamese. In past decades there have been regular exchange visits by high-ranking leaders that serve as a springboard for lifting bilateral relations to a new height. In 2002, Vietnam and Japan agreed to promote their relations as a "trusted and long-term stable partnership". In October 2006, the two governments decided to open a new phase of cooperation, "Toward a Strategic

Vietnam between China and Japan 167

Partnership for Peace and Prosperity in Asia". During a state visit to Japan by Vietnam's President Truong Tan Sang in March 2014, Hanoi and Tokyo decided to elevate their ties to a new level of "Extensive Strategic Partnership for Peace and Prosperity in Asia". Regular high-ranking visit exchanges and the strategic partnership framework have helped enhance political trust and the effectiveness of bilateral cooperation, especially via the Vietnam–Japan Cooperation Committee.

Japan's soft power in Vietnam also plays out in the international arena. Vietnam was one of the few ASEAN countries that gave its consistent support for Japan's bid for a permanent seat on the United Nations Security Council despite China's diplomatic pressure.[31] Japan recognizes the role that Vietnam, with its diplomatic ties with North Korea, could play in the politics surrounding the divided Korean peninsula. Prime Minister Abe has asked Vietnam to keep pressing North Korea to resolve the issue of its abduction of Japanese citizens, which prevents Tokyo and Pyongyang from normalizing relations.[32] Hanoi and Tokyo have also effectively coordinated on international and regional forums such as the East Asia Summit, ASEAN+3, and the Greater Mekong sub-regional development.

Lately Vietnam–Japan cooperation has become more strategic, particularly in the area of maritime security. This is a response to the growing tensions in the South China Sea, which is home to an important trade route for the Japanese economy, and Japan's expansion of its regional standing and role of its military. Given the lingering constitutional constraints, Japan has cautiously exercised a form of "indirect balancing" against China's rise and its growing assertiveness in the South China Sea by helping to strengthen Vietnam's economy to reduce its dependence on Chinese imports as well as enhancing Vietnam's capability in preserving its own security and territory in the South China Sea. Since 2012, Japan has used ODA for "strategic purposes". In December 2011, Tokyo decided to ease the restrictions imposed under its Three Principles on Arms Exports and is now seeking to promote direct arms exports to support the defence infrastructure of ASEAN countries.[33]

Against this background, Hanoi and Tokyo started enhancing their security and defence cooperation. In July 2010, they agreed to implement a subcabinet-level "two-plus-two" dialogue (a meeting involving the Foreign and Defence Ministries), a close security arrangement that Japan has only with the US, Australia, India (and Russia since late 2013). In 2011, the two defence ministers signed a Memorandum of Understanding on defence cooperation and exchange, which sets forth, among other items, the regular holding of vice-ministerial-level talks, the regular mutual visits by working-level officials, and cooperation on humanitarian assistance and disaster relief.[34] In 2013, during the Japanese defence minister's visit to Vietnam, the two Defence Ministries agreed to cooperate in human resource training, bomb and mine clearance, modernization of Vietnamese marine police forces, and military technical areas.[35] After the 2014 oil rig incident, Japan announced that it would provide Vietnam with six patrol vessels. More recently, Japan is the second country after Russia to get access to Cam Ranh Bay facilities (refuelling in late 2015 and early 2016), and the second country after Singapore to have naval ships visit Cam Ranh International Port.

168 *Alexander L. Vuving and Thuy T. Do*

In short, it can be said that Japan has become an increasingly important actor in Vietnam's decision-making. Japan's political and strategic leverage, however, is limited by Japan's secondary role to the US in the security and military realms, and by regime difference with Hanoi. The reality that Japan's military power and regional role is heavily constrained may also be responsible for negative effects on Vietnamese respect of Japanese power. In particular, the image of Japan as not having an independent foreign policy due to alliance with the US remains strong in Vietnam, as well as across Southeast Asia. Given this fact, Japan's influence on Vietnam to date generates mostly soft power effects of economic, political, cultural, and military exchanges. There have also been some structural effects of Vietnam's dependence on Japanese aid and trade, but this has not precipitated negative reactions among Vietnamese as in the case of China. Thus far, Japanese engagement of Vietnam has created the impetus to foster relations for some time to come.

Vietnam's responses to Chinese and Japanese power

Much of Vietnam's behaviour towards China is derived from structural conditions. The steep asymmetry of capabilities combined with geographic proximity and the prospects of living next door to China forever make deference a near constant in Vietnam's China policy. At the same time, the maintenance of a separate Vietnamese identity and Vietnam's political independence requires some resistance to the giant in the north. Deference and defiance have become the defining features of Vietnam's traditional approach towards China, honed by centuries of interaction in war and peace.[36] However, the subtle and complex ways of Vietnam's accommodation and resistance to China do not always reflect the structural conditions of their relations. Identity and interests are powerful variables that intervene to significantly modify the structural effects.[37] And this is true not particularly of Vietnam's behaviour towards China but more generally of Hanoi's conduct towards others, including Japan. Understanding Vietnam's behaviour requires the appreciation not just of the structural conditions of the country's strategic environment but also the identities and interests of its ruling elite.

For more than four decades after the end of what is known in the West as the Vietnam War but referred to in Vietnam as the American War, Vietnam has been ruled by the Communist Party. Beneath the continuity of a single-party regime, the elite that govern it have undergone substantial evolution. Starting in 1986, reform-era Vietnam has been marked by the selective and partial pursuit of Western-style modernization and integration into the Western-led international order by a party-state that remains wedded to an anti-Western ideology. As a consequence of these conditions, the political trajectories in the country reflect an evolving mixture of four policy currents. The first is driven by conservatives, who advocate political stability through regime preservation. The second current is represented by the reformers, who promote domestic modernization and international openness. The marriage of communism and capitalism in the reform era has led to the ascent of two other policy currents. One of these two, represented by the moderates,

Vietnam between China and Japan   169

follows the middle of the road, trying to bridge the diametrical differences between communism and capitalism. The other current, which can be called rent-seeking, pursues a dualistic approach, accumulating profit the capitalist way and power the communist way.[38]

The most important feature of the evolution of Vietnamese politics since the mid-1980s is the rise and crisis of a rent-seeking state. For a very short period from 1986 until 1989, reformers became slightly more influential than adherents to the other policy currents. However, conservatives regained primacy during 1989–1990, when communist regimes collapsed in Eastern Europe and the Soviet bloc practically disintegrated. Conservatives maintained their top position until the early 2000s. By 2006, rent-seekers emerged as the most powerful among Vietnam's four major policy currents. The decade between 2006 and 2016 was a time when rent-seekers reached hegemony but eventually lost ground.[39] The 12th Congress of the VCP in January 2016 ushered in a new period. In this, "Although rent-seeking may continue to dominate in the VCP Central Committee, modernisation is the most influential policy current in the Politburo."[40] Two events in 2016 illustrate well this new trend. While launching a major campaign to cut red tape, the new government under Prime Minister Nguyen Xuan Phuc also demonstrated its political will by undertaking a coordinated effort to punish local officials who harass and criminalize business. The Party leadership under General Secretary Nguyen Phu Trong also stepped up its campaign against rent-seeking, censuring former Minister of Industry and Trade Vu Huy Hoang, a prominent rent-seeker, for his wrongdoings over the last ten years.

Vietnam's response to foreign power is a patchwork of different, often mutually conflicting, strategies that are preferred by the country's four major policy currents. Conservatives perceive the greatest threat to Vietnam's security as coming from the West, most notably the US, in the form of what they term "peaceful evolution", which refers to sabotage activities to undermine and transform the Communist regime. Given this threat perception, they view China as the most important foreign ally in the struggle against regime change.[41] Conservatives thus strongly prefer solidarity with China, but this strategy is compromised by the Sino-Vietnamese territorial and maritime conflicts, and has met lukewarm reception from Beijing. As a result, while the conservatives' strategy towards China emphasizes solidarity, it more often takes the shape of deference.[42] Reformers, in contrast, perceive the country's underdevelopment as the largest threat and view advanced industrial countries, most prominently the US and Japan, as their pioneer in the quest for modernization. More nationalist than ideologist, reformers advocate close ties with the dynamic industrialized countries, while regarding China more as a competitor than a comrade. The reformers' preferred strategy towards China is to combine hard and soft balancing with enmeshment in an international web of interlocking interests.[43] Unlike both conservatives and reformers, rent-seekers are driven less by threat perception and more by opportunities.[44] They see the largest opportunity to thrive in economic engagement with the outside world. In the 1990s, rent-seekers looked primarily to capitalist Asia and the West, but since the turn of the century, China has emerged as their most preferred partner, with its way of doing business that prefers kickbacks and dislikes transparency.

170 *Alexander L. Vuving and Thuy T. Do*

Vietnam's approach to China since the renormalization of relations in 1991 has gone through four major phases. In the 1990s a combination of solidarity, deference, soft balancing, and enmeshment characterized Hanoi's strategy. In the 2000s, engagement was increasingly added to the mix, becoming the strongest component by the second half of the decade, while solidarity morphed into deference and enmeshment faded relative to the other approaches. Starting in the late 2000s, China's assertiveness in the South China Sea increasingly strengthened both hard and soft balancing while discrediting solidarity and enmeshment.[45] Sino-Vietnamese relations plunged into a severe crisis when China, from May 2 until July 15, 2014, unilaterally parked the US$1 billion oil platform HYSY-981 in Vietnam's EEZ. Following this oil rig crisis and to the present, Vietnam's strategy emphasizes a combination of hard and soft balancing and deference, while engagement is pursued more reluctantly, with more suspicion.[46]

If Vietnam's strategies towards China include both cooperative and competitive elements, covering nearly the full range of a continuum running between hard balancing on one extreme and solidarity on the other, Hanoi's responses to Japanese power are much less complex and far more cooperative than competitive. All four major policy currents in Vietnam emphasize economic engagement with Japan, although to different extents and for different reasons. Tokyo also serves as a partial counterweight to other major powers, most notably China, in Vietnam's balancing strategy. In other words, Hanoi's primary interest in relations with Japan is economic, but Vietnam also nurtures strong ties with Japan in order to keep its options open when dealing with the major powers. This geopolitical dimension of Vietnam's policy towards Japan has become more salient with the growth of Chinese assertiveness in the East and South China Seas, which pushes Japan and Vietnam closer than ever before. From a secondary component, strategic cooperation is becoming a major element on a par with economic engagement in Vietnam's approach to Japan.

Vietnam's options and role in the Sino-Japanese competition

If there was a rivalry between China and Japan for influence over Vietnam, it remained tacit and latent during most of the 1990s and 2000s. In the 1990s, Japan was more influential than China in the economic domain, while China was more influential than Japan in the political area. The balance of influence began to shift starting in the early 2000s. With the growth of its economic clout and the bilateral trade with Vietnam, China has become a major competitor of Japan in the economic realm. Since the late 2000s, with the rise of Chinese assertiveness in the East and South China Seas and Japan's support for Vietnam in the South China Sea, Japan has increasingly been China's competitor in the strategic field.

Several events marked this process. In 2004, China overtook Japan as Vietnam's top trading partner. In 2010, China surpassed Japan as Asia's largest economy and the world's second largest. Also in 2010, Japan Coast Guard officers boarded a defiant Chinese trawler in the Senkaku/Diaoyu Islands area and detained the Chinese captain, upsetting China, which responded by suspending political and cultural exchanges and stopping rare earth exports to Japan. Three times in 2011, Chinese vessels cut the exploration cable of Vietnamese vessels in the South China Sea, prompting several anti-China protests in Vietnam. Two recent events are illustrative of the Sino-Japanese strategic competition and Vietnam's role in it. On November 5, 2015, a few hours before Chinese President Xi Jinping arrived in Hanoi for a state visit, Japanese Defence Minister Nakatani Gen came to Cam Ranh Bay, starting his official visit to Vietnam. During this visit, Vietnam and Japan signed agreements on holding joint naval exercises and on Japanese military vessels and aircraft receiving refuelling and replenishment at Cam Ranh Bay.[47] With deep-water harbours protected seaward by a peninsula and with its location close to major transoceanic routes, Cam Ranh Bay is an ideal place for most strategic air and naval bases in the South China Sea area. In early 2016, Vietnam inaugurated an international port that would provide logistical services to foreign militaries. This international port is separate from the air and naval bases nearby, to which only the Vietnamese, Russian, and possibly Japanese militaries have access. In the ensuing months, Japan became the second country – after Singapore – to send naval ships to the international port facility, while China was the seventh – after India, France, Russia, and the US.

The growing Sino-Japanese competition is likely to widen rather than restrict Vietnam's strategic options. This can be seen in four major categories, depending on whether the major powers rely on cooptive or coercive measures, that is, whether they behave cooperatively, coercively or indifferently towards Vietnam. If China and Japan use co-optive measures, Vietnam is well positioned to benefit from its relations with both major powers as the two have an incentive to outcompete the other in gaining Vietnam's favour. This appears to be the case in the economic realm, where Japan is Vietnam's largest aid donor and second largest foreign direct investor, and China is Vietnam's largest foreign contractor and top trading partner. After the 2014 oil rig crisis, Vietnam handed the contract to build a 688-megawatt coal-fired power plant at the Duyen Hai complex on its southern coast to Sumitomo Corporation of Japan, although before the incident Japanese firms assumed a Chinese company could win the contract.[48]

If one major power uses coercive measures and the other behaves uncooperatively, Vietnam will have a hard time finding a third alternative. But this option remains more hypothetical than real. Japan has rarely used coercive measures against Vietnam, except for two major occasions in December 2008 and June 2014, when Tokyo suspended ODA due to kick-back scandals involving Japanese companies overseeing Japan-funded projects. However, none of these suspensions affected current loans. Moreover, Japan resumed its aid programmes three months after the announcement of the first suspension and less than two months after the second.[49] On the other hand, Japan has been one of the few governments that supported Vietnam when the latter faced challenges from China. In recent years, when China became more aggressive towards Vietnam in the South China Sea, and as Vietnam took steps to reduce its economic dependence on China, Japan responded by increasing its security and economic cooperation with Vietnam.

172 *Alexander L. Vuving and Thuy T. Do*

Japan has been comparatively far more reluctant than China to rely on coercive measures in dealing with Vietnam. This may result from China's greater power, Japan's greater risk-aversion, and the fact that Japan shares more strategic interests with Vietnam than China does with its little neighbour. Japan is on Vietnam's side in facing China in both regional security nodes that involve Vietnam, namely the South China Sea and the Mekong River Basin. As a countermeasure to China's growing economic influence in continental Southeast Asia, Japan has also stepped up its development assistance and economic cooperation with the Lower Mekong countries, including Vietnam, Thailand, Myanmar, Cambodia, and Laos. From both Vietnamese and Japanese perspectives, China is trying to alter the regional configuration of power at the expense of Vietnam and Japan. It is imperative for both Vietnam and Japan to join forces to balance China's expansion of influence. However, both Hanoi and Tokyo are well aware that, given Tokyo's restricted military power, any balancing effort that involves Vietnam and Japan only will not be sufficient to deter China. Thus, Japan's and Vietnam's balancing effort must be seen in the wider context of their coalition-building with a larger set of major and middle powers, notably the US, India, Russia, France, the UK, Australia, South Korea, and ASEAN states. In addition, the perception of China's overwhelming power also poses limitations on what Vietnam and Japan can do in strengthening and deepening their security cooperation.

Conclusion

The Vietnam–China–Japan triangle is embedded in a regional security complex that involves in its inner circle four major powers – China, Japan, the US, and India. Within this regional security complex, Vietnam is involved in two major security nodes: the South China Sea and the Mekong sub-region. While China is one of the local players there, major powers based outside such as Japan, the US, and India also play important roles in these two nodes. In the South China Sea, Vietnam and China are at odds over the ownership of the Paracel and Spratly Islands and the maritime boundaries along Vietnam's central and southeastern coasts. This conflict makes Vietnam feel insecure over China's growing influence in Laos and Cambodia, the two countries that flank Vietnam's western borders. In both security nodes, Vietnam is on the same side as Japan, the US, and India, facing China on the other side. It is the South China Sea disputes that give rise to the enmity between China and Vietnam and strengthen the amity between Vietnam and Japan, the US, and India. A pattern of enmity has also emerged between China and Japan, catalysed primarily by their disputes over the Senkaku/Diaoyu Islands and the maritime boundary in the East China Sea. These simple alignment patterns are, however, complicated by a pattern of amity between the two communist regimes ruling China and Vietnam, and a pattern of enmity between these regimes and the US.

With its strategic location and its capability as a sub-regional power in the South China Sea and the Mekong River Basin, Vietnam has the potential to act as a swing state in the balance of power between China and the other major powers in the Asian security complex. However, this swing-state role is more limited than it first appears. With respect to Japan, Vietnam can swing back and forth to maximize benefits from its relations with China and Japan. But the extent to which Vietnam can swing and still reap benefits is not large. China has shown no willingness to compromise in the South China Sea conflict. At the same time, Japan is one of the few governments that has strongly supported Vietnam in the South China Sea issue, at least comparatively. Veering to China and away from Japan will only worsen the predicament Vietnam faces in its asymmetric relations with its giant neighbour.

The balance of power between China on one side and Japan, Vietnam, and their security partners on the other is a set of complex inequalities. As a first cut, consider their GDP in market exchange rates. According to the World Bank estimates, China's GDP in 2015 was US$10,866.4 billion, while Japan's was US$4,123.3 billion, India's was US$2,073.5 billion, and Vietnam's was US$193.6 billion. The US GDP in the same year was US$17,947 billion.[50] With a GDP equal to 60.5 per cent of that of the US, whereas the latter has its home far away and can allocate up to 60–70 per cent of its resources to the Asian theatre, China has reached or is about to reach power parity with the US within the Asian security complex.[51] Without the US, a coalition including Japan, India, and Vietnam would be no match for China. The sum of these three states' GDP in 2015 amounts to only 58.8 per cent of China's. The only nuclear weapons state among the three, India has an arsenal of 120 weapons, less than half of China's 260.[52]

Of course, the GDP provides only a first cut, not the essence nor the big picture of the balance of power between states. It gives a first approximation of a state's economic power, which is also a foundation of the state's military power.[53] Power, in its wider application, refers not just to the powers to pay, buy, coerce, and prevail, but also to the powers to resist, coopt, gain trust, build coalitions, convince, set the agenda, shape the playing field, and manipulate. All these powers need material resources and the GDP provides a rough sense of the amount of material resources a country can generate. But to get a better view of the balance of power, one needs to take into account not only the total output a country produces but also many other factors, of which geography, technology, resolve, national identity, strategic culture, and organizational culture are the most important. Its GDP suggests that Vietnam can add very little to the balance of power between China and Japan. However, its strategic location, national identity, and strategic culture may amplify its strategic weight and make a difference in the Sino-Japanese competition.

Given the ongoing power shift in East Asia, the dynamics of Sino-Japanese amity and enmity will, to a large extent, shape the evolving regional security landscape. Like its many smaller regional neighbours, Vietnam fears a great power condominium that will be at the expense of its interests. Hanoi, however, would not want to see an open conflict between China and Japan because it has to choose a side. If anything, history has taught Vietnam bitter lessons about being a victim of great power rivalry. Therefore, Vietnam may prefer small-scale Sino-Japanese tensions and strategic competition so that it can attract resources from and swing

174 *Alexander L. Vuving and Thuy T. Do*

between both powers. Along that line, Hanoi has proactively sought to engage with Beijing while constantly reiterating its long-time non-alliance policy upon fostering strategic ties with Japan and other powers as a hedge against China's territorial ambition in the South China Sea. This strategic ambivalence of Vietnam has subsequently contributed to shape the pattern of ongoing Sino-Japanese competition and the dynamics of the evolving East Asian security complex.

Notes

1 This is a hierarchy of *partnerships*, in which only cooperative elements count, as opposed to *relationships*, which may include both cooperative and competitive elements. China, South Korea, North Korea, Russia, and Taiwan are always among the most important foreign states for Japan. But except for Taiwan, most of them are more often competitors than partners of Japan, thus their current value as Japan's partners is not very high. Taiwan can be seen as fairly close to Japan, but its lack of recognized statehood diminishes its strategic importance. Japan is a treaty ally of the US, a "special strategic partner" of Australia, and a "special strategic and global partner" of India. Tokyo also has a "strategic partnership with a special bond of friendship" with the Philippines and a "strategic partnership underpinned by sea and democracy" with Indonesia.

2 Nayan Chanda, *Brother Enemy: The War after the War* (New York: Harcourt Brace Jovanovich, 1986); Xiaoming Zhang, *Deng Xiaoping's Long War: The Military Conflict between China and Vietnam, 1979–1991* (Chapel Hill: University of North Carolina Press, 2015).

3 See the memoirs of then Vietnamese Vice Foreign Minister Tran Quang Co, "Hoi uc va Suy nghi" (Reminiscences and Reflections), unpublished manuscript, 2003, www.diendan.org/tai-lieu/ho-so/hoi-ky-tran-quang-co/hoiky-tqc-ch-0.

4 China has since formally declared a "comprehensive strategic cooperative partnership" with Laos in 2009, Cambodia in 2010, Myanmar and Russia in 2011, and Thailand in 2012. For a list of China's bilateral partnerships, see "China's 58 Partners Around the World", *Global Times Online*, July 29, 2014, www.globaltimes.cn/content/873141.shtml, and Peter Woods and Matt Brazil, "China's Foreign Relations: Levels of Commitment", September 18, 2016, www.p-wood.co/2016/09/18/chinas-foreign-relations.

5 Author's compilation using data from Vietnam's Customs Authority and Ministry of Industry and Trade. Note, however, that there is a large gap of about US$30 billion between Vietnam's and China's official statistics of the volume of their two-way trade. China's statistics for the China–Vietnam trade in 2015 is US$95.82 billion, while Vietnam's figure is US$66 billion. The Chinese figure for 2014 is US$83.6 billion, while the Vietnamese figure is US$58.7 billion. Some Vietnamese experts believe illicit trade and informal border trade account for most of the difference. See "Dang sau nhung con so thong ke kim ngach thuong mai Viet-Trung" (Behind the Statistical Figures of the Vietnam–China Trade), *Giao duc Viet Nam*, April 7, 2016, http://giaoduc.net.vn/Quoc-te/Dang-sau-nhung-con-so-thong-ke-kim-ngach-thuong-mai-Viet--Trung-post166959.gd

6 "Thuc trang su phu thuoc cua kinh te Viet Nam vao Trung Quoc" (The State of Vietnam's Economic Dependence on China), Central Institute for Economic Management (CIEM), Hanoi, August 29, 2014, www.vnep.org.vn/vi-vn/Hoi-nhap-kinh-te-quoc-te/Thuc-trang-su-phu-thuoc-cua-kinh-te-Viet-Nam-vao-Trung-Quoc.html; for the first half of 2016: Manh Nguyen, "Hang hoa Trung Quoc vao Viet Nam dang giam dan", *VietTimes*, June 25, 2016, http://viettimes.net.vn/hang-hoa-tu-trung-quoc-vao-viet-nam-dang-giam-dan-63727.html

7 CIEM, "Thuc trang su phu thuoc cua kinh te Viet Nam vao Trung Quoc"; for the 2015 figure, see Ngo Trang, "32 ty USD Viet Nam nhap sieu tu Trung Quoc nam 2015", *VnEconomy*, December 26, 2015, http://vneconomy.vn/thoi-su/32-ty-usd-viet-nam-nhap-sieu-tu-trung-quoc-nam-2015-20151226021543133.htm.

8 For some discussion of Vietnam's economic dependence on China, see CIEM, "Thuc trang su phu thuoc cua kinh te Viet Nam vao Trung Quoc"; Central Institute for Economic Management, *Phu thuoc kinh te giua Viet Nam va Trung Quoc* (Economic Dependence Between Vietnam and China) (Hanoi: Tai chinh, 2016); "Cac kich ban co the xay ra trong quan he kinh te Viet Nam – Trung Quoc – Giai phap han che su phu thuoc kinh te vao Trung Quoc" (Possible Scenarios in Vietnam–China Economic Relations: Solutions to Mitigate Economic Dependence on China), Central Institute for Economic Management, August 29, 2014, www.vnep.org.vn/vi-vn/Hoi-nhap-kinh-te-quoc-te/Cac-kich-ban-co-the-xay-ra-trong-quan-he-kinh-te-Viet-Nam-Trung-Quoc-Giai-phap-han-che-su-phu-thuoc-kinh-te-vao-Trung-Quoc.html. For a discussion of Vietnam–China trade, see Ha Thi Hong Van, "Nhung dac trung co ban cua quan he thuong mai Viet Nam-Trung Quoc trong giai doan hien nay" (Basic Characteristics of Contemporary Vietnam–China Trade Relations), *Nghien cuu Trung Quoc*, 1:161 (2015), 19–36.

9 Tran Ngoc Tho, "Von vay 'ODA' ma khong phai la ODA" (ODA Loans that are not ODA), *Thoi bao Kinh te Saigon*, August 19, 2016, www.thesaigontimes.vn/150191/Von-vay-ODA-ma-khong-phai-la-ODA.html; "Von vay tu Trung Quoc: Dieu chung ta khong nen chap nhan" (Capital Borrowed from China: What We Should Not Accept), *Dat Viet*, April 30, 2015, http://baodatviet.vn/kinh-te/tai-chinh/von-vay-tu-trung-quoc-dieu-chung-ta-khong-nen-chap-nhan-3265123.

10 CIEM, "Thuc trang su phu thuoc cua kinh te Viet Nam vao Trung Quoc".

11 See the history textbook for high school seniors published by the publishing house of the Ministry of Education in 2008.

12 "Cac quoc gia cong nhan Viet Nam la nen kinh te thi truong" (Nations Recognizing Vietnam as a Market Economy), Vietnam Chamber of Commerce and Industry (VCCI), December 12, 2013, http://chongbanphagia.vn/cac-quoc-gia-cong-nhan-viet-nam-la-nen-kinh-te-thi-truong-n4559.html.

13 Dinh Thi Hien Luong, "Vietnam–Japan Relations in the Context of Building an East Asian Community", *Asia-Pacific Review*, 16:1 (2009), 100–130, quotation on p. 108.

14 Foreign Minister Pham Binh Minh's interview "Vietnam–Japan Relations Will Continue to Grow Steadily", *Voice of Vietnam*, 21 September 2013, http://english.vov.vn/Politics/VietnamJapan-relations-will-continue-to-grow-steadily/265153.vov.

15 Ngo Quang Trung, "Dau tu truc tiep nuoc ngoai o Viet Nam: Thuc trang va van de" (Foreign Direct Investment in Vietnam: Reality and Issues), Institute for Policy and Development, Political Academy Region I, May 12, 2016, www.ipd.org.vn/nghien-cuu-truong-hop-noi-bat/dau-tu-truc-tiep-nuoc-ngoai-o-viet-nam-giai-doan-1988-2015:-thuc-trang-va-van-de-tac-gia:-ngo-quang-trung-a452.html.

16 "Japanese Gov't to Back 6 Key Industries in Vietnam", *Tuoi Tre News*, December 5, 2013.

17 Information was retrieved from the website of Vietnam's Customs, http://customs.gov.vn/Lists/ThongKeHaiQuan/ViewDetails.aspx?ID=958&Category=&Group=Ph%C3%A2n%20t%C3%ADch

18 "Việt Nam là đối tác ODA quan trọng nhất của Nhật" (Vietnam is the Most Important ODA Partner of Japan), *VnExpress*, January 31, 2013.

19 Dinh, "Vietnam–Japan Relations", p. 111.

20 Tom Wright and Misuru Obe, "Vietnam Plays Key Role in China–Japan Aid Battle", *Wall Street Journal*, March 27, 2015.

21 "Vietnam Asked to Return Bribe in Japan's ODA Project", *Thanh Nien News*, April 1, 2015.

22 Information was retrieved from the website of Vietnam's Tourism Bureau, http://vietnamtourism.gov.vn/index.php/items/19659.
23 Information was retrieved from the website of Japan National Tourism Organization, www.jnto.go.jp/eng/ttp/sta/PDF/E2015.pdf.
24 "Japan to Help Train 1000 Vietnamese Doctoral Students", *Hanoi Times*, 4 March 2008.
25 Japan Student Services Organization, "International Students in Japan 2015", www.jasso.go.jp/en/about/statistics/intl_student/data2015.html.
26 Vietnam's Government Portal, "Làm sâu sắc hơn quan hệ đối tác chiến lược VN-Nhật Bản" (Further Deepening the Vietnam–Japan Strategic Partnership), 9 December 2013.
27 "Japan's Foreign Population Climbs to All-Time High", www.nippon.com/en/features/h00137.
28 Kazuya Yamamoto, "Vietnam from the Perspective of the Asia Barometer Survey: Identity, Images of Foreign Nations, and Global Concerns", *Memoirs of the Institute of Oriental Culture*, 150 (2007), 320.
29 Ministry of Foreign Affairs of Japan, www.mofa.go.jp/region/asia-paci/asean/survey/qa0803.pdf, accessed January 12, 2014.
30 "Japan–Vietnam Relationship: Ever Beautiful as the Sakura", *Thoi Dai*, February 6, 2012, www.jica.go.jp/vietnam/english/office/topics/events120517_07.html
31 When Japan first bid for a permanent seat on the United Nations Security Council in 2005, only Singapore and Vietnam among the ASEAN states showed support for Japan due to diplomatic pressure applied to other nations in the region by China. See Corey J. Wallace, "Japan's Strategic Pivot South: Diversifying the Dual Hedge", *International Relations of the Asia-Pacific* 13:3 (2013), 479–517.
32 "Japan, Vietnam to Tighten Maritime Relations Amid China Threat", *Kyodo News*, October 7, 2013.
33 Ken Jimbo, "Japan Should Build ASEAN's Security Capacity", *AJISS Commentary*, 150, May 30, 2012.
34 Japan Ministry of Defense, www.mod.go.jp/e/jdf/no24/leaders.html, accessed January 15, 2014.
35 "Vietnam, Japan Vow to Strengthen Military Ties", *Tuoi Tre News*, September 13, 2013.
36 For more discussion, see Alexander L. Vuving, "Operated by World Views and Interfaced by World Orders: Traditional and Modern Sino-Vietnamese Relations", in Anthony Reid and Zheng Yangwen, eds, *Negotiating Asymmetry: China's Place in Asia* (Singapore: National University of Singapore Press, 2009), 73–92.
37 For more discussion, see Alexander L. Vuving, "How Experience and Identity Shape Vietnam's Relations with China and the United States", in Joon-Woo Park, Gi-Wook Shin, and Donald W. Keyser, eds, *Asia's Middle Powers? The Identity and Regional Policy of South Korea and Vietnam* (Stanford: Stanford University Shorenstein Asia-Pacific Research Center, 2013), 53–71.
38 This portion is adapted from Alexander L. Vuving, "Vietnam in 2012: A Rent-Seeking State on the Verge of a Crisis", in Daljit Singh, ed., *Southeast Asian Affairs 2013* (Singapore: Institute of Southeast Asian Studies, 2013), 325–347; Vuving, "Vietnam's Search for Stability", *The Diplomat*, October 25, 2012.
39 Alexander L. Vuving, "Power Rivalry, Party Crisis and Patriotism: New Dynamics in the Vietnam–China–US Triangle", in Li Mingjiang and Kalyan M. Kemburi, eds, *New Dynamics in US–China Relations: Contending for the Asia-Pacific* (London: Routledge, 2015), 271–273.
40 Alexander L. Vuving, "Why Trong's Re-election Doesn't Spell the End for Reform in Vietnam", *East Asia Forum*, April 5, 2016, www.eastasiaforum.org/2016/04/05/why-trongs-re-election-doesnt-spell-the-end-for-reform-in-vietnam.
41 Vuving, "How Experience and Identity Shape", 62–63.
42 Alexander L. Vuving, "Strategy and Evolution of Vietnam's China Policy: A Changing Mixture of Pathways", *Asian Survey*, 6:46 (2006), 805–824.

Vietnam between China and Japan   177

43 Vuving, "How Experience and Identity Shape", 63–64.
44 Alexander L. Vuving, "Vietnam: A Tale of Four Players", in Daljit Singh, ed., *Southeast Asian Affairs 2010* (Singapore: Institute of Southeast Asian Studies, 2010).
45 Vuving, "Power Rivalry, Party Crisis and Patriotism", 273–278.
46 Alexander L. Vuving, "A Tipping Point in the U.S.–China–Vietnam Triangle", *The Diplomat*, July 6, 2015.
47 "Bo truong Quoc phong Nhat tham quan cang Cam Ranh" (Japan's Minister of Defense Visits Cam Ranh Naval Base), *VietNamNet*, November 5, 2015, http://vietnamnet.vn/vn/thoi-su/bo-truong-quoc-phong-nhat-tham-quan-cang-cam-ranh-271472.html; "Japan to Strengthen Defence Ties with Vietnam", *Thanh Nien News*, November 6, 2015,www.thanhniennews.com/politics/japan-to-strengthen-defence-ties-with-vietnam-53372.html; "Japanese Patrol Aircraft to Stop at Vietnam Naval Base", *Thanh Nien News*, January 11, 2016, www.thanhniennews.com/politics/japanese-patrol-aircraft-to-stop-at-vietnam-naval-base-58001.html.
48 Wright and Obe, "Vietnam Plays Key Role".
49 "Japan Presses Bribery Charges against Execs in Vietnam Graft Scandal", *Thanh Nien News*, July 11, 2014, www.thanhniennews.com/politics/japan-presses-bribery-charges-against-execs-in-vietnam-graft-scandal-28398.html; "Japan Resumes ODA to Vietnam", *VietNamNet Bridge*, July 21, 2014, http://english.vietnamnet.vn/fms/business/107863/japan-resumes-oda-to-vietnam.html.
50 "Gross Domestic Product 2015", World Development Indicators database, World Bank, October 11, 2016, http://databank.worldbank.org/data/download/GDP.pdf.
51 Part of the US rebalance strategy towards Asia is to position 60 per cent of its Air Force and Navy forces to the Indo-Pacific region. See Cheryl Pellerin, "Budget Constraints Won't Halt Asia-Pacific Rebalance, Work Says", *Department of Defense News*, October 1,2014,www.defense.gov/News/Article/Article/603364/budget-constraints-wont-halt-asia-pacific-rebalance-work-says
52 "World Nuclear Weapons Stockpile Report", *The Bulletin of the Atomic Scientists*, March 2, 2016, www.ploughshares.org/world-nuclear-stockpile-report.
53 Paul Kennedy, *The Rise and Fall of the Great Powers: Economic Change and Military Conflict from 1500 to 2000* (New York: Random House, 1987).

10 Navigating between the Dragon and the Sun

The Philippines' gambit of pitting Japan against China in the South China Sea dispute

Renato Cruz De Castro

On April 8, 2012, a Philippine Air Force (PAF) reconnaissance plane spotted eight Chinese fishing boats around the Scarborough Shoal, 140 miles from the main Philippine island of Luzon. Immediately, President Benigno Aquino III ordered the Armed Forces of the Philippines (AFP) and the Philippine Navy (PN) to step up its monitoring activities and enforce the country's fisheries and maritime environmental protection laws. Accordingly, the PN deployed the PN's flagship *BRP Gregorio Del Pilar*, the recently purchased former US Coast Guard cutter, into the shoal. On April 10, 2012, the *BRP Gregorio Del Pilar* tried to apprehend several Chinese fishing boats at the Scarborough Shoal. However, two Chinese maritime surveillance vessels arrived and prevented the arrest. Realizing that the incident might escalate into armed confrontation, the Philippines replaced its surface combatant with a smaller Coast Guard vessel.

Instead of reciprocating, China raised the stakes by deploying the Yuzheng 310 – the most advanced and largest Coast Guard patrol ship, equipped with machine guns, light cannons, and electronic sensors. When the Philippines filed a diplomatic protest, the Chinese Embassy contended that the three Chinese surveillance vessels in Scarborough Shoal are "in the area fulfilling the duties of safeguarding Chinese maritime rights and interests", and added that the shoal "is an integral part of the Chinese territory and the waters around the traditional fishing area for Chinese fishermen".[1] These incidents underscore an international reality – Chinese power casts a long shadow over the Philippines which (along with Vietnam) is at the forefront of the South China Sea dispute with China.[2]

Coincidentally, in April 2012, at the start of the two-month stand-off between Philippine and Chinese civilian ships at Scarborough Shoal, then-Japanese Ambassador to the Philippines Urabe Toshio emphasized the "close-knit triangular relationship among Japan, the Philippines, and their closest (mutual) ally – the U.S.".[3] In May 2012, three Japanese Maritime Self-Defense Force (MSDF) surface combatants arrived in Manila for a four-day port call.[4] The visit came after Tokyo announced its plans to provide the Philippines with ten new patrol vessels to bolster the latter's maritime patrol capability. The newspaper *Yomiuri Shimbun* linked the ship visit to the ongoing Scarborough Shoal stand-off and editorialized that Japan could not stand by and wait for China and the Philippines to clash

Navigating between the Dragon and the Sun 179

openly.[5] It also stressed that it is in "Japan's national interest to ensure that its sea-lanes remain safe".[6] Interestingly, the MSDF's ship visit to the Philippines happened just a few days after the US Navy's *Virginia*-class attack submarine, the *USS North Carolina*, supposedly made a port call at Subic Bay.

This incident marked the beginning of the Philippines' active involvement in the evolving and expanding rivalry between Japan and China in East Asia. Interestingly, the Philippines takes advantage of this rivalry to strengthen its position in the South China Sea dispute. Conscious of its limited military capabilities, the Philippines aligns its diplomatic and strategic policy with Japan in order to balance an expansionist China in the South China Sea. This article examines how the Philippines has taken advantage of the Sino-Japanese rivalry by forging a security partnership with Japan in order to balance China in the South China Sea dispute. It also addresses the Sino-Japanese rivalry more broadly, investigating how rivalry affects each country's foreign policy towards the Philippines. Finally, it considers the possible outcomes of the Philippines' gambit of pitting Japan against China in the South China Sea dispute.

Navigating between the Dragon and the Sun

As two great powers in East Asia, China and Japan cast their respective shadows on Southeast Asia. On the one hand, the relations of the Southeast Asian states with China are complex and ambiguous.[7] This stems from their geographic proximity, historical baggage, and the implications of the constantly changing dynamics of China's comprehensive power and presence in maritime Southeast Asia. China claims almost 80 per cent of the South China Sea, along with the Paracel and Spratly Islands, which are also claimed by the Philippines, Brunei, Malaysia, and Vietnam. By consolidating its maritime claims, China enhances its territorial integrity and ensures its national security. The other claimant states, in turn, view this development as an ominous sign of Chinese maritime expansionism in an area of key strategic location and potential resources.[8]

On the other hand, Japan's policy relative to Southeast Asia is focused on balancing the power and influence of China.[9] This balancing strategy involves Japan's forging of economic partnership agreements with Southeast Asian countries such as Singapore, the Philippines, Indonesia, and Vietnam. These Japanese-sponsored agreements are meant to ensure economic cooperation among regional allies in the face of bilateral trade deals proffered by China in Southeast Asia.[10] Since 2005, Japan has also been alarmed by China's military modernization, especially Chinese naval build-up. The Japanese monitor China's maritime moves to protect their vital sea lanes of communication and trade, particularly in the Malacca Strait and the South China Sea. In effect, Japan pays serious attention to the South China Sea in particular, and to maritime Southeast Asia in general.

Historically, Philippines–China relations have always been problematic and challenging. Official relations between Manila and Beijing were established on June 9, 1975, when the two countries signed the "Joint Communiqué on the Establishment of Diplomatic Relations between the People's Republic of China

180   *Renato Cruz De Castro*

and the Republic of the Philippines". In 1986, the mechanism for bilateral consultations on a number of regional and international issues was established. High-level visits and exchanges of officials began in the early 1990s. After almost a decade of diplomatic exchanges and political consultations, however, the two countries' overall relations had been described as "cordial at the political level and only limitedly successful at the economic level".[11]

The lack of rapport in Philippines–China relations could be attributed to the fact that the relationship was conducted primarily on the basis of *realpolitik*. Manila established diplomatic ties with Beijing in the mid-1970s primarily because it found it expedient to both reduce Chinese support to the local communist movement, and to strengthen its non-alignment credentials with the socialist world. However, these motives were constrained by an overriding strategic consideration – Manila has always viewed Beijing as a long-term security challenge. Concern with China's long-term strategic intention made the Philippines (along with other Association of Southeast Asian Nations (ASEAN) states like Malaysia and Indonesia) extremely wary of its capability to provide assistance to the local communist insurgency, increase its naval build-up, and pursue its claim in the South China Sea.[12] This lingering fear of China, along with then prevailing view that Beijing had nothing substantive to offer Manila, prevented both countries from pursuing comprehensive relations.[13]

The Philippines' and China's efforts to pursue cooperative relations from the mid-1970s to the second decade of the twenty-first century have been beset by two systemic factors – the South China Sea dispute and the presence of the US as a Pacific power. In this trilateral relation, Manila has been a reactive participant, reacting to China's actions in the South China Sea and taking advantage of China's dynamic relations with the US when possible. Manila's concern over Chinese maritime expansion waned in the early twenty-first century as Philippines–China economic relations improved dramatically due to the latter's emergence as a major economic power in East Asia. During this period, Beijing's provision of economic largesse – part and parcel of its charm offensive – was designed to wean the Philippines away from its traditional ally, the US, and to draw the country into China's economic sphere of influence. China's charm offensive towards the Gloria Macapagal Arroyo Administration, however, failed to achieve its goals because the Philippines is an entrenched ally of the US and was still deeply suspicious of China's territorial ambitions in the South China Sea.[14]

In contrast to the problematic nature of Philippines–China relations, the Philippines and Japan have always maintained vibrant economic relations that have generated close diplomatic ties, and later a security partnership. Japan is one of the Philippines' most important trading partners and the country's biggest source of foreign direct investment.[15] According to the Organisation of Economic Cooperation and Development, Japan is also the Philippines' largest official development assistance (ODA) donor.[16] Since the early 1990s, Filipino and Japanese political leaders and high-ranking defence officials have conducted goodwill visits and high-level exchanges aimed at ensuring that the vigorous political interactions between the two US allies are sustained. Through these high-level dialogues and

Navigating between the Dragon and the Sun 181

consultations, the two sides have discussed important issues that affect their bilateral relations such as trade, investment, ODA, labour, immigration, and other consular matters. The most notable among these high-level exchanges occurred during the September 15, 2001 summit meeting with President Arroyo and Prime Minister Koizumi Junichiro. During the summit, the two heads of state agreed to elevate their relations to a higher level of partnership that would include discussion of bilateral, regional, and global security concerns. The two leaders also affirmed the need to hold an annual politico-security dialogue.

Conducted by Tokyo with a number of ASEAN countries, the dialogue aims to promote confidence-building measures between Japan and its Southeast Asian neighbours. In light of 9/11, the dialogue is designed to enhance joint efforts in addressing international terrorism. An interesting feature is the participation of military officials in these bilateral exchanges. The two US allies have also been discussing bilateral security concerns in a number of international forums such as the Nikkei International Conference on the Future of Asia, the Philippines–Japan Sub-Ministerial Meeting, the ASEAN–Japan Forum, the ASEAN–Japan Summit, and ASEAN+3. The two countries have also been cooperating on strengthening their enforcement capacity in preventing the proliferation of weapons of mass destruction and missile technology.

In February 2005, the Philippines and Japan conducted the First Political-Military-to-Military Consultation or Political-Security Dialogue. This consultation is part of Japan's overall security relationship with ASEAN countries aimed at fostering confidence-building measures and exploring possible areas of security cooperation.[17] During the meeting, Philippine and Japanese defence officials exchanged views on defence and security policies, situations, and challenges facing both countries, such as regional security, North Korea, the Spratly Islands, and nuclear non-proliferation in East Asia. In addition, they looked into the prospect of joint security cooperation, particularly in the areas of counter-terrorism and maritime security. The two sides agreed that addressing the threats of terrorism, piracy, human trafficking, and other transnational crimes must be their top priority. Tokyo then informed Manila that it will play a more active role in maintaining peace and stability in the international community.

The Philippine delegation followed up its request with its Japanese counterpart for joint maritime security cooperation on capacity-building and training, particularly in terms of acquiring new equipment and improving the communication infrastructure of the civilian Philippine Coast Guard (PCG). This would involve Japan's provision of equipment and training to the PCG in counter-terrorism and search-and-rescue operations, as well as civil aviation training for the personnel of the Philippine Air Transportation Office under a new office of transportation security.[18] Interestingly, the two sides again discussed current developments regarding their respective bilateral alliances with the US.[19]

In May 2005, Director Ono Yoshinori of the Japan Defense Agency (precursor to today's Ministry of Defense) visited Manila and raised the prospect of Philippines–Japan cooperation in defence and security matters, particularly in the areas of peacekeeping and the exchange of cadets and officers in military academies and

182　*Renato Cruz De Castro*

institutions.[20] He also proposed increased cooperation in the areas of maritime security, disaster management, and counter-terrorism training. Director Ono also discussed with then National Defense Secretary Avelino Cruz, Jr. the plan to establish a mechanism for an annual political-security dialogue, and joint military exercises between the AFP and the Self-Defense Forces (SDF), and the probable implications of redeploying American troops from Okinawa to the Japanese mainland. The two countries also explored their respective positions on the possibility of redeploying American troops from Japan to the Philippines, and the conduct of joint military exercises.[21]

In February 2006, the two countries held the second Political-Security Dialogue in Tokyo. During the meeting, the two sides reaffirmed their earlier agreement to focus their security cooperation on disaster preparedness and management, given the occurrence of these natural disasters in the region and Japan's expertise in dealing with them.[22] The two countries exchanged views on their visions of an East Asian Community and accentuated their commonalities: a robust alliance with the US and the defence-oriented nature of their security policies.[23] Tokyo expressed its growing concern with regard to maritime security and piracy, as well as issues related to capacity-building, information-sharing, and the protection of the environment in Southeast Asia. The Philippine delegation, for its part, raised the idea of a Philippines–Japan strategic partnership in regional ocean govern-ance.[24] This would involve cooperation in addressing mutual concerns relating to regional ocean governance, and maritime safety and security. The Japanese delegation showed interest in the Philippine initiative on "Coast Watch South". This schema is primarily a maritime situational awareness system aimed at secur-ing the long Philippine coastline from Palawan to Davao through the installation of a series of radar-capable watch stations located in a number of strategic areas. Each Coast Watch station will be provided with interdiction capabilities through the use of small attack-craft, gunboats, offshore patrol vessels, and aircraft.[25]

Consequently, the Philippines has consistently declared that it welcomes Tokyo's increasing political/security role as the current government seeks to revise its pacifist Constitution to enable the SDF to become more active in international peacekeeping and other military roles.[26] The two countries' armed forces have also been conducting low-key military-related activities such as table-top exercises and seminars on multilateral defence matters – for example, United Nations peace-keeping operations. The Philippine initiative on coastal patrols also presented an opportunity for Tokyo to forge a non-military but crucial security link with Manila. Japan has also become actively involved in the Mindanao peace process, as shown by Tokyo's deployment of Japanese personnel in the International Monitoring Team (IMT) tasked to monitor the ceasefire agreement between the Philippine government and the Moro Islamic Liberation Front since 2004. The Japanese personnel in the IMT specifically observed the rehabilitation and economic situation in conflict-affected areas in the Philippine southern province of Mindanao. Security ties between the two countries had a strong foundation in the first decade of this century. However, prior to 2012, Tokyo and Manila did not find the need to sign or even consider a formal agreement on defence cooperation.

Navigating between the Dragon and the Sun   183

That would change along with China's changing approach to its claims in the South China Sea after 2010.

Confronting China's maritime expansion

By early 2010, China's fervent nationalism, growing naval prowess, and unilateral moves were overtly directed against a militarily-weak Philippines. In the last quarter of 2010, the Philippine Department of Foreign Affairs (DFA) noted increased Chinese naval presence and activities in the Spratlys, and monitored six or seven major intrusions by Chinese vessels into the waters claimed by the Philippines.[27] In mid-2010, President Benigno Simeon Aquino III won the presidential election by capturing 42 per cent of the votes cast, the largest margin of victory since the Philippines adopted a multiparty system in 1987. Initially, President Aquino tried to maintain cordial relations with China. In late 2010, the Philippines joined a 19-state coalition led by China that boycotted the awarding ceremony in Oslo, Norway for Nobel Peace Prize winner and Chinese dissident Liu Xiaobo. In February 2011, President Aquino ordered the extradition to China of 14 Taiwanese accused of committing electronic fraud against Chinese nationals, causing a major diplomatic row between Manila and Taipei. In due time, however, President Aquino realized that kow-towing to China would not exempt the Philippines from becoming the target of Chinese aggressiveness in the South China Sea.[28]

On March 2, 2011, two Chinese patrol boats harassed a survey ship commissioned by the Philippine Department of Energy to conduct oil exploration in the Reed Bank (now called Recto Bank), 150 kilometres east of the Spratly Islands and 250 kilometres west of the Philippine island of Palawan. The Aquino administration was stunned by this maritime encounter, which happened within the Philippines' Exclusive Economic Zone (EEZ). Two days after the incident, the Philippine government filed a protest before the Chinese Embassy in Manila. A DFA spokesperson commented that "the Philippines is (simply) seeking an explanation for the incident". Brushing aside the Philippine complaint, a Chinese Embassy official insisted that China has indisputable sovereignty over the Spratly Islands and their adjacent waters. Beijing then went on to demand that Manila first seek Chinese permission before conducting oil exploration activities, even within the Philippine EEZ.

With these incidents confirming China's intent to pursue its claims at the Philippines' expense, the Aquino administration hastened to develop the AFP's territorial defence capabilities. The Philippines' immediate territorial defence goal was to establish a modest but "comprehensive border protection program" anchored on the surveillance, deterrence, and border patrol capabilities of the PAF, the PN, and the PCG. This monitoring and modest force-projection capability should extend from the country's territorial waters to its Contiguous Zone and EEZ.[29]

Shortly thereafter, developments in the East China Sea were changing Japan's threat perception with respect to China as well. Shinzō Abe came to power as Japan's prime minister amidst an intense territorial row between Japan and China over the Senkaku Islands. After the December 16, 2012 parliamentary election,

184 *Renato Cruz De Castro*

Prime Minister Abe declared "that the islands are the inherent territory of Japan . . . . We own and effectively control them. There is no room for negotiations about them." [30] In the first few months of his term, the Senkaku Islands dispute occupied centre-stage in the Japan–China relationship, which became extremely strained. Prime Minister Abe continued the policy of non-acknowledgement of disputes carried out by his predecessor. China responded by increasing the number and frequency of civilian ships deployed around the islands. [31] In the face of heightened tension in the Senkaku Islands, Prime Minister Abe took several significant steps to expand Japanese security policy, including with reference to its security relationships with other states. From his point of view, China's assertive behaviour in East Asia was a source of grave security concern for Japan. [32]

The Abe administration undertook three major security measures that could be regarded as defensive. During his first few months in office, Prime Minister Abe announced the first increase in defence spending in 11 years, as well as a review of the 2010 National Defense Program Guidelines. [33] In October 2013, Japan and the US convened a meeting of the Security Consultative Committee, or 2+2, in Tokyo. They issued a joint statement reaffirming the importance of the alliance and announcing a review of the US–Japan Defense Cooperation Guidelines, last updated in 1997, to reflect changes in the regional and global security environments. [34] The communiqué mentioned several priorities for cooperation, including ballistic missile defence, space and cyber defence, joint intelligence, surveillance and reconnaissance activities, dialogue on extended deterrence, joint training and exercises, realignment of US forces in Okinawa, and convening of trilateral and multilateral security cooperation among US allies in East Asia. [35] Finally, Japan launched "multilayered security cooperation" with like-minded countries that include US allies in the region such as South Korea and Australia, as well as with US alliance and partner countries whose coastal territories are critical to Japanese sea lanes of communications. [36] The *2013 National Security Strategy of Japan* specifically mentions that Japan will strengthen diplomacy and security cooperation with ASEAN countries concerned to settle disputes in the South China Sea, not by force, but in accordance with the rule of law. [37] Although the document did not name specific countries, the reference to Vietnam and the Philippines was implied, as two states located along Japan's sea lines of communication with ongoing disputes with China in the South China Sea.

The lowest point in Philippines–China relations: the Scarborough Shoal stand-off

The two-month stand-off between the Philippines and China at the Scarborough Shoal epitomized an international incident waiting to happen. Prior to the crisis, the Philippines sought the support of ASEAN for the creation of a "Zone of Peace, Freedom, Friendship, and Cooperation". This proposal aimed to clarify maritime boundary claims in the South China Sea by all parties, as well as to turn disputed areas into special enclaves where conflicting parties could jointly develop projects. [38] China, however, did not want the issue to be multilateralized, preferring

Navigating between the Dragon and the Sun   185

to resolve the dispute bilaterally. Furthermore, the delimitation of maritime borders required clarification of China's ambiguous, questionable, and expansive nine-dash line claim. Beijing also took note of Vietnam's and the Philippines' proposals for ASEAN to issue an official position on the South China Sea dispute during the ASEAN summit in Cambodia on April 3–4, 2012. However, China pressured the host country to keep the South China Sea dispute out of the summit agenda. Interestingly, on April 9, 2012, China's *Global Times* emphatically warned the Philippines against underestimating "the strength and will-power of China to defend its territorial integrity". [39]

On the morning of April 10, the *BRP Gregorio Del Pilar* verified the presence of eight Chinese fishing vessels anchored inside the Scarborough Shoal. Following the established rules of engagement, the PN ship dispatched a boarding team to inspect the fishing vessels. Large amounts of illegally collected corals, giant clams, and live sharks were found inside the compartments of the first fishing vessel boarded. Before the PN could apprehend the fishing vessels at the shoal, however, two Chinese marine surveillance vessels arrived and placed themselves between the arresting Philippine warship and the Chinese fishing boats. The surveillance vessels not only prevented the arrest of the Chinese fishermen but also informed the captain of the *BRP Gregorio Del Pilar* that he had strayed into Chinese territorial waters. Clearly, China's reaction was a complete turnaround from its previous stance on maritime encroachments. First, the Chinese patrol vessels prevented the PN from arresting the fishermen. Second, China defied Philippine territorial rights over the shoal, located only 224 kilometres from the province of Zambales in Luzon and well within the country's 200-nautical-mile EEZ.

The following day, Manila saw the possibility of a dangerous face-off with an assertive China. President Aquino recalled the *BRP Gregorio Del Pilar* and sent a smaller Coast Guard vessel to defuse the tension. Instead of reciprocating Manila's gesture, Beijing dispatched its most advanced fishery patrol ship, the *Yuzheng*-310, to join the two other civilian patrol vessels already in the shoal. *Xinhua News Agency* quoted the Chinese Foreign Ministry as saying that

> the Philippines' attempt to carry out so-called law enforcement activities in the waters of Huangyan Island [Scarborough Shoal] has infringed upon China's sovereignty, and runs counter to the consensus reached by both sides on maintaining the peace and stability in the South China Sea.

The Ministry likewise warned the Philippines "not to complicate and escalate the situation". [40]

While Chinese and Philippine patrol vessels were at an impasse in the Scarborough Shoal, the Chinese Embassy in Manila confirmed that both countries were engaged in a lengthy and tedious diplomatic negotiation. Again, the Chinese Embassy articulated the official mantra that the Scarborough Shoal is an integral part of Chinese territory. It also warned Manila not to take actions that could irreparably damage Philippines–China relations and affect the stability of the South China Sea. [41] By the end of April 2012, the Philippines–China negotiations

186 *Renato Cruz De Castro*

were getting nowhere. The Chinese Embassy accused Manila of negotiating in bad faith and of distorting the facts during the lengthy and tedious discussions. It also "urged the Philippines to stop illegal activities and leave this area", as it insisted once more that China had sovereign rights over almost the whole of the South China Sea. The Embassy spokesperson also said "that ever since the ancient times, numerous documents on Chinese history have put down definitely in writing that Huangyan Island belongs to Chinese territory". Manila, in turn, criticized China's aggressive stance against other claimant states like the Philippines.[42] Tersely, it reminded China that the "responsibility for resolving the stand-off in the South China Sea rests not just with one party but both parties" and challenged Beijing to let the International Tribunal for the Law of the Sea mediate the dispute.

In mid-June 2012, tension in the disputed area eased when the two countries withdrew their civilian vessels on the pretext of the onset of typhoon season. After the Philippines withdrew its lone Coast Guard vessel from the Scarborough Shoal, China began consolidating its control over the area. The China maritime surveillance vessels along with the China Fisheries Law Enforcement Command constructed a chain barrier across the mouth of the shoal to block Philippine access. China has also deployed surveillance vessels to protect the fleet of Chinese fishing boats operating deep into the Philippines' EEZ.

In October 2012, Chinese Foreign Minister Fu Ying, seeking a diplomatic solution to the dispute, visited Manila. However, instead of finding a mutually acceptable solution, the high-ranking official warned Manila not to do the following: (1) appeal to the UN; (2) internationalize the dispute in forums like ASEAN; (3) coordinate with other countries such as the US; or (4) issue any press release regarding the negotiations.[43] In effect, she advised the Philippines to accept China's exercise of de facto occupation of the Scarborough Shoal in silence.

The Philippines files a case against China and the aftermath

The tense two-month Scarborough Shoal stand-off and the later Chinese occupation of the shoal generated a sense of urgency on the part of Manila to react to what was perceived as a case of naked Chinese aggression against a weak power like the Philippines. Key Philippine officials were unanimous that they should not be cowed into accepting China's *fait accompli*. In January 2013, the Philippines directly confronted Chinese occupation of the Scarborough Shoal by filing a statement of claim against China in the Arbitral Tribunal of the United Nations Convention on the Law of the Sea (UNCLOS). In its Notification and Statement of Claim, the Philippines asked the Arbitral Tribunal to determine the country's legal entitlements under UNCLOS within its 200-nautical-mile EEZ, and to confirm the status of various land features within the EEZ (including the Scarborough Shoal) and the Spratly Islands, and therefore their maritime entitlements. These entitlements are based on the provisions of UNCLOS specifically to its rights to a Territorial Sea and Contiguous Zone under Part II, to an EEZ under Part V, and to a Continental Shelf under Part VI.[44]

As expected, China refused to participate in the international mediation and openly expressed its opposition to the Philippines' filing of a case with the Arbitral

Tribunal. On February 20, 2013, the Chinese Ambassador in Manila returned the notice of arbitration to the DFA. At the same time, Mr. Hong Lei, a Chinese Foreign Ministry spokesperson in Beijing, branded the filing as "factually flawed" and accused Manila of violating the non-binding 2002 Declaration of the Code of Conduct of the Parties in the South China Sea, which provides for ASEAN and China to settle their maritime disputes among themselves.

In April 2013, a visiting Chinese Foreign Ministry official warned Manila of the consequences of pushing the arbitration process against China.[45] In late August 2013, Beijing withdrew its invitation for President Aquino to attend the China–ASEAN Expo in Nanjing after the Philippine government refused to meet its precondition that Manila withdraw its arbitration case.[46] From early September to mid-October 2013, President Xi Jinping and Prime Minister Li Keqiang visited Indonesia, Malaysia, Brunei, Thailand, and Vietnam, mounting a public relations campaign underlining strong Chinese interest in fostering relations and managing differences with the Southeast Asian countries. The Philippines was not included as a stop on this campaign.

China's resentment towards the Philippines became more glaring in November 2013 after it donated a mere US$100,000 to the relief and rehabilitation efforts for the victims of Typhoon Yolanda (Haiyan) – a category-5 typhoon. As a result, the international media questioned China's ability to assume global leadership and responsibility.[47] In January 2014, the provincial government of Hainan passed a law requiring all vessels to get permission from China when fishing in almost all parts of the South China Sea.[48] The legislation was directed particularly to Vietnam and the Philippines, the two littoral countries at odds with China over this maritime area. Apart from the Scarborough Shoal stand-off, China's refusal to participate in the Arbitral Tribunal, its live-fire exercise in March 2013, its efforts to punish the Philippines for challenging its expansive maritime claim, and Hainan's provincial legislation on fishing are all telling of China's position regarding the South China Sea dispute in particular, and international law in general – that its sovereignty over the contested sea is non-negotiable. This stance is unlikely to change, as to do so would compromise China's long-held logic of indivisible territorial sovereignty.[49]

From July 7 to 13, 2015, the Permanent Court of Arbitration (PCA) in The Hague held its first hearing on the Philippine claims against China in the South China Sea. As expected, China did not participate in the proceedings, citing its policy of resolving disputes on territorial and maritime rights only through direct consultation and negotiation with the countries involved.[50] China repeatedly declared that "it will neither accept nor participate in the arbitration unilaterally initiated by the Philippines", and it also made it clear – through the publication of its 2014 December Position Paper and in other official statements – that, in its view the Tribunal lacks jurisdiction in this matter.[51] Since 2009, however, it has slowly shifted its strategy away from delaying the resolution of the dispute to one that emphasizes its sovereignty over the contested waters, to deter other claimant states like the Philippines and Vietnam from cementing their claims and to negotiate with these small powers from its position of strength.[52] Furthermore, it does not want to extend any legitimacy to the Tribunal since it holds other instruments of

188 *Renato Cruz De Castro*

power – economic, diplomatic, and strategic – that it can wield to settle the dispute on its own terms.[53]

Despite China's refusal to participate in the proceedings, then-Philippine Foreign Secretary Albert del Rosario made a presentation before the five-member tribunal hearing Manila's case filed against China's expansive maritime claim in the disputed waters. He admitted that the Tribunal does not have authority to make decisions on the issues of sovereignty. However, he said that the Philippines wanted to clarify its maritime entitlements in the South China Sea, a question over which the Tribunal has jurisdiction.[54] He also argued that the 1982 UNCLOS does not recognize or permit the exercise of so-called "historic" rights in areas beyond the limits of maritime zones that are recognized or established by UNCLOS.[55] He lamented that China has acted forcefully to assert its so-called right by exploiting the living and non-living resources in the areas beyond the UNCLOS limits while forcibly preventing other coastal states, including the Philippines, from exploiting resources in the same areas.[56] This marked the lowest point in Philippines–China relations in recent times.

Fostering a Philippines–Japan security partnership

Confronted by Chinese expansion in the South China Sea, the Philippines quickly found it necessary to foster a security partnership with Japan, China's main rival in East Asia. Moreover, Japan's early outreach to Manila suggested that Tokyo shared its interest in strengthened bilateral ties. Since 2011, Japan closely observed China's assertiveness in the South China Sea dispute, in which initially it has no direct interest since it is not a claimant state. In the aftermath of the Scarborough Shoal stand-off, however, Tokyo became more forthright in extending security assistance to the Philippines. In July 2012, Japanese Defense Minister Morimoto Satoshi and his Filipino counterpart, Defense Secretary Voltaire Gazmin, inked a bilateral agreement on maritime security. The agreement calls for high-level dialogue between defence officials and reciprocal visits by the MSDF chief of staff and the PN flag commander. A few days later, Philippine Foreign Affairs Secretary del Rosario announced that Tokyo was likely to provide the PCG with ten 40-metre boats as part of Japan's ODA to the Philippines by the end of the year. Newspapers also reported that two additional bigger vessels are being considered for transfer to the Philippine government under a grant.[57]

The election of the Abe government in December 2012 marked the beginning of renewed senior leader support to consolidate new agreements to strengthen Japan–Philippines relations in the security realm. A few weeks after his return to power, Prime Minister Abe sent Foreign Minister Kishida Fumio on a four-country Asia-Pacific diplomatic tour to convey Japan's growing concern over Beijing's expansive territorial claims in the South China Sea. In Manila, Minister Kishida met with Philippine Foreign Secretary del Rosario. They discussed the difficulties China's neighbours face in defending their positions vis-à-vis the East China and South China Sea issues while managing their economic relations with China, a major economic power.[58] The two foreign ministers agreed to closely work together in enhancing cooperation in maritime security.[59] Minister Kishida pledged ten multi-role response vessels to the PCG to better patrol Philippine maritime territories.[60] He also announced Japan's provision of essential communication system equipment to the PCG for maritime safety.[61]

On June 27, 2013, Japanese Defense Minister Onodera Itsunori and Philippine Defense Secretary Gazmin confirmed the continuous "exchanges of information aimed at strengthening Philippine–Japan defense relations and on working together to make U. S. strategic rebalancing a reality in Asia".[62] To further defence cooperation, the two security partners undertake the following activities:[63] reciprocal visits between the chiefs-of-staff of the Japanese MSDF and the flag officer of the PN; the holding of the Japan–Philippines Maritime Chief of Staff Meeting; port calls of MSDF vessels in the Philippines; and active participation in the Pacific Partnership 2012. During the same meeting, Secretary Gazmin raised the possibility of allowing the SDF access to the former American military bases in the Philippines, should Tokyo express interest.[64]

In December 2013, during a visit to Tokyo, President Aquino discussed China's establishment of an Air Defence Identification Zone in the East China Sea with Prime Minister Abe.[65] At their one-on-one meeting, the two leaders signed an agreement on yen-based soft loans to finance the ten Japanese patrol boats for the PCG. In June 2014, President Aquino and Prime Minister Abe met again in Tokyo and explicitly discussed China's ambition to become a major naval power in East Asia.[66] More significantly, former President Aquino endorsed Prime Minister Abe's move to expand Japan's security role in the region. Strongly supporting Prime Minister Abe's initiative to deploy Japan's SDF in overseas contingencies, he boldly declared:

> We believe that nations of goodwill can only benefit if the Japanese government is empowered to assist others and is allowed wherewithal to come to the aid of those in need, especially in the area of collective self-defense.[67]

During his state visit to Japan in early June 2015, then President Aquino continued his thorough consultation with Prime Minister Abe on the peace and stability in the Asia-Pacific region.[68] The two leaders signed a joint declaration on "A Strengthened Strategic Partnership for Advancing the Shared Principles and Partnership and Goals for Peace, Security, and Growth in the Region and beyond". They also agreed to further enhance the strategic partnership between their countries on the basis of shared principles and goals.[69] The document also expressed the two countries' commitment to ensure maritime safety and security in the South China Sea, and their opposition to unilateral actions to change the *status quo*, including large-scale reclamation and building of outposts.[70] The declaration included a detailed action plan for strengthening the two countries' strategic partnership. Areas of cooperation identified in the security realm include information exchange and policy coordination on respective security policies; collaboration on maritime matters (including maritime domain awareness); and humanitarian assistance; and, most importantly, the provision of defence equipment and technology.

190   *Renato Cruz De Castro*

With China pursuing maritime expansion in East Asia, the Philippines and Japan have explored a strategic partnership to complement their respective bilateral alliances with the US. This desire to build upon their alliances with the US and diversify their security relationships carries clear benefits for both Tokyo and Manila., On the one hand, the Philippines can leverage its alliances and defence engagements with foreign militaries to rectify the deplorable state of its military capability and effectively respond to security threats.[71] On the other hand, Japan can deter Chinese aggression in the East China Sea by assisting Southeast Asian countries in active dispute with China in the South China Sea.[72] Thus, strengthened Japan–Philippines ties make strategic sense to both partners in equal measure. This security partnership forged through leadership agreements under Prime Minister Abe and President Aquino is made operational by the two countries' regular bilateral consultations between their heads of states, defence exchanges between the Philippine Department of National Defense and the Japanese Ministry of Defense, naval exercises between the PN and MSDF, provision of defence equipment by Japan to the Philippines, and possibly the SDF's access to patrol in the South China Sea.

The Duterte administration and the Sino-Japanese rivalry: business as usual?

The election of President Rodrigo Duterte as the country's sixteenth president led to dramatic changes in Philippine foreign policy vis-à-vis China and the US. President Aquino pursued a proactive policy in the South China Sea dispute and openly challenged China's expansive maritime claim. As discussed above, he pursued this policy by building up the territorial defence capabilities of the AFP, enhancing Philippines–US political and strategic relations, and fostering a security partnership with Japan. In contrast to his predecessor, President Duterte is bent on a more accommodating policy towards China's maritime expansion in the South China Sea. Soon after his election, he expressed his openness to engaging Beijing in bilateral negotiations, to joint development of resources and, to downplay sovereignty issues if China could commit to do the same.[73] At the same time, he displayed a more ambivalent, if not hostile, attitude towards the US. [74]

President Duterte pursues a relatively balanced and calibrated policy character-ized by gravitating closer to China while creating some diplomatic distance from the Philippines' only strategic security ally, the US. On the one hand, he declared that he is open to direct bilateral negotiations with China. President Duterte's Foreign Secretary, Perfecto Yasay, announced in September 2016

> that the relationship between the two countries [China and the Philippines] was not limited to the maritime dispute. There were other areas of concern in such fields as investment, trade, and tourism and discussing them could open doors for talks on the maritime issues.[75]

On the other hand, President Duterte called for the withdrawal of American Special Forces operating in Mindanao in support of the AFP's counter-terrorism operations.[76] He also ordered the PN not to conduct joint patrols with the US Navy in the South China Sea lest these activities be seen by China as provocative, making it more difficult to peacefully resolve the territorial dispute.[77]

President Duterte's foreign policy approach of gravitating closer to Beijing while alienating Washington unsettled the US and Japan, and presumably some ASEAN countries as well. Many of the latter see the Philippines' arbitration case against China and its active support for American military presence in the region as potential game changers in the management of their own relations with both China and the US.[78] Puzzled by the changes in Philippine foreign policy, the Japanese government persevered with its uniquely nuanced approach to dealing with the Philippines. A senior Japanese official admitted that while Tokyo and Washington share the same goal in the Philippines, Japan takes a different approach in its relations with the Philippines. As a result, there are some things that Manila can only accept when Japan provides them.[79] President Duterte has been very critical about the Philippines–US alliance, but he has never criticized or even mentioned the Philippines–Japan security partnership.

In early August 2016, Japanese Foreign Minister Kishida met President Duterte in Davao City, where the two discussed how their two countries might work together for the peaceful resolution of the South China Sea dispute. Their discussion was based on the July 12 PCA Award, which was largely favourable to the Philippines, and which Japan considers final and legally binding. Minister Kishida explained to President Duterte that enhancing the PCG's and PN's capabilities in maritime security is an important pillar of Japan's assistance to the Philippines.[80] He then informed President Duterte that Japan intends to move ahead with providing patrol boats and leasing training aircraft to the PN to support enhanced maritime domain awareness.[81]

Both parties' continued commitment to deepening engagement was confirmed again at the ASEAN summit in Laos in 2016. There, Prime Minister Abe held his first meeting with President Duterte, during which he unveiled Japan's plan to provide two 90-metre patrol vessels in addition to the ten multi-role vessels that were delivered to the PCG to boost its search-and-rescue and fisheries protection capabilities.[82] These two large patrol vessels have thick armour to protect the crews from shells and are therefore likely to be treated as warships. Once transferred, the ships will be the first of their kind to be provided to a third country by Japan. Abe also informed his Filipino counterpart about Japan's decision to lend five MDSF TC-90 training aircraft to the Philippines, which will be useful for reconnaissance missions, disaster relief operations, and transporting supplies.[83] President Duterte responded by expressing his appreciation, and explained to Prime Minister Abe that these patrol vessels will enable the Philippines to strengthen patrols in its coastal waters and will enhance the Philippine presence in its EEZ.[84]

Prior to his October 2016 working visit to Japan, President Duterte expressed his willingness to advance defence cooperation between the Philippines and Japan.[85] While in Tokyo during his working visit, he showed his Japanese host that his resentment of the US does not necessarily extend to American allies, and offered praise for Japan while reiterating that he would not scale down security

192   *Renato Cruz De Castro*

cooperation with Washington.[86] The two leaders witnessed the signing of an agreement for Japan to provide two large patrol shops for the PCG that will be financed through yen loans.[87] They were also present during the signing of an agreement that Japan will lease five TC-90 training planes from the MSDF to the PN for maritime patrols in the South China Sea.[88] In his joint statement with Prime Minister Abe, President Duterte agreed

> That the Philippines will continue to work closely with Japan on issues of common concern in the region, and uphold the shared vision of democracy and adherence to the rule of law and the peaceful settlement of disputes, including the South China Sea.[89]

Probably due to Duterte's conciliatory approach, Japan has continued its comprehensive engagement with the Philippines.[90]

Japan's goal is to assist the Philippines to improve its maritime surveillance capabilities in the light of increasing Chinese maritime activities in the South China Sea and despite worsening Philippines–US relations. Aware that strained Philippines–US relations benefit China, Japan is strengthening its relations with the Duterte administration by fostering periodic consultations between the two countries, and strengthening the PN's and PCG's maritime domain awareness capabilities. For the Philippines, keeping its security partnership with Japan intact is necessary because it remains the country's most important trading partner, its largest investor, and the home of several thousand overseas Filipino workers and the millions of dollars of remittance income they send home each year, an important boost to the local economy.[91]

Moreover, currently, Japan is the only country in the Western alliance with a healthy and cordial relationship with the Philippines, making it an important countervailing force to an expected increase in Chinese influence in the light of President Duterte's efforts to gravitate closer to China's economic orbit.[92]

Conclusion

Philippines–China relations have been problematic since the establishment of diplomatic relations in 1976. Despite efforts by both countries to cooperate on a number of issues, their relations have been affected by the two countries' territorial and maritime disputes in the South China Sea. By contrast, Philippines–Japan relations have always been dynamic because of the two countries' strong economic relations. Japan is one of the Philippines' most important trading partners, its biggest foreign direct investor, and largest ODA donor. The two countries' vibrant economic relations have always generated dynamic diplomatic relations and now, in the second decade of the twenty-first century, they have evolved into a security partnership. This partnership was formalized during the Aquino administration and is being enhanced under Duterte.

In the second decade of the twenty-first century, the Philippines aligned its diplomatic and security policy with Japan as China became assertive in its maritime claims in the South and East China Seas. Confronted by an expansionist China in the South and East China Seas, the Philippines and Japan have forged a security partnership as a matter of course. The Philippines figured in hostile encounters with Chinese civilian vessels at the Reed Bank in March 2011 and again at the Scarborough Shoal in 2012. Japan experienced the same rough treatment from China over the Senkaku/ Diaoyu Islands first in the latter part of 2010, and second during a longer impasse between Chinese and Japanese Coast Guard vessels from late 2012 to mid-2013. This strategic partnership between the two US allies, however, is still in a tentative and evolving stage. It consists primarily of political and security consultations between Filipino and Japanese political leaders, ranking defence officials, and high-level military officers.

The election of President Duterte led to changes in the Philippine' policy towards China and the US, which both had implications for its relationship with Japan. President Duterte conducted a balanced and calibrated policy character-ized by gravitating closer to China while creating diplomatic distance from the US. Alarmed by the possible deterioration in Philippines–US security relations, Japan has persevered with its nuanced approach to dealing with the Philippines. Conscious that the deterioration in Philippines–US relations will only benefit China, Japan is currently strengthening its relations with the Duterte administra-tion by fostering periodic consultations between the two countries, and strengthen-ing its Navy's and Coast Guard's maritime domain awareness capabilities. This in turn provides the Philippines with the opportunity to continue its approach of playing one dragon against another as the East Asian powers' geostrategic rivalry evolves and expands into maritime Southeast Asia.

Notes

1 James Hookway, "Philippine, China Ships Square Off", *Wall Street Journal Asia*, April 12, 2012, 2, http://search.proquest.com/docview/993221572/fulltext/1368A3AE.
2 William Chong, "Path to Scarborough Far from Fair: South China Sea Rivals no Match for China's Economic, Military Clout", *The Strait Times*, April 21, 2012, 1, http://search.proquest.com/docview/1008636649/fulltext/1368A3A.
3 "Japan/Philippines/United States: Japan Envoy Notes Close-Knit Relations among Philippines, Japan, and U.S", *Asia News Monitor*, April 11, 2012, 1, http://search.proquest.com/docview/993161337/13A384763AF88.
4 "Philippine Navy Says Japan Sending Three Warships for Port Call to Manila", *BBC Monitoring Asia-Pacific*, May 26, 2012, 1, http://search.proquest.com/docview/10234 95212/13A384763AF48.
5 Ibid., 1.
6 Ibid., 1.
7 Alice Ba, "A New History? The Structure and Process of Southeast Asia's Relations with a Rising China", in Mark Beeson, ed., *Contemporary Southeast Asia* (New York: Palgrave, 2009), 193.
8 David Scott, *China Stands Up: The PRC and the International System* (Abingdon: Routledge, 2007), 104.
9 Michael J. Green, *Japan's Reluctant Realism: Foreign Policy Challenges in an Era of Uncertain Power* (New York: Palgrave, 2004), 189.
10 Julie Gilson, "Japan and Southeast Asia", in Mark Beeson, ed., *Contemporary Southeast Asia* (London: Palgrave, 2009), 6.

194   *Renato Cruz De Castro*

11   Aileen Baviera, "Turning Predicament in to Promise: A Prospective on Philippines–China Relations", in Aileen Baviera, ed., *Comprehensive Engagement: Strategic Issues in Philippines–China Relations* (Quezon City: Philippine–China Development Resource Center, 2000), 23.

12   Abdul Razak Abdullah Baginda, "PRC–ASEAN Relations: Strategic and Security Implication", in Theresa Carino, ed., *China ASEAN Relations: Political, Economic and Ethnic Dimensions* (Manila: China Studies Program, 1991), 89.

13   For an interesting account of this lack of mutual interest to each other, see Rizal C.K. Yuyitung, "Philippine Perception of the People's Republic of China", in Theresa Carino, ed., *China ASEAN Relations: Political, Economic and Ethnic Dimensions* (Manila: China Studies Program, 1991), 138–140.

14   Despite intensifying economic relations with China in the first decade of the twenty-first century, the Arroyo administration also strengthened its security ties with the US. To boost the AFP's counter-terrorist operation in Mindanao, the Philippine government allowed the American forces to set up semi-permanent military stations throughout the littorals of Southern Mindanao, and a more permanent facility in Manila. In March 2006, the Security Engagement Board (SEB), a consultative mechanism to address non-traditional security concerns in the twenty-first century, was created to complement the Philippines–US Mutual Defense Board (MDB). From January to September 2010, US Navy ships made 63 routine visits to various Philippines ports, and extended logistics support to AFP military operations. In early 2008, the Pentagon pledged US$15.5 million to finance the National Coast Watch System. The project entails the PN's and the Philippine Coast Guard's installation of high-frequency radio equipment and radar stations to ensure the broader protection, effective surveillance, and management of the country's maritime domains. Also the Pentagon formulated polices over the long-term period to cement the US's status as the Philippines' only formal strategic ally. From 2005 to 2006, it took concrete measures to enhance the AFP's capability to address internal security challenges; to increase the level of American security and defence assistance and explore new and potential areas for capability-building; and ensure the long-term readiness and interoperability of US–Philippines forces against external armed threats, which prophetically would include China in the second decade of the twenty-first century. See Co-Chair's Statement, "Philippines–United States Bilateral Strategic Dialogue", United States Embassy in Manila, January 27–28, 2011, 10.

15   Edwin Van Daar, "Philippine-Trade Policy and the Philippine Economic Partnership Agreement (JPEPA)", *Contemporary Southeast Asia*, 33:2 (2011), 118

16   Ibid.

17   Interview with an anonymous Japanese diplomat, Hotel Dusit, Makati City, November 2, 2006.

18   Office of the Asia-Pacific Affairs, *RP-Japan Political-Security Dialogue* (Pasay City: Department of Foreign Affairs, date unknown), 1.

19   Ibid., 2.

20   Carina I. Roncesvalles and Darwin T. Wee, "RP, Japan Agree to Step Up Security Cooperation", *Business World*, May 3, 2005, S1

21   Ibid.

22   Interview with an anonymous Japanese diplomat, Dusit Hotel, Makati City, November 2, 2006.

23   Office of the Asia-Pacific Affairs, *RP*-Japan, p 2.

24   Ibid, p.2.

25   Ibid, p. 3.

26   "GMA Welcomes Greater Global Role for Japan", *The Manila Times*, May 24, 2007, 1, http://proquest.umi.com/pqdweb?index=24&did=1276135921&SrchMode=1&sid=1&Fmt.

27   See Carl A. Thayer, "China's New Wave of Aggressive Assertiveness in the South China Sea", *International Journal of China Studies*, December (2011), 561–562.

Navigating between the Dragon and the Sun 195

28 "Singed by the Dragon; the Philippines Discovers that It doesn't Pay to Appease China", *Wall Street Journal*, March 31, 2011, 1, http://proquest.umi.com/pqdweb?index=96&did=2307204961&Src/
29 National Security Council, *National Security Policy 2011–2016* (Quezon City: National Security Council, 2011), 39.
30 James J., Przystup, "Japan–China Relations: Treading Troubled Waters", *Comparative Connections: A Triannual E-Journal on East Asian Bilateral Relations*, May (2013), 9, https://csis-prod.s3.amzonaws.com/ssfs-public/legacy-files/files/publication/1301 gjapan_china.pdf
31 Ibid., 7–8.
32 Bhubhindir Singh, "The Development of Japanese Security Policy: A Long-Term Defensive Strategy", *Asian Policy*, 19 (2015), 57.
33 Przystup, "Japan–China Relations", 9.
34 Michael J. Green and Nicholas Szechenyi, "U.S.–Japan Relations: Big Steps, Big Surprises", *Comparative Connections*, January (2014), 3.
35 Ibid., 8.
36 Yasuhiro Matsuda, "Engagement and Hedging: Japan's Strategy Toward China", *SAIS Review*, 32:2 (2012), 116.
37 Government of Japan, *The National Security Strategy of Japan* (Tokyo: Office of the Prime Minister, 2013), 60–61.
38 See International Crisis Group, "Stirring Up the South China Sea II: Regional Responses", *Asia Report*, 229(2012), 8.
39 Robert Sutter and Chin-huo Huang, "Hu Visits Cambodia as South China Sea Simmers", *Comparative Connections*, May (2012), 5, http://csis.org/files/publication/1201china_seasia.pdf.
40 Thai News Service Group, "China/Philippines: China Seeks Preservation of Over-All Friendly Relations with Philippines as Tension over Scarborough Shoal Ebbs Momentarily", *Asia News Monitor*, April 12, 2012, 1. http://search.proquest.com/docview/993552886/138B64F7C71082.
41 Ibid.
42 "Philippines/China: No Agreement Reached with Chinese Government on Pull-Out of Philippine Vessels from Scarborough Shoal – DFA", *Asia News Monitor*, April 26, 2012, 1, http://serach.proquest.com.docview/1009600955/138FC30C1134.
43 "Manila Takes a Stand", *Wall Street Journal Asia*, January 25, 2013, 1, http://search.proquest.com/docview/1272368093?accountid=28547.
44 Department of Foreign Affairs, "Notification and Statement of Claim to the United Nations Convention of Law of the Sea (UNCLOS) Arbitral Tribunal, Manila", January 22, 2013, 12–14.
45 Robert Sutter and Chin-hao Huang, "China's Growing Resolve in the South China Sea Dispute", *Comparative Connections: A Triannual E-Journal on East Asia Relations*, May (2014), 1–8, http://csis.org/files/publication/1301q-seasia.pdf.
46 Sutter, Robert and Chin-hao Huang, "China's Shifts to Positive, Downplays Disputes", *Comparative Connections: A Triannual E-Journal on East Asia Relations*, January (2014), 4, http://csis.org/files/publication/1303q_seasia.pdf.
47 Ibid., 4.
48 *The Economist*, "Hai-handed; The South China Sea", *The Economist*, January 18, 2014, 40, http://search.proquest.com/docview/1490545962?accountid=38643.
49 Kailash K. Prassad, "An Assessment of the Goals, Drivers, and Capabilities of China's Modernizing Navy", *Korean Journal of Defense Analysis*, 24:1 (2012), 56.
50 "China Not to Accept Third Party Decision over Sea Dispute with Philippines", *BBC Monitoring Asia-Pacific*, July 14, 2015, 5, http://search.proquest.com/docview/169596 2448?accountid=28547.
51 Permanent Court of Arbitration, "The South China Sea Arbitration (The Republic of the Philippines versus the People's Republic of China)", Press release July12, 2016, 1.

196 *Renato Cruz De Castro*

52 See Fravel M. Taylor, "China's Strategy in the South China Sea", *Contemporary Southeast Asia*, 33:3 (2011), 292–319, http://search.proquest.com/docview/921618988/accountid=28547.

53 Mather Waxman, "Legal Posturing and Power Relations in the South China Sea", Asian Maritime Transparency Institute, January 21, 2015, 3, http://amti.csis.org/chinas-mariime-actors-coordinate-and-directed-from-the-top.

54 Frank Ching, "Seeking a South China Sea Solution", *News Straits Times*, July 30, 2015, 1, http://search.proquest.com/docview/169973814?accountid=28547.

55 Michaela Callar, "China's Historical Claim over South China Sea Invalid under UNCLOS", *The Philippines News Agency*, July 8, 2015, 1, http://search.proquest.com/docview/1694690512?accountid=28547.

56 Ibid., 2.

57 "Japan to Provide Two Large Patrol Ships to Philippines", *Jiji Press English News Service*, September 6, 2016, 1, http://0-search-proquest.com.lib1000.dlsu.edu.ph/printviewfile?accountid=28547. Also see Ministry of Foreign Affairs of Japan, "Japan–Philippines Summit Meeting", September 6, 2016, 2, www.mofa.go.jp/s_sa/sea2/ph/page3e_000568.html.

58 Cris Larano and Jospehine Cuneta, "Japan, Philippines Pledge Greater Cooperation", *Wall Street Journal*, January 10, 2013, 1, http://search.proquest.com/1268166061?accountid=28547.

59 "Philippine/Japan: Philippines, Japan Agree to Enhance Cooperation in Maritime Security", *Asia News Monitor*, January 14, 2013, 1, http://search.proquest.com/docview/1269104724?accountid=28547.

60 Ibid., 2.

61 Ibid., 1.

62 "Philippines, Japan Agree to Strengthen Defense Ties", *BBC Monitoring Asia-Pacific*, June 27, 2013, 2, http://search.proquest.com/docview/137173115?accountid=28547.

63 Embassy of Japan in Manila, "Press Release on the Visit of His Excellency Mr. Itsunori Onodera, Minister of Defense of Japan to the Philippines", June 27, 2013, 1.

64 Ibid., 2.

65 "Japan, Philippines to Cooperate on China's Air Defense Zone", *Jiji Press English News Service*, December 13, 2013, 1, http://search.proquest.com/docview/1467745056?accountid=28547.

66 "Aquino and Abe Discuss Maritime Disputes", *Gulf News*, June 25, 2014, 1, http://search.proquest.com/docview/1539577105?accountid=28547.

67 Ibid., 1.

68 "Japan Shares Philippines Serious Concern Over China's Reclamation Activities in West Philippines Sea", *The Philippines News Agency*, June 5, 2015, 1, http://search.proquest.com/docview/1686051792?accountid=28547.

69 Ibid.

70 *Japan–Philippines Joint Declaration: A Strengthen Partnership for Advancing the Shared Principles and Goals of Peace, Security, and Growth in the Region and Beyond* (Tokyo: Ministry of Foreign Affairs, June 4, 2015).

71 Melanie Rodulfo-Veril, "AFP Modernization," in *Security Sector Reform: Modern Defense Force Philippines* (Quezon City: Ateneo University Press, 2012), p. 135.

72 National Institute for Defense Studies, *China Security Report 2011* (Tokyo: National Institute for Defense Studies, 2011), 26.

73 Aileen Baviera, "President Duterte's Foreign Policy Challenges", *Contemporary Southeast Asia*, 38:2 (2016), 203.

74 Sheldon Simon, "U.S–Southeast Asian Relations: Augmented Presence", *Comparative Connections: A Triannual E-Journal on East Asian Bilateral Relations*, 18:2 (2016), 53.

75 Jose Katigbak, "Philippines Eyes Talks with China Sans Preconditions", *The Philippine Star*, September 18, 2016, 1.

Navigating between the Dragon and the Sun 197

76 David Cagahastian, "Malacanang Clarifies Duterte Statement on Kickout of U.S. Troops in Mindanao", *Business Mirror*, September 13, 2016, 2.
77 Katigbak, "Philippines Eyes Talks", 2.
78 Baviera, "President Duterte's Foreign Policy Challenges", 204–205.
79 Alastair Wanklyn and Ayako Mie, "Japan Tries to Decode Duterte after Joint U.S. Patrols Halted", *TCA Regional News*, September 15, 2016, 1, http://0-search.proquest.comlib1000.dlsu.edu.ph/docview/1819126061?accountid=28547.
80 Ministry of Foreign Affairs of Japan, "Foreign Minister Kishida Pays Courtesy Call on the President of the Philippines", August 11, 2016, 2, www.mofa.go.jp/s_sa/sea2/page3e_000530.html
81 Ibid., 2.
82 "Japan to Provide Philippines with 2 Large Patrol Vessels", *The Japan News*, September 7, 2016, 1, http://0-search.proquest.com.lib1000.dlsu.edu.ph/docview/1816926113/fulltext/E8A1508CFEE44FE2PQ/42?accountid=28547.
83 Ministry of Foreign Affairs of Japan, "Japan–Philippines Summit Meeting", September 6, 2016, 2, www.mofa.go.jp/s_sa/sea2/ph/page3e_000568.html.
84 Ibid., 2.
85 "Duterte Willing to Advance Defense Cooperation with Japan", *Jiji Press English News Service*, October 25, 2016, 1, http://0-search.proquest.comlib1000.dlsu.edu.ph/docview/1831939351/fulltext/D08500A05DBB4259PQ/362?accountid=28547.
86 Mitsuru Obe, "Rodrigo Duterte Speaks Soothingly to Japan: Stronger Economic Ties with 'Longstanding Friend and Ally' are a Priority, He Tells Tokyo Investment Forum", *Wall Street Journal*, October 26, 2016, 1, http://0-search.proquest.com.lib1000.dlsu.edu.ph/printviewfile?accountid=28547.
87 "Japan, Duterte Vow Unity on South China Sea Dispute", *BBC Monitoring Asia-Pacific*, October 26, 2016, http://0-search.proquest.com.lib1000.dlsu.edu.ph/printviewlife?accountid=28547.
88 Ibid., 1.
89 "Japan–Philippines Joint Statement", issued in Tokyo, October 26, 2016, 1.
90 Wanklyn and Mie, "Japan Tries to Decode Duterte", 1.
91 See Anthony Rivera, "Simply by Design", *Business Mirror*, June 28, 2016, 1, http://0-search.proquest.com.lib1a000.dlsu.edu.ph/docview/1800132718/fulltext/C41F2428DA1E4763PQ/23?accountid=28547.
92 Alastair Wanklyn, "Amid Duterte–U.S. Row, Attention Turns to Japan", *TCA Regional News*, October 4, 2016, 2, http://0-search.proquest.com.lib1000.dlsu.edu.ph/printviewfile?accountid=28547.

11 Vying for influence

Sino-Japanese competition in perspective

Jeffrey Hornung, Kerry Lynn Nankivell, and Jeffrey Reeves

Transformation and uncertainty were arguably the defining characteristics of global and regional order in 2016. Moreover, uncertainty is likely to continue to dominate the foreseeable future. The election of Donald Trump as President of the United States, soft markets and shaken electorates in Europe following the successful Brexit referendum, and the resurgence of Russian geopolitical mano-euvring in the Middle East and elsewhere will also force unpredictability and change in the international system. Amid this global change, powerful forces for change will continue to reshape the East Asian region: growing nationalism, Beijing's 2017 scheduled leadership change, and Prime Minister Abe Shinzō's proactive regional engagement will all play a role in charting Asia's future. There are few scholars or analysts who do not expect Asia's environment to change significantly over the short term. Difference emerges, however, over how to think about regional dynamics: the source of change and where to look for evidence of potential futures.

This volume has put regional security complex theory (RSCT) forward as a plausible tool for thinking about the changing nature of East Asia. In doing so, the volume's contributors have largely passed over more common analytical frameworks – particularly the effect that US–China relations have on regional security – for the sake of a more nuanced approach that privileges regional players. The result is a timely consideration of East Asia *sui generis*. The works in this volume focus on Sino-Japanese competition as a primary feature of the region, shedding light on an often overlooked dynamic in East Asia to help explain the region's changing security landscape. Of course, rivalry between East Asia's giants does not paint the whole regional picture, which remains very much impacted by the US and its relations with regional players, particularly its allies. But it is a critical dimension. This may be particularly true if a new US administration adjusts its regional engagement or takes a tougher line with China. While the policy preferences of a new Trump administration remain unarticulated, both elements are foreshadowed by published commentary by incoming officials[1] available at the time of writing. In that context, we should anticipate the salience of Sino-Japanese relations to Asian security to increase.

To demonstrate the value of understanding Sino-Japanese rivalry through the lens of RSCT, the editors divided this volume along three thematic areas – security

Vying for influence 199

institutions, security issue areas, and security relations – to best capture the wide-ranging canvas on which Sino-Japanese rivalry plays out in Asian security affairs. Contributors identify specific patterns of security engagement in line with RSCT's approach that suggest an increasing regionalization of security, exclusive of US involvement. Sino-Japanese competition, for instance, has created specific patterns of security relations between East Asian states, patterns that are only visible through detailed examination of Sino-Japanese security rivalry in all its various manifestations throughout the region. This kind of approach uncovers the extent to which relations that take shape in the context of this rivalry form either a regional security web in which the majority of East Asian states are enmeshed, or as security nodes centred on Chinese and/or Japanese engagement.

Examination of patterns of amity and enmity between China and Japan, between regional states forced to respond to the two states' rivalry, and between security nodes aligned with either state also point to a definitive process of securitization at the regional level which exists exclusive of US involvement, even where the US is a referent object. Indeed, as the volume's contributors repeatedly show, securitization is increasingly an East Asian phenomenon, with states such as Vietnam, Australia, and the Philippines more likely to view China and Japan as regional great powers pursuing opposing national security strategies. These third states seem acutely attuned to the fact of Beijing and Tokyo's two-player game, outside the regular conceit of a US-centric Asian security paradigm. Taken together, they describe the process by which concerts of states align themselves along security poles with self-conscious reference to the Sino-Japanese security dyad. This gives credence to the claim that informal security partnerships between various East Asian states already exist outside the US security "hub and spoke" system.

This is not to say, however, that the US does not play a significant role in Asian security, even with respect to the Sino-Japanese relationship itself. US policy preferences, posture, and behaviours cast a long shadow on this discussion. This is so even in case studies where the primary focus is on Chinese and Japanese involvement alone. What this volume's findings do show, however, is that China and Japan enjoy considerable agency outside their ties to Washington, so much so that it is entirely necessary to consider their influence as stand-alone actors. This fact is increasingly significant as the uncertainty surrounding a new US administration's possible Asia-Pacific policies raise concerns over continued US engagement and hold out the possibility of more friction in the US–China relationship. It is also instrumental in understanding why, in this context, regional states, like those examined in this volume, choose to operate in line with a regional rather than global logic in ways that sometimes disadvantage US interests.

The overall effect of this broad consideration of rivalry and its consequences is a regional portrait that highlights the value of understanding China's and Japan's mutually informed behaviour through the lens of RSCT. Although considering different manifestations of their competition, the volume's examination of security institutions, security issue areas, and security relations captures the broad spectrum across which the Sino-Japanese rivalry already affects preferences, policies, and outcomes in Asian security affairs. Taken as a whole, the individual chapters

200 *Jeffrey Hornung et al.*

support the claim that East Asia is undergoing a process of security regionalization organized around rival poles. Significantly, when taken collectively, the work provides much insight into the nature of this rivalry, including suggestions for where agency lies, when rivalry began, where it is primarily located within Asian security, and how the US relates as an external variable. These insights are integral to a complete understanding of contemporary Asia, and invaluable for tracing the regional security complex's potential futures. To conclude, we will consider each in turn.

Agency

As noted in the introduction, examination of great power relations alone contributes to a lopsided understanding of Asia's regional security dynamics. The main argument set forth in this book is that there is a need to examine the regional and sub-regional factors that drive Asia's security environment instead of framing Asian security as contingent on US–China relations. Implicit in the great power literature is the narrative that the deterioration of regional security is due to a structural confrontation between China's rising power and the US's preponderance. The narrative arc of this volume substantiates a contrary view: that Japan has exercised considerable agency across Asia, to which China has reacted. As most of the existing literature understates Japanese agency in regional affairs, particularly where China is concerned, confirmation that Japanese policy can and often is a preceding factor in regional developments (including with respect to China) is an important insight carrying implications for the regional research agenda going forward.

Consider Japan's agency in the growing rivalry between China and Japan in the two security issues areas examined in this volume. While China's actions in the South China Sea and East China Sea are generally portrayed as overly assertive, Japan is often treated as a tertiary agent in the maritime domain, where it is considered at all. Yet, as Nankivell points out, Japan effects greater strategic change than it is often credited with. Tokyo has increasingly perceived its interests vis-à-vis China in the East China Sea as linked to developments in the South China Sea, which has led to a more proactive Japanese engagement with the South China Sea disputes. This engagement includes the establishment of several multilateral bodies that have reshaped maritime East Asia and its stakeholders, including China. A similar dynamic is seen in the cyber realm, where Saalman highlights the perceived Japanese threat as a motive for "patriotic" hacks into Japan's official networks. She describes how Japanese actions, like prime ministerial visits to the controversial Yasukuni Shrine and Japanese activities in the East China Sea, catalyse hacks perpetrated against Japan's National Police Agency, Defense Agency (now the Ministry of Defense), and Ministry of Foreign Affairs. Without attaching value-judgements to Japanese actions, Saalman is correct to put Chinese behaviour in the proper regional context, noting that Chinese perpetrators of illicit cyber activity cite Japanese "offences" as their rationale.

The chapters on security institutions also highlight Japan's ability to influence Chinese policy, threat perception, and behaviour. Vivoda's discussion on energy security argues that Tokyo has become increasingly assertive in its regional energy diplomacy, a significant departure from the Cold War precedent. For example, he suggests that China's securitization of energy supplies was encouraged by Japanese deal-making with Moscow. As Tokyo succeeded in securing Russian support for a longer pipeline route from Siberia to the Pacific Ocean, so Beijing saw its competitive bidding process in Iran against Japanese rivals with a new strategic imperative. Tracing a similar dynamic, Pacheco Pardo describes Japan's deftness at enmeshing member states of the Association of Southeast Asian Nations (ASEAN) in bilateral trade agreements through strategic use of incentives and official development assistance (ODA) funds. He explains that enmeshment was pursued by Tokyo for both the short-term gain to domestic companies in the form of regional infrastructure contracts, and for the long-term gain to the Japanese government of closer trade relations with recipient countries that might preclude or counterbalance growing Chinese economic leverage. Importantly, as Oba's chapter on institutions shows, though the Regional Comprehensive Economic Partnership (RCEP) has been cast as a manifestation of US–China competition, it originated with a 2005 Japanese proposal to create the Comprehensive Economic Partnership for East Asia. As in other instances already noted, with respect to RCEP, Chinese behaviour is arguably informed as much by its threat perception of Japan as it is by its threat perception of the US.

Japan has traditionally used economic tools or cultural means to exercise agency in the international arena. The state case studies contained in this volume suggest caution in privileging that assumption, highlighting the many additional means through which Japanese power is mediated across Asia. Both Cruz De Castro and Vuving and Do, for example, highlight the continuity with which Japan has engaged both Vietnam and the Philippines on political and security terms, even while acknowledging that these pillars have gained momentum in recent years through equipment transfers and operational interactions. Bisley's chapter on Australia explains how incremental "normalization" of Japan's foreign and security policy shapes security choices in Canberra as it thinks about potential futures for the regional security order. In this way, Japan's strategic partnerships, increasingly a prominent feature of its relations in Asia, reshape the security landscape in important ways, constructing new parameters within which China defines its own Asia policy. This reality confirms that Sino-Japanese rivalry is an important facet of contemporary Asia, and that scholarly understanding of its contours is a necessary, if not sufficient, undertaking for scholars of regional security.

Nature

The nature of Sino-Japanese rivalry is intuitively obvious to most scholars of East Asia, but difficult to define with precision. The preceding examination across a range of security institutions, nodes, and third states helps immeasurably in that task. While the chapter by Reeves and Hornung highlights observable instances of direct military balancing pursued by China and Japan, it is understandable to question whether their relations as a whole are characterized by rivalry. There are

202 *Jeffrey Hornung et al.*

simply too many arguments in favour of parallel, rather than competing, policy pursuits to take for granted that they are motivated by direct rivalry. Only by looking across a spectrum of issues does one begin to appreciate the breadth of an acute rivalry that often plays out only subtly in discrete institutions, issue areas, or countries. Comprehensive examination is needed to see the conceptual forest from the empirical trees.

The maritime domain provides the clearest example of this dynamic. As the chapter by Nankivell discusses, despite a relatively peaceful co-existence in the South China Sea throughout the Cold War that ran parallel to a contentious rivalry in the East China Sea, today the politics of the East China Sea are increasingly hard to consider in isolation from events farther south. As in previous decades, each sub-regional basin continues to be driven by many discrete factors and each maintains its own politics, applicable law, and strategic dynamic. But their increasing interconnectedness seems an incontrovertible fact and is importantly defined by Sino-Japanese rivalry. Japan's engagement with the South China Sea disputes is connected to its broader policy to protect its maritime interests and, in part, to its China policy. China, she shows, is very sensitive to Japanese involvement in the South China Sea and firmly committed to isolating its two-player game with Japan from the contested waters it tries to manage on its southern littoral. The former involves hardening its capacity to encircle the Japanese islands with military force; the latter involves a more ambivalent strategy of hardening capabilities without alienating partners and neighbours.

Yet rivalry, and their indirect attempts to counter each other, extends far beyond the maritime domain into a contest for influence in other realms. Saalman's chapter extends the analysis into the cyber domain. She contends that Beijing's cyber policy is motivated in part by a competitive drive directed at Japan, which it sees as harbouring both the malicious intent to contain China and the partnerships required to do so. While Saalman does not herself impute those motives to Japan, she argues that Sino-Japanese bilateral competition based on that assumption is driving regional developments in the cyber domain. A similar dynamic is found in both the economic and energy domains. In his discussion on economic security, Pacheco Pardo shows that while the two do not overtly engage in trade wars, they engage in economic competition with regional economies as a means not only to increase their overall profitability, but also to strengthen their political and strategic partnerships at the expense of the other. He argues that this logic underpins their competition over trade agreements, ODA, and major infrastructure programmes. It is also the logic behind their assumptions about energy security and the need for market intervention, as Vivoda argues. Here, rapid economic growth in the region has intensified their competition for increasingly scarce energy resources, leading both countries to promote overseas investment in order to secure both equity and self-developed oil and gas stakes as a means to enhance their energy security. Finally, in her look at the two countries' attempts to expand their roles in promoting regionalism and regional institutions, Oba examines how the development of regional institutions has been intertwined with Sino-Japanese competition over how and to what extent they should each take a leading role in constructing and maintaining a new order in the Asia-Pacific region. She argues that each wants to outperform the other and expand or maintain their leverage in regional politics. The theme is reinforced by the three state case studies, with each in their own context providing much-needed specificity to the claim that Sino-Japanese rivalry plays out within Asia's primary security institutions.

The nature of Sino-Japanese rivalry as understood through country case studies presents a more complex picture. Where security institutions are arenas for rivalry, third countries bring their own agency to the dynamic and complicate the analysis as a result. In all three cases presented, countries demonstrate a preference to secure the obvious and considerable economic gains of a developing China without risking political or strategic capture by Beijing. The chapters by Bisley and Vuving and Do specifically explore the ways in which this objective has shaped Australian and Vietnamese security policies, respectively. Both of these countries have found an effective hedge in Japan, with whom they have long enjoyed productive economic relations. They argue, in different ways, that Australia and Vietnam's longstanding relationships with Japan have increased in importance and intensity in recent years in direct proportion to their growing perception of threat from China. In looking at both countries, then, Sino-Japanese rivalry exists and is being instrumentalized, albeit to different degrees. Cruz De Castro's chapter on the Philippines takes on an even more pointed tone. Of course, like Hanoi, China has designs on territory that Manila claims for itself. Unlike Hanoi, Manila enjoys neither common geography nor ideological affinity with China. It is then not surprising, perhaps, that Cruz De Castro attributes Sino-Japanese rivalry with much more blatant explanatory power in various Philippine governments' overtures to Japan. In Manila's case, in the face of Chinese expansion in the South China Sea, the Philippines not only strengthened its ties with Japan, but actively began to seek security assistance as part of its multi-layered security cooperation with Tokyo. Complementing conclusions reached by Nankivell, Cruz De Castro characterizes the Philippines' Japan policy as explicitly aimed at leveraging Japan's concerns about Chinese aggressiveness in the East China Sea to build support for deepened defence ties as a bulwark to Chinese aggression in sea lanes farther south.

Each of these discrete discussions provide much-needed precision to the claim that competition between China and Japan not only exists, but defines East Asian security in important ways. Moreover, they also suggest the means by which this competition is realized. In each of the realms discussed, rivalry includes contest over foundational regional norms. As a case in point, Oba shows that Japan's creation of the East Asia Summit was motivated in part by a desire to construct a region based on global norms and rules, including democracy, human rights, and rule of law. Similarly, Saalman identifies competing conceptions of governance in cyberspace as a seminal point of contention between China and Japan. While China focuses on state-centric control over cyberspace and the need to block foreign interference, Japan prioritizes individual-centric cyber freedoms. A similar dynamic is at work in the economic security realm as well. As highlighted by Pacheco Pardo, in contrast to China's RCEP, which largely focuses on reducing barriers to trade in goods and services, the Japan-supported Trans-Pacific Partnership

204 *Jeffrey Hornung et al.*

aims to establish foundational norms in environmental rights and intellectual property. A contest over norms is also at work in maritime competition where, as Nankivell argues, Japan has firmly shifted its diplomatic approach from safety of navigation to freedom of navigation, drawing Chinese ire in the process. This, she argues, has strong normative overtones that also legitimates an expanded strategic geography for Japan; it implies that Japan understands itself as entitled to play an important role not just in its own claimed waters in the East China Sea, but in the South China Sea as well. Sino-Japanese rivalry is not just about access or presence, but also about diffuse contests for normative leadership of East Asia.

Timing

China and Japan have seen themselves as rivals at many junctures in their long history, but nothing in this history should be taken as evidence that rivalry is foreordained. As the current manifestation of Sino-Japanese rivalry has become a significant variable in today's Asian security landscape, locating the origin of its contemporary expression is important. While it is naively simplistic to pinpoint any exact date, the authors in this volume largely agree that Sino-Japanese relations took a new turn at the opening of the twenty-first century. Each of the analyses presented here assert that, until that time, Japan maintained a special position as an inconspicuous but uncontested leader in various fields, wielding a significant amount of regional influence as a result. As Oba argues, this is attributable to the fact that relations between Japan and other Asian countries, including China, were vertical. In various domains, the chapters in this volume nearly unanimously argue that this regional structure began to change in the last two decades. Only Vivoda, considering energy security, identifies contemporary rivalry prior to the mid-1990s. He notes that intensive competition over oil and gas supplies between the two Asian giants began around 1990. The reason for the emergence of rivalry is attributed by each author to the rather obvious fact that not only did China's economy grow at this time, it eventually surpassed Japan's. It is logical from this stand-point that competition over energy resources would precede more generalized rivalry, as China overtook Japan as a net importer of oil (in absolute volume) in 1996, before it overtook Japan's aggregate gross domestic product. At the same time, Japan's persistent recession and frequent leadership changes did not directly cause, but certainly did not help safeguard, its declining regional influence relative to a rising China. As a result of these structural changes, Japanese relations with China became more horizontal and China's influence vis-à-vis other regional countries grew. In turn, China's growing regional influence intensified its competition with Japan for expanding and maintaining leverage in the region.

The displacement of Japan as Asia's inconspicuous leader in a variety of domains served as an inflection point for bilateral relations. Both Oba and Vuving and Do point to shifts in economic balance of power and associated influence that this shift conferred on China as important milestones for the region and the dyad. Oba goes as far as to characterize the November 2001 ASEAN–China free trade agreement as the "direct trigger" of contemporary rivalry, noting the extent to

Vying for influence   205

which this enhancement of ASEAN–China ties shocked Japan. A similar sentiment is heard in Pacheco Pardo's chapter, which argues that, even in the face of overwhelming evidence, Tokyo has not yet come to terms with its own decreasing centrality to Asia-Pacific economic flows. This is in contrast to Beijing, which has once again become the self-consciously central nodal point of regional economic links. Bisley echoes these observations and, moreover, links them to strategic changes. He argues that the rise of China in the early 2000s, and the consequent disruption of East Asia's strategic balance, facilitated the convergence of Japan and Australia on a common view of regional and global security threats. Nankivell and Cruz De Castro push the analysis most explicitly in discussion of the Sino-Japanese military balance and associated activities. They each point to 2010 as a turning point in Japan's threat perception of its maritime neighbour, driven by notable strengthening of China's approach to pursuit of its maritime claims under the Xi Jinping administration. Taken together, the analyses here point to an observable evolution of contemporary rivalry that broadly mirrors structural shifts in their fundamental material indicators. Growing from structural changes to their positions as oil importers from 1990 to 1996, through inversion of their relative economic performance indicators in the early 2000s, all the way through to important changes in their hard power capabilities and behaviours, the authors collectively trace an arc of contemporary rivalry development from 1990 to 2010. Identification of this period as of specific significance is an important finding of these authors' collective work.

Location

As evidence of the value of RSCT, this book highlights the rivalrous dynamic between China and Japan over a broad set of issues that, in turn, shape regional relations. While the Asia-Pacific region writ large is an open arena for the two powers in their bilateral relations, the chapters in this volume demonstrate that (noting the important exception of cyberspace) their rivalry most often finds its centre of gravity in Southeast Asia. Not only does contemporary Sino-Japanese rivalry have a particular nature and timing then, but the prominence of Southeast Asia to the discussions in this volume suggests that it has a discrete geography as well.

The chapters highlight the increasing importance that Southeast Asia has as a reference point for both China and Japan and, in turn, the notable effect that their rivalry has for constructing the security landscape of third states. The chapters on Vietnam and the Philippines, for example, demonstrate Southeast Asia's centrality to the strategic interests of both Japan and China, while the study of Australia uses Southeast Asia as an important referent object of Canberra's calculations as well. And, as detailed in the chapters considering institutionalism, trade and investment, and maritime security, there is clearly pan-regional depth to China's and Japan's strategic interests vis-à-vis one another that expands beyond the borders of third states to the wider Southeast Asian geography.

Let us consider institutionalism. Oba shows that Japan's post-Cold War efforts at building regionalism and regional institutions centre on ASEAN and its member

206   *Jeffrey Hornung et al.*

states. Importantly, however, Japan is no longer alone in this endeavour. Reluctantly starting from the mid-1990s, China has also emerged as an active participant in ASEAN processes and forums as well as an aspiring leader in institution-building within an ASEAN-centric regional architecture. The same can be said about the economic realm, where both Beijing and Tokyo focus tremendous energy and political capital securing trade agreements with Southeast Asian countries that can be usefully understood as counterweights to initiatives underway with the other. The chapter by Pacheco Pardo shows that at the very moment that China secured trade agreements with ASEAN, Singapore, South Korea, and Thailand, Japan finalized agreements with ASEAN, Brunei, Indonesia, Malaysia, Mongolia, Philippines, Singapore, Thailand, and Vietnam. He goes on to highlight instances in which Chinese and Japanese companies and consortiums compete directly for infrastructure development projects throughout the sub-region, citing cases from Indonesia, Thailand, Malaysia, and Singapore. And whether it be resource nationalism or the importance of regional sea lanes, Vivoda's chapter demonstrates the importance of Southeast Asia for Sino-Japanese competition for access to finite energy resources.

This centrality of Southeast Asia is particularly acute in the issue of maritime security. Nankivell argues that, compared to traditional Japanese activities in maritime Southeast Asia, which focused on safety, Japan's view of these waters has become securitized commensurate with its concerns with Chinese activities in the East China Sea and, to some degree, China overall. As a result, Japan increasingly engages Southeast Asia along three distinct lines of effort: creating and leveraging multilateral diplomatic forums; introducing a normative dimension to its traditionally pragmatically directed maritime strategy; and direct operational involvement with states littoral to the South China Sea. On the other hand, China's growing economic dependence on Southeast Asia led to its own securitized perception of Japan's commercial safety assistance to Southeast Asian states, and its strategic discomfort with Tokyo's successful multilateralization of Southeast Asian maritime issues, including safety, throughout the 1990s. As this dynamic has become more pointed in the last decade, Chinese concerns with Japanese engagement in Southeast Asia have largely been operationally realized in the East China Sea, though a time may come when direct confrontation between Japan and China in Southeast Asian waters becomes a reality. China clearly stands to lose from Japan's shifting approach to maritime Southeast Asia, which invites coalition building among China's many rival claimants to territory and maritime jurisdiction.

Locating a centre of gravity of Sino-Japanese rivalry in Southeast Asia problematizes the assumption of parity or near-parity in their relations, which is what makes the exercise of locating rivalry so relevant. Just as the historical discussion suggests an evolution of "Japan-the-inconspicuous" to "Japan-the-contested-power" in Asia, the geographic discussion carries fundamental implications for understanding their relative positioning as well. China enjoys a proximity to Southeast Asia that Japan cannot easily match, due to cultural affinity, shared land and maritime boundaries, and its deepening direct infrastructure links. As the analyses here lay out, Japan counters this proximity in a range of domains by constructing

Vying for influence 207

strategic linkages of its own, establishing investment ties or support to human capital development as Pacheco Pardo outlines, or developing shared norms and values in the manner discussed by Oba, Saalman, and Nankivell. While both China and Japan expend a great deal of effort and capital developing these Southeast Asian links, Japan's engagement is conducted from a much less tangible base. In so far as Sino-Japanese rivalry can be understood as centred on a discrete Southeast Asian geography, China will always enjoy an advantage vis-à-vis Japan as Asia's inevitable power. It is a matter of geographic fact that China will continue to be deeply embedded in Southeast Asia across the spectrum of political, economic, and strategic affairs; in this space, Japan's engagement can be measured only by its effectiveness in acting as China's offshore balancer. Certainly each of the state case studies presented here, even including the analysis of Australia, leaves one with the sense that while Japan may be Asia's preferred partner in many respects, China, by dint of geography and sheer size, is Asia's inevitable power. If this structural observation holds true, Japan may opt to either continue to leverage its role as an offshore balancer, or to continue to seek external transformation of the regional security complex to shift the geographic boundaries of rivalry in directions that yield it greater structural advantage.

US penetration

The main argument of this volume is that patterns of security exist outside the larger international level of power relations and are not dependent on great power involvement. Yet, it is an abstraction to argue that regional dynamics exist wholly separate from great power interaction. For that reason, RSCT accounts for the influence of great powers in regional security dynamics via the notion of penetration. In that conception, the US is not the primary determinant of regional dynamics, but is an external variable that influences regional states via alliances and military power projection, among other means.

The case studies in this volume account for US penetration of Asia's regional security complex in various ways, reminding us of exogenous agency at work in Asia. As US allies, Australia and the Philippines necessarily and explicitly account for US position, capability, and preferences in their own policy calculation. Bisley's analysis of Australia confirms not only the strong consideration of the US in Australia's domestic debates over its bilateral relationship with Beijing, but also credits assumed or communicated US support for closer Australia–Japan relations as a key influence on Canberra's Japan policy. Likewise, Cruz De Castro's examination of rapidly developing Japan–Philippines security ties is framed in part as a complementary outgrowth of their respective bilateral alliances with the US. Vuving and Do acknowledge that US penetration also takes noted effect in non-US allies, claiming that Japan sometimes acts as a valuable bridge between Vietnam and the developed West, including the US.

US penetration is a theme common to other chapters as well, confirming its significance to understanding the regional complex. In her analysis of regional institutionalism, Oba shows the extent to which various Asian countries take US

208 *Jeffrey Hornung et al.*

reactions to regional initiatives under necessary consideration, due to its power to either bolster or undermine institutions through policy. She presents the failure of the Asian Monetary Fund as a case in point, an instance in which US opposition foreclosed on Japanese initiative. This influence is also found in the cyber realm, although not as directly. Saalman discusses the ways in which Japan's adherence to Western-centric cyber legal frameworks and military cyber umbrella opens a backdoor for Western "intrusion" into the region. Pacheco Pardo's treatment of economic security reminds us that Japan aims to ensure that the US remains committed to the Asia-Pacific region when looking at regional trade agreements, reflecting the extent to which trade and investment are securitized in Japan due to its rivalry with China. As already noted, the shadow of the US looms large over any discussion of Sino-Japanese rivalry and the Asian security complex. But that fact should not distract from the reality that great powers are not always determinants of regional events, despite their material capability. This volume's contributors add much texture to existing scholarship by privileging regional agency, taking account of US power as one among many factors to be considered in determining preferences, behaviours, and regional outcomes.

Conclusion

Read in line with RSCT's predictive scenarios, the volume's chapters present significant evidence that East Asia is moving towards internal transition where competition between China and Japan is consolidating regional-level change that already affects regional balance-of-power relations and significantly influences dominant patterns of enmity and amity across a wide geography and a range of issues. Whether with regard to institutions, security issue areas, or East Asian states' domestic and foreign policies, Sino-Japanese competition permeates the region as a dominant security driver. This dialogic dynamic mainly results in increased tensions, but also has a profoundly binding effect on the East Asian region. It constructs a shared regional paradigm that is powerful enough to animate the national security strategies that play out within it, but that is nonetheless exclusive of the US. Such an endogenously driven context has arguably not presented itself since the early part of the last century.

This contemporary manifestation is occurring at the same time that a new administration is coming to power in the US. It is still too early to know what a Trump administration will mean for the Asia-Pacific region in the years ahead. One can make a reasonable assumption, however, based on the discourse of the factious 2016 election, that President Trump will not implement the established status quo of American foreign policy. How President Trump will treat Asian allies, including Japan, how much his government will engage the region, and to what extent the administration will confront China remains unknown. Nonetheless, this volume establishes that the answers to these questions will have magnified impact on the regional security complex precisely because they will be mediated through Sino-Japanese rivalry. The US should not be read as the primary driver of Asian outcomes. Asia itself will provide its own destiny, and this will

Vying for influence 209

be disproportionately shaped by the central relationship between Tokyo and Beijing.

Of course, no destiny is preordained. A less rivalrous future is possible. As Oba demonstrates, because neither the Asian Development Bank (ADB) nor the Asian Infrastructure Investment Bank (AIIB) alone can match Asia's US$750 billion annual infrastructure deficit, institutional cooperation facilitating development investment could underwrite a common responsibility for security. Pacheco Pardo suggests as much, indicating that the two development banks have already started to work together, contrary to the dominant narrative that the AIIB is China's direct challenge to Japan's ADB. He extends the argument to regional finance as well, outlining instances in which the two have worked together to establish an institutional network to mitigate financial risk while stabilizing flows. Assuming that China and Japan realize that a more prosperous and financially stable Asia-Pacific is of mutual benefit, they have the potential to move towards a win-win scenario. Vivoda notes that, working from within a similar energy security paradigm, China and Japan have ample opportunity to cooperate on renewable energy, and clean technologies to reduce their respective dependence on foreign energy supplies and vulnerable sea lanes. State-led co-investment in alternative energy markets in Asia would move the two energy giants away from pointed rivalry over finite supplies to collaborators for the future. Japan's role in this is particularly important, as stressed by both Saalman and Vuving and Do's characterization of Japan as a bridge between West and East. As Japan can traverse and interpret Eastern and Western normative conceptions of the legal and strategic definitions of cyberspace, so it could promote mutual understanding between China and the rest of the world. At the very least, Japan has theoretical access to an understanding of China that is much more elusive in Western circles.

Most trends, unfortunately, suggest that rivalry will persist and possibly cleave to conflict. If the countervailing trends of China's ascendancy and Japan's relative decline pertain, tensions will likely be exacerbated. This is particularly the case if China's "One Belt, One Road" policy and AIIB continue to grow in regional prominence, accruing growing ancillary politico-economic leverage to China. Without similar vision and resources applied to its Asia policy, Japan risks marginalization in this context. Intensified rivalry over infrastructure development programmes, ODA, and regionalism overall will become increasingly key to gaining regional access and influence. Economics aside, Japan must also be conscious of the risk of marginalization due to its adherence to "Western" norms like cyber freedom or freedom of navigation over a more traditionally Asian, sovereignty-centric paradigm.

Nowhere is the potential for conflict more pronounced than in the maritime domain. China's inflexible position on South China Sea and East China Sea disputes, its refusal to participate or recognize the arbitral tribunal award in the Philippines case, and its efforts to punish those that challenge its claims confirm that China holds its sovereign claims as non-negotiable. As long as this does not change, compromise with China is unlikely. On the other hand, if Japan continues to deploy seapower to engage the South China Sea disputes, it will raise the ire of

210 *Jeffrey Hornung et al.*

China and risk escalation of rivalry. This does not portend a hopeful future. To be certain, neither China nor Japan has shown a proclivity for the use of force to settle what until now have been largely political or economic lines of competitive effort. That the two states increasingly see their security interests in zero-sum opposition to one another, however, suggests more, not fewer, arenas in which conflict could arise.

From an academic perspective, these findings are significant as they identify an alternative lens through which to view regional security to the often-dominant US-centric trope. In raising China and Japan as regional actors with regional-level agency to affect East Asian security, this volume has made a significant contribution to the study of Asia. Moreover, the contributors to this volume have collectively placed defined boundaries around an appropriate research agenda for Sino-Japanese rivalry by specifying its critical time period, its geography, attribution of agency, and what it implies for great power penetration of Asia. In many ways, the existing field of international relations has reached an explanatory ceiling imposed by overweening concern with US-dominated structures and events at the expense of regionally focused investigation. Admitting that the US does, of course, play a significant role in Asia, this volume offers a new avenue of inquiry about how twenty-first century Asia operates as a security complex outside and above the US ability to shape and direct security dynamics. It raises Asia as a worthy object of study rather than a tertiary variable to great power conflict.

From a policy viewpoint, this volume provides important insight into areas of potential conflict in Asia that are often overlooked by outside actors (and some East Asian states). By parsing China and Japan's activities within East Asian security from the US role, this volume's contributors have outlined a more complex and, admittedly, unstable security environment that requires policy-specific responses. This outcome is particularly relevant for the US policy community, which often shortchanges the nuance of regional dynamics for the sake of simplicity in US policy making. Remembering Churchill's adage that the trouble with allies is that they have their own interests, stepping outside the US-centric view and understanding the region on its own terms can pay important dividends for US policy aimed at reducing Washington's relationship with East Asia without risking its decades-old stability and prosperity. The analysis here should not be read as a prescription against the evolution of US policy, but only a caveat that changes to the US's Asia policy must be undertaken with clear-eyed appreciation of the regional forces imposing on resident states and their security relations.

Importantly, the volume also provides a clear way forward for both academic and policy researchers interested in developing a research agenda on ways to mitigate growing instability in Sino-Japanese relations. Most contributors to this volume, for instance, identify areas and opportunities where cooperation could take place between the two states to ensure greater regional stability. From regional institutions to the two states' shared interests in regional state-level stability, Beijing and Tokyo could pursue common national security interests over the perceived need to compete along zero-sum lines. For cooperation to triumph over competition, however, both states must work to create greater strategic trust. Such a development requires both political will and mutual sociability, conditions within the Sino-Japan dyad that are currently in short supply. As the chapters contained in this volume demonstrate, the two countries continue to vie for influence in many domains across the Asia-Pacific. While the future of the regional security complex in this context is yet to be written, it will be very much dependent on getting the central Sino-Japanese relationship right.

Note

1 Besides the many campaign statements given by Donald Trump promising a tougher China policy, incoming senior officials including Gen. (ret) James Mattis, nominee for Secretary of Defense, have published views on the need to be tough on China while also encouraging Japan to assume a greater share of the burden for its own defence. See, *inter alia*, Alex Gray and Peter Navarro, "Donald Trump's Peace Through Strength Vision for the Asia-Pacific", *Foreign Policy*, November 7, 2016; and General Jim Mattis, "A New American Grand Strategy", *Defining Ideas*, February 26, 2015, www.hoover.org/research/new-american-grand-strategy.

Selected bibliography

"2003–2013 nian quanqiu wangluo he xinxi anquan fazhan dongtai" (2003–2013 Global Network and Information Security Development Dynamics), *Xinxi anquan yu tongxun baomi* (Information Security and Communication Confidential), 12 (2013), 48–56.

"2011 nian shijie zhuyao guojia he diqu xinxi anquan jianshe zhuangkuang" (2011 Condition of Cyber Security Formation in the World's Primary Countries and Regions), *Zhongguo xinxi anquan (China's Information Security)*, 1 (2012), 68.

Aalto, P. and D. Korkmaz Temel. "European Energy Security: Natural Gas and the Integration Process", *Journal of Common Market Studies* 52:4 (2014), 758–774.

Acharya, Amitav, "Thinking Theoretically about Asian IR" in David Shambaugh and Michael Yahuda, eds, *International Relations of Asia* (New York: Rowman & Littlefield, 2014).

Acharya, Amitav, "Global International Relations (IR) and Regional Worlds: A New Agenda for International Studies", *International Studies Quarterly*, 58:4 (2014), 653.

Acharya, Amitav, *The End of American World Order* (Cambridge: Polity Press, 2014).

Aggarwal, Vinod K., "Mega-FTAs and Trade–Security Nexus: The Trans-Pacific Partnership (TPP) and Regional Comprehensive Economic Partnership (RCEP)", *Asia Pacific Issues*, 123 (2016).

Aixian, Dong, "Guoji wangluo kongjian zhili de zhuyao jucuo, tedian ji fazhan qushi" (Major Initiatives, Characteristics, and Development Trends in International Cyberspace Governance), *Xinxi anquan yu tongxin baomi (Information Security and Communication Confidential)*, 1 (2014), 36–41.

Ang, Cheng Guan, *Lee Kuan Yew's Strategic Thought* (London: Routledge, 2013).

Asian Development Bank, *Asian Economic Integration Report 2016: What Drives Foreign Direct Investment in Asia and the Pacific* (Manila: Asian Development Bank, 2016).

Aslam, Mohamed, "The Impact of ASEAN–China Free Trade Agreement on ASEAN's Manufacturing Industry", *International Journal of China Studies*, 3:1 (2012), 43–78.

Athukorala, Prema-chandra, "Production Networks and Trade Patterns in East Asia: Regionalization or Globalization", ADB Working Paper Series on Regional Economic integration 56 (2010).

Ba, Alice, "A New History? The Structure and Process of Southeast Asia's Relations with a Rising China", in Mark Beeson, ed., *Contemporary Southeast Asia* (New York: Palgrave, 2009).

Bader, Jeffrey A., *Obama and China's Rise: An Insider's Account of America's Asia Strategy* (Washington, DC: Brookings Institution Press, 2012).

Baginda, Abdul Razak Abdullah, "PRC–ASEAN Relations: Strategic and Security Implication", in Theresa Carino, ed., *China ASEAN Relations: Political, Economic and Ethnic Dimensions* (Manila: China Studies Program, 1991).

Selected bibliography 213

Baldwin, David A., "Security Studies and the end of the Cold War", *World Politics*, 48:1 (1995), 117–141.

Ball, Desmond, *The Transformation of Security in the Asia-Pacific Region* (London: Routledge, 2015).

Baviera, Aileen, "Turning Predicament into Promise: A Prospective on Philippines–China Relations", in Aileen Baviera, ed., *Comprehensive Engagement: Strategic Issues in Philippines–China Relations* (Quezon City: Philippine–China Development Resource Center, 2000).

Baviera, Aileen, "President Duterte's Foreign Policy Challenges", *Contemporary Southeast Asia*, 38:2 (2016), 202–208.

Bekkevold, Jo Inge, Ian Bowers, and Michael Raska, *Security, Strategy and Military Change in the 21st Century: Cross-Regional Perspectives* (London: Routledge, 2015).

Bisley, Nick, "'The Japan–Australia Security Declaration and the Changing Regional Setting: Wheels, Webs and Beyond?", *Australian Journal of International Affairs* 62:1 (2008), 38–52.

Bisley, Nick "Never Having to Choose", in James Reilly and Jing-Dong Yuan, eds, *Australia and China at 40* (Sydney: New South Publishing, 2012).

Bisley, Nick "'An Ally for All the Years to Come': Why Australia is Not a Conflicted Ally", *Australian Journal of International Affairs*, 67:3 (2013), 403–418.

Bisley, Nick, "Australia and Asia's Trilateral Dilemmas: Between Beijing and Washington?", *Asian Survey*, 54:2 (2014), 297–318.

Blair, Dennis C. and John T. Hanley, "From Wheels to Webs: Reconstructing Asia-Pacific Security Arrangements", *The Washington Quarterly*, 24:1 (2001), 7–17.

Blusse, Leonard. "Gang Zhao: The Qing Opening to the Ocean – Chinese Maritime Policies, 1684–1757", *The American Historical Review*, 119:3 (2014).

Booth, K. and N.J. Wheeler, *The Security Dilemma: Fear, Cooperation and Trust in World Politics* (Basingstoke: Palgrave Macmillan, 2007).

Brautigam, Deborah, "Aid 'With Chinese Characteristics': Chinese Foreign Aid and Development Finance Meet the OECD-DAC Aid Regime", *Journal of International Development*, 23:5 (2011), 752–764.

Breckenridge, Carol A. and Peter van der Veer, *Orientalism and the Postcolonial Predicament: Perspectives on South Asia* (Pennsylvania: University of Pennsylvania Press, 1993).

Bush, Richard C., *The Perils of Proximity: China–Japan Security Relations* (Washington, DC: Brookings Institution Press, 2013).

Buzan, Barry and Ole Wæver, *Regions and Powers: The Structure of International Security* (Cambridge: Cambridge University Press, 2003).

Buzan, Barry, Ole Wæver, and Jaap de Wilde, *Security: A New Framework for Analysis* (Boulder: Lynne Rienner Publishers, 1998).

Cable, Vincent, "What is International Economic Security", *International Affairs*, 71:2 (1995), 305–324.

Cai, Kevin G., *The Political Economy of East Asia: Regional and National Dimensions* (Basingstoke: Palgrave Macmillan, 2008).

Calder, K.E., *Asia's Deadly Triangle: How Arms, Energy and Growth Threaten to Destabilize Asia-Pacific* (London: Nicholas Brealey Publishing, 1997).

Calder, K.E., *The New Continentalism: Energy and Twenty-First-Century Eurasian Geopolitics* (New Haven: Yale University Press, 2012).

Campbell, Kurt, *The Pivot: The Future of American Statecraft in Asia* (New York: Hatchette, 2015).

214 *Selected bibliography*

Capannelli, Giovanni and Masahiro Kawai, *The Political Economy of Asian Regionalism* (New York: Springer Science & Business Media, 2014).

Chanda, Nayan, *Brother Enemy: The War After the War* (New York: Harcourt Brace Jovanovich, 1986).

Chang, F.K., "Chinese Energy and Asian Security", *Orbis*, 45:2 (2001), 211–240.

Chin, Gregory T., "Asian Infrastructure Investment Bank: Governance Innovation and Prospects", *Global Governance: A Review of Multilateralism in International Organizations*, 22:1 (2016), 11–25.

Christensen, Thomas J., "China, the U.S.–Japan Alliance and the Security Dilemma in East Asia", *International Security*, 23:4 (1999).

Christensen, Thomas J., *The China Challenge: Shaping the Choices of a Rising Power* (New York: W.W. Norton & Company, 2015).

Chua, Beng Huat and Koichi Iwabuchi, *East Asian Pop Culture: Analysing the Korean Wave* (Hong Kong: Hong Kong University Press, 2008).

Clough, Ralph N., *East Asia and US Security* (Washington, DC: Brookings Institution Press, 1974).

Cohen, Paul A., *Discovering History in China: American Historical Writing on the Recent Chinese Past* (New York: Columbia University Press).

Coker, Christopher, *The Improbable War: China, the United States and Logic of Great Power Conflict* (Oxford: Oxford University Press, 2015).

Cordesman, Anthony H., *Chinese Strategy and Modernization in 2015: A Comparative Analysis* (Washington, DC: CSIS, 2015).

Cunliang, Sun, "One Belt, One Road", Cultural Exchanges: Significance, Practice, and Mechansims" ("Yidai, yilu", renwen jiaoliu: zhongda yiyi, shijian lujing he jiangou jizhi), *International Aid* (2015), 14–20.

Danzi, Liao, "'Duoyuanxing', feichuantong anquan weixie: Wangluo anquan tiaozhan yu zhili" ("Pluralism" Non-Traditional Security Threats: Cyber Security Challenges and Governance), *Guoji anquan yanjiu* (*International Security Research*), 3 (2014).

Dittmer, Lowell, "China's New Asia Policy", *China: An International Journal*, 12:2 (2014), 116–117.

Downs, E.S., "The Chinese Energy Security Debate", *The China Quarterly* 177 (2004), 21–41.

Drifte, R., "Japan's Energy Policy in Asia: Cooperation, Competition, Territorial Disputes", *Oil, Gas & Energy Law*, 4 (2005).

Eichengreen, Barry and Masahiro Kawai, eds, *Renminbi Internationalization: Achievements, Prospects, and Challenges* (Tokyo: Asian Development Bank Institute, 2015).

Eldridge, Robert D., *The Origins of U.S. Policy in the East China Sea Islands Dispute: Okinawa's Reversion and the Senkaku Islands* (New York: Routledge, 2014).

Enemark, Christian, *Disease and Security: Natural Plagues and Biological Weapons in East Asia* (London: Routledge, 2007).

Feigenbaum, Evan A., "The New Asian Order: And How the United States Fits In", *Foreign Affairs*, February 2, 2015.

Feng, Zhang, "Rethinking the 'Tribute System': Broadening the Conceptual Horizon of Historical East Asian Politics", *Chinese Journal of International Politics*, 2:4 (2009), 597–626.

Feng, Zhang, "How Hierarchic was the Historical East Asian System?", *International Politics*, 51:1 (2014), 1–22.

Feng, Zhang, *Chinese Hegemony: Grand Strategy and International Institutions in East Asian History* (Stanford: Stanford University Press, 2015).

Selected bibliography 215

Foot, R., "Asia's Cooperation and Governance: The Role of East Asian Regional Organizations in Regional Governance: Constraints and Contributions", *Japanese Journal of Political Science*, 13:1 (2012), 133–142.

Fravel, M. Taylor, "Territorial and Maritime Boundary Disputes in Asia", in Saadia M. Pekkanen, John Ravenhill, and Rosemary Foot, eds, *Oxford Handbook of the International Relations in Asia* (Oxford: Oxford University Press, 2014).

Friedberg, Aaron L., *A Contest for Supremacy: China, America, and the Struggle for Mastery in Asia* (New York: W.W. Norton & Company, 2012).

Fuchs, Andreas, Peter Nunnekamp, and Hannes Ohler, "Why Donors of Foreign Aid Do Not Coordinate: The Role of Competition for Export Markets and Political Support", *The World Economy*, 38:2 (2015), 255–285.

Gallagher, Kevin P., Rohini Kamal, and Yongzhong Wang, "Fueling Growth and Financing Risk: The Benefits and Risks of China's Development Finance in the Global Energy Sector", GEGI Working Paper 2 (2016).

Gamble, Andrew and Anthony Payne, eds, *Regionalism and World Order* (London: Macmillan, 1996).

Gansen, N., *Bilateral Legacies in East and Southeast Asia* (Singapore: Institute of Southeast Asian Studies, 2015).

Gilson, Julie, "Japan and Southeast Asia", in Mark Beeson, ed., *Contemporary Southeast Asia* (New York: Palgrave, 2009).

Goh, Evelyn, "Great Powers and Hierarchical Order in Southeast Asia: Analyzing Regional Security Strategies", *International Security*, 32:3 (2008), 113–157.

Graham, Euan, *Japan's Sea Lane Security, 1940 – 2004: A Matter of Life and Death?* (Abingdon: Taylor & Francis: 2005).

Green, Michael J., *Japan's Reluctant Realism: Foreign Policy Challenges in an Era of Uncertain Power* (New York: Palgrave, 2004).

Green, Michael J., "U.S.–Japan Relations: Traversing a Rough Patch", *Comparative Connections*, 10:4 (2009).

Green, Michael J. and Nicholas Szechenyi, "U.S.–Japan Relations: Big Steps, Big Surprises", *Comparative Connections*, January (2014).

Gunaratna, Rohan and Muh Taufiqurrohman, "Insurgency and Terrorism in East Asia: Threat and Response", in Ramon Pacheco Pardo and Jeffrey Reeves, eds, *Non-Traditional Security in East Asia: A Regime Approach* (London: Imperial College Press, 2015).

"Guoji wangluo he xinxi anquan fazhan dongtai" (Development Dynamics in International Cyber and Information Security), *Xinxi anquan yu tongxin baomi* (*Information Security and Communication Confidential*), 6 (2015), 10–11.

Haiping, Wang and Zhu Jie, "2013 nian wuzhuang chongtu fa yanjiu zongshu" (A Summary of Studies on Armed Conflict Law), *Xian zhengzhi xueyuan xuebao* (*Journal of Xi'an Politics Institute*), 3 (2014), 98–102.

Hancock, K.J. and V. Vivoda. "International Political Economy: A Field Born of the OPEC Crisis Returns to its Energy Roots", *Energy Research & Social Science* 1 (2014): 206–216.

Harris, Mark, *et al.*, *Transnational Organized Crime in East Asia and the Pacific: A Threat Assessment* (Bangkok: United Nations Office of Drugs and Crime, 2013).

Hayton, Bill, *The South China Sea: The Struggle for Power in Asia* (New Haven: Yale University Press, 2014).

Helm, D., *Energy, the State, and the Market: British Energy Policy since 1979* (Oxford: Oxford University Press, 2004).

216 Selected bibliography

Herz, J.H., *Political Realism and Political Idealism: A Study in Theories and Realities* (Chicago: University of Chicago Press, 1951).

Ho, Joshua. "Combating Piracy and Armed Robbery in Asia: The ReCAAP Information Sharing Center (ISC)", *Marine Policy*, 33:2 (2009), 432–434.

Hobson, John H., *The Eastern Origins of Western Civilization* (Cambridge: Cambridge University Press, 2004).

Howe, Brendan and Joel Campbell, "Continuity and Change: Evolution, Not Revolution, in Japan's Foreign and Security Policy Under the DPJ", *Asian Perspectives*, 37:1 (2013), 99–123.

Hughes, Christopher W., *Japan's Foreign and Security Policy Under the "Abe Doctrine": New Dynamism or New Dead End?* (London: Palgrave, 2015).

Hughes, Christopher W., *Japan's Remilitarization* (Abingdon: Routledge, 2009).

Humphrey, Chris and Katharina Michaelowa, "Shopping for Development: Multilateral Lending, Shareholder Composition and Borrower Preferences", *World Development* 44 (2013), 142–155.

Ikenberry, G. John, *Liberal Leviathan: The Origins, Crisis, and Transformation of the American World Order* (Princeton: Princeton University Press, 2012).

Ikenberry, G. John, "Between the Eagle and the Dragon: America, China, and Middle State Strategies in East Asia", *Political Science Quarterly*, 20 (2015), 1–35.

Inderst, Georg, "Infrastructure Investment, Private Finance, and Institutional Investors: Asia from a Global Perspective", ADBI Working Paper Series 555 (2016).

Itoh, S., "Russia's Energy Policy Towards Asia: Opportunities and Uncertainties", in C. Len and E. Chew, eds, *Energy and Security Cooperation in Asia: Challenges and Prospects* (Stockholm: Institute for Security and Development Policy, 2009).

Jacques, Martin, *When China Rules the World: The End of the Western World and the Birth of a New Global Order* (New York: Penguin Books, 2012).

Jain, Purnendra, "Japan's Foreign Aid: Old and New Contests", *The Pacific Review*, 29:1 (2016), 93–113.

Jervis, R., "Cooperation under the Security Dilemma", *World Politics* 30:2 (1978), 167–174.

Jiangyong, Liu, "China's Peripheral Diplomacy: Continuity and Innovative Development" (Zhongguo zhoubian waijiao: zai jicheng zhong fazhan chuangxin), *Contemporary International Relations (xiandai guoji guanxi jiqi sikao)*, 10 (2013).

Jianhe, Sun, "Zhong ri wangluo duihua chenggong de jushi" (Revelations from the Successful China–Japan Dialogues), *Duiwai da chuanbo (External Communication)*, 6 (2007), 41–43.

Jianzhong, Ren and Zhang Xin, "2012 nian jisuanji bingdu fazhan qingkuang ji fan bingdu jishu fazhan qushi" (2012 Developments of Computer Viruses and Anti-Virus Technology Development Trends), 10 (2013), 211–214.

Jukes, Geoffrey, *The Soviet Union in Asia* (Berkeley: University of California Press, 1973).

Kalkuhl, M., Edenhofer, O., and K. Lessmann, "The Role of Carbon Capture and Sequestration Policies for Climate Change Mitigation", *Environmental and Resource Economics* 60:1 (2015), 55–80.

Kang, David C., *East Asia Before the West: Five Centuries of Trade and Tribute* (New York: Columbia University Press, 2012).

Kaplan, Robert D., *Asia's Cauldron: The South China Sea and the End of a Stable Pacific* (New York: Random House, 2014).

Katada, Saori N., "At the Crossroads: The TTP, AIIB, and Japan's Foreign Economic Strategy", *Asia Pacific Issues*, 125 (2016).

Selected bibliography 217

Katsumara, Hiro, "Establishment of the ASEAN Regional Forum: Constructing a 'Talking Shop', or a Norm Brewery?", *The Pacific Review*, 19:2 (2006), 181–198.

Kawai, Masahiro and Ganeshan Wignaraja, "Trade Policy and Growth in Asia", ADBI Working Paper Series 495 (2014).

Kawai, Masahiro, "From the Chiang Mai Initiative to an Asian Monetary Fund", ADBI Working Paper Series 527 (2015).

Kennedy, A.B., "China's New Energy Security Debate", *Survival* 52:3 (2010), 137–158.

Kim, Hyo-sook and David M. Potter, eds, *Foreign Aid Competition in Northeast Asia* (Boulder: Lynne Rienner Publishers, 2012).

Kim, Ji Young, "Dismantling the Final Barrier: Transforming Japan into a 'Normal' Country in the Post-Cold War Era", *Pacific Focus*, 16:3 (2015), 223–248.

Kissinger, Henry, *On China* (New York: Penguin, 2012).

Kitano, Naohiro, "China's Foreign Aid at a Transitional Stage", *Asian Economic Policy Review*, 9:2 (2014), 301–317.

Kitano, Yohei, "Development of Asian Local Currency Bond Markets and Remaining Challenges", *Nomura Journal of Capital Markets*, 6:3 (2015), 1–16.

Kivimaki, Timo, *The Long Peace of East Asia* (Farnham: Ashgate, 2014).

Koike, M., G. Mogi, and W.H. Albedaiwi, "Overseas Oil-Development Policy of Resource-Poor Countries: A Case Study from Japan", *Energy Policy* 36:5 (2008), 1764–1775.

Kojima, Kiyoshi, "The 'Flying Geese' Model of Asian Economic Development: Origin, Theoretical Extensions, and Regional Policy Implications", *Journal of Asian Economics*, 11:4 (2000), 375–401.

Kong, B., "Governing China's Energy in the Context of Global Governance", *Global Policy* 2:1 (2011), 51–65.

Kong, B. and J.H. Ku. *Energy Security Cooperation in Northeast Asia* (London: Routledge, 2015).

Kongxiang, Wang, "Wangluo anquan de guoji hezuo jizhi tanxi" (Analysis on International Cooperative Mechanisms on Cyber Security), *Guoji luntan* (*International Forum*), 5 (2013), 1–7.

Lai, H., *Asian Energy Security: The Maritime Dimension* (New York: Palgrave, 2009).

Lake, David A. and Patrick M. Morgan, *Regional Orders: Building Security in a New World* (University Park: Pennsylvania State Press, 1997).

Lanteigne, Marc, *China and International Institutions: Alternate Paths to Global Power* (London: Routledge, 2005).

Lee, John, "Divergence in Australia's Economic and Security Interests", in James Reilly and Jingdong Yuan, eds, *Australia and China at 40* (Sydney: UNSW Press, 2012), 142–161.

Lewis, Martin W. and Kären Wigen, *The Myth of Continents: A Critique of Metageography* (Berkeley: University of California Press, 1997).

Liang, Qiao and Wang Xiangsui, *Unrestricted Warfare: China's Master Plan to Destroy America* (Beijing: PLA Literature and Arts Publishing House, 1999).

Libing, Mao, "Xinxi anquan ma? Quanqiu daxiang xinxi anquan baowei zhan" (Is Information Secure? The Global War for Information Security Protection), *Zhishi jingji* (*Information Economy*), 6 (2013), 38–42.

Linli, Ma, "'Zhaobing maima' qiangzhan 'zhiwang quan' – Jinnian guowai bufen ji zuzhi wangjun jianshe zuixin dongtai" (Recruitment "To Seize the Network" – Some Foreign Countries in Recent Years and Their New Developments in Building Their Cyber Armies), *Wangjun jianshe* (*Building a Cyber Army*), *Zhonggyo xinxi anquan* (*China's Information Security*), 8 (2012).

218   Selected bibliography

Liu, Fu-kuo and Philippe Regnier, *Regionalism in East Asia* (London: Routledge, 2013).

Lu, Tang, "Qianxi yi falv xingshi kongzhi wangluo junbei jingsai de biyaoxing" (An Analysis on the Necessity of Controlling Cyber Arm- [sic] Race Juristically [sic]), *Guofang keji* (*Defense Technology*), 3 (2010), 33–36.

Luong, Dinh Thi Hien, "Vietnam–Japan Relations in the Context of Building an East Asian Community", *Asia-Pacific Review*, 16:1 (2009), 100–130.

Mahbubani, Kishore, *Can Asians Think?* (Singapore: Marshall Cavendish, 2009).

Manicom, James, *Bridging Troubled Waters: China, Japan, and Maritime Order in the East China Sea* (Washington, DC: Georgetown University Press, 2014).

Maslow, Sebastian, "A Blueprint for a Strong Japan? Abe Shinzo and Japan's Evolving Security System", *Asian Survey*, 55:4 (2015), 739–765.

Mastanduno, Michael, "Realism and Asia", in Saadia M. Pekkanen, John Ravenhill, and Rosemary Foot, eds, *The Oxford Handbook of the International Relations of Asia* (Oxford: Oxford University Press, 2014).

Maurin, C. and V. Vivoda, "Shale Gas and the Energy Policy 'Trilemma'", in T. Hunter, ed., *Handbook of Shale Gas Law and Policy* (Cambridge: Intersentia, 2016).

Mearsheimer, John J., "The Gathering Storm: China's Challenge to US Power in Asia", *The Chinese Journal of International Politics*, 3:4 (2010), 381–396.

"Mei ri zhendui zhong e gao wangluo junyan" (The United States and Japan Engage in Military Cyber Exercises Against China and Russia), *Guofang shibao* (*Defense Times*), August 22, 2011.

Midford, Paul, "Japan's Approach to Maritime Security in the South China Sea", *Asian Survey*, 55:3 (2015), 525–547.

Mifune, Emi, "Impact of the American 'Re-Balance' Strategy on Japanese Naval Power", in Greg Kennedy and Harsh V. Pant, eds, *Assessing Maritime Power in the Asia-Pacific: The Impact of American Strategic Re-Balance* (Aldershot: Ashgate, 2015).

Miller, Alice and Richard Wich, *Becoming Asia: Change and Continuity in Asian International Relations Since World War II* (Stanford: Stanford University Press, 2011).

Nakatani, K., "Energy Security and Japan: The Role of International Law, Domestic Law, and Diplomacy", in B. Barton, C. Redgwell, A. Rønne, and D.N. Zillman, eds, *Energy Security: Managing Risk in a Dynamic Legal and Regulatory Environment* (Oxford: Oxford University Press, 2004).

Nankivell, Kerry Lynn, "The Stories Nations Tell: In Three Voices", *Asian Security*, 11:1 (2015), 89–97.

Nesadurai, Helen E., *Globalisation and Economic Security in East Asia: Governance and Institutions* (London: Routledge, 2012).

Nicolas, Francoise, "The Political Economy of Regional Integration in East Asia", *Economic Change and Restructuring* 41:4 (2008), 345–367.

Oba, Mie, "Regional Arrangement for Trade in Northeast Asia", in Vinod Aggarwal and Min Gyo Koo, eds, *Asia's New Institutional Architecture: Evolving Structures for Managing Trade, Financial and Security Relations* (New York: Springer, 2007).

Oba, Mie, "TPP, RCEP, and FTAAP: Multilayered Regional Economic Integration and International Relations", *Asia-Pacific Review*, 23:1 (2016), 100–114.

Pacheco Pardo, Ramon and Pradumna B. Rana, "Complementarity between Regional and Global Financial Institutions: The Case of ASEAN+3 and the Global Financial Safety Net", *Global Governance: A Review of Multilateralism and International Organizations*, 21:3 (2015), 413–433.

Pacheco Pardo, Ramon, "The Quest for Economic Security in East Asia", in Ramon Pacheco Pardo and Jeffrey Reeves, eds, *Non-traditional Security in East Asia: A Regime Approach* (London: Imperial College Press, 2015), 119–141.

Selected bibliography 219

Park, Susan and Jonathan R. Strand, eds, *Global Economic Governance and the Development Practices of the Multilateral Development Banks* (London: Routledge, 2016).

Peng Er, Lam, "Japan and the Spratlys Dispute: Aspirations and Limitations", *Asian Survey*, 36:10 (1996), 995–1010.

Peng Er, Lam, *Japan's Relations with Southeast Asia: The Fukuda Doctrine and Beyond* (Abingdon: Routledge, 2013).

Phillips, A., "A Dangerous Synergy: Energy Securitization, Great Power Rivalry and Strategic Stability in the Asian Century", *The Pacific Review*, 26:1 (2013), 17–38.

Pillsbury, Michael, *The Hundred-Year Marathon: China's Secret Strategy to Replace America as the Global Superpower* (New York: Henry Holt and Co., 2015).

Poddar, Prem and David Johnson, *A Historical Companion to Postcolonial Thought in English* (New York: Columbia University Press, 2005).

Prantl, J., "Crafting Energy Security Cooperation in East Asia", S. Rajaratnam School of International Studies, Centre for Non-traditional Security Studies, Policy Brief 9 (2011).

Prassad, Kailash K., "An Assessment of the Goals, Drivers, and Capabilities of China's Modernizing Navy", *Korean Journal of Defense Analysis*, 24:1 (2012).

Prasso, Sheridan, *The Asian Mystique: Dragon Ladies, Geisha Girls, & Our Fantasies of the Exotic Orient* (New York: Public Affairs, 2006).

Pyle, Kenneth B., *Japan Rising: The Resurgence of Japanese Power and Purpose* (New York: The Century Foundation, 2007).

Qi, Xin, Yuan Yi, and Zhu Danlong, "Chu meiguo wai, e, ri, yin, han, fa, ying deng guo ye bugan luohou – fazhan wangluo zhan, geguo you zhaoshu" (Aside from the United States, Russia, Japan, India, Korea, France, Britain and Other Countries are Not Far Behind – The Development of Cyber Warfare, Each Country has its Tricks), *Jiefangjun bao* (*People's Liberation Army Daily*), April 17, 2015.

Qingguo, Jia, "Zhong-mei guangxi de jingzheng yu weilai" (Competition and the Future of China–US Relations) *Caixin*, September 22, 2014.

Radetzki, M., "European Natural Gas: Market Forces Will Bring about Competition in Any Case", *Energy Policy*, 27:1 (1999), 17–24.

Ravenhill, J., "Resource Insecurity and International Institutions in the Asia-Pacific Region", *The Pacific Review* 26:1 (2013), 39–64.

Reeves, Jeffrey, *Chinese Foreign Relations with Weak Peripheral States: Asymmetrical Economic Power and Insecurity* (London: Routledge, 2015).

Ren, Xiao, "China as an Institution-Builder: The Case of the AIIB", *The Pacific Review* 29:3 (2016), 435–442.

Roberts, Cain and Malcolm Fraser, *Dangerous Allies* (Melbourne: Melbourne University Press, 2014).

Said, Edward, *Orientalism* (New York: Knopf Doubleday Publishing Group, 2014).

Schimmelpenninck van der Oye, David, *Russian Orientalism: Asia in the Russian Mind from Peter the Great to the Emigration* (New Haven: Yale University Press, 2010).

Scott, David, *China Stands Up: The PRC and the International System* (New York: Routledge, 2007).

Shaoul, R., "An Evaluation of Japan's Current Energy Policy in the Context of the Azadegan Oil Field Agreement Signed in 2004", *Japanese Journal of Political Science* 6:3 (2005), 411–437.

Shimodaira, Takuya, "The Japan Maritime Self Defense Force in the Age of Multilateral Cooperation", *Naval War College Review*, 67:2 (2014), 52–68.

Singh, Bhubhindir, "The Development of Japanese Security Policy: A Long-Term Defensive Strategy", *Asian Policy* 19 (2015).

220 Selected bibliography

Smith, Jeff, "Beware China's Strategy: How Obama can Set the Right Red Lines", *Foreign Affairs*, May 20, 2015.

Smith, Sheila. "Japan and the East China Sea Dispute", *Orbis*, 56:3 (2012).

Snyder, Scott, "The Korean Peninsula and Northeast Asian Stability", in David Shambaugh and Michael Yahuda, eds, *International Relations of Asia* (New York: Rowman & Littlefield, 2014).

Solis, Mireya and Saori N. Katada, "Unlikely Pivotal States in Competitive Free Trade Agreement Diffusion: The Effects of Japan's Trans-Pacific Partnership Participation on Asia-Pacific Regional Integration", *New Political Economy* 20:2 (2015), 155–177.

Songyang, Han, "Cong zhihai quan dao zhiwang quan: Tanxi dashuju shidai zhengzhi wangluo yingxiao de zhongyaoxing" (From Sea Control Rights to Network Control Rights: An Analysis of the Importance of Political Network Markets in the Big Data Era), *Nanfang lunkan (Southern Journal)*, 9 (2014), 34–35.

Sovacool, B.K. and V. Vivoda, "A Comparison of Chinese, Indian, and Japanese Perceptions of Energy Security", *Asian Survey*, 52:5 (2012): 949–969.

Stockholm International Peace Research Institute, *SIPRI Yearbook 2015: Armaments, Disarmaments and International Security* (Oxford: Oxford University Press, 2015).

Stoddard, E., "Reconsidering the Ontological Foundations of International Energy Affairs: Realist Geopolitics, Market Liberalism and a Politico-Economic Alternative", *European Security*, 22:4 (2013), 437–463.

Storey, Ian, "Japan's Maritime Security Interests in Southeast Asia and the South China Sea Dispute", *Political Science* 65(2), 135–156.

Swaine, Michael D., *America's Challenge: Engaging a Rising China in the Twenty-first Century* (New York: Carnegie Endowment, 2011).

Takuya, Shimodaira, "The Japan Maritime Self-Defense Force in the Age of Multilateral Cooperation: Nontraditional Security", *Naval War College Review*, 67:2 (2014), 52–68.

Tan, Seng, "Asian Multilateralism in an Age of Japan's 'New Normal': Perils and Prospects", *Japanese Journal of Political Science*, 16:3 (2015), 296–314.

Tan, Seng, *Multilateral Asian Security Architecture: Non-ASEAN Stakeholders* (London: Routledge, 2015).

Terry, Edith, *How Asia Got Rich: Japan, China and the Asian Miracle* (London: Routledge, 2015).

Thayer, Carlyle, "China's Rise and the Passing of U.S. Primacy: Australia Debates its Future", *Asia Policy*, 12 (2011).

Tow, William T. and H.D.P. Envall, "Australia Debates American Primacy", in Yoichiro Sato and See Seng Tan, eds, *United States Engagement with the Asia-Pacific: Perspectives from Asia* (Amherst: Cambria Press, 2015).

Van Daar, Edwin, "Philippine-Trade Policy and the Philippine Economic Partnership Agreement (JPEPA)", *Contemporary Southeast Asia*, 33:2 (2011).

Verschaeve, Joren and Jan Orbie, "The DAC is Dead, Long Live the DCF? A Comparative Analysis of the OECD Development Assistance Committee and the UN Development Cooperation Forum", *The European Journal of Development Research* 28:4 (2016), 571–587.

Victor, D.G. and L. Yueh, "The New Energy Order: Managing Insecurities in the Twenty-First Century", *Foreign Affairs*, 89:1 (2010), 61–73.

Vivoda, V., "Evaluating Energy Security in the Asia-Pacific Region: A Novel Methodological Approach", *Energy Policy*, 38:9 (2010), 5258–5263.

Vivoda, V., *Energy Security in Japan: Challenges after Fukushima* (Abingdon: Routledge, 2014).

Selected bibliography 221

Vivoda, V., "LNG Import Diversification in Asia", *Energy Strategy Reviews*, 2:3/4 (2014), 289–297.

Vivoda, V., "Natural Gas in Asia: Trade, Markets and Regional Institutions", *Energy Policy*, 74 (2014), 80–90.

Vivoda, V., "Energy Security in East Asia", in J. Reeves and R. Pacheco Pardo, eds, *Non-Traditional Security in East Asia: A Regime Approach* (London: Imperial College Press, 2015).

Vivoda, V., "State–Market Interaction in Hydrocarbon Sector: The Cases of Australia and Japan", in A.V. Belyi and K. Talus, eds, *States and Markets in Hydrocarbon Sectors* (Basingstoke: Palgrave Macmillan, 2015).

Vivoda, V. and J. Manicom, "Oil Import Diversification in Northeast Asia: A Comparison between China and Japan", *Journal of East Asian Studies* 11:2 (2011), 223–254.

Vu, Tuong and Wasana Wongsurawat, *Dynamics of the Cold War in Asia: Ideology, Identity, and Culture* (London: Palgrave Macmillan, 2009).

Vuving, Alexander L., "Strategy and Evolution of Vietnam's China Policy: A Changing Mixture of Pathways", *Asian Survey*, 6:46 (2006), 805–824.

Vuving, Alexander L., "Operated by World Views and Interfaced by World Orders: Traditional and Modern Sino-Vietnamese Relations", in Anthony Reid and Zheng Yangwen, eds, *Negotiating Asymmetry: China's Place in Asia* (Singapore: National University of Singapore Press, 2009).

Vuving, Alexander L., "Vietnam: A Tale of Four Players", in Daljit Singh, ed., *Southeast Asian Affairs 2010* (Singapore: Institute of Southeast Asian Studies, 2010).

Vuving, Alexander L., "How Experience and Identity Shape Vietnam's Relations with China and the United States", in Joon-Woo Park, Gi-Wook Shin, and Donald W. Keyser, eds, *Asia's Middle Powers? The Identity and Regional Policy of South Korea and Vietnam* (Stanford: Stanford University Shorenstein Asia-Pacific Research Center, 2013).

Vuving, Alexander L., "Vietnam in 2012: A Rent-Seeking State on the Verge of a Crisis", in Daljit Singh, ed., *Southeast Asian Affairs 2013* (Singapore: Institute of Southeast Asian Studies, 2013).

Vuving, Alexander L., "Power Rivalry, Party Crisis and Patriotism: New Dynamics in the Vietnam–China–US Triangle", in Li Mingjiang and Kalyan M. Kemburi, eds, *New Dynamics in US–China Relations: Contending for the Asia-Pacific* (London: Routledge, 2015).

Wallace, Corey J., "Japan's Strategic Pivot South: Diversifying the Dual Hedge", *International Relations of the Asia-Pacific*, 13:3 (2013), 479–517.

Waltz, Kenneth N., "Structural Realism after the Cold War", *International Security*, 25:1 (2006), 5–41.

Watson, Iain and Chandra Lal Pandey, *Environmental Security in the Asia-Pacific* (London: Palgrave Macmillan, 2015).

Weatherbee, Donald E., *International Relations in Southeast Asia: The Struggle for Autonomy* (London: Routledge, 2008).

Wenbo, Cui, "'Talin shouce', dui wo guo wangluo anquan liyu de yingxiang" (The Impact on Chinese Cyber Security Interest [sic] of [sic] Tallinn Manual), *Jiangnan shehui kexueyuan xuebao (Journal of Jiangnan Social University)*, 3 (2013), 23–26.

Wenyan, Wang, Zhao Yan, Lu Shan, and Zhao Meng, "Hai zhanchang wangdian kongjian zuozhan xitong yanjiu (Research on Marine Battlefield Network Space Warfare Systems), *Xin Jujiao (New Focus)*, issue unavailable (date unavailable), 9–10.

Wesley, Michael, *Energy Security in Asia* (London: Routledge, 2007).

222 Selected bibliography

White, Hugh, "Power Shift: Australia's Future Between Beijing and Washington", *Quarterly Essay*, 39 (2010).

White, Hugh, *The China Choice: Why the US Should Share Power* (Melbourne: Black Ink, 2012).

Wilkins, Thomas S., "From Strategic Partnership to Strategic Alliance? Australia–Japan Security Ties and the Asia-Pacific", *Asia Policy*, 20 (2015), 81–111.

Wilson, J.D., "Northeast Asian Resource Security Strategies and International Resource Politics in Asia", *Asian Studies Review*, 38:1 (2014), 15–32.

Wilson, J.D., "Resource Security: A New Motivation for Free Trade Agreements in the Asia-Pacific Region", *The Pacific Review* 25:4 (2012), 429–453.

Woods, Ngaire, "Whose Aid? Whose Influence? China, Emerging Donors and the Silent Revolution in Development Assistance", *International Affairs*, 84:6 (2008), 1205–1221

Woolcock, Stephen, *Trade and Investment Rule-making: The Role of Regional and Bilateral Agreements* (Tokyo: United Nations University Press, 2006).

World Trade Organization, *International Trade Statistics 2015* (Geneva: World Trade Organization, 2015).

Wu, S. and H. Nong, *Recent Developments in the South China Sea Dispute: The Prospect of a Joint Development Regime* (London: Routledge, 2014).

Xianlong, Zhang, "Hulianwang shidai weihu guojia anquan de zhanlue sikao" (Strategic Thinking on Safeguarding National Security in the Internet Age), *Zhongguo xinxi anquan* (*China Information Security*), 7 (2013).

Xiguang, Li, *Soft Power and the China Dream (ruanshili yu Zhongguo meng)* (Beijing: Falu Chubanshe, 2014).

Xinmin, Liu, "Reflection on United Nations Security Council Reform and China/Japan/US Relations" (*An Lihui gaige shijiao xia de Zong Ri Mei guanxi*) *Theory Horizon* (*Lilun jie*), 8 (2014).

Xueping, Tan and Yu Feng, "Ri ziweidui zengjia yusuan zhaobing maima: Yusuan zengjia 0.6% youxian goumai hai, kong zhuangbei, bing sida wangluo tanhuanzhan" (Japan Self-Defense Forces to Increase Budget for Recruiting: Budget Increased by 0.6%, Giving Priority to the Purchase of Sea and Air Equipment, Intended for Paralyzing War), *Waijun liaowang* (*Foreign Military Lookout*), October 11, 2011.

Xuetong, Yan and Sun Xuefeng, *Zhongguo jueqi jiqi zhanlue* (*China's Rise and Strategy*) (Beijing: Beijing Daxue Chubanshe, 2005).

Yamamoto, Kazuya, "Vietnam from the Perspective of the Asia Barometer Survey: Identity, Images of Foreign Nations, and Global Concerns", *Memoirs of the Institute of Oriental Culture*, 150 (2007).

Yamei, Shen, "Japan Responds to and Influences US Strategy to Shift East" (Riben yinying meiguo zhanlue Dong yi de jucuo jiqi yingxiang), China Institute of International Studies, November 26, 2013.

Yergin, D., "Ensuring Energy Security", *Foreign Affairs*, 85:2 (2006), 69–82.

Yew, Leong, *Alterities in Asia: Reflections on Identity and Regionalism* (London: Routledge, 2010).

Yi, Yuan, "Zhihui chengshi de wangluo anquan yinhuan ji duice" (Hidden Dangers and Countermeasures of Network Security in Smart Cities), *Wangluo kongjian zhanlue luntan* (*Cyberspace Strategy Forum*), 7 (2016), 30–32.

Yinhong, Shui, "Zhong-mei guanxi pingjing zaiyu quanshi fenxiang er fei huxin" (Power Sharing and Mutual Distrust are the Bottle Neck in Chinese–US Relations) *Phoenix TV*, February 2, 2015.

Yongsheng, Zhou, "Riben weihe xuanran zhongguo wangluo weixie" (Why Japan Poses a Threat to China's Networks), *Renmin Luntan (People's Tribune)*, 8 (2011).

Yuqing, Liu and Gong Yanli, "Wangluo zhan shidai de anquan weixie ji duice yanjiu" (Study on Security Threats and Countermeasures in Era of Cyber warfare), *Qingbao tansuo (Intelligence Exploration)*, 11 (2014), 61–64.

Zala, Benjamin, "The Australian *2016 Defence White Paper*, Great Power Rivalry and a 'Rules-Based Order'" *Australian Journal of International Affairs*, 70:5 (2016), 441–452.

Zhang, Xiaoming, *Deng Xiaoping's Long War: The Military Conflict between China and Vietnam, 1979–1991* (Chapel Hill: University of North Carolina Press, 2015).

Zhang, Z., "The Overseas Acquisitions and Equity Oil Shares of Chinese National Oil Companies: A Threat to the West but a Boost to China's Energy Security?" *Energy Policy*, 48: 698–701.

Zhe, Jia and Zhang Linjie, "Zizhu wangluo kongjian anquan jishu yanjiu" (Research on Independent and Controllable Cyberspace Security Technology), *Jisuanji yu wangluo (Computers and Networks)*, 6 (2015), 59–61.

Zheng, Ye and Zhao Baoxian, "Guanyu wangluo zhuquan, wangluo bianjiang, wangluo guofang de sikao" (Thoughts on Cyber Sovereignty, Cyber Borders, and Cyber Defense), *Wangluo kongjian zhanlue luntan (Cyberspace Strategy Forum)*, 1 (2014), 28.

Zhixiong, Huang, "Guojifa shijiao xia de 'wangluo zhan' ji zhongguo de duice – yixizhe wuliquan wei zhongxin" (International Legal Issues Concerning "Cyber Warfare" and Strategies for China: Focusing on the Field of Jus ad Bellum), *Xiandai faxue (Modern Law Science)*, 5 (2015), 145–158.

Zhongping, Feng and Huang Jing, *China's Strategic Partnership Diplomacy: Engaging with a Changing World* (Brussels: European Strategic Partnership Observatory, 2014).

Zhuangdong, Wang, "Wangluo anquan guanxi guojia mingyun" (Cyber Security Relations and National Fate), *Jisuanji anquan (Computer Security)*, 3 (2004), 3–4.

Index

Abbott, Tony 152, 153

Abe, Shinzō: defence spending rises 36, 184; foreign policies 34–5; maritime law, adhering to 39–40, 108, 114–15; maritime security, East Asia 117, 183–4, 188, 189; Philippines security partnership 189–90, 191; South and East China Seas linkages 109; strategic partnerships 38–9, 41, 153, 167

Acharya, Amitav 108

Aquino, Benigno III 118, 178, 183, 185, 187, 189–90

Arroyo, Gloria Macapagal 180, 181

ASEAN (Association of Southeast Asian Nations): AIIB funding 67; China-ASEAN relations 32, 56–8, 73–4, 206; Japan-ASEAN relations 38–9, 56, 58, 172, 181, 201; members' economic growth 61; regional trade statistics 30–1

ASEAN+3 56, 58–9, 79–80, 167

ASEAN Defense Ministers Meeting-Plus (ADMM+) 7, 62, 147

ASEAN Regional Forum: freedom of navigation issue 110, 113–14; security focused 7, 55, 111, 206; South China Sea dispute 184–5

ASEAN Treaty of Amity and Cooperation 58, 62

Asian Bond Markets Initiative 80

Asian Development Bank (ADB): AIIB's China backed challenge 31–2, 41; cooperative aid provision 67, 76, 81; intraregional development aid 7, 54–5

Asian financial crisis (1997) 55–6, 71, 78–9, 80

Asian identity 7, 33–4

Asian Infrastructure Investment Bank (AIIB): aid provision, Chinese targeting 26, 31–2, 63–4; Australian membership

debate 147–8, 150; cooperative aid provision 67, 76, 80–1; intraregional development 7; investment security 81–2; operational scrutiny 40–1, 66–7

Asian security: Asia, peripheral in global power politics 3–5; China's New Asian Security concept 62–3; energy demand and challenges 86, 89–96; US and US/China relations 1–2, 5–6; *see also* regionalism

Asia-Pacific Economic Cooperation (APEC) 7, 55, 86, 94, 147

Australia: Asia-Pacific regional order, engagement debate 18–19, 144–6, 154–6, 201, 207; China's economic partnership 144, 146–7, 150, 155; defence upgrades and regional security ties 148–50, 152; Japanese security partnership 39, 116, 150–4, 184, 203; multilateral policies 147–8; partnership conflicts 65, 150; regional institutions 55, 59, 111; trade relations and agreements 65, 73, 91, 146–7

balance of power dynamics: China's role 54, 59–62, 68, 155–6, 209; Indonesia's role 11; Japan's role 54, 59–62, 68, 209; Vietnam's role 11, 20–1, 169–74, 203

Brunei 58, 66, 68, 73, 179

Bush, George W. 62

Bush, Richard 27

Buzan, Barry 8, 108

Cambodia 32, 39, 48n, 56, 172

Chang Mai Initiative 56, 79

Chang Mai Initiative Multilateralization 59, 69n, 79

China: A2/D2 (Anti-Access/Aerial Denial) strategy 38, 39, 107; AIIB, involvement

Index 225

criticism 40–1, 66; ASEAN, strategic relations 32, 56–8, 65, 73–4, 206; Asian periphery diplomacy 26–7, 187; balance of power dynamics 54, 59–62, 68, 155–6, 209; China/Australia economic partnership 144, 146–7, 150, 155; China/Japan, oppositional framing 33–4; Chinese media's propaganda role 28–9, 112; comprehensive strategic partnerships 32–3, 73, 74, 147, 174n; cyber governance, Japan critiqued 128–30, 131, 133–4, 135, 200; cyber sovereignty advocacy 130–1, 133; cyber warfare, US led threat 132–4; East China Sea, territorial dispute 28, 29, 36–7, 61, 106, 121; economic engagement, Japan as obstacle 29–31; energy securitization 86, 90–2, 93, 95–6, 200–1; financial and aid initiatives 26, 31–2, 40–1, 59, 65, 75–6; foreign direct investment 31, 41–2, 77–8, 144, 163; fossil fuel reduction challenge 94–5; freedom of navigation issue 114; Japan as regional peer 27, 65, 72, 206–7; Japan's diplomatic threat 33, 112; maritime security, post-war policies 105, 106–7, 108; military capability and strategy building 117, 119, 126n; military policies and the Japanese threat 27–9, 110; New Asian Security concept 62–3; One Belt, One Road initiative 26, 30, 41, 49n, 63, 78; Philippines, problematic relations 179–80, 183, 184–8; regionalism, revaluated strategy 53–4, 55–6, 206; renminbi, potential impact 80; Scarborough Shoal incident and stand-off 67, 108, 178, 184–6; Silk Road Fund 7, 26, 63, 82; South and East China Seas, operational segregation 119, 121, 122; South China Sea, territorial dispute 33, 35, 57, 58, 67–8; UNCLOS Tribunal and Philippine claims 186–8; US/China relations 32, 65; Vietnam's dependent partnership 160–3; Xi's regional security vision 62–3
China Development Bank 26
Christensen, Thomas 5, 95
climate change mitigation 94–5
Clinton, Hillary 113–14
Cohen, Paul 3–4
cultural chauvinism 3, 4
cybersecurity: contrasting approaches to 17–18; cyber sovereignty, China's advocacy 130–1, 135; cyber warfare, ideology and capabilities 132–5, 200,

202, 203; international mechanisms 131, 134, 135; Japan and East/West integration 135–6; Japan's Western-centric strategy, China's critique 128–30, 131, 135

Del Rosario, Albert 188–9
development aid: AIIB funding 26, 67; Asia-Pacific donor competition 75–6; Chinese challenge for dominance 31–2, 40–1, 76; Japan's ODA for 'strategic use' 118, 119, 120, 165, 167; Japan's ODA policy 38, 40, 75; recipient dilemma 14; Vietnam, Japan's top beneficiary 164–6
Do, Muoi 162
Duterte, Rodrigo 190–2, 193

East Asian security: China, Japan and third state relations 18–21, 154–6, 168–75, 203; China's rhetoric on Japanese 'militarization' 27–9; comprehensive strategic partnerships 32–3; geographic area 21n; military escalation 9, 10–11; regional security complex, applicability factors 9–10, 71–2; rules-based order, Australian support 149–50; Sino-Japanese rivalry, growing influence 2, 10–11, 13–14, 200–1, 208–11; soft power competition 33; Vietnam's cooperative ties with Japan 166–7
East Asia Summit: Australian membership 147; Japan's contributory principles 203; Japan/Vietnam cooperation 167; maritime issues 39; regional organizations 7; regional vision 58–9, 60; US membership 62, 111
East China Sea: Air Defence Identification Zone (China) 29; energy reserve rights 86, 92; Senkaku (Diaoyu) Islands, territorial dispute 28, 36–7, 61, 103–4, 113, 121, 170-1; *see also* South and East China Seas
economic security: Asian financial crisis, impact of 55–6, 71, 80; China and Japan as economic poles 10, 14–15, 72–3, 82, 204–5, 209; China/Australia economic partnership 144, 146–7; Chinese engagement, Japan as obstacle 29–31; development banks, potential cooperation 80–1; financial sector, intraregional cooperation 78–80, 209; free trade areas, East Asia 59; infrastructure funding, contract rivalry 41–2, 77–8, 171; partnership conflicts 64–8; regional development, assistance rivalry 26, 31–2,

226 *Index*

40–2, 63–4, 75–6, 202; trade relations and agreements 30–1, 57–8, 59, 64–6, 73–5, 206; Vietnam's Chinese dependency 162–3; Vietnam's cooperative ties with Japan 164–6

energy security: cleaner energy potential 94–5, 96; concept of 87; financially aided supplier agreements 91–2; fossil fuel subsidies 93–4; geographic and political issues 92–3; policy approaches and trends 87–9; regional demand impacts 10, 86–7; resource nationalism 92, 94; Sino-Japanese rivalry 15–16, 34, 86–7, 204; Sino-Japanese securitization policies 89–91, 95–6, 200–1

Expanded ASEAN Maritime Forum (EAMF) 111–12

financial sector, intraregional cooperation 78–80, 209

foreign direct investment (FDI): Asia-originated increase 7, 65; China-Japan competition 31, 77–8; China's role in Australia 144; Japan and ASEAN countries 77, 180

freedom of navigation (FON) 38, 106, 110, 113–15, 125n

free trade agreements (FTA): ASEAN-China agreement (2002) 57–8, 73; bilateral and multilateral expansion 7, 73; China and Australia 146–7; energy supply linked 91; Japan and ASEAN countries 58

Fukuda, Takeo 56, 105–6

Fukuda Doctrine (1977) 56, 106

Gazmin, Voltaire 188, 189

Hatoyama, Yukio 60–1

Hobson, John 6

Hu, Jintao 27, 61, 162

Ikenberry, John 5

India 42, 59, 65, 93

Indonesia: Asian financial crisis (1997) 78–9; balance of power dynamics 11; financial aid 56; foreign direct investment 31, 41–2, 77; fossil fuel subsidies 93; Sino-Japanese strategic partnerships 32, 33, 39, 57; South China Sea dispute 68; trade relations and agreements 30–1, 58, 59, 73, 74, 179

infrastructure funding, contract rivalry 41–2, 77–8, 171

Jacques, Martin 5

Japan: ASEAN, strategic relations 38–9, 56, 58–9, 181, 201; Australian security partnership 39, 116, 150–4, 203; balance of power dynamics 54, 59–62, 68, 209; China as regional peer 27, 65, 72, 206–7; China/Japan, oppositional framing 33–4; China's military power concerns 35–6; cyber governance, Chinese critiques 128–30, 131, 133–4, 135; cybersecurity, integrated roles 134, 135–6; East China Sea, territorial dispute 28, 29, 36–7, 61, 103–4, 106, 183–4; energy securitization 90–2, 95–6, 200–1; financial and aid initiatives 40–1, 59, 75–6, 80, 180; foreign direct investment 31, 41–2, 77, 180; freedom of navigation diplomacy 114–15, 119; Fukuda Doctrine (1977) 56, 106; Japan/US defence alliance strengthened 37, 47n; maritime security, post-war policies 105–7, 108, 122n, 123n; militarization, Chinese claims 28–9; militarization, Japanese justification 35–8, 107, 110; military capability and strategy building 116, 117–21, 184, 206; multilateral diplomacy in East Asia 110–12; National Security Strategy 35; Official Development Assistance (ODA) policy 38, 40, 75, 120; Philippines security partnership 28, 39, 49n, 118–19, 180–3, 188–93; regionalism, promotional strategies 53, 54–5, 56, 58–61, 201, 206–7; regional security, proactive role 34–5, 37–8, 167, 179, 200; regional trading obstacle to China 30–1; Scarborough Shoal incident 178–9; South and East China Seas linkages 109, 112–13, 115–16, 120, 200, 202; South China Sea, military presence 116–17, 120–1, 167; South China Sea, territorial dispute 34, 39–40, 104, 106, 109–10; strategic partnerships 38–40, 48n, 152–4, 166–7, 174n; Trans-Pacific Partnership (TPP) 41, 64–5, 74; US economic alliance, importance of 64, 68, 74–5, 208; Vietnam, soft power and strategic relations 49n, 160, 164–8, 170, 176n

Jia, Qingguo 5

Jiang, Zemin 27, 162

Kang, David 6

Kishida, Fumio 188–9, 191

Kissinger, Henry 5

Koizumi, Junichiro 57–8, 59, 111, 120, 181
Kotani, Tetsuo 114

Laos 31, 32, 33, 39, 48n, 172
lawfare 128–9
Le, Kha Phieu 162
Lewis, Martin W. 4
Li, Keqiang 26, 28, 187

Malaysia: development aid 75; financial aid 56, 66, 68; maritime claims 179; Sino-Japanese strategic partnerships 32, 33, 39, 59; trade relations and agreements 58, 73, 74
maritime security: anti-crime and enforcement agencies 111; China's post-war policies 105, 106–7, 108; East China Sea disputes 28, 29, 36–7; freedom of navigation (FON) 38, 106, 110, 113–15; Japan's post-war policies 105–7, 108, 122n, 123n; military capabilities and strategy building 116–21, 178–9, 184, 206; South and East China Seas, Japan's linkage 109, 112–13, 115–16, 120, 202, 204; South China Sea, China's claims 33, 57; South China Sea, Japan's involvement 34, 39–40, 104, 109–10, 112, 206; South China Sea, regional policies 49n; territorial disputes, potential impact 9, 16–17, 209–10; see also individual countries
Maritime Self-Defence Force (MSDF) 29, 36, 107, 117, 124n, 178–9
Maritime Silk Road initiative 30, 63
Midford, Paul 111, 122n
Mongolia 32, 73
Myanmar: Chinese strategic partnership 32; energy exports 93; financial and development aid 56, 76; foreign direct investment (FDI) 31; Japanese diplomacy 39, 48n, 172

New Miyazawa Plan 56
New Zealand 59, 65, 73, 111
Noda, Yoshihiko 48n, 61
Nong, Duc Manh 162
North Korea 9, 167

Obama, Barack 47n, 62
Ohira, Masayoshi 55
One Belt, One Road initiative 26, 30, 33, 41, 49n, 63, 78
Onodera, Itsunori 115, 189

Paracel Islands: China and ASEAN country claims 179; China's seizure from Vietnam 57, 163, 173; Japan's security responses 106, 119, 123n
People's Liberation Army Navy (PLA(N)) 27, 110, 117
periphery diplomacy 26
Philippines: China, problematic relations 33, 179–80, 183, 192; Duterte and Japan 191–2, 193; Duterte's Chinese bias and US hostility 190–1; financial aid 56, 68, 180; Japanese security partnership 28, 39, 48n, 118–19, 180–3, 188–90, 201; maritime entitlements, UNCLOS Tribunal 186–8; maritime security 49n, 116, 118–19, 127n, 181–2, 184–5, 203; regional relations and alliances 19–20; Scarborough Shoal incident and stand-off 67, 108, 178–9, 184–6; Spratly Islands, China's activities 183; trade relations and agreements 58, 66, 73; US security ties 190–1, 194n, 207

Qian, Qichen 55, 57

Regional Comprehensive Economic Partnership (RCEP) 7, 59, 64–5, 74, 201
regionalism: ASEAN ties, Sino-Japanese competition 56–9, 201, 205–6; China's revaluated strategy 53–4, 55–6; concept of 53; economic security, partnership conflicts 64–8; forums and frameworks 58–61; Japan's promotional strategies 54–5, 56, 58–61, 206–7; Japan/US initial dominance 53; US engagement 53, 62, 64–5, 207–8
regional organizations: political and diplomatic 7, 64; see also ASEAN related associations
regional security complex theory (RSCT): complex types 11; great power involvement 11; objectives 11; operational approach 11–12; regional dynamics and linkages 8–9; regional powers and relationships 10–11, 198–200; theoretical contribution 8
regional security order: China, Japan and third state relations 18–21, 154–6, 169–74, 199, 203, 205; East and South China Seas 103–4, 107, 204; rules-based order, Australian support 149–50; US involvement 62, 64–5, 68, 74–5, 153–4, 207–8; Vietnam's balance of power role 172–4

228 *Index*

rent-seeking state 169
resource nationalism 92, 94

Said, Edward 4
Scarborough Shoal: Chinese boat incident and stand-off 67, 108, 178, 184–6; Japan's security responses 118, 178–9
securitization, concept of 8
security multiplex 108
Senkaku (Diaoyu) Islands, territorial dispute: Chinese trawler incident 110, 113, 170–1; Japanese 'militarization' 28, 36–7; Shinzō Abe's security policies 109, 183–4; sovereignty claims 61, 103–4, 106, 121
Shi, Yinhong 5
Silk Road Fund 7, 26, 63, 82
Singapore: Chinese diplomacy 57; Chinese strategic partnership 32; Japanese diplomacy 48n; South China Sea dispute 68; trade relations and agreements 58, 66, 73, 179
Smith, Shelia 113
soft power competition 33
South and East China Seas: Japan's linked engagement policies 109, 112–13, 115–16, 120, 202, 204
South China Sea: Declaration of Conduct 58, 115; energy reserve rights 86, 92; Japan's increased engagement 116–17, 120–1, 167; maritime law, Japan's advocacy 34, 39–40, 109–10, 112, 115–16, 206; military capabilities and strategy building 116–19, 122, 167, 179; multilateral responses and policies 49n, 113–14; Scarborough Shoal incident and stand-off 67, 108, 178–9, 184–6; Sino-Japanese post-war positioning 105–6; territorial disputes 9, 16, 57, 67–8, 103–4, 106; UNCLOS Tribunal and Philippine claims 186–8
South Korea 65, 73, 75, 135, 184
Spratly Islands, China's activities: ASEAN countries' negative reactions 67–8, 179; China-Vietnam conflicts 67–8, 106, 160, 163, 172; Japan's security responses 109, 110, 118, 119, 123n, 181; Philippine responses to incidents 183, 186

Thailand: Asian financial crisis (1997) 55, 78; development aid 75; financial aid 56; foreign direct investment 31, 42; fossil fuel subsidies 93; Sino-Japanese strategic partnerships 32, 33, 48n, 172; trade relations and agreements 58, 66, 73

Trans-Pacific Partnership (TPP) 7, 41, 62, 64–6, 73, 74, 203–4
Turnbull, Malcolm 148, 152

UNCLOS: Arbitral Tribunal, Philippine entitlements 186–8; freedom of navigation advocacy 49n, 114, 115, 116
UN Group of Governmental Experts (UNGGE) 131, 135
United States (US): Asian middle powers' essential ally 173; Asian regionalism, impact on 53, 62, 64–5, 68, 74–5, 153, 207–8; Australia/US security alliance 149; cybersecurity threat, China's perception 132–4; freedom of navigation advocacy 113–14, 125n; Japan/US defence alliance strengthened 37, 47n, 184; Japan/US relations, China's opposition 32; maritime security, East Asia 114, 116–17, 121–2, 184; security ties in Philippines 190–1, 194n; Trump administration 208, 211n; Vietnam's contrasting strategies 169

Vietnam: balance of power dynamics 11, 20–1, 169–74, 203; Cam Ranh Bay's strategic facility 119, 160, 167, 171; China's military influence and regime affinity 160–2; Chinese oil rig incident 67, 163, 167, 170; development aid 75; financial aid 56, 66, 68, 163; foreign direct investment 31, 163; Green Growth policies 94–5; Japan's soft power and strategic relations 160, 164–8, 171–2, 179, 201, 207; maritime security 116, 119, 165, 167, 179; North Korea, diplomatic ties 167; political identity and foreign power relations 168–70; Sino-Japanese strategic partnerships 28, 32, 33, 39, 48n, 119, 166–7; South China Sea dispute 49n, 57, 67–8, 160, 164, 170–1, 172–3; trade relations and agreements 31, 58, 73, 74, 162–3, 164–5, 174n

Wæver, Ole 8
Wigen, Kären 4

Xi, Jinping: Japanese 'militarization' 28; periphery diplomacy 26, 187; regional security vision 62–3

Yan, Xuetong 5

Zhang, Feng 6